INTELLECTUAL
PROPERTY LAW

Other books in *Essentials of Canadian Law* Series

Criminal Law

The Law of Evidence

Statutory Interpretation

Media Law

The Law of Trusts

Income Tax Law

ESSENTIALS OF
CANADIAN LAW

INTELLECTUAL PROPERTY LAW
Copyright, Patents, Trade-marks

DAVID VAVER

Professor of Law
Osgoode Hall Law School, York University

IRWIN
LAW

INTELLECTUAL PROPERTY LAW
© David Vaver, 1997

Published in 1997 by
Irwin Law
1800 Steeles Avenue West
Concord, Ontario
L4K 2P3

ISBN: 1-55221-007-3

Canadian Cataloguing in Publication Data

Vaver, D.
   The law of intellectual property: copyright, patents, trademarks

(Essentials of Canadian law)
Includes bibliographical references and index.
ISBN 1-55221-007-3

1. Intellectual property – Canada.   I. Title.   II. Series.

KE2779.V38 1996   346.7104'8   C96-932181-3
KF2979.V38 1996

Printed and bound in Canada.

1   2   3   4   5   01   00   99   98   97

SUMMARY
TABLE OF CONTENTS

DETAILED
TABLE OF CONTENTS

FOREWORD

Communication, invention, and commerce are the engines that propel our society. It comes as no surprise, then, that the branches of law which govern the rights of people to the products of mind fuelling these engines should enjoy increasing prominence as we approach the twenty-first century.

Canada is responding in its own unique way to the needs for better law in the field of intellectual property. As a result, our law of copyright, patent, and trade-marks has undergone important changes in recent decades. The law of intellectual property not only touches more people than ever before but touches them in new and different ways.

Canadians, more than ever before, stand in need of a guide to mark the new and emerging boundaries of the law of copyright, patent, and trade-marks. To meet that need, David Vaver has written this book. On a subject noted for its complexity, it offers simplicity. The rules are set out with clarity and concision. Exceptions are succinctly detailed. Policy issues are objectively discussed. This is the type of book that interested persons — non-lawyers and lawyers alike — can access with ease. It constitutes an important addition to the legal literature on copyright, patent, and trade-marks. I recommend it unreservedly to lawyers, students, and the creators of ideas whose rights it addresses.

The Honourable Madam Justice Beverley McLachlin
Supreme Court of Canada

To

My mother and late father

and to

the students whom I have taught and who have taught me

PREFACE

Intellectual property suddenly is hot. Comedians joke about it. The mainstream press features it. We read of some rock star's "patented" lifestyle, of someone "copyrighting" an idea, of a hockey player's "trademark" slapshot, and of nations fighting trade wars over "piracy" of videotapes, compact disks, and computer software. Anyone with an idea talks of his or her "intellectual property" in it. Discussion groups on the Internet buzz about intellectual property — and its impending death. The preserve of a select group of specialist lawyers has suddenly shifted to the screens and the streets. Or so it seems. Like the old story about the blind men trying to tell the shape of an elephant by standing at different ends and touching different parts of it, what one sees and hears about intellectual property is often confusing and sometimes downright wrong.

This book examines the three main branches of modern intellectual property law: copyright (chapter 2), patents (chapter 3), and trade-marks (chapter 4). Chapter 5 discusses how the rights are managed and enforced, and chapter 6 concludes by looking at reform and the future. The account is necessarily abbreviated. One text on Canadian copyright law alone runs into thousands of pages, and the detail and nuance possible in such a work cannot be achieved in a shorter and more general book.

This book is directed towards anyone who wants to know more about these subjects: the general reader, as much as the university student or the non-specialist lawyer. The footnotes are there for lawyers and law students, who would otherwise not believe a word of what is said in the text; but citation and a detailed discussion of many disputed points have often been condensed or omitted. General readers can safely avert their eyes from the bottom of most pages without missing anything of substance except cross-references. A glossary at the back deals with technical terms and abbreviations.

Aficionados of industrial designs, integrated circuit topographies, and plant varieties may be disappointed, for space limitations have meant that these topics have been relegated to a paragraph or two, though they are integrated into the discussion in chapters 5 and 6. Various common law actions that protect intellectual property — breach of confidence, passing-off, and misappropriation of personality — also receive short shrift, though again they are woven into the general discussion. Those seeking further elucidation should look to the suggested readings at the end of each chapter. The body of literature on intellectual property law is enormous, so these listings represent only a personal selection.

I have tried to state the law as I understand it, while simultaneously providing a critical context. Intellectual property law is far from static. New legislation, judicial decisions, and technology constantly work to reshape it. I have sought to give some sense of the changes and how the law may be affected by them. Not everyone may agree with all the views presented here. For the last three centuries or more, any suggestion that intellectual property law, in its then current state, has not attained a state of ultimate perfection has managed to touch a raw nerve somewhere. This book repeats that suggestion in respect of the present state of the law, in the hope of stimulating further constructive thought and debate.

A number of people have made this book possible. In particular, William L. Hayhurst, QC, Professor Harry Glasbeek, George Klippert, and Natalie Derzko provided detailed criticism from their special experience and perspective. Professor Reuben Hasson, besides reading the manuscript, has over the years assiduously passed on copious intellectual property material that I surely would not otherwise have come across. Maxine Vaver made sure that the details of the culinary example in chapter 3 were plausible. Tai Nahm and Michael Crinson provided research assistance on various aspects of the work. Rebecca Thompson checked the quotations and citations and compiled the table of cases. Rosemary Shipton performed the final edit with care and sensitivity. I am grateful to them all. I also thank William Kaplan for suggesting the project and providing support as it proceeded, Jeffrey Miller for gracefully guiding the work through its technical phases, and Madam Justice Beverley McLachlin for agreeing to read the text and provide a foreword.

DV
Toronto, November 1996

INTELLECTUAL PROPERTY: AN OVERVIEW

A. INTRODUCTION

What is intellectual property law? It starts from the premise that ideas are free as the air — a common resource for all to use as they can and wish. It then proceeds systematically to undermine that principle.

Some trace the desire to privatize the fruits of the mind back to time immemorial, but the common law recognized no such right and, indeed, legislation was needed to create it.[1] The regulation of patents protecting industrial inventions, the oldest form of intellectual property, goes back to a Venetian decree of 1474 (or the English *Statute of Monopolies* of 1624, depending on one's taste and chauvinism), but the practice of encouraging new enterprise by granting monopolies may be even older. Copyright started as a response to the protectionist bent of the early eighteenth century London book trade, then reeling from the demise of its role as the Crown's censor of books. France repackaged this protectionist urge more attractively as a basic human right after the French Revolution of 1789. In that guise, copyright expanded to cover the whole gamut of the creative arts and beyond, into the murky world of tax tables, lottery numbers, and now computer programs. Industrial

---

1   *Donaldson v. Beckett* (1774), 4 Burr. 2408, 1 E.R. 837 (H.L.), rejecting a common law copyright for published works outside the *Copyright Act, 1710* (U.K.), 8 Anne c. 19.

design protection came out of late eighteenth-century England to give the textile trade lead time against foreign competition. Trade-marks were used by ancient merchants to identify their goods, and later by guild craftsmen as guarantees of quality. Modern trade-mark law is, however, a product of the Industrial Revolution, when judges started protecting business names and symbols. Such attitudes led to systems of national trade-mark registration in the second half of the nineteenth century. More recently, semi-conductor chip makers and seed companies have persuaded the relevant authorities that integrated circuit topographies and new plant varieties need and deserve protection as well.

The argument has always been that, without protection, people would not let the public have the benefit of the good ideas they had, through fear of competition from imitators. Those who sowed had to be protected from those who wanted to reap without sowing. The Bible could be used to support that sentiment.

Even before Confederation, Canada's settlers took the need to protect intellectual property as a self-evident truth. Today's copyright, patent, trade-mark, and industrial design laws are direct descendants of laws tracing back before 1867. Upper Canada passed a trade-mark law in 1860, anticipating Britain's by fifteen years, but Canadian statutes were mostly modelled on earlier British and, occasionally, U.S. laws. Although recent Canadian revisions have moved away from their foreign forebears in form, they are typical of those established by other major nations in substance.

This outcome is no accident. The late nineteenth century saw the creation of two major international multilateral treaties on intellectual property. The *Paris Convention for the Protection of Industrial Property* of 1883 covered patents, trade-marks, designs, and unfair competition. The *Berne Convention for the Protection of Literary and Artistic Works* of 1886 covered authors' rights. Britain, as an initial signatory, brought itself and its empire into these folds. So, early in its history, Canada came to protect foreign authors and enterprises alongside its native born — at least those native born descended from settlers. Both the *Paris* and the *Berne* conventions were highly Eurocentric treaties that ignored the culture of indigenous peoples. Native culture was thought to be free for the taking, the product of many and so the preserve of none — except when it was transformed by the mediation of Europeans, whereupon it magically gained cultural legitimacy.

The pattern of reciprocal and intensifying international protection continued after Canada attained full control over its foreign policy in the early twentieth century. Canada actively participated in the periodic revisions of *Paris* and *Berne* that took place during the century. But, until recently, Canada had adhered only to the 1934 revision of *Paris*; the 1967 revision was ratified only in 1996. Ratification of *Berne*'s 1971 version is yet to come.

The most recent major international developments have been the *North American Free Trade Agreement* of 1992 and the *Agreement on Trade-Related Aspects of Intellectual Property Rights* appended to the *World Trade Organization Agreement* of 1994 [*WTO*]. These agreements mandated the entrenchment of national treatment and high standards of protection for intellectual property, first in North America and then worldwide.[2] Non-observance can lead to trade sanctions against offenders. The process continues as revisions to *Berne* are proposed to intensify and expand copyrights further, especially to regulate digital technology. International corporate power has effectively curbed national sovereignty in the field of intellectual property policy.

1) Why "Intellectual"? Why "Property"?

Why were these rights thought necessary? Why do they even deserve the labels "intellectual" or "property"? It was not always so. The talk once was more of "privilege" than "property," as grants of monopoly depended on the favour of the monarch and the royal entourage. This favouritism changed in the West during the eighteenth century as the forces of the Enlightenment and the Industrial Revolution consciously worked to switch discourse from privilege to property. Capitalists want to "own" whatever their enterprise produces and to exclude everyone else from its enjoyment except on their terms. Ownership includes control of not merely *tangible* items of commerce exchangeable for profit but also the *intangible*: ideas, schemes, product and business imagery, even relationships with the public, or "goodwill." Everything can be turned into cash. Those who imitate or appropriate such assets can then be called thieves and pirates, whether the activity took place on land or at sea. Judges can rule that taking intellectual property is not actually

---

2   Ratification by Canada of the latest versions of the *Paris Convention for the Protection of Industrial Property*, 20 March 1883, 828 U.N.T.S. 107 [*Paris*], and the *Berne Convention for the Protection of Literary and Artistic Works*, 9 September 1886, 828 U.N.T.S. 221 [*Berne*] therefore seems little more than a formality, since the *North American Free Trade Agreement*, 17 December 1992 (Ottawa: Supply & Services, 1993) [*NAFTA*], and the *Agreement on Trade-Related Aspects of Intellectual Property Rights, Including Trade in Counterfeit Goods*, (1994) 25 I.I.C. 209 [*TRIPs*], obliged Canada to bring all its intellectual property laws substantively in line with what *Paris* (1967) and *Berne* (1971) required; Canada has, of course, now done so.

theft, since it is not property — its owner is still left in possession after the taking[3] — but such decisions can be treated as pettifoggery.

Lawyers and lawmakers have sometimes joined in the rhetoric that treats property as a transcendental notion. A 1985 parliamentary sub-committee report on copyright reform took as its lodestar the assertion "that 'ownership is ownership is ownership': the copyright owner owns the intellectual works in the same sense as a landowner owns land."[4] As a prescription for policy making, this notion is fatuous at best and question-begging at worst: unsurprisingly, the committee did not rec-ommend that copyright should embrace 999-year leases, zoning, and a registry that guarantees title. As description, the statement is a half-truth. The half that is not true is as important as the half that is. Intellectual property in this sense is a peculiarly Western conceit. It is founded on a modern emphasis on the individual and on individual rights, and on encouraging and celebrating creativity and innovation as paths to both self-fulfilment and social advance. By contrast, Eastern and traditional cultures that emphasize social obligation, submersion of the self, respect for tradition, and the replication of traditional forms and themes provide inhospitable soil for Western conceptions of intellectual prop-erty. They do, however, create fertile sources for serious misunder-standing and conflict between peoples and nations.

What is indisputable is that intellectual property has become the new wealth of the late twentieth century, and wealth must be measur-able and hence commoditized. The law in Canada and most Western nations has come to accept this capitalist imperative. For many pur-poses, intellectual property is classed as personal property (or *chose in action*, for those who like legal mystique). It can be bought and sold, licensed, and used to obtain credit. It may be part of the matrimonial assets available to spouses on marriage breakdown; on death, it may form part of an estate. It can be charged, taxed, subjected to a trust, and often taken in satisfaction of a judgment debt. On insolvency, it can pass to the official assignee in bankruptcy or to a corporate receiver to be sold off for the benefit of creditors. It cannot — any more than any other asset — be expropriated without compensation.

---

3   *R. v. Stewart*, [1988] 1 S.C.R. 963.
4   House of Commons, Standing Committee on Communications and Culture, *Report of the Sub-Committee on the Revision of Copyright: A Charter of Rights for Creators* (Ottawa: Supply & Services, 1985) at 9.

Yet not all intellectual property rights can technically be called property.[5] Even those that can may not everywhere have all the usual attributes of property. The right to stop one's name or image from being used in advertising may, according to some provincial privacy laws, die with the person and cannot be assigned, although at common law the right may pass to the estate and may also be licensed.[6] Authors' "moral rights" — rights to attribution and to prevent distortion and unfavourable association of an author's work — also cannot be assigned, but do pass to the estate on the author's death.[7] Trade secrets are in even more of a twilight zone: they are a mishmash of contract, equity, and property law,[8] and are probably capable of being passed on in bankruptcy, but are otherwise of uncertain assignability. Most trade-marks are assignable to others, but some may not be. The trade-mark a famous artist puts on her works to indicate authorship may fall into this latter class, because nobody else may be able to use it without deceiving the public.

In short, we can talk about intellectual property as we talk about military intelligence: as useful shorthand for a phenomenon, but with no implication that its components — intellectual or property — do or should exist. In particular, the property part of intellectual property should not close off debate about what rights attach or should attach to a particular activity. There is, after all, property and property. To compare the rights someone has in a manuscript or a trade-mark with those he has in an automobile or a piece of land is an exercise in contrast more than anything else.

What intellectual property law needs, whenever a policy or a concrete dispute is being debated or resolved, is a careful weighing and balancing of interests. How the appropriate balance may be struck is discussed in the chapters that follow and is reconsidered structurally in the conclusion. At this point, it is necessary to say only that throwing property onto the scales contributes nothing to this balancing exercise. At worst, it unfairly tends to bias the process in favour of protection, at the expense of other values. For against intellectual property as an absolute ideal are ranged values of at least equal importance: the right of people

---

5   Compare *Compo Co.* v. *Blue Crest Music Inc.* (1979), [1980] 1 S.C.R. 357 at 372–73: "copyright law is neither tort law nor property law in classification, but is statutory law. . . . Copyright legislation simply creates rights and obligations upon the terms and in the circumstances set out in the statute."

6   *Gould Estate* v. *Stoddart Publishing Co.*, [1996] O.J. No. 3288 (Gen. Div.) (QL) [*Gould*].

7   *Copyright Act*, R.S.C. 1985, c. 42, s. 14.1(2). See section I, "Authors' Moral Rights," in chapter 2.

8   *LAC Minerals Ltd.* v. *International Corona Resources Ltd.*, [1989] 2 S.C.R. 574, 61 D.L.R. (4th) 14 at 74.

to imitate others, to work, compete, talk, and write freely, and to nurture common cultures. The way intellectual property should be reconciled with these values — or vice versa — has changed much over time and continues to vary among countries and among legal systems. The adjustments occur for social and economic reasons; they are not preordained by natural law. Where a particular line should be drawn can certainly not be answered by circularities like "intellectual property is property" or "ownership is ownership is ownership." For example, at one time, newspapers freely borrowed news items from one another. Western writers and dramatists used to recycle stories and plots that had come down from old Graeco-Roman times — and some still do. Popular works used to be translated without any thought of seeking the author's consent; indeed, the original author would as likely thank the translator for causing the author's thoughts to be brought before a wider audience. Practices like these may now be frowned on in many Western countries as inconsistent with the cult of originality and individualism. Will the denizens of cyberspace be as censorious tomorrow? Are many even as censorious today?

2) Justifying Intellectual Property

How is legal protection for intellectual property commonly justified?[9] Morally, a person may be said to have a "natural right" to the product of her brain; a variant is to say that society should reward persons to the extent that they have produced something useful for society: as one sows, so should one reap. However plausible as prescriptions, these arguments have never been accepted to the full — or even the half full. We know that ideas are not protected once they leave their producer's brain and, when society does protect ideas after they have taken some concrete shape, the protection is always limited in time and in space: nobody anywhere has ever argued for worldwide protection of every new idea in perpetuity. Nor, if social reward is the criterion, can we say exactly what services deserve what reward. Does a pulp novelist read by millions merit as much as the inventor of insulin, even if readers are shown to need the pulp for their sustenance as much as a diabetic needs insulin to survive? And why should an intellectual property right be the appropriate reward? Isaac Newton could get no patent for the principle of gravity, yet his idea has proved more scientifically and socially useful over time than the finest Stephen King thriller, for which society thinks

---

9   Based on D. Vaver, "Some Agnostic Observations on Intellectual Property" (1991) 6 I.P.J. 125 at 126–28.

fit to award King or his assignee a copyright for the author's life plus fifty years. The decision on who gets the monopoly right where two or more persons invent something independently, without knowing of the other's work, is often more a matter of luck than anything else: the history of science and invention suggests that the phenomenon of simultaneous discovery is the rule, not the exception.[10] The sower who first turns up at a patent office will reap; the other sower will rue.

On the economic plane, patents and copyrights are supposed to encourage work to be disclosed to the public and to increase society's pool of ideas and knowledge. Yet much inventiveness and research are kept secret, and the law rigorously protects that decision, whether or not disclosure would be more socially useful than secrecy. Whoever finds the cure for AIDS or cancer can lock the recipe in a drawer forever. Copyright law, too, allows an author not to publish his work and shades off into a tool of censorship. The Australian government stopped the publication of embarrassing official documents about its duplicitous policy towards East Timor by asserting copyright in its literary creativity.[11] J.D. Salinger also used copyright to stop an unofficial biography that quoted from the author's correspondence. The biographer could paraphrase the ideas found in the publicly archived correspondence, but could not use Salinger's expression without the author's permission.[12] The law of confidential information can sometimes stop even paraphrase, as historian William D. Le Sueur found out at the beginning of the twentieth century. His biography of William Lyon Mackenzie was suppressed because Mackenzie's heirs had given him access to their forebear's papers so he could depict Mackenzie as one of the "Makers of Canada," not the "puller down" that Le Sueur ultimately suggested he was. Le Sueur owned the copyright in his manuscript, but Mackenzie's heirs were able to enjoin its publication as a breach of confidence.[13]

At a more basic level, intellectual property regimes are said to encourage the initial creative act. Yet, in the centuries before copyright and patent laws were established or were rigorously enforced, inventive and creative

---

10 R. K. Merton, *The Sociology of Science: Theoretical and Empirical Investigations* (Chicago: Chicago University Press, 1973) at 356. Compare *Kewanee Oil Co. v. Bicron Corp.*, 416 U.S. 470 (1974) at 490–91: "If something is to be discovered at all very likely it will be discovered by more than one person. . . . Even were an inventor to keep his discovery completely to himself, . . . there is a high probability that it will be soon independently developed."

11 *Australia v. John Fairfax & Sons Ltd.* (1980), 147 C.L.R. 39 (Austl. H.C.).

12 *Salinger v. Random House Inc.*, 811 F.2d 90 (2d Cir. 1987).

13 *Lindsey v. Le Sueur* (1913), 29 O.L.R. 648 (C.A.); C. Harvey & L. Vincent, "Mackenzie and Le Sueur: Historians' Rights" (1980) 10 Man. L.J. 281.

work flourished throughout the world. And if the *Statute of Monopolies* of 1624 really did encourage greater inventiveness, why did the Industrial Revolution take more than a century to arrive in England? Such a time lag suggests a lack of, or at least a serious discrepancy between, cause and effect in the law. In any event, much creative and inventive work today is carried out by employees who work for reasons other than intellectual property. The system celebrates quite trivial advents compared with the body of public knowledge on which they have built. The pygmy standing on the giant's shoulders may well see further than the giant, but the giant usually represents the contributions of many communities and individuals over centuries. In focusing on the present and the individual, intellectual property tends to discount the accumulated social wisdom of the past.

The strongest economic argument for intellectual property is utilitarian: without such rights, much research and creativity would not be carried on or would not be financed by capitalists. But this argument is only partly true. No doubt, less activity would occur — but how much less, and in what areas? It seems impossible to argue that the current laws encourage just the right amount of research, creativity, and financing, and in just the right areas. In any event, the rationale fails to make the case for intellectual property. If the allocation of these property rights is simply a means to an end — to make the fruits of creativity and research available to users — one must ask if the means is the most effective way to that end. If the rights restrict availability and use more than they increase them, they are unjustifiable; if the converse, one must ask if there are better means of increasing availability and use, either by modifying the rights or by finding alternative means.

3) Intellectual Property versus Other Means

Questions about how intellectual property is justifiable tend to be ignored. They sit uncomfortably with capitalist societies driven by notions of property, fences, privatization, and markets. Alternatives to intellectual property are often denounced as government subsidies or as other "interferences" in the free play of market forces. This designation conveniently ignores the fact that establishing a property right is in itself a form of subsidy. True, the state may pay no money from general revenue, but it sheds this responsibility by dictating that one person or one class of people should pay another person or another class a fee — that is, subsidize them — ostensibly for the benefit of the community as a whole. It is a subsidy with a difference. Questions of who can benefit directly and who must pay directly or indirectly are constrained by the classification of intellectual property.

One example will suffice. Assume for argument's sake that it is a good idea to compensate musicians for the unauthorized taping of their records, as the *Act to Amend the Copyright Act* of 1996, Bill C-32, advocates. There are many ways to achieve this end. Direct grants may be made from central funds, as is the case with Canadian authors, who are compensated annually for public library lending of their books. Or the Canada Council or the provincial arts councils may be funded to subsidize struggling musicians. Or tax write-offs may be allowed for private contributions to societies representing such musicians. Or buyers of blank tapes may be given vouchers, redeemable on later record purchases.[14] The money could come from general revenue or from direct taxes imposed on blank tapes. The beneficiaries could be precisely targeted: struggling performers could be preferred over the well-heeled; or Canadian performers, or certain record companies could be favoured over others.

Bill C-32, however, proposes a private tax, though it is not called that. The euphemism employed is a "right to remuneration."[15] Makers and importers of blank audio tapes would be obliged to pay sums to the holders of this right: composers, lyricists, performers, and record companies. The cost would be passed on to all buyers of tapes. Whether they use the tapes to record their friends' records or their own performances, or to transfer a compact disk they own onto a tape for the car, would not matter. Packaged as a copyright, this tax cannot discriminate between the wealthy and the struggling musician, the Canadian-owned record company and the branch plant of a major foreign company. It must conform to Canada's international treaty obligations, such as the *Berne* requirement of equal treatment for all foreign composers and lyricists. It also has a political consequence. Other governments will undoubtedly pressure Canada, under threat of trade reprisals, to give their performers and record companies equal treatment, too. Canada would extend the benefits of this tax at least to countries that provide Canadians with like benefits. This coverage means either that the local tax would go up or that the amount each performer receives would go down. If the tax goes up, demand for tapes may decline as people search for cheaper substitutes, and the returns to beneficiaries will also further decline.

---

14 See, for example, the voucher scheme proposed in the Federal Cultural Policy Review Committee, *Report* (Ottawa: Supply & Services, 1982) (Co-chairs: L. Applebaum & J. Hébert) at 244.

15 The Australian High Court ruled the blank tape levy to be a tax and invalidated it, since the Australian constitution forbids tax measures from being mixed up in a bill with other non-tax matters like copyright: *Australian Tape Manufacturers Assn. Ltd. v. Australia* (1993), 176 C.L.R. 480 (Austl. H.C.).

This approach is different from the way intellectual property is usually discussed today. The discourse is of intellectual property as opposed to subsidy, whereas it could equally be framed around intellectual property as itself subsidy. Thomas Macaulay could in 1841 speak frankly in the British House of Commons of copyright as "a tax on readers for the purpose of giving a bounty to writers"; but talk today of taxes and subsidies is even more emotionally charged than in nineteenth-century Britain. The result is to prevent the fullest range of policy options for a given objective from being openly aired and debated. Instead, entrepreneurs — who have no difficulty co-opting authors and performers with the lure of untold riches — press for rights. Direct subsidies or taxes mean more government involvement, an outcome inimical to the political agenda of most entrepreneurs. Worse still, subsidies and taxes can come and go with governments. Rights, on the other hand, once granted, can rarely be taken away, at least for long. Record companies in 1971 lost the right to charge for the playtime their records got on radio and television. Twenty-five years later, Bill C-32 would give the right back to them. The difference is that, this time, the right would be fully entrenched by international law, since Canada would adhere to the international treaty (*Rome*, 1961) guaranteeing the right.

4) Traditional Perspectives

Two other traditional ways of viewing intellectual property trace back to the Western Enlightenment. Both reject the idea that intellectual property rights are somehow "natural." Both recognize them as limited by other values. One, which still retains some attraction today, sees intellectual property law as a device to balance creator and user interests. The other, now less persuasive, considers intellectual property a contract between the creator and the state, representing the public.

a) Balancing Owner and User Interests

Since the eighteenth century it has been common in Anglo-American theory to treat intellectual property as the product of competing interests and values. Lord Mansfield expressed copyright's dilemma in this way:

> [W]e must take care to guard against two extremes equally prejudicial; the one, that men of ability, who have employed their time for the service of the community, may not be deprived of their just merits, and the reward of their ingenuity and labour; the other, that the world may not be deprived of improvements, nor the progress of the arts be retarded.[16]

---

16   *Sayre v. Moore* (1785), 1 East. 361n, 102 E.R. 139n.

In practice, this policy produces two poles in constant tension. One, driven by the "rough practical test that what is worth copying is prima facie worth protecting," pulls towards protection.[17] The second pole pulls towards broad rights of use. It holds that culture and the economy need a dynamically functioning public domain, so "care must always be taken not to allow . . . [patent and copyright laws] to be made instruments of oppression and extortion."[18]

Even within a liberal democratic framework, modern courts — often composed of judges who, as lawyers, acted for entrepreneurs and so easily empathize with their viewpoint — often favour protection for most products that result from intellectual endeavour or for which a demand exists, just as they extend property rights to the tangible creations of manual labour. If they deny property status to an intellectual creation or other valuable intangible, they decide in effect that everyone is free to use it; the originator can benefit from her creation only in competition with others who did not share its cost of creation and development. There is, of course, a tendency to gloss over the fact that the person claiming protection is often not the originator, but the firm to which the originator is bound in contract. But this slippage also occurs when property rights in the products of manual labour are allocated, and is treated as inevitable under capitalist modes of production.

Despite the tendency of some judges to let their natural rights instincts roam free, no intellectual property law says that every tangible product or idea deserves protection. Indeed, the opposite is true. The way intellectual property laws are carefully circumscribed shows that copying or independently producing an identical item is acceptable, even to be encouraged, unless it is clearly prohibited. Keeping a broad public domain itself encourages experimentation, innovation, and competition — and ultimately the expectation of lower prices, better service, and broader public choice.

Further, the decision to protect, once taken, must be matched by an equally careful decision on how far to protect. Overprotection imposes social costs by stopping or discouraging others from pursuing otherwise desirable activities. Before the public is excluded, clear harm should first be found to the particular right-holder or the intellectual property system

---

17 *University of London Press Ltd.* v. *University Tutorial Press Ltd.,* [1916] 2 Ch. 601 at 610. The aphorism conveniently begs all questions of initial eligibility, protectability, and even infringement.

18 *Hanfstaengl* v. *Empire Palace,* [1894] 3 Ch. 109 at 128 (C.A.), approved 100 years later in *Canadian Assn. of Broadcasters* v. *Society of Composers, Authors & Music Publishers of Canada* (1994), 58 C.P.R. (3d) 190 at 196 (Fed. C.A.).

as a whole. The restrictive treatment of parody by trade-mark and copyright law — penalizing humorous comments on products or business activity — is an example of business interests being overly protected to the disadvantage of an effectively operating public domain. Intellectual property law as written does not mandate these results. They come from knee-jerk tendencies to interpret the law to prefer business investment over critical comment, and not to ignore some grievances as *de minimis*. Intellectual property's legitimacy suffers with each such decision. Protection should be confined to intellectual property's "just" merits. The "progress of the arts" of which Mansfield spoke two centuries ago must, overall, not be retarded. The contribution of a later actor to this progress must be assessed as carefully as that of the first on the scene.

b) Contract

Patents were once treated as bargains between the state and the inventor. The inventor introduced a new trade or, more recently, disclosed a new invention; in return, the state paid the entrepreneur or inventor with a temporary protection from competition. The patent explicitly set out the conditions and representations (the "consideration") on which it was granted. Legal arguments could then be made that patents must be benevolently construed and that any failure of the consideration (such as not disclosing the invention fully) invalidated the grant.[19] Conversely, it could be argued that grants could not be unilaterally revoked or modified by the state once the consideration was fully performed. The theory was also politically expedient for patent proponents. A patent for invention was not just any old monopoly; it was one the public offered in consideration of getting a new trade or a public disclosure. Attacks on the grant were attacks on the sanctity of this contract — a more daunting hurdle to overcome than an attack on a simple monopoly.[20] Copyrights and other intellectual property could also be fitted into a similar theoretical mould: the rights flowed from a public offer of a monopoly in return for an author's producing and giving to the world a work that had never existed before.

These rhetorical flourishes may have made sense in the eighteenth century. The statutes then were cryptic. Patents were largely self-contained, spelling out the conditions of grant on their face. The magic word "contract" tended to shield almost any institution from criticism. None of

---

19   For example, *Pioneer Hi-Bred Ltd.* v. *Canada (Commissioner of Patents)*, [1989] 1 S.C.R. 1623, 60 D.L.R. (4th) 223 at 232 (S.C.C.).

20   Compare H.G. Fox, *Monopolies and Patents: A Study of the History and Future of the Patent Monopoly* (Toronto: University of Toronto Press, 1947) at 202.

these conditions exists today. What serves to invalidate grants is now largely settled by case law or is explicit in the legislation. Where doubt exists, contract analysis will hardly explain whether some infirmity is serious enough to invalidate a grant. The lexicon of contract may therefore be dropped from intellectual property law, with no corresponding loss of understanding. One may as plausibly claim that welfare beneficiaries or other receivers of statutory benefits make bargains with the state. Several questions remain to be answered: What are or should be the terms or duration of these "contracts"? Are they susceptible to change or revocation? What contract doctrines apply? Is it plausible today to claim that legislation that increases or decreases benefits mid-term is invalid, merely because the people it targets do not consent or provide fresh consideration?

B. SOME COMMON FEATURES OF INTELLECTUAL PROPERTY LAW

The specifics of copyright, patent, and trade-mark law are examined in the chapters that follow. In this introduction, however, some features and themes common to intellectual property law as a whole are noted.

1) Territoriality

Intellectual property rights are both territorial and international. They are territorial in that a Canadian right is effective in Canada only. It cannot be infringed by acts occurring entirely in France. Nor can a French intellectual property right be infringed by acts done in Canada. Similarly, an infringement in France must be pursued there according to French law; a French owner whose right is infringed in Canada must pursue the infringer according to Canadian law in a Canadian court. Some rights may cross boundaries. For example, a foreign trade-mark may be so well known in Canada that the Canadian Trade-marks Office [TMO] will refuse to register it in anyone else's name, and a Canadian court will enjoin its use by anyone else as passing-off.

On the other hand, intellectual property rights are international in that their existence does not depend on where the activity creating them took place. A book written by a French author in France automatically has a Canadian copyright; a Canadian patent can be granted for something invented abroad (indeed most Canadian patents are). The rights are protected by a web of interlinking international treaties by which almost every country in the world is bound. These treaties ensure that national laws do not discriminate against foreign producers and owners. Canadian laws implement these treaties, which are therefore essential background material for understanding and even interpreting Canadian law.[21] But harmonization as a goal, one that is striven for in the European Union [EU], is still far off the world agenda. Significant differences in approach and detail exist between national laws. So an infringement in country A may not necessarily infringe in country B; a right valid in country A may without incongruity be denied or found invalid in country B.

The dual national and international face of intellectual property rights has its controversial aspect. The rights are often used to create non-tariff barriers to trade by preventing parallel imports. Since a Canadian patent is in law a separate and different right from a French patent, a patented product lawfully made in France but exported to Canada may infringe a Canadian patent. This phenomenon allows intellectual property rights to be manipulated to prevent parallel imports where the same entity owns or controls both patents. Far from disapproving, the international treaties reinforce this right, and free-market unions like the EU, initially hostile, are succumbing to it. The result is to reinforce the policies of multinational corporations, which can set the price and quality of items differently in one country from another.

The most serious challenge to these structures and tendencies may come from a different direction: instantaneous communication technology. A Canadian may upload her writings or artwork electronically onto an Internet server located in Germany. From there, the material may be downloaded by another user located in Canada, Uganda, or Thailand. What law applies to the uploading: Canadian, German, or both? What law applies to the downloading: German, Canadian, Ugandan, Thai, or some combination? The rules governing conflicts of laws work even more arbitrarily in cyberspace. Critical events like uploading, accessing, downloading, and redistribution of material may occur anywhere. Concepts of territoriality may simply create chance applications of one or another country's laws. In the extreme, those laws may become practically unenforceable.

2) Cumulative Rights

Intellectual property rights are distinct from property rights in the tangible item to which they relate. Selling a patented machine or a book

---

21 *National Corn Growers Assn. v. Canada (Import Tribunal)*, [1990] 2 S.C.R. 1324, 74 D.L.R. (4th) 449 at 482–83 (S.C.C.) (*GATT*); *Milliken & Co. v. Interface Flooring Systems (Canada) Inc.* (1993), 52 C.P.R. (3d) 92 (Fed. T.D.), aff'd (1994), 58 C.P.R. (3d) 157 (Fed. C.A.) (copyright and *Berne*).

does not transfer any interest in the patent or copyright, but the intellectual property owner cannot prevent the buyer from using the article, at least in its expected way. For example, while articles may usually be repaired without problem, substantial changes or complete reconstruction may infringe the intellectual property owner's rights.[22] Those with thoughts of livening up some dreary artwork will find that distortions or other prejudicial changes may infringe the moral rights of the artist.[23]

Intellectual property rights are also distinct from one another. So, for example, a copyright owner cannot rely on its copyright to insulate it from other wrongs it may commit in relation to the work. The material in the work may have been obtained in breach of confidence. The title may be objectionable as a tortious passing-off if it suggests that the work is a sequel of another well-known work. The contents may also violate an author's moral right of attribution or integrity.

Many rights are also held cumulatively. A firm's logo may be registered as a trade-mark, a textile pattern may be registered as an industrial design, a computer program can be protected by a patent, yet copyright protection for all three is often cumulatively claimed and courts have usually accepted it unless a statute positively limits overlap. This is a debatable policy, for multiple protection is usually overprotection. If material is adequately protected by trade-mark law, why stretch copyright law to protect it more? If material such as a computer program has a copyright, why should it also be patented? If dual protection, such as copyright and patent, is available, why should the copyright not be forfeited on the voluntary acquisition of a patent?

3) Registration

Some rights exist without registration: trade-marks, business names, trade secrets, and other business confidences are protected at common law. Copyrights are also automatically protected under the *Copyright Act*, although they can optionally be registered, too. But many intellectual property rights depend for their existence on registration with the Canadian Intellectual Property Office in Hull, Quebec. Different branches are concerned with different rights: the Patent Office handles patents; the Trade-marks Office handles registration of trade-marks,

---

22 See "Repairs and Modifications" in section J(3) in chapter 2, section H(6) in chapter 3, and section I(5) in chapter 4.
23 Moral rights live on for fifty years after the author dies and may be exercised by the estate. See section I, "Authors' Moral Rights," in chapter 2.

and so on. Except for copyrights, the application for registration is first carefully checked by a specialized examiner to determine that the statutory conditions for obtaining the right exist. The procedure is usually between the applicant and the examiner only. Plant breeders' right and trade-mark applications are exceptions, in that third parties can oppose applications. Trade-mark oppositions are particularly frequent.

Once registered, the right is presumed valid in all judicial and administrative proceedings — but not indefeasibly so. Those with a legitimate interest can always challenge validity or title by applying to the Federal Court to have the right struck off the register, or by defending an infringement action by pleading invalidity or cross-claiming to expunge the right. The person challenging validity usually carries the burden of proof.[24]

4) Marking Optional

It is common to see references to intellectual property rights on goods or on their advertising or packaging. Reflecting U.S. practice, trade-marks are often seen accompanied by some notation: a registered trade-mark ®, an unregistered trade-mark ™, or, less commonly, a service mark[SM]. Books, films, and advertising often carry a legend such as "© Jane Bloggs 1997" or "Copyright Jane Bloggs 1997." Patented articles are also often marked with a patent number, country of patent, and patent owner's name. Still other products are sometimes marked "patent or trade-mark pending."

None of this marking is mandatory in Canada, but it is nonetheless legally useful.[25] It notifies the existence of a right or a claim and reduces the ranks of potential "innocent" infringers who might win a judge's sympathy. Marking may also help to create or to maintain rights, particularly for trade-marks. The first maker of shredded wheat breakfast cereal may have had a fighting chance of privatizing "shredded wheat" as its own brand had it consistently referred to its product as "SHREDDED WHEAT™ brand breakfast biscuit." Instead, "shredded wheat" fell into the public domain, becoming the common name of the product itself.[26]

---

24   See section C(2), "Presumption of Validity," in chapter 5.

25   A false marking can, however, be disadvantageous, particularly if the lie is deliberate: if persisted in, the practice may cause the refusal of discretionary relief (injunctions, accounts of profits, etc.) for lack of "clean hands." False marking does not, however, usually prevent registration or cause invalidation of the intellectual property right; compare *Enterprise Rent-A-Car Co.* v. *Singer* (1996), 66 C.P.R. (3d) 453 at 486–87 (Fed. T.D.).

26   See section C(1)(b), "Generic Marks" in chapter 4.

Marking can also clarify a right-holder's intentions where users are uncertain of their rights. Thus, on the Internet, right-holder notices often spell out what users may and may not do with material that can easily be accessed, downloaded, manipulated, reproduced, and redistributed electronically or in hard copy. The notices may technically be licences,[27] so disobedience may mean infringing the owner's copyright. But since the difficulties of detecting and enforcing such infringements are well known, the notices often operate on another level: as appeals to users' sense of honesty and fair play. In cyberspace, a version of the golden rule — do unto your neighbour as you would have your neighbour do unto you — may gain in moral force what it lacks in legal sanction.

Because marking is not mandatory, the onus is nonetheless squarely on all users to ensure that an activity does not infringe some intellectual property right of which they may be totally unaware. Even courts sympathetic to the innocent usually do not hesitate to grant injunctions and issue orders to withdraw offending goods.

5) Constitutional Problems

Some rights that protect intellectual property, such as actions for passing-off or breach of confidence, fall under provincial jurisdiction as "Property and Civil Rights in the Province" or "Matters of a merely local or private Nature in the Province."[28] Most intellectual property, however, comes under federal jurisdiction. Thus, the *Patent* and the *Copyright Acts* come under Parliament's exclusive power to legislate in respect of "Patents of Invention and Discovery" and "Copyrights," respectively.[29] The *Industrial Design Act* also draws on the "copyrights" power; indeed, design rights in the nineteenth century were commonly called "copyrights."

Surprisingly, trade-marks are not mentioned in the *Constitution Act, 1867* but immediately after Confederation Canada continued the trade-marks register established by the Province of Canada; trade-marks

---

27 See chapter 5.

28 *Constitution Act, 1867* (U.K.), 30 & 31 Vict., c. 3, ss. 92(13) & 92 (16) [*1867 Act*].

29 *1867 Act, ibid.*, ss. 91(22) & 91(23). The setting up and disbanding of compulsory licence schemes and rate-fixing tribunals have come within these powers: *Smith, Kline & French Laboratories Ltd. v. Canada (A.G.)*, [1986] 1 F.C. 274 (T.D.), aff'd [1987] 2 F.C. 359 (C.A.); *Society of Composers, Authors & Music Publishers of Canada v. Landmark Cinemas of Canada Ltd.* (1992), 45 C.P.R. (3d) 346 (Fed. T.D.); *Apotex v. Tanabe Seiyaku & Nordic* (1994), 59 C.P.R. (3d) 38 (Ont. Gen. Div.).

legislation therefore clearly was considered part of the "Regulation of Trade and Commerce."[30] The trade and commerce power may also support other rights, including the *Plant Breeders' Rights* and the *Integrated Circuit Topography Acts*, although patent-like PBRs can be based on the Parliament's exclusive jurisdiction over "Patents of Invention and Discovery," and design-like ICTs on its similar jurisdiction over "Copyrights." Of course, the fact that these laws may have been enacted to fulfil international treaty obligations does not by itself bring them within federal power.

A law may be constitutional as a whole, yet individual provisions may not be. For example, performers' rights over their live performances, found in the *Copyright Act*, are categorically different from copyrights historically, and so might not qualify constitutionally as "copyrights"; but, if enacted as a *World Trade Organization Agreement* obligation, such rights can be supported by reference to the "Trade and Commerce" power. Alternatively, they may validly "round out" intellectual property schemes if, for instance, a "rational functional connection" between the provision and a valid-as-a-whole scheme can be shown. Otherwise, they enter provincial territory and become invalid exercises of the federal legislative power.

Parts of the *Trade-marks Act* have been under attack as not sufficiently connected to trade and commerce. The complaints come typically from local businesses that rely on provincial law for their protection, while the *Trade-marks Act* is more designed to protect businesses operating interprovincially or across Canada. The resulting conflict has given neither the local merchant nor the national registrant much satisfaction when their businesses collide in a particular locality.[31]

Sections 7 and 9 of the *Trade-marks Act*, dealing with offensive business practices and "official" marks, have also drawn fire. Indeed, subsection 7(e), allowing civil actions for acts or business practices "contrary to honest industrial or commercial usage in Canada," has been struck down for attempting to create a tort within sole provincial competence.[32] Similarly, subsection 7(a), allowing civil actions for misleading statements that discredit a competitor's business, has been limited to statements about existing intellectual property rights. It has not been applied to statements about inchoate intellectual property rights (as where a claimant has only applied for a patent) or about a competitor's

---

30   *1867 Act, ibid.*, s. 91(2); *Macdonald v. Vapor Canada Ltd.* (1976), [1977] 2 S.C.R. 134 [*Vapor*].

31   *Reference Re Constitution Act, 1867, ss. 91 & 92* (1991), 80 D.L.R.(4th) 431 at 451–52 (Man. C.A.).

32   *Vapor*, above note 30.

business generally.[33] On the other hand, the passing-off tort created by subsection 7(b) of the *Trade-marks Act* has been upheld, since protecting the goodwill of unregistered trade-marks "rounds out" the registered marks system. The protection section 9 of the *Act* gives to official marks has also so far been ruled valid.[34]

The question remains, however, of how far guarantees of freedom of the media and of expression in the *Canadian Charter of Rights and Freedoms* affect intellectual property rights — an issue that has been as yet little developed in the jurisprudence. For example, may comparative advertising, or parody that includes copyright and trade-marked material, be constitutionally protected from being infringement? If the *Charter* protects commercial speech (as the Supreme Court has held), should it not also protect speech in furtherance of a labour dispute?[35] Will the Internet be recognized as a new form of communication that may require all present intellectual property constraints to be reshaped in the light of the imperatives of free expression?[36]

FURTHER READINGS

ALFORD, W.P., "Don't Stop Thinking About . . . Yesterday: Why There Was No Indigenous Counterpart to Intellectual Property Law in Imperial China" (1993) 7 J. Chinese L. 3

AMERICAN ASSOCIATION OF LAW SCHOOLS INTELLECTUAL PROPERTY SECTION, "Symposium on Compliance with the TRIPs Agreement" (1996) 29 Vand. J. Transnat'l L. 1

BRUSH, S.B., & D. STABINSKY, eds., *Valuing Local Knowledge: Indigenous People and Intellectual Property Rights* (Washington, D.C.: Island Press, 1996)

---

33   *Safematic Inc.* v. *Sensodec Oy* (1988), 21 C.P.R. (3d) 12 (Fed. T.D.).

34   *Asbjorn Horgard A/S* v. *Gibbs/Nortac Industries Ltd.*, [1987] 3 F.C. 544 (C.A.); *Canadian Olympic Assn.* v. *Konica Canada Inc.* (1991), [1992] 1 F.C. 797 (C.A.).

35   Not according to *Rôtisseries St-Hubert Ltée* v. *Syndicat des Travailleur(euses) de la Rôtisserie St-Hubert de Drummondville (CSN)* (1986), 17 C.P.R. (3d) 461 (Que. S.C.), dismissing *Charter* argument and awarding damages for copyright infringement against a union using caricatures of the St-Hubert rooster logo on stickers during a labour dispute with the restaurant chain.

36   Compare *American Civil Liberties Union* v. *Reno*, 929 F. Supp. 824 (D. Pa. 1996), invalidating the part of the *Communications Decency Act 1996* that criminalized "patently offensive" material that was not obscene or child pornography.

CHROMECEK, M., & S. C. MCCORMACK, *World Intellectual Property Guidebook: Canada* (New York: Matthew Bender, 1991)

CORNISH, W., *Intellectual Property: Patents, Copyright, Trade Marks and Allied Rights*, 2d ed. (London: Sweet & Maxwell, 1989)

ECONOMIC COUNCIL OF CANADA, *Report on Intellectual and Industrial Property* (Ottawa: Information Canada, 1971)

GORDON, W.J., & K.L. PORT, eds., "Symposium on Intellectual Property Law Theory" (1993) 68 Chi.-Kent L. Rev. 1

HAYHURST, W.L., "Intellectual Property Laws of Canada: The British Tradition, the American Influence and the French Factor" (1996) 10 I.P.J. 265

LADAS, S.P., *Patents, Trademarks and Related Rights: National and International Protection* (Cambridge, Mass: Harvard University Press, 1975)

MCKEOUGH, J., & A. STEWART, *Intellectual Property in Australia* (Sydney: Butterworths, 1991)

PHILLIPS, J., & A. FIRTH, *Introduction to Intellectual Property Law*, 2d ed. (London: Butterworths, 1990)

REICHMAN, J.H., "Charting the Collapse of the Patent-Copyright Dichotomy: Premises for a Restructured International Intellectual Property System" (1995) 13 Cardozo Arts & Ent. L.J. 475

RICKETSON, S., *The Law of Intellectual Property* (Sydney: Law Book Co., 1984)

RICKETSON, S., *Intellectual Property: Cases, Material & Commentary* (Sydney: Butterworths, 1994)

ROTHNIE, W.A., *Parallel Imports* (London: Sweet & Maxwell, 1993)

TREBILCOCK, M.J., & R. HOWSE, *The Regulation of International Trade* (New York: Routledge, 1995), c. 10

WALLERSTEIN, M.B., M.E. MOGEE & R.A. SCHOEN, eds., *Global Dimensions of Intellectual Property Rights in Science and Technology* (Washington, D.C.: National Academy Press, 1993)

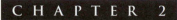

CHAPTER 2

COPYRIGHT

A. INTRODUCTION

Copyright is protected solely under the *Copyright Act*.[1] This statute was enacted in 1921 as a substantial copy of the 1911 U.K. copyright law. It came into force in 1924 and underwent major amendments in 1931, 1988, and, more recently, in 1993 and 1994 as a result of the *North American Free Trade Agreement* and the *Agreement on Trade-Related Aspects of Intellectual Property Rights*. Its central aim is to grant rights of exploitation to authors of original literary, dramatic, musical, and artistic works.[2] The works may be created through old or new technology: an artist using a paintbrush computer program today should be as fully protected as one with a real brush and real canvas was in the nineteenth century. An electronic multimedia work or database should also be as fully protected as the traditional encyclopedia or card-index. Quality and legality are irrelevant: trash and the sublime — even works that are pornographic or that themselves infringe copyright (e.g., an unauthorized

---

1   R.S.C. 1985, c. C-42, [*C Act*]; [unless otherwise indicated, references are to the *Act* as amended].

2   *C Act*, *ibid.*, s. 5(1), s. 2, defines "every original literary, dramatic, musical and artistic work." This tracks the latest (1971) version of the *Berne Convention for the Protection of Literary and Artistic Works*, 9 September 1886, 828 U.N.T.S. 221 [*Berne*]. The *North American Free Trade Agreement*, 17 December 1992 (Ottawa: Supply & Service, 1993) [*NAFTA*], compelled Canada, then bound only by the 1928 version of *Berne*, to protect copyright to the 1971 level of *Berne*.

translation) — all have been found equal under the copyright law.[3] Protection is automatic and usually lasts for the author's life plus fifty years.

The original purpose of copyright may have been to encourage culture — by providing incentives to authors and artists to produce worthy work, and to entrepreneurs to invest in the financing, production, and distribution of such work. Whether copyright, as presently configured, achieves those ends is an interesting question. Many works, as we shall see, have little to do with culture and are simply industrial products. Protection for these products, as well as for fine art, runs for the author's life plus fifty years. The work may be produced by an employee, who never sees the copyright because it belongs to the employer; yet protection lasts as long, even though the original purpose of benefiting an author's surviving family is no longer there. No rational employer, financier, or entrepreneur needs protection that can run for well over a century.

By contrast, industrial designs for mass-produced items like automobiles or dishwashers are typically excluded from copyright protection. They, however, may be protected for ten years on registration under the *Industrial Design Act*.[4] Protection like this might seem more apt for the many purely industrial items that presently fall automatically under copyright. For many other items, such as business letters, outmoded trademark designs and advertisements, and most computer programs, long-term protection seems equally unnecessary: Has not the cost of producing now obsolete WordPerfect 4.0 been amortized many times over? Needless to say, producers of such items would violently disagree. Nobody wants to give up a benefit that one day may possibly have some value, even though the item was originally produced without any thought of such opportunism.

1) Contours of Protection

The key features of copyright protection are as follows:

- Only original work is protected. This stipulation does not mean new work, but that the work must originate from the author, cannot be copied, and must involve some minimal intellectual effort. The level required can be judged from the fact that most private and commercial correspondence, however banal and cryptic, qualifies.[5]

---

3   *Aldrich v. One Stop Video Ltd.* (1987), 17 C.P.R. (3d) 27 (B.C.S.C.); D. Vaver, "Translation and Copyright: A Canadian Focus" (1994) 16 E.I.P.R. 159 at 161.
4   See section B(7), "Industrial Design," in this chapter.
5   See section C(1), "Originality," in this chapter.

- Copyright law prevents copying only. Nobody infringes unless they somehow copied a protected work. This requirement is what supposedly makes the long term of copyright tolerable and makes copyrights different from patents, industrial designs, or trade-marks, where the right may be infringed despite a defendant's independent creation.
- Copyright protects expression only: not ideas, schemes, systems, artistic style, or "any method or principle of manufacture or construction."[6] Anyone was (and is) free to paint funny-looking people holding guitars: what they cannot do is imitate Picasso's expression of these subjects.

2) Non-traditional Subject Matter: Bill C-32 of 1996

Copyright has traditionally been the preserve of authors and artists, but performers, record producers, and broadcasters have internationally been accorded rights akin to copyright (sometimes called *droits voisins*: "neighbouring" or "allied" rights) by the *Rome Convention* [*Rome*]. Theoretically, none of these persons is an author, none does anything "original," none produces a "work." Performers interpret or execute works, record producers record them, broadcasters transmit them, so none is entitled to a traditional copyright.

Nonetheless, since 1924, Canada has protected sound recordings by copyright for a flat fifty-year period. A bill to amend the *Copyright Act*, Bill C-32, introduced into Parliament on 25 April 1996, would extend copyright coverage to broadcasters and increase the coverage now available to performers, both for a similar flat fifty years. Even though performers are often like authors, and indeed, when spontaneously improvising, can be authors, the protection is for the performance itself, not for any originality that went into it. Thus one hundred identical performances, whether recorded or not, of the same tune each have separate copyrights. Broadcasters do nothing original in transmitting or carrying a signal: it is their investment in distribution that would be protected.

Most traditional copyright principles would nonetheless be extended to these non-traditional subject matters. In applying them, however, one should recall that performances, sound recordings, and broadcasts differ in justification and practice as much from one another as they do from traditional copyright works.

---

6   *C Act*, above note 1, s. 64.1(1)(d).

3) Application to Register

Registration with the Copyright Office at Hull is optional, since copyright is fully protected automatically on creation of the work. Registration, however, creates a presumption of validity in litigation and some priority for registered grants of the copyright.[7] Registration is particularly useful where the plaintiff's claim to title in the copyright is obscure or results from a chain of events, or where the work in question was produced far away in time or in place, for the person disputing what the register reveals bears the onus of proof. There is no time limit for registering. Certificates are often obtained at the last moment, just before infringement proceedings issue, causing some courts to baulk at giving them their full effect.[8]

Registration is a simple process: it involves filling out the prescribed application form and sending it with $35 to the Copyright Office, which registers the details and issues a certificate, without even looking at the work.[9] About 10,000 registrations are issued annually.

B. WHAT IS PROTECTED?

First we shall examine the traditional subject matter that is protected, and, second, the less traditional matter — sound recordings, performances, and, as Bill C-32 proposes, broadcasts.

1) Literary, Dramatic, Musical, and Artistic Works

Every original "literary, dramatic, musical and artistic work" is protected "whatever may be the mode or form of its expression."[10] The categories are further defined and illustrated in the *Act*, an approach that often seems like categorization for categorization's sake, but there seems to be enough flexibility to include evolving technologies. For example, the *Act* does not refer to multimedia works on CD-ROM, but this material can be protected as a "compilation":[11] the "mode or form"

---

7   See section C, "Registration and Expungement," in chapter 5.

8   For example, *R. v. Laurier Office Mart Inc.* (1994), 58 C.P.R. (3d) 403 at 413–14 (Ont. Prov. Div.), aff'd (1995), 63 C.P.R. (3d) 229 (Ont. Gen. Div.) [*Laurier*].

9   *C Act*, above note 1, ss. 36–58; similarly, Bill C-32, *An Act to Amend the Copyright Act*, 2d Sess., 35th Parl., 1996, new Part V [Bill C-32].

10   *C Act*, *ibid.*, s. 5(1), s. 2, def. "every original literary, dramatic, musical and artistic work"; compare *Berne*, above note 2, art. 2(1).

11   See section B(9), "Compilation," in this chapter.

in which works are expressed is irrelevant, and a mixture of different forms — literary, musical, and so on — melded into a composite whole is expressly mentioned as being protectable as a compilation.[12] Still, there are difficulties where works cross formal boundaries; yet classification is sometimes practically unavoidable because not every item is protected by the *Act* for the same duration or in the same way.[13]

Copyright protection extends to almost anything written, composed, drawn, or shaped. It therefore recognizes the diversity of cultural activity. In practice, however, copyright has sprawled into the realm of purely industrial products. Lottery tickets, advertisements, jingles, product instructions, company logos, computer programs, and internal company memoranda all jostle for protection under the law with the work of Margaret Atwood, Roch Carrier, Gordon Lightfoot, Carol Shields, and Michael Snow — not to mention Danielle Steele, Irving Berlin, and Roland Barthes. Since it does not matter whether a work is good or bad art, almost anything has come to be protected — both works whose creation was induced by the prospect of life-plus-fifty year protection and those that were not.

This comprehensiveness may or may not be a good thing. Its defenders claim it is the only practicable way to run the system, unless judges are to become arbiters of aesthetics. But easy entrance to copyright entails a corresponding need to monitor and delineate the scope of protection very carefully. For example, a lottery ticket can be reproduced in many different ways: by an artist who enlarges and frames a reproduction as a form of social commentary; by a magazine that illustrates an article on chaos theory by reproducing a stylized photograph of the ticket; by an employee who scans the ticket into her computer and uses elements from it to decorate her employer's web site and letterhead; or by a lottery operator who takes the ticket for his own competing enterprise. Granted the ticket has copyright and granted all these acts may, on the face of it, be infringements: the question is, which should and which should not be treated legally as infringements? In other words, how far ought a copyright owner be able to control what others do with its work? Questions like these may ultimately be more crucial than the threshold question of whether a work is capable of having copyright protection. True, gatecrashers should be kept out, but courts should be at least as concerned to police what entrants do on copyright's expansive terrain — and what others may do with or to them.

---

12   *C Act, ibid.,* s. 2.1(1).

13   Photographs, for example, are protected for a flat fifty years, while other artworks are usually protected for the artist's life plus fifty years. See section F, "Duration," in this chapter.

That said, one must be aware of the enormous range of material that may be protected.

2) Literary Work: Books and Other Writings

Literary work covers everything "expressed in print or writing": the form in which this occurs (paper, diskette, and the like) is irrelevant.[14] The *Act* mentions tables, computer programs,[15] books, pamphlets, and other writings, lectures (including addresses, speeches, and sermons), and translations as examples.[16] Also obviously included are novels, poems, biographies, histories, academic theses, newspaper articles, instruction manuals, preliminary drafts and working notes, and private diaries. Less obvious items have also been protected: *billets doux*, routine business letters,[17] examination papers, medical records, legal contracts and forms, telegraph codes, even a list of computer-generated winning lottery numbers![18] But short combinations of words (e.g., trade-marks like EXXON and slogans lacking any literary composition) or simple product instructions are not protected, since granting protection risks monopolizing the ideas behind the expression.[19]

Spontaneous speech and signing are obviously not protected, but what of e-mail? Some e-mail may qualify as literary work, just as tradi-

---

14 *Apple Computer Inc.* v *Mackintosh Computers Ltd.* (1987), [1988] 1 F.C. 673 (C.A.), aff'd [1990] 2 S.C.R. 209 [*Apple*].

15 See section B(3), "Computer Programs," in this chapter.

16 *C Act*, above note 1, s. 2, defs. "literary work" and "every original literary, . . . [etc.] work."

17 Thus, in *Tett Brothers Ltd.* v. *Drake & Gorham Ltd.* (1934), [1928–1935] MacG. Cop. Cas. 492 (Ch.), the following letter (omitting "Dear Sir" and "Yours etc.") was protected as an "original literary work":

> Further to the writer's conversation with you of to-day's date, we shall be obliged if you will let us have full particulars and characteristics of "Chrystalite" or "Barex." Also we shall be obliged if you will let us have your lower prices for 1, 2, 3, 4 and 5 ton lots and your annual contract rates.
>
> We have been using a certain type of mineral for some time past and have not found it completely satisfactory, and as we shall be placing an order in the very near future we shall be obliged if you will let us have this information at your earliest convenience.

18 *Express Newspapers* v. *Liverpool Daily Post and Echo*, [1985] 1 All E.R. 680 (Ch.); D. Vaver, "Copyright in Legal Documents" (1993) 31 Osgoode Hall L.J. 661 ["Copyright"].

19 *Exxon Corp.* v. *Exxon Insurance Consultants International Ltd.*, [1982] Ch. 119 (C.A.) [*Exxon*]; *Promotions Atlantiques Inc.* v. *Hardcraft Industries Ltd.* (1987), 17 C.P.R. (3d) 552 (Fed. T.D.).

tional letters do. But much activity on the Internet resembles conversation: person-to-person messages, "forums," and "discussion boards," where users instantly communicate with one another using a computer keyboard and screen instead of a telephone. This use could be analogized to instant versifying and a medium's automatic writing, which are considered protectable,[20] though these forms lack the interactivity that distinguishes speech, signing, and Internet exchanges from ordinary literary compositions. The Internet may have spawned a new hybrid: a communication literary in form, but oral in substance. Unlike most other laws, copyright usually celebrates form over substance. Whether this will continue with communication flows on the Internet remains to be seen.

3) Literary Work: Computer Programs

A computer program is defined as "a set of instructions or statements, expressed, fixed, embodied or stored in any manner, that is to be used directly or indirectly in a computer in order to bring about a specific result."[21] It includes source and object codes for operating and application programs, component routines such as a table of numbers operating as a program lock, the screen display generated by the program, and perhaps even the language in which the source code is written.[22] Most complex programs, such as a word-processing program, include many smaller linked programs and so are also a compilation[23] of literary works. But a literary work produced using a word-processing program is obviously not part of the program: the work's copyright belongs to the writer, not the programmer.

Copyright protection for programs is awkward and causes many practical problems. Programmers may enjoy being called "binary bards," and the codes they produce may look like telegraph code books (long considered literary works). But the purpose of the program is to embody the code in electronic circuitry, where it functions like, and often replaces, machine parts. Infringement trials resemble patent trials in scope and expense, except that they are more amorphous: no claims[24] stake out

---

20   *University of London Press Ltd.* v. *University Tutorial Press Ltd.*, [1916] 2 Ch. 601 at 609 [*University of London*]; *Cummins* v. *Bond*, [1927] 1 Ch. 167.

21   *C Act*, above note 1, s. 2, def. "computer program."

22   *Autodesk Inc.* v. *Dyason* (1992), 173 C.L.R. 330 (Austl. H.C.); *Delrina Corp.* v. *Triolet Systems Inc.* (1993), 47 C.P.R. (3d) 1 at 28 (Ont. Gen. Div.) [*Delrina*]; *Data Access Corp.* v. *Powerflex Services Pty. Ltd.* (1996), 33 I.P.R. 194 (Austl. Fed. Ct.).

23   See section B(9), "Compilation," in this chapter.

24   See section C(4)(b), "Claims," in chapter 3.

what parts of the program are protected, causing major arguments over what exactly may or may not be taken from a program or its output. As a U.S. judge recently wrote:

> [T]o assume that computer programs are just one more new means of expression, like a filmed play, may be quite wrong. The "form" — the written source code or the menu structure depicted on the screen — look hauntingly like the familiar stuff of copyright; but the "substance" probably has more to do with the problems presented in patent law or . . . in those rare cases where copyright law has confronted industrially useful expression. Applying copyright law to computer programs is like assembling a jigsaw puzzle whose pieces do not quite fit.[25]

4) A Digression: Integrated Circuit Topographies[26]

In the late 1970s semiconductor chip-makers operating out of Silicon Valley in the United States became worried that their output might not be fully protected worldwide under copyright and patent laws. They therefore persuaded the U.S. Congress to pass the *Semiconductor Chip Protection Act* of 1984. Shortly afterwards, the World Intellectual Property Organization convened an international meeting for the same purpose. It resulted in the *Washington Treaty on Intellectual Property in Respect of Integrated Circuits* of 1989, which almost nobody has ratified.

Canada nonetheless passed the *Integrated Circuit Topography Act* of 1990 to mirror the main aspects of the treaty. The *Act* excludes integrated circuit topographies — essentially layout designs embedded in computer semiconductor chips or circuit boards — from copyright protection, except for any computer program contained in a topography.[27] Integrated circuit topographies (ICTs) registered under the *Act* are protected for ten years against copying or independent creation. Time runs from the earlier of the date when the application was first filed or when the topography was first commercially exploited. The work must be

---

25 *Lotus Development Corp.* v. *Borland International Inc.*, 49 F.3d 807 at 820 (1st Cir. 1995), aff'd 116 S. Ct. 804 (1996) [*Lotus*].

26 Integrated circuit topographies are not really literary works, but are so closely connected with computer programs that it was found convenient to deal with them here.

27 *C Act*, above note 1, s. 64.2(1). How far *Anacon Corp. Ltd.* v. *Environmental Research Technology Ltd.*, [1994] F.S.R. 659 (Ch.), extending U.K. copyright protection to a circuit board diagram, may apply in Canada is unclear. See J. Choksi, "The Integrated Circuit Topography Act: Approaching Ministerial Review" (1996) 12 Can. Intell. Prop. Rev. 379.

"original," which in this context means it must (a) not be copied, (b) be the result of an "intellectual effort," and (c) not be "commonplace" among ICT designers or manufacturers.[28]

The *Act* is open to members of the World Trade Organization, but, compared with the United States, traffic to date has been light. Between 1993 and 1995, sixteen applications were filed and ten registrations were issued. Whether the *Act* benefits Canada much is unclear. Elsewhere the main effect of comparable legislation has been to stop the parallel import of videogames, an enterprise already adequately protected in Canada by the copyright and patent laws.

5) Dramatic Work: Plays, Films, Choreography

Dramatic works such as plays, operas, and operettas traditionally involve a thread of related events that are narrated or presented by dialogue or by action. Protection extends to the structure: the characters' "relationships with and integration into the sequence of incidents, scenes, locale, motivation, and dramatic expression" through which the story evolves.[29] Historical characters or events, however, cannot be monopolized; incidents and characterizations ("ideas") may be taken from earlier nonfiction if the treatment and development ("form") are different.[30]

Choreography, mime, and recitation pieces are also protected if their "scenic arrangement or acting form" is "fixed in writing or otherwise."[31] This definition should also cover abstract dance and mime if it has been previously recorded (e.g., by Labanotation) or if it is recorded as it occurs (e.g., by videotape). Choreographed marching bands and parades, ice-figure skating performances, sales promotions, and circus productions may also be included.[32] Oddly, only choreography is mentioned as requiring no story line for the work to be protected.[33] One trusts that this example intends to clarify, not amend, the law: otherwise, mime and other work within the dramatic arts would be unprotected if it lacked a story line.

---

28   *Integrated Circuit Topography Act*, S.C. 1990, c. 37, ss. 2(2), 5, 4(1) and 4(2) [*ICT Act*]. The ten-year period runs to the end of the calendar year.

29   K.A. Raskin, "Copyright Protection for Fictional Characters" (1971) 2 Performing Arts Rev. 587 at 590.

30   *Harman Pictures NV v. Osborne*, [1967] 2 All E.R. 324 (Ch.) [*Harman Pictures*].

31   *C Act*, above note 1, s. 2, def. "dramatic work."

32   M.M. Traylor, "Choreography, Pantomime and the Copyright Revision Act of 1976" (1981) 16 New Eng. L. Rev. 227 at 229.

33   *C Act*, above note 1, s. 2, def. "choreographic work."

Spectacles like football, hockey, or roller derbies, however thrilling, have been found not to be dramatic works. One reason given was their unpredictability: "no one bets on the outcome of a performance of *Swan Lake*," as one court put it.[34] Someone might very well bet on the outcome of an amateur or postmodernist version of the ballet, but, that apart, this test unwittingly excludes much improvisational theatre and performance art. Perhaps it is getting harder to distinguish between sport and theatre, but it is not hard to see why dramatists and performers might, more than sports participants and coaches, need copyright to protect their livelihoods. A test that relies more on sociology than on essentialism may work better here. It would also serve to explode a developing myth that sports competitors have some copyright in their "moves," despite the intriguing prospect of enlivening Olympic medal ceremonies by the added spectacle of writ service.

a) Film, Video, and Formats

The *Act* protects "any cinematograph." This term includes "any work expressed by any process analogous to cinematography," such as movies and material recorded electronically on any medium (e.g., video or computer disk), including probably the soundtrack.[35] A work may qualify even though it is not a "cinematograph production where the arrangement or acting form or the combination of incidents represented give the work an original character."[36] Before 1994, only such "original character" productions were classed as "dramatic"; films without this characteristic — telecasts of live events like football or of hosted rock video programs like Terry David Mulligan's *Good Rockin' Tonight* — were simply protected as a series of photographs.[37] Today, both classes of production are considered to be dramatic works.

Radio and television formats are problematic. In 1933 the format for a children's radio sketch was protected because the structure of the show was clearly worked out,[38] but, more recently, a British television

---

34   *FWS Joint Sports Claimants v. Canada (Copyright Board)* (1991), [1992] 1 F.C. 487 at 495 (C.A.) [*FWS*].

35   *C Act*, above note 1, s. 2, defs. "dramatic work" and "cinematograph." Compare W.L. Hayhurst, "Audiovisual Productions: Some Copyright Aspects" (1994) 8 I.P.J. 319, at 326–28. The Bill C-32 (above note 9) def. of "sound recording" provides that a film soundtrack has no separate copyright as a sound recording.

36   This "original character" criterion is still relevant to the length of protection. See section F, "Duration," in this chapter.

37   *Canadian Admiral Corp. v. Rediffusion Inc.* [1954] Ex.C.R. 382 at 401 [*Canadian Admiral*].

38   *Kantel v. Grant,* [1933] Ex.C.R. 84 [*Kantel*].

game-show format was denied copyright because it lacked certainty or unity: each show was different and did not "perform" the format.[39] The format for Mulligan's *Good Rockin' Tonight* was also thought to be unprotected because it had no story line or dramatic incident; but a format structured around the concept of a place where information on the "Top of the Pops" was gathered with high-tech equipment "lent enough dramatic incident and seminal story line" to qualify as a "dramatic work."[40] The distinction seems arbitrary.

6) Artistic Work

The following artistic works are specified in the *Act*: "paintings, drawings, maps, charts, plans, photographs, engravings, sculptures, works of artistic craftsmanship, . . . [and] architectural works," and "illustrations, sketches and plastic works relative to geography, topography, architecture or science."[41] For a non-specified work to qualify as artistic, one court has insisted that it "to some degree at least, be a work that is intended to have an appeal to the aesthetic senses not just an incidental appeal, . . . but as an important or one of the important objects for which the work is brought into being."[42] Coloured rods for teaching arithmetic to youngsters were found to fall outside this definition. More recently, however, coloured labels for file folders were thought to be artistic works. The court said that "artistic work" was simply "a general description of works which find expression in a visual medium as opposed to works of literary, musical or dramatic expression."[43] This approach seems the better view.

---

39   *Green v. Broadcasting Corp. of New Zealand*, [1989] 3 N.Z.L.R. 18 (C.A.), aff'd [1989] 2 All E.R. 1066 (P.C.).

40   *Hutton v. Canadian Broadcasting Corp.* (1989), 102 A.R. 6 at 39 (Q.B.), aff'd (1992), 120 A.R. 291 (C.A.). Formats may be alternatively protected on breach of confidence or unjust enrichment principles: *Promotivate International Inc. v. Toronto Star Newspapers Ltd.* (1985), 53 O.R. (2d) 9 (H.C.J.) [*Promotivate*]; R. Casswell, "A Comparison and Critique of Idea Protection in California, New York, and Great Britain" (1992) 14 Loyola L.A. Int'l. & Comp. L.J. 717.

41   *C Act*, above note 1, s. 2, defs. "artistic work" and "every original . . . artistic work."

42   *Cuisenaire v. South West Imports Ltd.*, [1968] 1 Ex.C.R. 493 at 514, aff'd on other grounds [1969] S.C.R. 208.

43   *DRG Inc. v. Datafile Ltd.* (1987), [1988] 2 F.C. 243 at 253 (T.D.), aff'd (1991), 35 C.P.R. (3d) 243 (Fed. C.A.) [*DRG*]. The design, however, lacked copyright protection because it should have been registered as an industrial design. See section B(7) in this chapter.

a) Drawings, Plans, Paintings

A drawing is simply "lines drawn on paper" or any other medium; included are sketches, illustrations, silhouettes, and pattern sheets cut from drawings.[44] The subject is irrelevant: landscapes, cartoons, engineering and architectural drawings and plans, even ideograms depicting items in a food store, are all included.[45]

There is an anomalous U.K. decision that asserts that "painting" does not include facial make-up and, moreover, that "[t]wo straight lines drawn with grease-paint with another line in between them drawn with some other colouring matter . . . by itself could not possibly attract copyright."[46] Neither comment is particularly persuasive. Most paintings are intended for hanging, but not all: body painting and tattooing are among the oldest known arts. Similarly, the court's views on minimalist art is inconsistent with the legal position on drawings and would discriminate among different schools of art. Constable's expressionism and Barnett Newman's vertical stripe on a plain coloured field should be equal candidates for copyright.

b) Photographs

This category includes photolithographs and "any work expressed by any process analogous to photography."[47] Both amateur and professional photographs are protected. No negative or other plate is required, so images produced by electronic cameras or xerography, photographs stored on computer disks, and holograms should all be protectable.[48] The fleeting images seen on a television screen or a computer monitor should, however, not qualify.[49] A single frame of a movie — perhaps enlarged for use as a poster — was formerly considered a photograph, since very often the whole film was classed in this way; but today the frame is probably protected as part of the dramatic work (the cinematograph) in which it appears.[50]

---

44   *Lerose Ltd.* v. *Hawick Jersey International Ltd.* (1972), [1974] R.P.C. 42 at 47 (Ch.).

45   *Spiro-Flex Industries Ltd.* v. *Progressive Sealing Inc.* (1986), 13 C.P.R. (3d) 311 (B.C.S.C.); *2426–7536 Quebec Inc.* v. *Provigo Distribution Inc.* (1992), 50 C.P.R. (3d) 539 at 543 (Que. S.C.) [*2426–7536*].

46   *Merchandising Corp. of America Inc.* v. *Harpbond* (1981), [1983] F.S.R. 32 at 47 (C.A.). The case involved pop singer Adam Ant's three coloured lines of greasepaint, supposedly mimicking Native Indian warpaint.

47   *C Act*, above note 1, s. 2, def. "photograph."

48   *C Act, ibid.*, ss. 10(1)(b) & 10(2)(b).

49   See *Canadian Admiral,* above note 37, although the conservative approach there taken on what constitutes photography and its analogues no longer holds.

50   *Spelling Goldberg Productions Inc.* v. *BPC Publishing Ltd.*, [1981] R.P.C. 283 (C.A.).

What of a photograph that is scanned into a computer and then electronically manipulated, so that some or all of its features no longer resemble the original? At some stage, the photograph presumably loses its identity as such and dissolves into a generic artistic work or perhaps an original electronic "painting."[51] This classification presumably will depend on the degree of artistry used and the extent to which the result differs from the original scanned work.

c) Engraving and Sculpture

Engravings include "etchings, lithographs, woodcuts, prints and other similar works, not being photographs"; sculpture includes "casts and models," presumably for the purpose of sculpture.[52] Both the original engraved plate and the prints made from it are included, as are moulds and graphic labels produced by a non-photographic process from a photographic plate.[53]

Work outside traditional art, such as Hogarth or Rodin, can qualify. In New Zealand a wooden model of a frisbee was classed as a sculpture — the expression in three-dimensional form of a sculptor's idea — but not the frisbees themselves, which were produced through injection-moulding.[54] Elsewhere machine parts and the moulds used to stamp them have been denied protection. They were not engravings, because this technique "has to do with marking, cutting or working the surface — typically, a flat surface — of an object," not (as the New Zealand case had claimed) shaping an object by cutting. Nor were they sculptures: while "some modern sculptures consist of or include parts of machines, . . . that does not warrant the conclusion that all machines and parts thereof are properly called sculptures."[55] These decisions will hardly be the last word on this subject.

d) Artistic Craftsmanship

A work of artistic craftsmanship is usually the product — typically durable and handmade — of an artist-craftsperson. The work need have no artistic merit, nor need be bought for its aesthetic appeal. Whether a

---

51   Categorization may be important because photographs are protected for a flat fifty years, while generic art works and paintings are protected for fifty years past the author's death. See section F, "Duration," in this chapter.

52   *C Act*, above note 1, s. 2, defs. "engraving" and "sculpture."

53   *DRG*, above note 43 at 546.

54   *Wham-O Manufacturing Co. v. Lincoln Industries Ltd.*, [1984] 1 N.Z.L.R. 641 (C.A.).

55   *Greenfield Products Pty. Ltd. v. Rover-Scott Bonnar Ltd.* (1990), 95 A.L.R. 275 at 284–85 (Austl. Fed. Ct.). See section B(7), "Industrial Design," in this chapter.

work qualifies is judged objectively, aided by the expert evidence of designers and artisans. What the producer intended, how she proceeded, and what resulted are key issues. Chippendale chairs, Cellini candelabra, Coventry Cathedral tapestry, stained-glass windows, hand-painted tiles, and wrought-iron gate work have been instanced as works of artistic craftsmanship. Clothing, coloured rods for teaching children mathematics, and mass-produced toys have not qualified.[56]

e) Architecture

An "architectural work" means "any building or structure or any model of a building or structure."[57] This description, like some modern architecture itself, has shed its rococo elements over the years. Between 1924 and 1988 the definition referred to an architectural work of art, demanded an artistic character or design of the building or structure, and confined protection to that character or design. Judges progressively elevated this requirement virtually into one of novelty, over and above the requirement of originality.[58] Prefabricated cottage kits were found to lack copyright since they had no "panache," "flair," "individualism," "distinctiveness," or "uniqueness": "Are the homes novel in an artistic sense? Are they set apart in some way from what one *generally* sees?" asked one judge, sounding like a real estate broker's questionnaire.[59] Finding "panache" or its synonyms should no longer be needed. Designs for any sort of building (even mass-produced low-cost housing) and products of landscape architecture, such as garden or golf course layouts, are protectable.[60]

Architecture may also be protected through the copyright in underlying drawings and plans. To copy the interior or exterior design of a house or store, or distinctive features that make up a substantial part of the design, may be to copy indirectly the two-dimensional plans

---

56   *George Hensher Ltd.* v. *Restawile Upholstery (Lancaster) Ltd.* (1974), [1976] A.C. 64 (H.L.); *Merlet* v. *Mothercare* (1984), [1986] R.P.C. 115 (Ch.), appeal dismissed (1985), [1986] R.P.C. 129 (C.A.), leave to appeal refused, [1986] R.P.C. 135 (H.L.); *Eldon Industries Inc.* v. *Reliable Toy Co.* (1965), [1966] 1 O.R. 409 (C.A.).

57   *C Act*, above note 1, s. 2, def. "architectural work."

58   *C Act, ibid.*, s. 5(1).

59   *Viceroy Homes Ltd.* v. *Ventury Homes Inc.* (1991), 34 C.P.R. (3d) 385 at 389–91 (Ont. Gen. Div.), appeal dismissed, filed on minutes of settlement (22 October 1996), (Ont. C.A.) [unreported] [emphasis in original].

60   *Hay* v. *Sloan*, [1957] O.W.N. 445 (H.C.J.); *Half Court Tennis Pty. Ltd.* v. *Seymour* (1980), 53 F.L.R. 240 (Q.S.C.). Naval architecture may also possibly be protected; *Bayliner Marine Corp.* v. *Doral Boats Ltd.* (1985), [1986] 3 F.C. 346 (T.D.), rev'd on other grounds [1986] 3 F.C. 421 (C.A.), to the contrary, on the pre-1988 definition, may not apply today.

from which the house was built; the copier may infringe without having ever seen the plans.[61]

7) Industrial Design

Much artistic work is devoted to making products attractive to buyers and users. The *Copyright Act* removes full copyright protection from some of this "applied" artwork, applied as a design to a finished "useful article" such as a vase, kettle, or boat, but not an ornamental sculpture, if more than fifty copies of the article are made.[62] This means that a Chanel "original" may be fully protected by copyright; so may any other original dress design, until the fifty-first dress is made anywhere with the copyright owner's consent. Then anybody can copy the dress (a useful article) without infringing any copyright in it or any preliminary sketches and patterns. They cannot, however, copy or photograph the sketches or patterns themselves; these are merely "carrier[s] for artistic or literary matter," and so are not useful articles.[63]

The only protection that designs for mass-produced useful articles may receive comes from the *Industrial Design Act*.[64] The design must first be registered on the industrial design register after an application for it is examined and accepted by the Industrial Design Branch of the Canadian Intellectual Property Office. All World Trade Organization members may apply for this protection, which runs for ten years from registration against copiers and independent creators alike.[65] The design must be "original," in that it must (a) not be copied, (b) result from some "spark of inspiration," and (c) either differ from earlier designs or be applied to a new use.[66] About 2000 design registrations are issued annually.

---

61   *New Brunswick Telephone Co.* v. *John Maryon International Ltd.* (1981), 33 N.B.R. (2d) 543 (C.A.) [*John Maryon*]; 2426–7536, above note 45 at 543–44.

62   *C Act*, above note 1, s. 64.

63   *C Act*, ibid., *Industrial Design Act*, R.S.C. 1985, c. I-8, s. 2 [*ID Act*], defs. "useful article" and "utilitarian."

64   Common law protection may occasionally be had for product shapes that function like trade-marks, where the market recognizes them as coming from a particular producer (whose identity need not be known): *Reckitt & Colman Products Ltd.* v. *Borden Inc.*, [1990] 1 All E.R. 873 (H.L.) (the yellow, lemon-shaped JIF lemon-juice container could not be imitated).

65   *C Act*, above note 1, s. 10(1).

66   *ID Act*, above note 63, s. 7(2); *Bata Industries Ltd.* v. *Warrington Inc.* (1985), 5 C.I.P.R. 223 at 231–32 (Fed. T.D.). This is a stiffer test than originality for copyright; see section C(1) in this chapter.

Such design artwork has been treated differently from regular fine artwork at least since the nineteenth century. The originals that Turner produced from his atelier were thought to deserve long-term copyright protection more than the long runs of pottery that the Wedgwood factory turned out. Today, this differential treatment may perhaps be justified because (1) designers are more likely to be on a payroll than are artisans, who (together with their heirs) may depend more on copyright for their subsistence; (2) industrial designs change frequently and firms can usually amortize their costs and reap a profit within a decade; (3) imitation is more desirable in the commercial sphere than in the fine arts. This distinction is, of course, highly debatable, and some of it applies equally to the utilitarian articles that copyright does protect. Copyright continues to benefit from the image of the starving author in the garret, whereas the designer sitting in front of a computer monitor in an air-conditioned high-rise office tower rarely excites much parliamentary sympathy.[67]

The attempt to draw a bright line between fine art and industrial design is unfortunately undermined by the list of bric-à-brac that is specifically allowed to retain full copyright: trade-mark designs, labels, architectural works, textile designs, character merchandising items, pictures on mugs, articles sold in a set (unless more than fifty sets are made), and anything else the government feels like adding by regulation.[68] These items may also qualify for cumulative protection under the *Industrial Design Act*. Moreover, designers of mass-produced cloth receive full copyright protection, but designers of mass-produced clothing do not, revealing the arbitrariness of the policy separating industrial designs from copyright. Design policy in many other jurisdictions is equally incoherent.

8) Musical Work

A musical work is defined as "any work of music or musical composition, with or without words." This definition replaces one in effect until 1993 which covered only "any combination of melody and harmony, or either of them, printed, reduced to writing or otherwise graphically produced

---

67   In fact, both employees and freelancers under contract have no design rights; these rights vest automatically in their employer: *ID Act*, above note 63, s. 12(1).

68   *C Act*, above note 1, s. 64(3); D. Vaver, "The Canadian Copyright Amendments of 1988" (1988) 4 I.P.J. 121 at 132–38; W.L. Hayhurst, "Intellectual Property Protection in Canada for Designs of Useful Articles" (1989) 4 I.P.J. 381.

or reproduced.[69] Experimental and aleatory music that had difficulty complying with the pre-1993 definition should now qualify more easily.

Problems with avant-garde music were not, however, the main reasons for the 1993 amendments. They were prompted by some odd interpretations of the *Act* that exonerated microwave and cable transmitters of music from any obligation to pay royalties to right-holders. These operators argued that copyright extended to communication of "the work"; their transmissions were not of "the work" because they did not transmit any "graphically produced" version; all they communicated was an acoustic presentation of the work. This, they claimed, fell outside the copyright owner's control. The courts agreed.[70] These decisions meant that virtually the only communications a copyright owner could control were those that featured a picture of the sheet music! Protests from the musical performing rights societies caused Parliament to drop the "graphic reproduction" requirement. At the same time, the "melody and harmony" requirement was also removed, presumably to avoid arguments that such works as drum solos were not protected.

Rearrangements, such as different piano versions of an opera score, have also long been protected as musical works. Each different arrangement can have its own separate copyright.[71] In practice, much early classical and jazz music remains in copyright, though its composer is long dead and buried; for the arranger who rejigs Beethoven's "Moonlight" Sonata for beginners by simplifying the source and including fingering, dynamic marks, tempo indications, slurs, and phrasing has copyright in her original arrangement.[72] Beethoven's descendants are entitled only to bathe in their forebear's reflected glory.

Similarly, a performer also has a limited copyright in his or her performance, distinct from any copyright in the work performed.[73]

---

69   *Copyright Act*, R.S.C. 1985, c. C-42, as am. by S.C. 1993, c. 23, s. 1.
70   *C Act*, above note 1, s. 3(1)(f); *C.A.P.A.C. Ltd.* v. *CTV Television Network,* [1968] S.C.R. 676; *Canadian Cable Television Assn.* v. *Canada (Copyright Board),* [1993] 2 F.C. 138 (C.A.) [*Canadian Cable*].
71   *Wood* v. *Boosey* (1867), L.R. 2 Q.B. 340.
72   *Consolidated Music Publishers Inc.* v. *Ashley Publications Inc.,* 197 F. Supp. 17 at 18 (1961).
73   See section B(12), "Performances," in this chapter.

9) Compilation

Compilation is defined as a work resulting "from the selection or arrangement of literary, dramatic, musical or artistic works or of parts thereof" or of data.[74] A compilation of literary works is itself a literary work, a compilation of artistic works is an artistic work, and so on. A compilation of data — such as an electronic database — is classified according to the type of data: for example, literary material becomes a compilation of literary works. A mixed compilation — such as literary and artistic work — is classed according to whether the literary or artistic work makes up its "most substantial part."[75] This formula may prove troublesome. Is a catalogue of paintings that intersperses text "literary" or "artistic" in its "most substantial part"?

Just gathering data and sorting them in an obvious way may not involve "selection or arrangement," and so may not result in a protectable compilation.[76] In the United States this restriction has meant there is no protection for white pages telephone directories: either they lack any selection or arrangement at all or the purely alphabetic selection or arrangement is too commonplace or mechanical to be original.[77] Items like encyclopedias, dictionaries, anthologies, radio and television guides, betting coupons, and advertising brochures that select and arrange material from various sources, collections of "one-write" business forms, and trade catalogues, all protected before 1994,[78] may still qualify under the more rigorous test because they involve more than industrious collection. Items like book or customer lists, sports pro-

---

74   *Copyright Act*, R.S.C. 1985, c. C-42, s. 2, def. "compilation," as am. by *North American Free Trade Agreement Implementation Act*, S.C. 1993, c. 44, s. 53(3) [*NAFTA I A*]. This overturns the view that only compilations of *literary* works were protected in Canada: *Re Royalties for Retransmission Rights of Distant Radio and Television Signals* (1990), 32 C.P.R. (3d) 97 at 146 (Copyright Bd.), aff'd (*sub nom. Canadian Cable Television Assn./Assn. Canadienne de Télévision par Cable* v. *American College Sports Collective of Canada Inc.*) [1991] 3 F.C. 626 (C.A.) [*Royalties*]. The "broadcast day," denied protection by this decision, has since been protected as a compilation of dramatic works: *Re Royalties for Retransmission Rights of Distant Television Signals 1995–1997* (28 June 1996), (Copyright Bd.) [not yet reported] [*Royalties 1995–7*].

75   *C Act*, above note 1, s. 2.1(1).

76   *Laurier*, above note 8 at 415–16.

77   *Feist Publications Inc.* v. *Rural Telephone Service Co.*, 499 U.S. 340 (1991) [*Feist*]. See section C(1), "Originality," in this chapter.

78   *Bulman Group Ltd.* v. *"One Write" Accounting Systems Ltd.*, [1982] 2 F.C. 327 (T.D.); *Slumber-Magic Adjustable Bed Co.* v. *Sleep-King Adjustable Bed Co.* (1985), 3 C.P.R. (3d) 81 (B.C.S.C.).

grams or fixtures, yellow pages business directories, and driver training manuals collecting mainly government material may involve little more than industrious collection and so may now attract closer scrutiny.[79]

10) Title of a Work

A "work" is defined to include "the title thereof when such title is original and distinctive."[80] The idea that this definition might confer a separate copyright on titles was rejected in 1939: the song title "The Man Who Broke the Bank at Monte Carlo" could be used for a movie without any permission from the song's copyright owner. Titles neither had a separate copyright nor were a substantial part of the work, unless they involved substantial literary composition, as did eighteenth-century full-page book titles that epitomized the book.[81] But the fancy graphics in which a book or film title is presented may have copyright. The unauthorized marketing of T-shirts carrying the *Crocodile Dundee* movie logo was stopped this way.[82]

Titles for periodicals or series (e.g., "Essentials of Canadian Law") may be registered as trade-marks, and any title may also be protected through passing-off law if it is not descriptive and if it has a market reputation.[83] So nobody may issue a rival *Globe and Mail*, except perhaps as an isolated spoof. By contrast, the publisher of a book called *Intellectual Property Law* cannot stop later texts from bearing the same descriptive name, so long as their get-up and marketing do not misrepresent the one as the other. The employee who quit the firm that was marketing a work under the descriptive name *Who's Who in Canada* could start up a rival publication called *The Canadian Who's Who*. The imprint, appearance, and price of the two works differed enough to prevent buyers from confusing the two.[84]

---

79 Compare *Tele-Direct (Publications) Inc. v. American Business Information Inc.* (1996), 113 F.T.R. 123 (T.D.), (listings in yellow pages directory not "original") [*Tele-Direct*]; *École de Conduite Tecnic Aube Inc. v. 1509 8858 Québec Inc.* (1986), 12 C.I.P.R. 284 at 298ff (Que. S.C.); *Index Téléphonique (N.L.) de Notre Localité v. Imprimerie Garceau Ltée* (1987), 18 C.I.P.R. 133 at 140–41 (Que. S.C.).

80 *C Act*, above note 1, s. 2, def. "work"; R. Stone, "Copyright Protection for Titles, Character Names and Catch-Phrases in the Film and Television Industry" (1996) 7 Ent. L. Rev. 178.

81 *Francis, Day & Hunter Ltd. v. Twentieth Century Fox Corporation Ltd.* (1939), [1940] A.C. 112 (P.C.). There was no passing-off, since nobody thought the film was based on or included the song.

82 *Paramount Pictures Corp. v. Howley* (1991), 39 C.P.R. (3d) 419 at 426 (Ont. Gen. Div.).

83 Generally, see chapter 4, "Trade-marks."

84 *International Press Ltd. v. Tunnell*, [1938] 1 D.L.R. 393 (Ont. C.A.).

11) Sound Recordings

Records, "perforated rolls and other contrivances by means of which sounds may be mechanically reproduced" have their own separate copyright distinct from that in the music or lyrics recorded. The recording may in fact be protected even though what it records is not — if, for example, it is public domain music, bird calls, crashing waves, or spontaneous conversation.[85] Bill C-32 would modernize the antiquated language of such phrases as "perforated rolls." Sound recording would become "a recording, in any material form, consisting exclusively of sounds, whether or not of a performance of a work." Film soundtracks would be specifically excluded: they would come under the film's copyright.[86]

Bill C-32 would also allow record companies to collect money from public performances and broadcasts of their records, and also blank audio tape royalties.[87]

12) Performances

Since 1996 performers from World Trade Organization states have been able to prevent the unauthorized recording and broadcasts of their performances. This coverage includes improvisations, whether the work performed is in or out of copyright.[88] Protection applies retrospectively to unauthorized recordings made up to fifty years before — for example, of live Beatles or Elvis Presley concerts.

Bill C-32 would allow performers also to collect money from the rental, public performance, or broadcast of records containing their performances, as well as blank tape royalties.[89]

13) Broadcasts

Presently, a broadcaster who televises or broadcasts a live event acquires copyright in it as a cinematograph work if the event is simultaneously recorded. There is no protection for unfixed broadcasts, but the selection of programs transmitted during a twenty-four-hour or other longer

---

85   *C Act*, above note 1, s. 5(3); *Bouliane v. Service de Musique Bonanza Inc.* (1986), 18 C.I.P.R. 14 (Que. C.A.).

86   Bill C-32, above note 9, def. "sound recording."

87   *Ibid.*, introducing cls. 18(1), 19–20, & 81.

88   *C Act*, above note 1, s. 14.01(1) & s. 2, def. "performer's performance."

89   Bill C-32, above note 9, cls. 15–17, 19–20, & 81. See section A(1), "Copyright for Non-traditional Subject Matter: Bill C-32 of 1996," and section H, "Owner's Rights: Sound Recordings, Performances, Broadcasts," in this chapter.

period ("the broadcast day"), unprotected before 1994, was recently held to be protectable as an original compilation of dramatic works.[90]

Bill C-32 would give broadcasters located in a World Trade Organization or *Rome Convention* state a copyright over unauthorized recording and reproduction of their transmissions.[91]

C. CRITERIA FOR COPYRIGHTABILITY: LITERARY, DRAMATIC, MUSICAL, AND ARTISTIC WORKS

To be protected by copyright, a work must be (1) original, (2) fixed, and (3) appropriately connected to Canada, or to a *WTO, Berne,* or *Universal Copyright Convention* member state.

1) Originality

Copyright protects only original work. The product must (a) originate from its author, (b) not be copied, and (c) involve some intellectual effort.[92] Novelty or non-obviousness in the sense of the patent law[93] is not required; indeed, little would qualify, if it were. So A and B, working independently, can each produce a similar or even identical "original" work and each will have his own copyright. This duplication can happen if they are both working to a similar plan or idea and using common sources. In such a case, A's work will not infringe B's copyright even if B's was made first. Someone copying B's work will infringe only B's copyright, not A's.

In aesthetics, originality is very much a contested idea. The notion of the Author as Romantic Genius, who, like the original Creator, makes something out of nothing, has been under siege at least since Marcel Duchamp exhibited an up-ended urinal signed with a concocted name

---

90 *Royalties 1995–7*, above note 74, distinguishing *FWS*, above note 34. See section B(5)(a), "Film, Video, and Formats," in this chapter.

91 Bill C-32, above note 9, cl. 21. The broadcasters envisaged are conventional radio and television stations, but not cable retransmitters: *ibid.*, cl. 2 def. "broadcaster." See section H, "Owner's Rights: Sound Recordings, Performances, Broadcasts," in this chapter.

92 *C Act*, above note 1, s. 5(1) & s. 2, def. "every original literary, dramatic, musical and artistic work"; *Ladbroke (Football) Ltd.* v. *William Hill (Football) Ltd.*, [1964] 1 All E.R. 465 (H.L.).

93 See chapter 3, "Patents."

("R. Mutt"). Was this "original" "art"? What made it so? The additions? The putting of a familiar object in a different context? The fact that an artist purported to sign it? What of Roy Lichtenstein's large-scale reproductions of frames from popular cartoons or of sketches from art history manuals? Would George Brecht's text, *Two Signs*, which reads in its entirety

TWO SIGNS
• SILENCE
• NO VACANCY

qualify as original?

The disintegration of Romanticism, at least outside Europe, has had its effect. Originality has been found in the most unlikely places. A poster of an out-of-copyright painting was called "original" because, inadvertently, it was not an exact copy. With an apparently straight face, the judge said that "[a] copyist's bad eyesight or defective musculature, or a shock caused by a clap of thunder" was enough to make the result original if the author "adopt[ed] it as his."[94] This decision meant that the more exact the copy, the less likely it was to have a copyright! Veering away from that conclusion, another court relocated originality in the preliminary work involved in converting a two-dimensional work into a three-dimensional engraving before running off multiple prints.[95]

In practice, originality may serve several public policy functions. First and foremost, it signals that enough has been done to create a potentially marketable commodity.[96] Production and distribution finance can then be attracted from investors who know that their outlay cannot be undercut by cheap copies. Second, the insistence that a work not be copied and that it emanate from an "author" prevents photocopiers, reprinters, tracers, or computer scanners from claiming copyright for mechanical work or for simply making material more available without added value. Third, originality helps police the borders between copyright and other rights. Words used as trade-marks, book and song titles, and slogans have all been called unoriginal, however much effort went into

---

94   *Alfred Bell & Co.* v. *Catalda Fine Arts Inc.*, 191 F.2d 99 at 105 (2d Cir. 1951).

95   *Martin* v. *Polyplas Manufacturers Ltd.*, [1969] N.Z.L.R. 1046 at 1049–50 (S.C.).

96   At least enough to make copyright something other than a cure for any act of unfair competition or misappropriation, torts the federal parliament cannot constitutionally enact: *Macdonald* v. *Vapor Canada Ltd.* (1976), [1977] 2 S.C.R. 134. The constitutionally unrestricted U.K. view that anything beyond a "single straight line drawn with the aid of a ruler" (*British Northrop Ltd.* v. *Texteam Blackburn Ltd.* (1973), [1974] R.P.C. 57 at 68 (Ch.) [*British Northrop*]) may be original may therefore need reconsideration in Canada, because it seems little more than a rule against people reaping where they have not sown.

devising them.[97] This last task is, however, too great for originality to perform alone. Judges unversed in art are sometimes too impressed by the effort in producing trivial matter — for example, the sloping VISA mark — and seem loath to let trade-mark law alone do the job that is its *raison d'être*.[98]

In fact, originality's requirement of some intellectual effort has caused it to lose its way in the twentieth century. As usual, operations at either end of the spectrum are relatively uncontroversial. Originality is rarely questioned where someone has done a translation, written her own computer program, composed her own song or painting, drafted her own engineering drawings, selected and arranged the best work of a single author or group of authors into an anthology, or even written a book on intellectual property. At the other end of the spectrum, originality also serves a useful purpose in guarding against over-easy extensions or grants of copyright when work is in, or about to go into, the public domain. Strategies concocted to extend copyrights beyond the fifty years after an author's death by bringing out "new editions" can be policed by insisting on substantial — not merely cosmetic — changes before a new copyright is allowed over the new matter. Changing a single word — however important — in a poem cannot create a fresh copyright for the poem or the word.[99] Other trivialities are also routinely denied copyright: (re-)arranging existing material in obvious ways, listing starters for a competition, composing a few sentences for an advertisement, producing simple application forms, shortening books with scissors and paste (or their electronic equivalent), or making minor changes to drawings without affecting their overall visual impact.[100]

But, while a low threshold test of originality may protect artists in their livelihood, it does not carry over well into the world of commerce. There it supports almost irresistible pressures to call virtually anything

---

97   For example, *Exxon,* above note 19; *Sinanide v. La Maison Kosmeo* (1928), 139
L.T. 365 (C.A.).

98   For example, *Motel 6 Inc. v. No. 6 Motel Ltd.* (1981), [1982] 1 F.C. 638 (T.D.); *Visa International Service Assn. v. Auto Visa Inc.* (1991), 41 C.P.R. (3d) 77 at 87 (Que. S.C.). See section G, "Owner's Rights," in chapter 4.

99   *Black v. Murray & Son* (1870), 9 Macph. 341 (Ct. Sess., Scot.), where one (albeit critical) word changed in a poem in the second edition of Walter Scott's novel *Antiquary* was not enough to create a new copyright in the poem or the book.

100 For example, *Commercial Signs v. General Motors Products of Canada Ltd.,* [1937] O.W.N. 58 (H.C.J.), aff'd without written reasons [1937] 2 D.L.R. 800 (C.A.); *Interlego AG v. Tyco Industries Inc.* (1988), [1989] A.C. 217 (P.C.); *FAI Insurances Ltd. v. Advance Bank Australia Ltd.* (1986), 68 A.L.R. 133 at 140–41 (Austl. Fed. Ct.); compare *Caron v. Assoc. de Pompiers de Montréal Inc.* (1992), 42 C.P.R. (3d) 292 (Fed. T.D.) [*Caron*] (pocket scheduler original).

original and protected. If someone wants to pay a lot of money for an amateur home video — perhaps because, like Zapruder, the photographer happened to have his camera rolling when President Kennedy was assassinated — then, so the argument goes, surely the filmer must have "rights" in it. Or if time and money is spent scanning public domain material into a databank and making the result publicly available for a fee, surely the scanner must have "rights" in this material. So, why not a *copy*right?

How copyright deals with transcriptions of speeches or interviews is symptomatic. Perhaps a transcriber who turns incoherent babbling into polished prose may deserve to have her work called original. What, though, of the transcriber who, like a tape recorder, provides an accurate transcript, perhaps with only the occasional correction for grammar or syntax? In the United Kingdom and perhaps Canada this version is considered original because it protects the transcriber's investment of skill, time, and labour.[101] In the United States, the opposite holds: a court reporter there apparently has no copyright in his transcript of evidence.[102]

The problem with originality therefore starts from its own internal incoherence. Although all concur that the author has to exercise some skill, ingenuity, judgment, labour, or expense (or some combination of these) in making the work, the type and amount of effort is left unclear. Courts often fudge matters by saying that it is all a question of degree and fact; that quality matters more than quantity; and that what qualifies as original for one class of work (say, compilations) is not the same as for another (say, painting). On the degree of work, some would require "little more than negligible" work, others "substantial." On the type of work, some seem happy with industry or even experience; others demand "creativity" or the expression of the author's own thoughts. On the latter theory, a judge's written reasons for judgment would no doubt be original, while the listing of subscribers in a white or yellow pages telephone directory would not.[103] How short e-mail messages or the written "conversations" that occur on Internet "chat corners" may fare is unclear.[104]

---

101   *Express Newspapers* v. *News (UK) Ltd.*, [1990] 3 All E.R. 376 (Ch.); *Gould Estate* v. *Stoddart Publishing Co.*, [1996] O.J. No. 3288 (Gen. Div.) (QL) [*Gould*]; compare *Cala Homes (South) Ltd.* v. *Alfred McAlpine Homes East Ltd.*, [1995] F.S.R. 818 at 835 (Ch.) [*Cala*].

102   *Lipman* v. *Massachusetts*, 475 F.2d 565 (1st Cir. 1973) (Mary Jo Kopechne inquest).

103   For example, *Tele-Direct*, above note 79, and *Caron*, above note 100; compare *Feist*, above note 77; *C Act*, above note 1, s. 2, def. "compilation." But what if the telephone directory were exhibited as an artwork, as A.C. Danto playfully suggested in *The Transfiguration of the Commonplace: A Philosophy of Art* (Cambridge, Mass.: Harvard University Press, 1981) at 136–38?

104   It is questionable, in the first place, whether these communications qualify as literary work.

Unfortunately, nobody can tell in advance what quality or quantity of work, skill, judgment, research, or time a court will demand before calling something original. The quantitative and qualitative "tests" used are notoriously unpredictable. An incentive-based test — requiring evidence that, without the stimulus of copyright, the work would not have been created[105] — might be more consistent with overall copyright policy; but the law, as presently understood, would need realignment, and a number of precedents, such as those finding originality in ordinary personal and business correspondence, would have to be overruled.

This preoccupation with originality has had at least one adverse result. It has tended to divert attention from other possibly more critical issues, such as when, by whom, and how far copyright should be asserted. The resolution of future disputes might be easier if more thought was given to providing guidance on these issues than on the elusive height of the copyright threshold.

2) Fixation

The *Act* nowhere specifies that fixation is a general condition of protection. Sometimes this condition is explicit for particular classes of work. Choreography, mime, or recitation pieces must have their "scenic arrangement or acting form" fixed in writing or otherwise. Live broadcasts or telecasts are considered fixed if they are recorded while being transmitted. Computer programs may be "expressed, fixed, embodied or stored in any manner," although what the virtual synonyms of "fixed" add is unclear.[106] At other times, fixation is implicit, as for photographs. In fact, most works are fixed in some way — in writing or on tape or computer disk.

From all these considerations, one court deduced that "for copyright to subsist in a 'work' it *must* be expressed to some extent at least in some material form, capable of identification and having a more or less permanent endurance."[107] This proposition is a *non sequitur*. The fact that some, even most, works are so fixed does not mean that all are or must be. After all, every work is supposedly protected "whatever may be the mode or form of its expression": this language is expansive enough to cover oral works, too.[108] Thus, "lectures, addresses, sermons and other works of the

---

105   J.S. Wiley Jr., "Copyright at the School of Patent" (1991) 58 U. Chi. L. Rev. 119 at 145–54.

106   *C Act*, above note 1, s. 2, defs. "dramatic work" and "computer program," s. 3(1.1).

107   *Canadian Admiral,* above note 37 at 394 [emphasis added].

108   *C Act*, above note 1, s. 2, def. of "every original literary, dramatic, musical and artistic work," tracking *Berne*, above note 2, art. 2(1), although art. 2(2) allows states optionally to make fixation a precondition of protection.

same nature" are protectable under *Berne*, even though they are expressed in sign language or an oral "mode or form."[109] By not explicitly requiring fixation for these works, the *Copyright Act* may as plausibly imply that these and other works are protected without fixation.

On the one hand, this flexibility may seem beneficial. Even in the print era, which gave birth to the notion, fixation was an ambiguous concept. Literary critics point to the difficulty of establishing a "fixed" version of a work that has gone through various revisions by the writer and her editors. Digital technology makes the point more starkly: How is an electronic database, on which the data change by the minute, "fixed"? Far from being a general precondition for protection, fixation may function better simply by providing evidence of the existence or character of a work. Otherwise, much improvisational, performance, and kinetic art, as well as interactive art generated by "virtual reality" products, may end up unprotected.[110] This distinction would discriminate among artistic endeavours that, on the face of them, seem equally worthy.

On the other hand, a fixation requirement does add some certainty to the law. It prevents arguments that spontaneous activity, signing, and oral conversation automatically qualify for protection and helps identify (although sometimes artificially) who can claim to be the author of a work.[111] The whole concept of fixation may need some rethinking, for either imposing or removing it across the board may result in an unnecessary injustice.

3) Connection with Canada, or with a *WTO*, *Berne*, or *UCC* State

Works created by a Canadian national or a usual resident of Canada (e.g., a landed immigrant or even a refugee claimant), or works first published in Canada, should obviously be protected in Canada. But copyright eligibility extends well beyond this definition. Virtually every original literary, dramatic, musical, or artistic work qualifies for Canadian protection. It does not matter when or where it was first published (indeed, whether it is published at all), and what its author's nationality was.

---

109 *Berne, ibid.,* art. 2(1); S.P. Ladas, *The International Protection of Literary and Artistic Property* (New York: Macmillan, 1938) at 216–17.

110 *Komesaroff* v. *Mickle* (1986), [1988] R.P.C. 204 at 210 (Vict. S.C.), refusing protection to a moving sand sculpture.

111 Thus, in *Gould,* above note 101, the reporter to whom Glenn Gould gave an oral interview had copyright in his transcript, while Gould had no rights at all.

Until very recently, it was impossible to generalize in this way. Even after *NAFTA* compelled clearer eligibility criteria to be introduced in 1994, a work's eligibility for copyright still depended on poorly drafted provisions dating from the 1921 *Act*. This restriction was swept aside after 1 January 1996 by Canada's implementation of the *Agreement on Trade-Related Aspects of Intellectual Property Rights* [*TRIPs*]. A work is now protected in Canada if its author was, when the work was made, a citizen, subject, or ordinary resident of a *Berne, Universal Copyright Convention* [*UCC*], or *World Trade Organization Agreement* [*WTO*] state or a Commonwealth resident (even if not "ordinarily" resident in a Commonwealth state).[112] Alternatively, the work is protected if it is first published[113] in a *Berne, UCC, WTO,* or Commonwealth country by issuing enough copies to satisfy reasonable public demands. Publication in different countries within thirty days of the actual first publication is treated as simultaneous publication in all, apparently allowing the copyright owner to choose any as the country of origin.[114] Films are protectable on yet another optional basis: if the maker has its corporate headquarters in a *Berne, UCC,* or *WTO* country or, if an individual, is a citizen, subject, or ordinary resident there.[115]

It used to be critical to know what a work's country of origin was, since works made or published before the country joined *Berne* or the *UCC* fell into and remained in the public domain in Canada. This knowledge is important now only to find out whether the work was still in copyright in the country of origin when it joined *Berne* or the *WTO*. If so, the work is now automatically protected in Canada even if it was made before the country joined.[116]

Since almost every significant state belongs to at least one of the *WTO, Berne,* or *UCC,* few works fall outside the net of protection. For those that do, the Minister of Industry can, by notice in the *Canada*

---

112 *C Act*, above note 1, s. 5(1)(a).

113 "Publication" has a technical meaning: *C Act, ibid.*, s. 4(1) & (2): see section G(1), "First Public Distribution," in this chapter.

114 *C Act, ibid.*, ss. 5(1)(c)(i) & 5(1.1). The "reasonable public demand" criterion does not apply to the construction of architecture or the incorporation of artwork in architecture: s. 5(1)(c)(ii)).

115 *C Act, ibid.*, s. 5(1)(b). Commonwealth residence (not necessarily "ordinary" residence) also qualifies. The film's "maker" is whoever undertook the arrangements necessary for its making (*C Act*, s. 2, def. "maker"); typically, a film production company, but sometimes an individual producer.

116 *C Act, ibid.*, ss. 5(1.01) & 5(1.02). Transitional provisions apply to protect reliance on a work's previous lack of copyright: ss. 29 & 70.8.

Gazette, extend protection if a non-treaty state protects Canadians similarly to its own nationals.[117]

D. CRITERIA FOR COPYRIGHTABILITY: SOUND RECORDINGS, PERFORMANCES, BROADCASTS

Sound recordings, performances, and broadcasts have different copyrightability criteria from traditional works. Sound recordings alone require "originality" — presumably some intellectual effort in the act of recording — although Bill C-32 would eliminate even this requirement.[118] So only fixation and connection need discussion.

1) Sound Recordings

Sound recordings are protected as if they were musical, literary, or dramatic works.[119] The same criteria of nationality and publication in a *Berne, UCC,* or *WTO* state apply to them. Their "author" is whoever undertook the arrangements necessary to make the initial plate (matrix, tape, etc.); the residence of a corporate "author" is any Commonwealth or *Berne* state where it has a place of business. The copyright owner then has rights to first distribute, reproduce, rent, or authorize these acts.[120]

Bill C-32 would change some of these criteria. The "deemed author" fiction would be dropped. The sound recording would then be protected if its maker was a record company with its headquarters in a *Berne, Rome,* or *WTO* state when the record was first fixed or first published there, or a citizen or permanent resident of one of those states at that time.[121]

However, the new rights the bill proposes would not apply to all records. Blank audio tape royalties would be payable on records first fixed by a Canadian citizen, permanent resident, or record company with its headquarters in Canada.[122] Public performance and broadcast

---

117   *C Act, ibid.,* s. 5(2). This power existed under the original 1921 *Act*, and works protected on this basis (i.e., U.S. works since 1924) continue with this protection, too.

118   Bill C-32, above note 9, cl. 18(1).

119   *C Act*, above note 1, s. 5(3).

120   *C Act, ibid.,* s. 11; s. 2 def. "maker"; s. 5(4). See section C(3), "Connection with Canada, or with a *WTO, Berne,* or *UCC* State," in this chapter.

121   Bill C-32, above note 9, introducing cl. 18(2).

122   *Ibid.,* cl. 79 def. "eligible maker."

royalties would apply if the maker of the record had its corporate head-quarters in Canada or a *Rome* state, or was a citizen or permanent resident of any of them, or if all the records were made there.[123]

2) Performances

Performers are protected against unauthorized fixation, reproduction, or broadcast of their live performances if the performance occurred in a *WTO* state.[124]

The expanded rights Bill C-32 proposes covering rental, public performance, and broadcasts would apply only to some performances. The performance would have to occur in Canada or in a *Rome* state; alternatively, it would have to be simultaneously broadcast from Canada or a *Rome* state by a broadcaster headquartered in such a state. For performances on sound recordings, the record would have to be protected by copyright in Canada through its connection with Canada or a *Rome* state: that is, the maker would have to be headquartered there or be a citizen or a permanent resident, or first publication would have to take place there.[125]

To qualify for blank audio tape royalties, the performer would have to be a citizen or a resident of Canada.[126]

3) Broadcasts

Bill C-32 would give broadcasters with their headquarters in a *WTO* or *Rome Convention* state a copyright if the signal was broadcast from that state.[127]

4) Additional Powers of the Minister

Bill C-32 would also allow the Minister of Industry to extend the rights given to performances, sound recordings, and broadcasts to other *NAFTA* members, or to other states on a reciprocal basis.[128] The Minister could also eliminate a right proposed for broadcasters — in respect of

---

123 *Ibid.*, cl. 20(1).
124 *C Act*, above note 1, s. 14.01(1).
125 Bill C-32, above note 9, cl. 15(2).
126 *Ibid.*, cl. 79 def. "eligible performer."
127 *Ibid.*, cl. 21. See section B(13), "Broadcasts," in this chapter.
128 *Ibid.*, cl. 17(4), 20(2), 22, & 85.

television programs shown wherever the public is charged an entrance fee to view — for signals coming from countries that do not grant a similar right in their legislation.[129]

E. TITLE

The author owns the moral rights in a work and usually first owns the copyright, too. To market their work, however, authors may have to waive their moral rights or transfer copyright to a distributor. If the author is employed, her employer usually owns the copyright automatically, but the position with freelancers and with firms acting as independent contractors is different. Paying a freelancer or a firm does not by itself give the customer full rights to the work.[130] The livelihood of freelancers or such firms may depend on the copyright inventories they maintain. The *Act* therefore allocates first ownership to them, rather than to the client who hires them.[131]

Unfortunately, there is little consensus internationally on ownership rules. Most states adopt *Berne*'s rhetoric, which makes the author the central figure on the copyright stage, but then adopt legal rules or practices that quickly allow him to be pushed out of sight.[132] In the United States, for example, many freelancers can, by simple signed agreement, be assimilated to employees; so a person or a corporation ordering such a "work made for hire" from them automatically becomes both the author and the first copyright owner.[133] The U.S. owner who sues for infringement in Canada will, however, fail unless it is the owner according to Canadian law or it joins whoever is the owner.[134] Whether *NAFTA* will force a different approach for U.S. and Mexican works

---

129   *Ibid.*, cls. 21(1)(d) & 21(3).
130   Except for industrial designs and integrated circuit topographies (ICTs), where the person ordering the work under contract is the first owner of the design or ICT, whether the maker is an employee or a freelancer: *ID Act*, above note 63, s. 12(1); *ICT Act*, above note 28, s. 2(4).
131   Compare section E(5), "Changing Ownership and Implying Rights of Use," in this chapter.
132   *Berne,* above note 2, art. 5(1); J. Seignette, *Challenges to the Creator Doctrine* (Deventer: Kluwer, 1994).
133   *Copyright Act,* 17 U.S.C., §§ 101 ("work made for hire") & 201(b) (1976) [*Copyright Act 1976*]; similarly for ICTs in Canada (*ICT Act*, above note 28, s. 2(4)). Compare section E(1), "Author," in this chapter.
134   *Frank Brunckhorst Co. v. Gainers Inc.* (1993), 47 C.P.R. (3d) 222 (Fed. T.D.).

remains to be seen.[135] Meanwhile, Canadian owners who try to enforce their copyrights abroad may have to comply with the foreign forum's law on ownership.[136]

1) Author

Who is an "author"? The term compendiously describes whoever writes a book, letter, or play, as well as every other producer of creative work: scriptwriters, music composers, artists, choreographers, and computer programmers alike. In Canada the status is reserved to the individual actually making the work. A corporation can be the author of a traditional work in only one case: a photograph. Nothing of course ever prevents it from being a copyright owner.[137]

a) The Unoriginal Author

Some say that "author" and "original work" are "correlative; the one connotes the other."[138] This is not entirely true: the author of a straight line may create something too trivial to be original. A person who does fresh work on an existing work may, however, claim to be author of the resulting product. So a musical arranger may claim authorship and copyright in her arrangement and sue those who infringe it, even if she failed to get clearance for her activity from the source work's copyright owner.[139]

b) Idea Providers Generally Not Authors

Copyright exists in the expression of ideas, not in the ideas themselves. An author is the person who puts ideas into their copyright form: the painter of a canvas, the sculptor of a monument, the architect of a building or the engineer of its structural work, but not the builder who exe-

---

135 *NAFTA*, above note 2, art. 1705(3)(b), provides that "any person acquiring or holding such economic rights by virtue of a contract, including contracts of employment underlying the creation of works and sound recordings, shall be able to exercise those rights in its own name and enjoy fully the benefits derived from those rights." No amendment to the *Act* reflects this provision.

136 *Enzed Holdings Ltd.* v. *Wynthea Pty. Ltd.* (1984), 57 A.L.R. 167 at 179–81 (Austl. Fed. Ct.); Seignette, above note 132 at 74–79.

137 *Massie & Renwick Ltd.* v. *Underwriters' Survey Bureau Ltd*, [1940] S.C.R. 218 at 232–34 [*Massie & Renwick*]. See section F(3), "Sound Recordings, Performances, Broadcasts," in this chapter.

138 *Sands & McDougall Pty. Ltd.* v. *Robinson* (1917), 23 C.L.R. 49 at 55 (Austl. H.C.). See section C(1), "Originality," in this chapter.

139 *Redwood Music Ltd.* v. *Chappell & Co. Ltd.* (1980), [1982] R.P.C. 109 at 120 (Q.B.).

cutes the architect's or the engineer's instructions.[140] "Ideas people" are generally not authors:

> A person may have a brilliant idea for a story, or for a picture, or for a play, and one which appears to him to be original; but if he communicates that idea to an author or an artist or a playwright, the production which is the result of the communication of the idea to the author or the artist or the playwright is the copyright of the person who has clothed the idea in form, whether by means of a picture, a play, or a book, and the owner of the idea has no rights [i.e., copyright] in that product.[141]

A lawyer drafting an agreement on a client's instructions should be its author, even though the client has sent her specimen forms as aids. But if the lawyer simply approves or makes minor corrections to a draft the client has sent, the client should remain the author; the lawyer may be legally responsible for the document's inadequacies, but that may not make her an author, any more than a libel lawyer passing a book for publication becomes its author.[142]

c) Joint Authors

The rule that the provision of ideas can never count as authorship is nevertheless coming under siege. Much work is the result of team, rather than individual, effort. Even a simple song may involve the intermingled contributions of a tunesmith, lyricist, and arranger. A collaboration like this may produce a work of joint authorship, with one copyright co-owned by the co-authors. If the contributions are distinct, each author has a separate copyright in her contribution.[143] The participants' conduct may help establish their relationship. So if A and B sign an exploitation agreement stating they are co-authors or, with their knowledge, are so named on their publication or in promotional material, they may be precluded from denying co-authorship, at least in any dispute between themselves.[144]

---

140 *John Maryon*, above note 61.
141 *Donoghue* v. *Allied Newspapers Ltd.* (1937), [1938] 1 Ch. 106 at 109. See also *Gould*, above note 101. The idea provider might, however, claim an equitable interest or constructive trust in the copyright. He or she might also have rights other than copyright — for example, those arising from an express or implied contract, or from a relationship of trust or confidence.
142 D. Vaver, "Copyright," above note 18 at 665–66; compare *Delrina*, above note 22.
143 *C Act*, above note 1, s. 2, def. "work of joint authorship"; *Ludlow Music Inc.* v. *Canint Music Corp.*, [1967] 2 Ex.C.R. 109 at 124–25.
144 *Prior* v. *Lansdowne Press Pty. Ltd.* (1975), 12 A.L.R. 685 at 688 (Vict. S.C.).

What contribution warrants co-authorship may be contentious. Trivial editing is obviously not enough. Correcting punctuation, grammar, and syntax in another's manuscript before publication should not qualify; nor should providing chapter titles or suggesting a few ideas or lines.[145] On the other hand, contributions to a work's expression that would independently create an original work are obviously enough. In between these two extremes is the case, for example, where A supplies B with all the ideas for the plot of a play and B turns them into a finished work. This collaboration has sometimes not counted as joint authorship unless A's ideas were independently copyrightable[146] — a result that may promote certainty but that still seems hard. There would have been no play at all without A's input. To elevate B's contribution and entirely discount A's may discourage some fruitful collaborations. It may also undesirably invite a minute examination and dissection of who said and did what, often long after the event when memory is unreliable. Any substantial intellectual contribution to a work's composition pursuant to a common design should, in principle, count as co-authorship. A house designer whose detailed instructions to the drafters enabled them to draw the house plan was held to be a co-author with the drafters.[147]

An apparent reluctance on the part of some courts to admit joint authorship may spring partly from the romantic view of the author as Lone Genius, or from a more pragmatic desire to avoid problems that plague co-ownership generally but that are particularly acute for copyright. For example, in what shares do co-owners hold? If one co-author contributed more than another, does she deserve a greater share? How is "more" to be assessed, without encountering aesthetic difficulties? What if one co-owner refuses to agree on whether or how to exploit a work? Can the court "partition" this property or order a sale? If there is a partition, what part goes to which owner, and how can exploitation practically occur without affecting the other owner's interest? U.K. law avoids some of these questions by allowing any one co-owner to prevent all forms of exploitation and to obtain an injunction and its share of

---

145 *Dion v. Trottier* (23 July 1987), (Que. S.C.) [unreported] at 29–31.

146 *Kantel,* above note 38; *Ashmore v. Douglas-Home* (1982), [1987] F.S.R. 553 at 560 (Ch.).

147 *Cala,* above note 101 at 835–37; see also *Najma Heptulla v. Orient Longman Ltd.* (1988), [1989] F.S.R. 598 at 609 (India H.C.). The common law could partly mitigate the results of denying co-authorship — for example, through principles of unjust enrichment, trust, confidence, or implied agreement: see *Promotivate,* above note 40.

damages or profits from infringement.[148] U.S. law, by contrast, allows a co-owner to exploit a work by non-exclusive licensing without the other co-owners' consent, subject to accounting to the others for their share of the proceeds.[149] Canadian courts might prefer a similar solution to that of the United Kingdom, where one co-owner can play "dog in the manger." Until Canadian law is clarified, the tendency to avoid finding joint authorship wherever possible may perhaps continue being justified by pragmatic considerations.[150]

d) Photographs and Films

For photographs, extraordinarily, the owner of the initial negative (or if none, of the photograph) is also the author and first copyright owner. The owner may be a corporation.[151] Presumably, the person whose photo is taken in a coin-operated automatic photograph booth is the author of the photo, since the payment made by or for her would usually cover ownership of the negative.

The authorship of films is surprisingly unclear. For an unedited movie of live events shot before 1994, the position is the same as for photographs: the owner of the initial negative is the author, as the movie was then considered merely a series of photographs.[152] Such movies are now classed as dramatic works, along with regular commercial movies and television drama. The "author" of these dramatic works presumably is the person who gave the "arrangement or acting form or the combination of incidents represented" in the production "an original character." This would usually be the director. This copyright is separate from those in the underlying work — the script, the scenario, and the soundtrack.

For a home movie lacking the requisite original character, the author would presumably be whoever shoots the film, for he or she is the "effective cause of the representation when completed."[153] Whether scenes taken by an automatic surveillance camera are authored by any-

---

148   For example, *Cescinsky v. George Routledge & Sons Ltd.*, [1916] 2 K.B. 325; *Redwood Music Ltd. v. B. Feldman & Co.*, [1979] R.P.C. 1 (Ch.); similarly in Canada, *Massie & Renwick,* above note 137.

149   U.S. Senate, Subcommittee on Patents, Trademarks and Copyrights, *Joint Ownership of Copyrights* (Study No. 12) by G.D. Cary (U.S.: Comm. Print, 1958) 85.

150   B. Torno, *Ownership of Copyright in Canada* (Ottawa: Consumer & Corporate Affairs, 1981) at 63–67.

151   *C Act*, above note 1, s. 10(2). See section E(3), "Ownership: Commissioned Engravings, Photographs, and Portraits," in this chapter.

152   *Canadian Admiral*, above note 37 at 401; *NAFTA I A*, above note 74, s. 75(2).

153   Compare *Nottage v. Jackson* (1883), 11 Q.B.D. 627 at 637 (C.A.), on old-time photography.

one is doubtful: the person responsible for positioning the camera is no Atom Egoyan. Such authorless films may have no copyright at all.

2) Ownership: Employees

The author is usually the first owner of copyright, unless (a) she is employed under a contract of service or apprenticeship, and (b) the work was made in the course of that employment or apprenticeship. Her employer then usually first owns the copyright.[154] This arrangement squares with the common expectation under capitalist modes of production. A person hired to produce material as part of her work normally expects copyright to be her employer's; for, without the hire, the work would probably not have been produced at all. Where expectations are different or the work would have been produced anyway, it is consistent with copyright policy to leave ownership with the author.

a) Contract of Service
The employer first owns the copyright only if the author is employed under a contract of service. The author must be an employee, not a freelancer. This distinction involves interpreting the parties' relationship according to familiar principles of labour law. As more employees work from home and many consultants come to the workplace, the actual site where work is done tells little about whether the worker is an employee or a freelancer. Instead, the hiring contract and the surrounding circumstances must be examined to see how the worker is treated. If she is called an employee and treated as part of the staff, is paid a salary with income tax deducted at source, is given pension and other benefits, has to attend staff meetings or report on how she spends her time, the worker will probably be found to be an employee. The fewer such factors are present, the more likely the worker will be found to be a freelancer, who *prima facie* owns the copyright in her work product.[155]

---

154 *C Act*, above note 1, s. 13(3) (apprentices are not separately considered). This position can be modified by simple agreement: See section E(5), "Changing Ownership and Implying Rights of Use," in this chapter. See generally K. Puri, "Copyright and Employment in Australia" (1996) 27 I.I.C. 53, where similar principles apply.

155 For other factors, see the standard labour law cases. Copyright cases include *Goldner v. Canadian Broadcasting Corp.* (1972), 7 C.P.R. (2d) 158 at 161–62 (Fed. T.D.) (television consultant not employee); *Stephenson Jordan & Harrison Ltd. v. MacDonald & Evans* (1951), [1952] 1 T.L.R. 101 (C.A.) [*Stephenson*] (management consultant partly employee, partly freelancer); *Community for Creative Nonviolence v. Reid,* 490 U.S. 730 (1989) (sculptor freelancer). See also, Y. Gendreau, "La titularité des droits sur les logiciels créés par un employé" (1995) 12 Can. Intell. Prop. Rev. 147 at 149ff.

Establishing a worker's status has been likened to determining the subject of an impressionist painting which is built up from an accumulation of detail.[156] Unfortunately, such a painting may strike different viewers differently. Thus, the inmate of a federal penitentiary was recently held to be not only an involuntary tenant of Her Majesty but also (unbeknownst to him) her employee too — paid $6 a day. The government of Canada therefore owned the copyright in a painting he had done as part of his rehabilitation, as well as the painting itself. After serving his time and opening an art business, the painter was not allowed even to photograph the work for his portfolio![157]

b) Work Produced "in the Course of Employment"

Not everything an employee does for her employer is necessarily done "in the course of . . . [her] employment" under her contract. The employment contract may not compel a work to be created at all or in a form that attracts copyright. A worker who then chooses to produce in that form does so outside the course of her employment. The copyright may then be hers. One test is to ask whether the worker would have broken her contract by not producing the work the way she did. If the answer is yes, her employer owns the copyright; if no, it is the worker's.

Take the case of a university professor. Suppose his employment contract compels him to teach, but leaves how he does that — spontaneously, from jotted notes, or from fully prepared text — entirely up to him.[158] The copyright in any lecture notes or text he prepares should *prima facie* be his. This result could also be supported for policy reasons. Were the copyright his employer's, incentives for the production of worthy work may be reduced; employers would receive a windfall; employee mobility would be reduced, for professors could not effectively deploy their expertise elsewhere once they lost copyright in their notes to their university; and employers, who typically are responsible for preparing job descriptions, can always bargain for a different result.[159]

---

156 *Hall (Inspector of Taxes)* v. *Lorimer,* [1992] 1 W.L.R. 939 at 944 (Ch.), aff'd (1993), [1994] 1 W.L.R. 209 (C.A.).

157 *Hawley* v. *Canada* (1990), 30 C.P.R. (3d) 534 (Fed. T.D.) [*Hawley*].

158 H.S. Bloom, "The Teacher's Copyright in His Teaching Materials" (1973) 12 J. Soc. Pub. T.L. 333 at 341; *Stephenson* , above note 155; *Noah* v. *Shuba,* [1991] F.S.R. 14 (Ch.) [*Noah*]. Compare *Greater Glasgow Health Board's Application* (1995), [1996] R.P.C. 207 at 222–24 (Pat. Ct.) (copyright approach applies also to patents).

159 See *Williams* v. *Weisser,* 78 Cal. R. 542 (2d Dist. 1969). A similar analysis might have left the copyright in the prisoner's painting in *Hawley,* above note 157, with the prisoner, even assuming he was rightly held to be an employee.

c) Journalist Employees

Copyright law treats journalist employees differently in one respect from other employees. For articles or other contributions (e.g., cartoons) to a newspaper, magazine, or similar periodical, the author retains "a right to restrain" publication of the work otherwise than as part of a newspaper, magazine, or similar periodical. This appears to be only a right of veto. The author has no positive right to publish. Still, unless the journalist has waived the right, the employer or any other person may be unable to republish the work in book or any other non-periodical form (e.g., on an electronic database) without first coming to terms with the author. Cartoonists may also reap the benefit of their characters' popularity on T-shirts and other bric-à-brac.[160]

3) Ownership: Commissioned Engravings, Photographs, and Portraits

Freelancers usually first own copyright in work they produce, even on order. A special rule, however, applies to ordered engravings, photographs, and portraits. If the original, or the negative or matrix from which it derives, is created by a freelancer to fulfil an order given for valuable consideration, the customer is the first copyright owner of the work, any images made from it, and any preparatory material.[161] This rule includes cases where the customer is liable to pay a reasonable price because she has impliedly requested the work. Someone who asks that his photograph be taken does not automatically get the copyright; this happens only if he became expressly or impliedly liable to pay for the original or the prints. Just making oneself available for a photo session may not be enough.[162] With wedding photos, the bride or groom who places the order with the photographer usually does so for both of them. The copyright may then be owned jointly by the spouses.[163]

Freelancers sometimes think that, because they own the copyright, they can do what they like with a work. This is not true. For example, a photographer has no business giving or selling prints or negatives of commis-

---

160 *C Act*, above note 1, s. 13(3); *Sun Newspapers Ltd.* v. *Whippie* (1928), 28 S.R. (N.S.W.) 473 (Eq. Ct.); see *De Garis* v. *Neville Jeffress Pidler Pty. Ltd.* (1990), 18 I.P.R. 292 (Austl. Fed. Ct.); K. Puri, "Journalists' Copyright in Australia" (1994) 9 I.P.J. 90.

161 *C Act, ibid.*, s. 13(2); *James Arnold & Co. Ltd.* v. *Miafern Ltd.*, [1980] R.P.C. 397 at 403–4 (Ch.) [*Arnold*]; *Planet Earth Productions Inc.* v. *Rowlands* (1990), 73 O.R. (2d) 505 (H.C.J.). This position can be modified by simple agreement: see section E(5), "Changing Ownership and Implying Rights of Use," in this chapter.

162 *Sasha Ltd.* v. *Stoenesco* (1929), 45 T.L.R. 350 (Ch.); *Arnold, ibid.* at 404.

163 *Mail Newspapers* v. *Express Newspapers* (1986), [1987] F.S.R. 90 at 93 (Ch.).

sioned photographs to a newspaper, where the subjects later come into the public limelight. Conduct like this, while not infringing copyright, may violate a duty of confidentiality, privacy, or implied contractual obligation of exclusivity owed to the subject or the customer, and may expose the photographer and possibly the newspaper to an injunction and damages.[164] On the other hand, Glenn Gould's estate was unsuccessful in trying to stop the use of photographs of the pianist in a biography about him. A claim that Gould's personality had been mis-appropriated failed: the shots had been taken with Gould's consent during an interview and were used on an occasion of public interest, not merely to exploit Gould's personality to sell products.[165]

4) Government Work

Federal, provincial, and municipal governments and Crown corporations can own and acquire copyrights, just like any private employer. Thus, the copyright in works produced by a municipal employee on the job belongs to the municipality. Such disparate material as departmental memoranda, cabinet or policy documents, prison manuals, and, more dubiously, artwork produced by a federal prisoner as part of his rehabilitation, has been included.[166]

The *Act* vests copyright ownership of any work prepared or published "by or under the direction or control of Her Majesty or any government department" in the federal or provincial government.[167] This includes artwork produced by employees or commissioned from freelancers, and reports written by government employees and published under the aegis of their departments.[168] In addition, "any rights or privileges of the Crown" are specifically preserved.[169] This language refers to

---

164 *Pollard* v. *Photographic Co.* (1888), 40 Ch.D. 345; see also *Cala* above note 101 at 836 (drafter producing design for home builder). British Columbia, Manitoba, Newfoundland, Quebec, and Saskatchewan have special privacy legislation that might also be violated by such actions. In Ontario, such action may breach a common law right of privacy: *Saccone* v. *Orr* (1981), 34 O.R. (2d) 317 (Co. Ct.).

165 *Gould*, above note 101.

166 For example, *Ontario (A.G.)* v. *Gowling & Henderson* (1984), 47 O.R. (2d) 449 (H.C.J.); *Australia* v. *John Fairfax & Sons Ltd.* (1980), 147 C.L.R. 39 (Austl. H.C.) [*Fairfax*]; *Hawley*, above note 157.

167 *C Act*, above note 1, s. 12; B. Torno, *Crown Copyright in Canada: A Legacy of Confusion* (Ottawa: Consumer & Corporate Affairs, 1981). This position can be modified by simple agreement: see section E(5), "Changing Ownership and Implying Rights of Use," in this chapter.

168 *Kerr* v. *R.* (1982), 66 C.P.R. (2d) 165 (Fed. T.D.); [*Kerr*]; *R.* v. *James Lorimer & Co.*, [1984] 1 F.C. 1065 at 1069 (C.A.) [*James Lorimer*].

169 *C Act*, above note 1, s. 12.

the government's prerogative power to control publishing. In seventeenth-century Britain, when talk of treason and sedition was rife, the power was asserted as a form of censorship over everything published. Three centuries later, a Canadian court gave this power a more limited range. It now encompassed only "a somewhat miscellaneous collection of works, no catalogue of which appears to be exhaustive."[170] One of the most important items today may be legislation. Both the provincial and the federal governments continue to claim a perpetual monopoly in statutes, proclamations, orders in council, and regulations.[171] This monopoly may operate loosely in practice, as legislation is made available online and on compact disk, and what users do with it becomes less traceable.

It is interesting to note that the Crown today still claims a prerogative power over publishing judicial decisions. The power may be exercised through delegates like provincial law societies. The idea may have seemed plausible when the monarch claimed to rule by divine right and the publication of judicial proceedings in the House of Lords was punishable as a contempt of Parliament. It seems less plausible today, especially in light of the untrammelled rise of private law reporting in Britain since at least the mid-eighteenth century. No European state, other than the United Kingdom, Eire, and Italy, claims to protect "official texts of a legislative, administrative and legal nature, and . . . official translations of such texts."[172] Nor does the United States. Judges there have since the nineteenth century asserted that the people's laws belong to the people. In the United States, there is therefore no copyright on federal and state court opinions and legislation as a matter of public policy.[173] U.S. copyright may, however, exist in added value like headnotes, annotations, indexes, compilations, and, less plausibly, pagination.[174]

---

170 R. v. *Bellman,* [1938] 3 D.L.R. 548 at 553 (N.B.C.A.) (hydrographic and admiralty charts of the Bay of Fundy).

171 Upheld in *New South Wales (A.G.)* v. *Butterworth & Co. (Australia) Ltd.* (1938), 38 S.R. (N.S.W.) 195 (Eq. Ct.), although the New South Wales government recently waived its rights over this material.

172 *Berne,* above note 2, art. 2(4); see also J.A.L. Sterling, "Crown Copyright in the United Kingdom and Other Commonwealth Countries" (1996) 10 I.P.J. 157.

173 This policy may, however, not extend to assertions of copyright in such material outside the U.S.: D. Vaver, "Copyright and the State in Canada and the United States" (1996) 10 I.P.J. 187 at 209.

174 *Howell* v. *Miller,* 91 F. 129 (6th Cir. 1898) (state statutes); *Banks* v. *Manchester,* 128 U.S. 244 (1888); *Callaghan* v. *Myers,* 128 U.S. 617 (1888) (judicial decisions); *West Publishing Co.* v. *Mead Data Central Inc.,* 799 F.2d 1219 (8th Cir. 1986), cert. denied 479 U.S. 1070 (1987) (pagination); see also L. Patterson & C. Joyce, "Monopolizing the Law: The Scope of Copyright Protection for Law Reports and Statutory Compilations" (1989) 36 U.C.L.A. L. Rev. 719.

The U.S. and majority European position seems more compatible with the idea of a modern democracy. When or whether Canada's governments will eventually see things this way is a matter for speculation.

5) Changing Ownership and Implying Rights of Use

Copyright may always be transferred by written assignment.[175] Two special cases where this rule is qualified should be noted.

a) Changing First Ownership by Simple Agreement

First ownership may be varied by simple agreement in the three situations just discussed: employees, government works, and freelance engravings, photographs, and portraits. So the *prima facie* rule that an employer owns the copyright in works employees produce on the job can be changed with no formality at all before the work is begun or even (possibly) completed. An oral agreement may work; so may an agreement implied or inferred from conduct. No special rules govern the terms and duration of the agreement, which needs to be established according to standard common or civil law principles. The person alleging a variation from the standard position established by the *Act* carries the burden of proving the variation.[176]

One major area where copyright ownership is often reallocated in this way is in the business of photography. Independent studios may, for example, have their customers sign an agreement allocating copyright to the studio, to prevent rival studios from making cheaper prints and enlargements from the negatives. In a recent interesting case, a freelance photographer took a photograph of Member of Parliament Sheila Copps at the request of *Saturday Night* magazine. The photograph turned up on the cover of the magazine and the photographer was duly paid. The *Toronto Star* newspaper later reproduced the magazine cover, without anyone's consent, for a story it ran on Copps. The photographer sued the *Star*. The court accepted evidence of a trade custom — an implied agreement contrary to the standard position — under which freelancers doing such media work continued to own copyright in their work. *Saturday Night* could use the photo once, but had to get the freelancer's consent for reuse and pay customary reuse fees. It could not authorize others to use the photograph. So the *Star* had to pay the photographer damages for infringing his copyright.[177]

---

175   See chapter 5.
176   *Noah*, above note 158 at 25–27.
177   *Allen v. Toronto Star Newspapers Ltd.* (1995), 63 C.P.R. (3d) 517 (Ont. Gen. Div.) [under appeal].

b) Freelancers: Implied Use Rights for Clients

Many people contracting with freelancers are but dimly aware, if at all, of their copyright position. They may think that, having paid for the work, they can do what they like with it — that they own the full copyright. Firms paying for a computer program to be upgraded have sometimes been surprised to find that the programmer owns the copyright on the upgrade and can even sell it to the firm's competitors.[178] Courts have sometimes tried, within the *Act*'s framework, to avoid such results and to produce instead an outcome that meets their perception of the parties' expectations and the equities of the situation. Techniques such as express or implied agreements, trusts, estoppels, waivers, implied licences, proved trade custom, and finding the client to be a joint copyright owner have all been used. For example, engineers or architects hired to produce plans for a building usually keep their copyright. Courts have nevertheless held that the site owner was impliedly licensed to copy the plans when, for example, the structure needed repair or redesign.[179] A site owner could even prevent a freelancer from reusing plans that included significant design features provided by the site owner, for the latter may be a joint author and owner of the copyright.[180] Similarly, clients may be able to switch lawyers and have their documents redrafted without their ex-lawyers' using copyright to hinder the process.[181]

Contests to redraw rights of ownership and use in ways different from those the *Act* prescribes are becoming more common as works are increasingly available online and in new formats such as multimedia CDs. Publishers are finding that their right to put works in electronic databases and to distribute them in new formats is not always crystal clear. Challenges may come from freelancers, who say the publisher was granted merely a licence to use the material once. The *Act* obviously did not envisage how ownership and use should play out in an electronic universe. It nevertheless is the backdrop against which arrangements have been and continue to be made. Skirmishes in other fields may prove relevant to the electronic era.

A graphic artist, for example, may be hired to design promotional material for a client: a neon sign with the client's name or improvements to the logos used by the client. Can the artist use her copyright to prevent

---

178 *Amusements Wiltron Inc. v. Mainville* (1991), 40 C.P.R. (3d) 521, at 525ff (Que. S.C.).

179 *Netupsky v. Dominion Bridge Co. Ltd.* (1971), [1972] S.C.R. 368, rev'g (1969), 58 C.P.R. 7 (B.C.C.A.) [*Netupsky*]; *ADI Ltd. v. Destein* (1982), 41 N.B.R. (2d) 518 (Q.B.).

180 See also *Cala*, above note 101 at 835–36.

181 Vaver, "Copyright," above note 18.

the client from using the sign or logo generally in the business, perhaps for a completely new use? May the artist demand a further fee, or must the client stop the new use? So far at least, common law courts have sided with the client, finding an implied licence in the client's favour.[182] Since the artist could not herself honestly reuse such tailor-made work without the client's consent, courts could even have inferred a common intention that the client should be the copyright owner, not a mere licensee. British courts have done so in comparable cases. A client that had its computer program enhanced by a freelancer was found to own the copyright because of a presumed intention between the parties to this effect. The same argument applied where a producer had a choreographer work on a ballet in which the producer already owned the musical and literary copyright.[183] Implied agreements like these may be fully effective between the parties to make the client the second copyright owner in equity, although a written assignment is necessary to perfect title.[184]

It seems wrong to find such an implied or presumed licence or agreement where the freelancer would be unfairly prejudiced — for example, where a client knew or should have known it was obtaining only limited rights. Such an implication seems justifiable, however, where the artist should, from the start, have made her expectations clear to the client that only rights of limited use were being acquired. This would be so, for instance, where the artist is a professional and the client is a tyro in the copyright world. A professional who fails to explain the copyright position to a novice can hardly complain if a court rules that the beginner's belief that it is buying clear title is preferable. This is really a finding that the client's belief is "more" reasonable and thus the presumed intent of both parties. The writing requirement, intended partly to protect freelancers from imprudent assignments, should not work as a trap for unsuspecting clients.[185]

---

182   *Silverson v. Neon Products Ltd.* (1978), 39 C.P.R. (2d) 234 (B.C.S.C.); *Cselko Associates Inc. v. Zellers Inc.* (1992), 44 C.P.R. (3d) 56 (Ont. Gen. Div.).

183   *John Richardson Computers Ltd. v. Flanders* (1993), 26 I.P.R. 367 at 383–84 (Ch.); *Massine v. de Basil* (1938), [1936–45] MacG. Cop. Cas. 223 (C.A.); compare *Saphena Computing Ltd. v. Allied Collection Agencies Ltd.* (1988), [1995] F.S.R. 616 (Q.B.) appeal dismissed (1989), [1995] F.S.R. 649 (C.A.) [*Saphena*].

184   *C Act*, above note 1, s. 13(4). For the consequences of equitable ownership, see section B(4), "Equitable Assignments and Licences," chapter 5.

185   Artists' unions may impose an ethical obligation (that can readily turn into a legal one) on the artist to clarify the copyright position in the initial contract with the client: for example, Graphic Artists Guild (U.S.), *Graphic Artists Guild Handbook: Pricing and Ethical Guidelines,* 8th ed. (New York: Graphic Artists Guild Inc., 1994) at 27, on U.S. practice.

6) Sound Recordings, Performances, Broadcasts

The first copyright owner in a sound recording is whoever undertook the arrangement necessary for making the recording, typically the recording company. The ownership provisions for traditional works, detailed above, apply as if the maker were an author.[186] A performer is the first owner of the right in his or her performance.[187]

Bill C-32 would retain these ownership rules for sound recordings and performances, and similarly would make the broadcaster the first owner of the signal it broadcasts.[188] Record companies would not, however, be able to resort to the ownership provisions applying to traditional works; for example, first ownership may not be able to be reallocated by a simple agreement. The bill proposes that all the rights may be assigned or licensed like traditional copyrights.[189]

F. DURATION

1) Literary, Dramatic, Musical, and Artistic Works

Copyright terms have grown over the years. What started in early eighteenth century Britain as a twenty-eight-year term (fourteen years plus an optional fourteen years renewal) was added to incrementally over the years until, by the early twentieth century, it had internationally become the life of the author plus fifty years. This has been Canada's term since 1924.[190] All terms now run to 31 December of the year in which they are due to expire. The term of copyright for an author who died on 1 January 1956 therefore expires after 31 December 2006.[191]

For jointly authored work, copyright lasts until fifty years after the last author dies.[192] For anonymous and pseudonymous works, copyright lasts for the shorter of fifty years from first publication or seventy-five years from making; but, if during that period, the author's identity

---

186 *C Act*, above note 1, s. 11; s. 2 def. "maker." See section E(4), "Government Work," in this chapter.

187 *Act, ibid.*, s. 14.01(4).

188 Bill C-32, above note 9, cl. 24.

189 *Ibid.*, cl. 25.

190 *C Act*, above note 1, s. 6; compare *Berne*, above note 2 (1908), art. 7, & (1971), art. 7. In Europe the term was recently increased to author's life plus seventy years, and a similar bill is presently being urged in the United States.

191 *C Act, ibid.*, s. 6. This "year's end" formula is repeated throughout the *Act* and Bill C-32, above note 9, for all works and beneficiaries.

192 *C Act, ibid.*, s. 9.

becomes commonly known, the standard life-plus-fifty-year term then applies.[193] For literary, dramatic, musical works, lectures, or engravings unpublished or (except for engravings) unperformed in public when the author dies, copyright lasts perpetually until publication or performance and then ceases fifty years later; but Bill C-32 proposes that the standard life-plus-fifty term would apply here, too.[194]

Some periods drop all reference to an author's life and provide a flat fifty-year term. Copyright in photographs thus runs for fifty years from the date when the initial photograph, negative, or plate was made.[195] Cinematographs that lack an original character arising from their arrangement, acting form, or combination of incidents (e.g., unedited films of live events) are also protected for fifty years. Thus, copyright runs from the date the film was made. If the film was first published during this period, the copyright is prolonged to fifty years past that publication.[196] For works prepared or published under the direction or control of the federal or provincial government and first owned by it, copyright lasts for fifty years after first publication.[197] There is, however, no term specified for works falling under the Crown prerogative.[198] If statutes indeed come under this power, the result is that every pre- and post-Confederation statute, regulation, and order in council, whether repealed or still in force, is still under the exclusive control of the federal and provincial governments.

2) Reversion

Any assignment or grant of interest in copyright (e.g., exclusive licence) by an author ends twenty-five years after he dies, and the copyright reverts to his estate. The idea is to enable the estate directly to benefit from the copyright and free itself of any improvident deal made during the author's lifetime.[199] Exceptions are where (a) the author was not the first copyright owner;[200] (b) the author was a corporation (as is possible

---

193   *C Act, ibid.*, s. 6.1. The same applies to jointly authored work: *C Act, ibid.*, s. 6.2.

194   *C Act, ibid.*, s. 7; Bill C-32, above note 9, cl. 6 (replacing s. 7) also proposing transitional measures for existing works.

195   *C Act, ibid.*, s. 10.

196   *C Act, ibid.*, s. 11.1. The same applies to compilations of these films.

197   *C Act, ibid.*, s. 12.

198   See section E(4), "Government Work," in this chapter.

199   *C Act*, above note 1, s. 14; *Chappell & Co. Ltd. v. Redwood Music Ltd.*, [1980] 2 All E.R. 817 at 828–29 (H.L.). Any waiver of moral rights presumably ceases too.

200   This is the case for employees' work, freelancers making a commissioned photograph, engraving, or portrait, and government works — at least, where no contrary agreement initially vesting copyright in the author was made: *C Act, ibid.*, ss. 13(3), (2), & 12. See section E, "Title," in this chapter.

for photographs and sound recordings);[201] (c) copyright in a "collective" work is assigned, or a licence is granted to publish a work or a part in a collective work protected by copyright;[202] or (d) an author not falling within these exceptions disposes of the copyright by will.

3) Sound Recordings, Performances, Broadcasts

Sound recordings and performances both have a fifty-year term. For sound recordings, this term presently runs from the date when the initial plate (e.g., matrix, tape) was made and is subject to reversion.[203] For a performance, it runs from the date when the performance first took place.[204]

Bill C-32 proposes two changes. Performers would have rights over their recorded performances running for fifty years from the first fixation of the performance in a sound recording. Broadcasters would have rights in the communication signal they transmit for fifty years from the date when the signal was broadcast.[205]

G. OWNER'S RIGHTS: LITERARY, DRAMATIC, MUSICAL, AND ARTISTIC WORKS

The list of activities set out in the *Act* over which the copyright owner has control has grown longer over the years and will likely continue to do so as right-holders try to tighten control over the newer forms of electronic delivery. Bill C-32 is part of this trend. When Parliament baulks, owners sometimes try to achieve their ends by persuading courts to interpret already listed items expansively; for unless an activity is listed, it is no infringement to do it, however harmful or unfair right-holders might think the use is. Since it is easy for a product to qualify

---

201 *C Act, ibid.*, ss. 10 & 11. The reversion provisions seem to apply to photographs, non-dramatic cinematographs, and sound recordings, even though the language in the *C Act* seems geared more to works with a term of life plus fifty years than to those with a flat fifty-year term.

202 *C Act, ibid.*, s. 2, defines "collective work" as "(a) an encyclopaedia, dictionary, yearbook or similar work; (b) a newspaper, review, magazine or similar periodical, and (c) any work written in distinct parts by different authors, or in which works or parts of works of different authors are incorporated."

203 *C Act, ibid.*, s. 11.

204 *C Act, ibid.*, s. 14.01(5).

205 Bill C-32, above note 9, cls. 23(1)(a), (c), & (2).

for copyright, courts should exercise great care in delineating protection suitable for that type of product. As suggested earlier,[206] a lottery ticket may not merit the same extent and intensity of protection as a book or a computer program. These distinctions must be borne in mind when one interprets whether a user has a formal justification[207] and whether an activity falls under the copyright owner's control in the first place: "the too rigorous application of legal logic" should not replace "common sense," as one court chose to put it.[208]

In the list of activities that follows, anyone doing any of them for whatever reason without the owner's consent may infringe copyright.[209] The owner may or may not give its consent as it wishes, and may impose whatever conditions it wishes.

At least a part of the activity must occur in Canada to be within the owner's control. An offshore Internet service making copyright material available to Canadian subscribers may need Canadian copyright clearance. So may a Canadian user who uploads or downloads material coming from a foreign server.[210] But a Canadian composer may not be able to sue in Canada for any unauthorized reproduction of her music in the United States, even if the copier's company is located in Canada: a U.S. copyright is infringed only in the United States.[211]

1) First Public Distribution

The copyright owner has the right to first distribute an unpublished work — to "mak[e] copies. . . [of it or a substantial part] available to the public."[212] Once the first copies of a work have been put on the market, the first distribution right has gone for those works and all other copies of the work. The owner cannot control later distribution of copies of the work, whoever puts them on the market.[213] Some jurisdictions — for example, France, Italy, Chile, and California — allow artists to recap-

---

206   See section B(1), "Literary, Dramatic, Musical, and Artistic Works," in this chapter.

207   Compare sections J and K, "Users' Rights," in this chapter.

208   *Autospin (Oil Seals) Ltd.* v. *Beehive Spinning,* [1995] R.P.C. 683 at 700 & 701 (Ch.).

209   *C Act,* above note 1, ss. 27(1) & 3(1).

210   *C.A.P.A.C.* v. *International Good Music Inc.,* [1963] S.C.R. 136 at 143 (border television station).

211   *Def Lepp Music* v. *Stuart-Brown,* [1986] R.P.C. 273 (Ch.). See section G(5), "Telecommunication," in this chapter.

212   *C Act,* above note 1, ss. 3(1), 4(1) & (2).

213   *Infabrics Ltd.* v. *Jaytex Ltd.* (1981), [1982] A.C. 1 (H.L.); *Avel Pty. Ltd.* v. *Multicoin Amusements Pty. Ltd.* (1990), 171 C.L.R. 88 (Austl. H.C.). See section G(10), "Distributing and Importing Infringing Copies," in this chapter.

ture a percentage of an artwork's price on resale, but no such right (sometimes called *droit de suite*) exists in Canada.[214]

The right to distribute is confusingly called a right of publication, reflecting the *Act*'s print bias. It has nothing to do with publication in, say, the law of defamation. Performing, exhibiting, broadcasting, or otherwise telecommunicating a work may publicize it, but does not technically publish it.[215] A question arises whether the presence of the word "copies" (plural) in the above definition requires more than one copy to be made available. The plural form traces back to a *Berne* provision that has given equal trouble internationally.[216] "Copies" is capable of meaning "copy";[217] and one copy of a piece of serious music, a movie, a dreary book, or any posting on the Internet may be quite enough to satisfy public demand. This usage suggests that "copies" may well include a single copy. The key is whether it is made available "to the public." This requirement is not satisfied by making it available to a restricted group of people; this use may be "private," not "public."[218] So first publication occurs only when at least one physical copy is made publicly available free or for sale or hire, with or without advertising or dispositions occurring.[219] Work available online or sitting in a public database may therefore be considered "published."[220]

---

214 For a recent critique, see J.H. Merryman, "The Wrath of Robert Rauschenberg" (1993) 40 J. Copr. Soc. U.S.A. 241.

215 *C Act,* above note 1, s. 4(1)(d) to (g). Sculpture or architecture is also not published by issuing photographs or engravings of it: s. 4(1), closing words.

216 *Berne,* above note 2, art. 4(3), def. "published works" (art. 4 of the 1908 and 1928 versions is the same for present purposes); S. Ricketson, *The Berne Convention for the Protection of Literary and Artistic Works; 1886–1986* (London: Centre for Commercial Law Studies, Queen Mary College, 1987) at 182–86.

217 *Interpretation Act,* R.S.C. 1985, c. I-21, s. 33(2).

218 These disclosures, if unauthorized, may amount to an actionable breach of confidence, but that is another matter.

219 *Massie & Renwick,* above note 137; *British Northrop,* above note 96. Exceptionally, to construct architecture or to include artwork incorporated into architecture is also to publish the architecture or artwork: *C Act,* above note 1, s. 4(1)(b).

220 *C Act, ibid.,* ss. 4(1)(a) to (c); Information Highway Advisory Council, *Final Report of the Copyright Subcommittee: Copyright on the Information Highway* (Ottawa: The Council, 1995) at 11; compare *R. v. M. (J.P.)* (1996), 67 C.P.R. (3d) 152 at 156 (N.S.C.A.) [*M. (J.P.)*], where a seventeen-year-old computer bulletin board operator who made infringing copies of computer software available to selected users was held guilty of the criminal offence of "distribut[ing]" them to the copyright owner's prejudice: *C Act, ibid.,* s. 42(1)(c).

2) Reproduction

A central right is "to produce or reproduce the work . . . in any material form whatever."[221] To come under this right, the owner's work must be copied. This means copying the form in which the ideas are expressed — not the ideas themselves, which are free to all. There may be a "reproduction" even if the source work has not been seen by its copier. An engraver may, for example, produce an artwork according to a third party's verbal description of the original, as happened with "knock-offs" of Hogarth's engravings in the eighteenth century; or a photographer may infringe copyright in boat plans by photographing the boat itself. A copy of a copy is still a copy.[222]

The process by which a work is made is critical in deciding if reproduction has occurred. For example, no historian can monopolize her research and sources: a second comer can write a similar history relying on those sources, among others, but he must check them out independently.[223] Similarly, a filmmaker cannot base his treatment on the incidents, dialogue, and treatment of a historical event as interpreted by just one historian, without getting her prior consent.[224] Compilers of information or anthologies may take the idea of making a compilation from previous sources, but they must do their own work. They can use earlier work only to ensure that their own is complete; they cannot proceed the other way round and take a substantial part of the earlier compilation's original selection or arrangement, even if they add their own material.[225]

"Any material form whatever" has been interpreted broadly to cover all forms in which a source work is recast, however much work went into the transformation. So changing direct speech to indirect speech, transcribing a work into or out of code, braille, or shorthand, and video- and audio-taping have all been held to reproduce the source works, whether or not the new format was immediately humanly perceptible as

---

221   *C Act, ibid.*, s. 3(1).
222   *Dorling* v. *Honnor Marine Ltd.* (1964), [1965] Ch. 1 at 22–23 (C.A.).
223   *Jarrold* v. *Houlston* (1857), 3 K. & J. 708 at 714–17, 69 E.R. 1294 (Ch.).
224   *Harman Pictures*, above note 30. Compare *Hoehling* v. *Universal City Studios Inc.*, 618 F.2d 972 (2d Cir. 1980): facts and information have no copyright; infringement occurs only when actual expression is lifted.
225   *Macmillan & Co. Ltd.* v. *Cooper* (1923), 93 L.J.P.C. 113 at 117–21; compare *Cambridge University Press* v. *University Tutorial Press* (1928), 45 R.P.C. 335 (Ch.): an annotated compilation of thirteen Hazlitt essays with notes was not infringed by a later compilation of twenty essays that included the same thirteen but differently arranged and annotated.

a copy.[226] Similarly, two-dimensional artwork is "reproduced" in three dimensions, and vice versa, if the copy looks like its source. So the copyright owner of a cartoon character may control the making of toy doll replicas from it. Similarly, *tableaux vivants* may infringe a painting, and a building may infringe drawings or plans.[227]

Whether such transformed work should legally infringe the source work is another question. Too often courts mechanically assume that any unauthorized reproduction must be an infringement, whatever the nature and extent of the transformation. Thus postmodernist artist Jeff Koons was found by a U.S. court to have infringed copyright in a commonplace photograph by mimicking it in a large sculpture he designed and exhibited, even though the sculpture was meant to critique modern culture.[228] A century ago, when art flourished at least as much as today, this result would have been unthinkable.[229] And had the U.S. court been applying law like this in Shakespeare's time, a very different opus from the Bard would be with us now. In deciding issues of infringement, especially in an era of high experimentation with digital technology, courts must consider not only the parties' immediate interests but also how any decision may affect future artistic behaviour.[230] So, in Koons's case, why postmodernism had to suffer at the hands of modernism certainly requires explanation, if not justification.

a) Computer Programs and Files

Copying source or object codes may reproduce the program as a literary work. The fact of reproduction may be demonstrated through expert evidence. Even rewriting code to achieve the same effect as a previous program may "reproduce" the latter. Thus, non-literal copying of a program's structure — for example, its flow charts and organization of modules — has been held to "reproduce" the program, just as a dramatic work can be infringed by adopting its overall structure, charac-

---

226 *C Act*, above note 1, s. 2, def. "infringing"; *Apple*, above note 14. Bill C-32, above note 9, cl. 32, would allow works to be put in more suitable format for the blind in some circumstances.

227 *King Features Syndicate Inc. v. O. & M. Kleeman Ltd.*, [1941] A.C. 417 (H.L.); *Bradbury, Agnew & Co. v. Day* (1916), 32 T.L.R. 349 (K.B.); *Netupsky*, above note 179.

228 *Rogers v. Koons*, 960 F.2d 301 (2d Cir. 1992) [*Rogers*]; K. Bowrey, "Copyright, the Paternity of Artistic Works, and the Challenge Posed by Postmodern Artists" (1994) 8 I.P.J. 285 at 311ff.

229 *Hanfstaengl v. Empire Palace*, [1894] 3 Ch. 109 (C.A.).

230 See R. Posner, *Law and Literature: A Misunderstood Relation* (Cambridge, Mass.: Harvard University Press, 1988) at 343ff.

ters, plot development, and dénouement.[231] Similarly, the displays of a videogame may be protected as an artistic or dramatic work.[232] But any idea or "any method or principle of manufacture or construction"[233] is not protectable, so any features of a program dictated by functional considerations can be copied. Copyright in a user interface and screen display has therefore been denied, for there were only a few ways to design these elements. To force later programmers to design around them would indirectly protect the underlying ideas.[234] More recently, a U.S. court held the menu command tree on the Lotus 1-2-3 program an unprotectable "method of operation." Without the commands, the program was as useless as a VCR with no operating buttons.[235]

Computer files are certainly "reproduced" when copied to a computer's permanent memory (hard disk, tape, or diskette). U.S. courts have even held that it is infringement to download a file into temporary volatile memory so it may be viewed on a monitor — thereby creating for works in electronic form a new right: the exclusive right to read. One hopes this result will be avoided in Canada, but one cannot be confident.[236]

The concept of reproduction in relation to works in electronic form raises many difficulties. For example, artwork scanned into a computer file may be converted into a binary form that does not look at all like the source, but the artwork is probably "reproduced" in the file. But what if the file is later electronically manipulated so that the artwork no longer looks like its source? It should no longer be a "reproduction" of the former artistic work if the result is judged visually. But what if substantial parts of the underlying binary code are still the same? Can this be a reproduction of the underlying literary work? One trusts not. An impressionist painter may copy another's brushstrokes, and yet produce a painting that would strike the ordinary art lover as quite different. Why should this painting be held a "reproduction" of the first work, just

---

231   *Computer Associates International Inc.* v. *Altai Inc.*, 982 F.2d 693 (2d Cir. 1992).

232   *Stern Electronics Inc.* v. *Kaufman*, 669 F.2d 852 at 855 (2d Cir. 1982).

233   *C Act*, above note 1, s. 64.1(1)(d).

234   *Delrina* , above note 22 at 44.

235   *Lotus*, above note 25.

236   *MAI Systems Corp.* v. *Peak Computer Inc.,* 991 F.2d 511 (9th Cir. 1993) [*MAI*], criticized by J. Litman, "The Exclusive Right to Read" (1994) 13 Cardozo Arts & Ent. L.J. 29 at 40; D. Vaver, "Rejuvenating Copyright, Digitally," in *Symposium of Digital Technology and Copyright* (Ottawa: Department of Justice, 1995) 1 at 3–5. Compare Information Highway Advisory Council, *Final Report: Connecting Community Content: The Challenge of the Information Highway* (Ottawa: The Council, 1995) at 114–15 [*Challenge*] (copyright owner should be able to control "browsing").

because an art expert can trace the influences? The brushstrokes, like the electronic bits and bytes, are a means to an end. Art may best be judged by its impact on its intended market — typically, art buyers and spectators, not experts on artistic technique.

b) Subconscious Copying

Reproduction implies that there is a causal connection between an earlier and a later work, although the copier may not have intended to reproduce or may not have known he or she was doing so. Moreover, close similarity between the two works, if the defendant had access to the first, presents a *prima facie* case the defendant must answer to avoid infringement.[237]

In combination, these two rules create a dilemma for anyone who may have seen or heard a work long ago, retained it in his subconscious memory, and later reproduced a major part without knowing it. A U.S. court found infringement in such a case against ex-Beatle George Harrison for subconsciously copying the Chiffons' 1962 hit "He's So Fine" in his 1970 composition "My Sweet Lord."[238] In upholding a substantial award of damages against Harrison, the appeal court said that "as a practical matter" any other rule "could substantially undermine" copyright protection.[239]

The issue is more complex than it would appear: cryptomnesia — involuntarily recalling something one's memory chose to retain — is not uncommon today, when so much of the manufactured environment to which everyone is daily exposed is protected by copyright. All authorship has even been called the "astigmatic repackaging of others' expression."[240] The problem is the defendant's lack of moral culpability: his subconscious, not he, was in control, without his knowing or being able to influence it. Society does not usually hold people legally responsible where their mind does not prompt or direct their actions. Sleepwalkers, automatons, the very young, and the insane are not usually liable for assaults or trespasses, because they cannot appreciate the nature or quality of what they are doing. The same sort of "somewhat uneasy compromises"[241] struck for such people may need to evolve for cryp-

---

237 *Francis Day & Hunter Ltd.* v. *Bron*, [1963] Ch. 587 (C.A.).

238 *Bright Tunes Music Corp.* v. *Harrisongs Music Ltd.*, 420 F. Supp. 177 (D.N.Y. 1976); compare *Gondos* v. *Hardy* (1982), 38 O.R. (2d) 555 (H.C.J.).

239 *ABKCO Music Inc.* v. *Harrisongs Ltd.*, 722 F.2d 988 at 999 (2d Cir. 1983).

240 J. Litman, "The Public Domain" (1990) 39 Emory L.J. 965 at 1011.

241 *Williams* v. *Williams* (1963), [1964] A.C. 698 at 752 (H.L.) (insanity). The fear that cryptomnesia will become a defence *à la mode* is unrealistic, any more than insanity or somnambulism have become such defences in civil cases.

tomnesiacs. The copyright owner may sometimes perhaps deserve protection, but it seems hard to justify the full schedule of remedies against the "infringer": perhaps at most an injunction and an account of profits, deducting any added value. As copyright-protected material comes to occupy more and more of everyone's physical and mental space, copyright holders as a group may have to make do with a lower overall level of protection if society is to be allowed to function reasonably or at all. This relaxed approach may not, of course, apply against the habitual involuntary recaller: courts will no doubt help him "get out of the author business and go to digging ditches, where his mind will not be able to pilfer."[242]

3) Subsidiary Rights

Some rights are variants on the right to reproduce.

a) Abridgment

Abridgments and condensations are within the owner's right to "reproduce . . . [a] substantial part" of the work.[243] This category includes both "scissors and paste" versions (e.g., trimming a seven-volume report down to one volume) and *Coles' Notes*–like condensations.[244] Short abstracts that whet the reader's appetite — such as those found at the head of articles in many periodicals — should usually fall outside this right. Abstracts that substitute for the original are different: a newspaper's systematic abstraction of analyses from a financial newsletter "suck[ed] the marrow from the bone" of the source work and was enjoined.[245]

b) Translation

The right to translate is specifically mentioned in the *Act*.[246] It encompasses changing a work in one language or dialect into another. Even

---

242   E.P. Butler, "'Pigs Is Pigs' and Plagiarists Are Thieves," in M. Salzman, *Plagiarism: The "Art" of Stealing Literary Material* (Los Angeles: Parker, Stone & Baird, 1931) at 70.

243   *C Act*, above note 1, s. 3(1); D. Vaver, "Abridgments and Abstracts: Copyright Implications" [1995] 5 E.I.P.R. 225.

244   *James Lorimer*, above note 168; *Sillitoe* v. *McGraw-Hill Book Co. (U.K.) Ltd.* (1982), [1983] F.S.R. 545 (Ch.) [*Sillitoe*].

245   *Wainwright Securities Inc.* v. *Wall Street Transcript Corp.*, 418 F. Supp. 620 at 625 (D.N.Y. 1976), aff'd 558 F.2d 91 (2d Cir. 1977).

246   *C Act*, above note 1, s. 3(1)(a); D. Vaver, "Translation and Copyright: A Canadian Focus" [1994] 4 E.I.P.R. 159.

some computer programming may be included — for example, changing code from Pascal to Fortran.[247] But just as changing text into braille is reproduction, not translation, converting source to object code should not be translation either: one set of symbols is simply switched for another or for electrical circuitry.

c) Novelization, Dramatization, Movie Adaptation

Novelization, dramatization, and movie adaptation are separate rights in the *Act*.[248] They can cover quite unusual cases. Thus, *Coles' Notes'* version of Shaw's *St. Joan* infringed the novelization right by converting the play into a non-dramatic work. The summary was in indirect speech, interspersed with criticism, and intended as a study aid; but none of this mattered.[249] More typically, making a play or a movie will usually engage these rights. Taking a substantial part of either the dialogue or the plot of the source work may then infringe. Just taking one or two ideas or situations may not be enough, but reproducing the combination and sequence of incidents and characters has been held to be infringement.[250]

The protectability of characters alone has been much debated. Cartoon characters are usually more easily recognizable, and hence protectable, in movie or other adaptations than are literary characters. So Walt Disney has stopped Goofy, Mickey, and other characters from being recast in counter-culture comic books and films.[251] Courts are more reluctant to protect literary characters, even "obvious" copies of characters "as distinctive and remarkable" as Falstaff, Tartuffe, or Sherlock Holmes. A U.S. judge put it neatly:

> If Twelfth Night were copyrighted, it is quite possible that a second comer might so closely imitate Sir Toby Belch or Malvolio as to infringe, but it would not be enough that for one of his characters he cast a riotous knight who kept wassail to the discomfort of the household, or a vain and foppish steward who became amorous of his mistress. These would be no more than Shakespeare's "ideas" in the play, as little capable of monopoly as Einstein's Doctrine of Relativity, or

---

247   *Prism Hospital Software Inc.* v. *Hospital Medical Records Institute* (1994), 57 C.P.R. (3d) 129 at 278 (B.C.S.C.).

248   *C Act*, above note 1, ss. 3(1)(b), (c) & (e).

249   *Sillitoe*, above note 244 at 550–51.

250   *Kelly* v. *Cinema Houses Ltd.* (1932), [1928–35] MacG. Cop. Cas. 362 (Ch.), aff'd (1932), [1928–35] MacG. Cop. Cas. 371 (C.A.) [*Kelly*]; *Harman Pictures*, above note 30 (John Osborne film script for *The Charge of the Light Brigade* infringed Cecil Woodham-Smith's book).

251   *Walt Disney Productions* v. *Air Pirates*, 581 F.2d 751 (9th Cir. 1978).

Darwin's theory of the Origin of Species. It follows that the less developed the characters, the less they can be copyrighted: that is the penalty an author must bear for marking them too indistinctly.[252]

A Canadian court also indicated its willingness to protect the characters in a script for a science fiction movie if they were "sufficiently clearly delineated," but found they did not meet this test on the facts.[253]

d) Film, Audio and Video Recording

These "mechanical" rights are part of "the sole right . . . to make any record, perforated roll, cinematograph film or other contrivance by means of which the [literary, dramatic, or musical] work may be mechanically performed or delivered."[254] Sound and video recordings are obviously "contrivances," while record pressers, film processors, and the persons ordering the pressing or processing are included as "makers."[255] Even ephemeral recordings, such as those a broadcaster makes for technical reasons, have fallen under this right. So a broadcaster who transfers a work, for which it has telecommunication rights, onto a more suitable medium for broadcast in a different time zone must pay an additional fee to the owner of the mechanical reproduction right.[256] A temporary synchronization like this is specifically exempted in some countries, but Canada is not yet one of them.

4) Public Performance

Public performance is a major means by which copyright owners make money from music, drama, and movies.[257] Since a performance is defined as "any acoustic representation of a work or any visual representation of a dramatic work," both live and recorded performances are included. Performance includes whatever is seen or heard when a radio, television set, or an audio or video player is turned on.[258]

---

252 *Nichols v. Universal Pictures Corp.*, 45 F.2d 119 at 121 (2d Cir. 1930) [*Nichols*], criticized as involving vague aesthetic judgment by F.M. Nevins Jr., "Copyright + Character = Catastrophe" (1992) 39 J. Copr. Soc. U.S.A. 303 at 309ff.

253 *Preston v. 20th Century Fox Canada Ltd.* (1990), 33 C.P.R. (3d) 242 at 275, aff'd (1993), 53 C.P.R. (3d) 407 (Fed. C.A.) (Ewoks in *Return of the Jedi*).

254 *C Act*, above note 1, s. 3(1)(d). Bill C-32 would modernize this language.

255 *Warner Brothers–Seven Arts Inc. v. CESM–TV Ltd.* (1971), 65 C.P.R. 215 at 241 (Ex. Ct.); *Compo Co. v. Blue Crest Music Inc.* (1979), [1980] 1 S.C.R. 357 [*Compo*].

256 *Bishop v. Stevens*, [1990] 2 S.C.R. 467.

257 *C Act*, above note 1, s. 3(1). The right also encompasses public delivery of lectures, addresses, speeches, sermons, and the like.

258 *C Act, ibid.*, ss. 3(1) & 2 def. "performance."

Actors and musicians obviously qualify as performers, but so may anyone who causes a performance to be represented. This includes everyone from the owner of the cabaret where the band or radio plays down to the person who actually switches on the radio or television set.[259] Broadcasters and cablecasters also perform in public where a studio audience is present, but not when they transmit their programming: a separate right of public telecommunication[260] is designed not to overlap with public performance.[261]

A special provision extends liability where theatres and other places of entertainment are used for private profit for a public performance. If the performance has no copyright clearance, anyone "permitting" the premises to be used for it also infringes copyright, unless he was unaware and had no reasonable ground for suspecting the lack of clearance. Simply leasing or licensing premises to a performing group is not in itself "permission"; there must be some control over the performers, knowledge of the particular work to be performed, and permission to use the premises for that performance.[262]

Everyone is of course fully entitled to play records or the radio in private. What is not permissible is to perform a work "in public" without the copyright owner's consent. What amounts to a performance "in public" usually depends on the character of the audience. On the one hand, private or domestic performances are excluded: this exclusion should cover those in private homes and apartments, or in rooms hired for weddings, confirmations, or batmitzvahs, where the guests are family and friends and the premises are an extension of the host's home. On the other hand, performances occurring "openly, without concealment and to the knowledge of all," have been said to be "in public," whether or not anyone intends to make money from the performance. This test would include restaurants, cabarets, arenas, members' clubs open to invited guests, and offices, factories, or elevators where music plays to relax staff or customers.[263] Grey areas still abound. What of a performance at a firm's Christmas

---

259 *Vigneux v. Canadian Performing Right Society,* [1945] A.C. 108 (P.C.) [*Vigneux*].

260 See section G(5), "Telecommunication," in this chapter.

261 *C Act,* above note 1, s. 3(4), overruling *Canadian Cable,* above note 70.

262 *C Act, ibid.,* s. 27(5); *Corporation of the City of Adelaide v. Australasian Performing Right Assn. Ltd.* (1928), 40 C.L.R. 481 (Austl. H.C.); *de Tervagne v. Beloeil (Town),* [1993] 3 F.C. 227 (T.D.). See also section G(8), "Authorization," in this chapter.

263 *Canadian Cable,* above note 70; *Performing Right Society Ltd. v. Rangers F.C. Supporters Club,* [1975] R.P.C. 626 (Ct. Sess., Scot.); compare *NAFTA,* above note 2, art. 1721, defining "public." The performance must be for "private profit" only where liability is extended to someone "permitting" a theatre or other place of entertainment to be used: *C Act, ibid.,* s. 27(5), discussed in the previous paragraph.

party: Are the employees there privately or as members of the public? An Australian case, interestingly, suggests the latter. An employer who played an instructional video at the workplace to a small group of employees was found to have put on a public performance. The ties that bind employees were thought to be commercial, not private or domestic.[264]

What of hotels that rent movies to guests to play in their rooms? In Australia, the hotel was said to be causing public performances; not so in the United States.[265] The U.S. rule seems preferable. The guest is, in relation to the hotel, certainly a member of the public; but the performance is surely in private, because the hotel room is merely a person's temporary home. Had the guest hired the movie from a separate rental store, the performance in her room would have been "in private." How can the identity of the supplier change the character of the performance? Finding the performance to be private nonetheless creates an anomaly: rental gets a competitive edge over in-house cable delivery systems that must pay copyright fees for "[tele]communicat[ing] to the public."[266] Substitute delivery systems should compete on their merits. Either both or neither should pay. Copyright law here should strive for technological neutrality.

5) Telecommunication

The right to communicate "to the public by telecommunication" covers transmission by "wire, radio, visual, optical or other electromagnetic system."[267] Sending works by radio, television, cable, fax, modem, satellite, or microwave involves telecommunication. But, to attract liability, the communication must be "to the public."[268] Such communication should exclude point-to-point e-mail and faxes, and transmissions between a network and its affiliate television stations.[269] It would, how-

---

264   *Australasian Performing Right Assn. Ltd.* v. *Commonwealth Bank of Australia* (1992), 40 F.C.R. 59 (Austl. Fed. Ct.).

265   *Rank Film Production Ltd.* v. *Dodds* (1983), 76 F.L.R. 351 (N.S.W.S.C.); compare *Columbia Picture Industries Inc.* v. *Professional Real Estate Investors Inc.*, 866 F.2d 278 (9th Cir. 1989).

266   *Canadian Cable*, above note 70; see section G(5), "Telecommunication," in this chapter.

267   *C Act*, above note 1, s. 3(1)(f); s. 2 def. "telecommunication."

268   Perhaps broader than the corresponding words "*in* public" [emphasis added] in the public performance right: *Canadian Cable*, above note 70 at 148–49.

269   A public communication occurs only when the affiliate airs the program; the network and the affiliate are then jointly liable: *CTV Television Network Ltd.* v. *Canada (Copyright Board)*, [1993] 2 F.C. 115 (C.A.) [*CTV*]; *C Act*, above note 1, s. 3(1.4). The provider of the means of carrying the communication is not liable: *C Act, ibid.*, s. 3(1.3).

ever, include programming — ordinary, scrambled, or interactive — delivered by cable to private subscribers.[270] A mass unsolicited faxing of material to telephone subscribers may also be included. So may data posted on publicly accessible electronic bulletin boards as the Internet, even if people access the data at different times from different places.[271]

Special schemes regulate the licensing and payment for cable retransmissions and music used in public telecommunication.[272] Indeed, the Society of Composers, Authors and Music Publishers of Canada recently filed a proposal with the Copyright Board to require Internet providers of musical works to pay royalties from 1996 at the greater of the rate of twenty-five cents per month per subscriber or 3.2 percent of gross revenue from advertising.[273] The Copyright Board is expected to give a decision shortly on whether this activity falls within this right and, if so, what method of charging for it would be appropriate.

6) Public Exhibition of Artwork

The copyright owner of an artistic work (except a map, chart, or plan) has the right to present it "at a public exhibition," other than for sale or hire. This rights applies to works made after 7 June 1988, the date the right was first introduced.[274] Galleries and museums that exhibit such works are typically included; dealer galleries are not, unless the work is there purely for exhibition. Works hanging in public lobbies may not be covered either, although the point is unclear.[275] Whether finger-paintings hung in school hallways come under the right is a problem that caused some school boards initial anxiety, but no budding Picasso has yet come forward to sue.

Like the public performance right, this right is supposed to return some benefit to artists for the public exposure of their work. It is often more symbolic than practical. Institutions may be loath to exhibit a

---

270 *CTV, ibid.* This includes a communication exclusively to occupants of apartments, hotel rooms, or dwelling units in the same building: *C Act, ibid.*, s. 3(1.2).

271 Compare *Challenge,* above note 236 at 114; *M.* (*J.P.*), above note 220, where a computer bulletin board operator, who made infringing copies available to selected users, was found guilty of "distribut[ing]" them to the copyright owner's prejudice, contrary to s. 42(1)(c) of the *C Act.*

272 See sections K(1) and K(2) in this chapter.

273 Further on SOCAN, see section K, "Users' Rights: Paying Uses," in this chapter.

274 *C Act,* above note 1, s. 3(1)(g). See W. Noel, *The Right of Public Presentation: A Guide to the Exhibition Right* (Ottawa: Canadian Conference of the Arts, 1990).

275 Compare French version of *C Act, ibid.*, s. 3(1)(g): "présenter [une oeuvre artistique] au public lors d'une exposition."

work unless the artist waives her right to demand a fee. If the artist holds out, there is usually plenty of pre-1988 material that can be shown free.

7) Rental

Canadian authors have, since 1987, received money from a fund administered by the Public Lending Rights Commission (now under the Canada Council) to compensate for book loans made through public libraries. Around $6 million per year is distributed to 7000 writers. The scheme does not operate within the copyright system, partly to avoid any obligation to pay foreign authors.

No right to control renting exists under copyright, except for computer programs rented out "for motive of gain."[276] Only easily reproducible over-the-counter operating or application programs are targeted. Videogame cartridges, encrypted programs reproducible only by experts, or hard-wired programs that help run items like dishwashers or automobiles are outside the right. For programs that are caught, all types of rental (including sham transactions) should be encompassed. Loss leading and cross-subsidization practices may not avoid liability; businesses that try to attract custom by offering free rentals are obviously pursuing a motive of gain, for their purpose is to profit financially.[277] Genuine sales or inventory financing involving lease-back or rent-to-own schemes should, however, be excluded. So should loans by non-profit libraries, members' clubs, or other cases where no more than a cost recovery, including overhead, charge is made.[278]

The rental right is an exception to the rule that copyright owners cannot control dispositions past the first public distribution.[279] It was created because the computer industry claimed that renting cut into sales, since some renters illicitly copied programs before returning them. So far, this right is used by owners more to close down operations than to provide an alternative means of exploiting their products. This practice may change as owners experiment with rental as one form of delivery on the Internet.

---

276   C Act, ibid., s. 3(1)(h) & s. 3(2); D. Vaver, "Record and Software Rentals: The Copyright Spin" (1995) 10 I.P.J. 109. A similar rental right also applies to sound recordings: C Act, ibid., ss. 5(4)–(6); see section D, "Sound Recording, Performances, Broadcasts," in this chapter.

277   Compare C.A.P.A.C. v. Western Fair Assn., [1951] S.C.R. 596 [Western Fair].

278   C Act, above note 1, ss. 3(2)(a) & (3).

279   See section G(1), "First Public Distribution," in this chapter.

8) Authorization

The owner can "authorize" any of the above rights that fall under the definition of copyright.[280] In practice, the authorization right attaches liability to people beyond those who actually commit the infringing act. Thus, whoever grants, or purports to grant, expressly or impliedly, the right to reproduce or perform a work in public has been held to "authorize" the reproduction or performance. The authorizer is then as liable as the reproducer or the performer.[281] A publisher or a record company placing orders with a printer or a presser has been found to "authorize" the reproduction. Someone hiring a dance orchestra and giving it full discretion to play whatever the conductor chooses also impliedly authorizes the performance. A cablecaster, too, has been held liable for impliedly authorizing bars that are its subscribers for the public performance that occurs when the television set is turned on for the patrons to watch cable.[282] Liability attaches only if the "authorized" act occurs, although *quia timet* relief is available where the act authorized has not yet been committed.

Buyers of blank tapes may use them to record music without authority. Similarly, VCR users may record programming off air or from other tapes. It is, of course, difficult and politically embarrassing to pursue individual private users. Copyright owners have therefore moved against manufacturers and sellers or lenders of records, blank tapes, and copying and recording machines to try to hold them liable for the infringing acts of buyers or hirers. These attempts have typically failed.[283] Courts have said that merely to provide the means of infringement is not the same as authorizing it, any more than someone selling a gun thereby authorizes a buyer to hunt without a licence or to commit a crime.[284] A supplier of a jukebox and records at a fixed rental to a restaurant was found not to authorize the hirer to publicly perform the music on the records.[285]

---

280 *C Act, ibid.*, s. 3(1), closing words; see section G(4), "Public Performance," in this chapter.

281 *Muzak Corp. v. C.A.P.A.C.*, [1953] 2 S.C.R. 182 at 189 [*Muzak*].

282 *Compo*, above note 255; *Canadian Performing Right Society v. Yee* (1943), 3 C.P.R. 64 (Alta. Dist. Ct.); *Canadian Cable*, above note 70.

283 *CBS Songs Ltd. v. Amstrad Consumer Electronics*, [1988] A.C. 1013 (H.L.); *Sony Corp. of America v. Universal City Studios Inc.*, 464 U.S. 417 (1984).

284 *Muzak*, above note 281.

285 *Vigneux*, above note 259. The hirer and its customers, however, both performed the work in public. Had the supplier told the hirer that public performances could occur without fee, or if they were partners or joint venturers, authorization might have been found: *Muzak, ibid.*, at 189.

For a time, "authorize" was equated with "sanction, approve, and countenance" or even "permit."[286] This equation fell out of favour in the United Kingdom in the 1980s, when attempts to turn passivity into authorization were rejected. This broader meaning, however, led to liability in Australia against a university library that let photocopying occur on its premises without taking reasonable steps to discourage suspected infringements.[287] This is doubtful law in the United Kingdom and probably in Canada, too. Bill C-32 would remove any risk of this or other liability from non-profit educational institutions, libraries, archives, and museums that operate photocopiers on their premises. A copyright notice in a form to be prescribed would, however, have to be exhibited.[288]

9) Substantial Infringement

A copyright owner controls what may be done not only with her whole work but with any substantial part of it.[289] Taking half a book may be infringement; so, too, may changing direct to indirect speech or even paraphrasing every sentence, as these acts change nothing of substance. A substantial part of a book may be not merely its collocation of words but its structure: its relationship of characters, incidents, and development. To lift this structure is as much infringement as lifting a chapter bodily. But structure cannot be abstracted too highly: had William Shakespeare and Leonard Bernstein been contemporaries, *West Side Story* should have opened despite its being inspired by *Romeo and Juliet*. The general stock of incidents in fiction or drama is free for all to use — a substantial part of everyone's culture, not of any one individual's work. "Substantial part" thus polices the line dividing what belongs to one and what belongs to all.

Nineteenth-century copyright statutes did not usually include any "substantial part" language, but judges nevertheless rightly wrote it into the law. Infringement then was a question of fact, often decided by a jury. The questions asked interchangeably were whether a taker had "unfairly" or "wrongfully" appropriated a claimant's labour and skill, or

---

286 *Falcon v. Famous Players Film Co.*, [1926] 2 K.B. 474 at 491 (C.A.); *Muzak, ibid.*, at 193.

287 *Moorhouse and Angus & Robertson (Publishers) Ltd. v. University of New South Wales*, [1976] R.P.C. 151 (Austl. H.C.).

288 Bill C-32, above note 9, cls. 30.3 & 30.4.

289 *C Act*, above note 1, s. 3(1), refers to "any substantial part" of a copyright work only in reference to the opening rights (reproduce, publish, publicly perform), but it applies to *all* the rights: for example, *Kelly*, above note 250 at 371.

whether he had "unfairly used" a claimant's material. Clearly, a value judgment was being made, depending on a number of considerations. Judges who today say that infringement is "all a question of fact and degree" mean much the same.

a) Taking a Particle Does Not Infringe

One should first screen out what cannot in law be a substantial part. "Part" means portion, not "particle."[290] A copyright owner cannot therefore control every particle of her work, any little piece the taking of which cannot affect the value of her work as a whole. So to carry two minor scenes from one play into another was found not to infringe copyright. More recently, transferring 60 of 14,000 lines of computer program source code into another program was found not to take a substantial part of the former work, especially since writing this routine material from scratch would have taken a competent programmer twenty minutes.[291] The occasional hyperbole to the contrary — that the taking of even a single sentence from the likes of a Dickens or a Shakespeare may infringe[292] — is simply nonsense. It falsely supports more mischievous assertions, such as that the inclusion in an audio recording of a single sound, however distinctive, from an earlier record infringes copyright. But two or three seconds from a three-minute recording is a mere particle; the sound, while perhaps of value to the taker, should not affect the value of the source work as a whole and so should be outside the copyright owner's control. Performers and record companies nevertheless continue to make such claims.[293]

b) Taking an Essential or Material Part Infringes

All concede that "substantial" connotes quality as much as or even more than quantity: so taking a material or essential part alone infringes another's copyright. A line or note count is relevant, but not conclusive.

---

290 *Chatterton v. Cave* (1878), 3 App. Cas. 483 at 492 (H.L.) [*Chatterton*].

291 *Ibid.*, at 495: "their extent was so slight, and their effect so small, as to render the taking perfectly immaterial"; *Delrina*, above note 22.

292 For example, *Rockford Map Publishers v. Directory Service Co. of Colorado Inc.*, 768 F.2d 145 at 148–49 (7th Cir. 1985): "Dickens did not need to complete *Bleak House* before receiving a copyright; every chapter — indeed every sentence — could be protected standing alone," citing (of course) no authority.

293 *Grand Upright Music Ltd. v. Warner Bros. Records Inc.*, 780 F. Supp. 182 (D.N.Y. 1991) finds unauthorized sampling to be an infringement, but the part taken appears to have been substantial. *Jarvis v. A & M Records*, 827 F. Supp. 282 (D.N.J. 1993) suggests that a distinctive bridge and keyboard riff may be a substantial part of a musical work.

On the one hand, to take a major chapter from a novel must be infringement except in the rarest of cases. So is the taking of a few bars from the refrain of a popular song — presumably more than the few notes necessary for anyone to "name that tune" — for what else is left?[294] On the other hand, to take four lines from a poem may not infringe: the context in which they are put may be critical. To feature the lines in an advertisement would most likely infringe; to stand them at the head of a magazine article probably would not.[295] Asking whether the part taken could have been protected on its own, as sometimes happens, is not helpful. Let us admit that *haiku* can be protected. How does that answer the question whether what *this* defendant did in taking *these* four lines from *this* poem infringes *this* claimant's rights?

What activities have been found to infringe or not to infringe has been indicated during the discussion on owner's rights.[296] Matters are often judged by how the ordinary reasonable buyer or user would react on seeing the two products involved together. Expert evidence may be needed to put the court in the position of someone reasonably versed in the relevant art or technology, so it may view the products through the eyes of such a person.[297] The following factors then become relevant in reaching a decision on infringement:[298]

- Is the part taken distinctive — something on which the first author spent much skill, effort, or ingenuity? The simpler a work, and the closer the line between its idea and its expression, the less need there is to grant broad control — indeed, the greater the care that must be taken that ideas do not end up being protected.
- Does the author merit the degree of protection sought, to her and others, to produce works of that sort? Would takings like this significantly impair the incentive to create for other similarly placed authors?

---

294   *Hawkes & Son (London) Ltd.* v. *Paramount Film Service Ltd.*, [1934] Ch. 593 (C.A.); compare *G. Ricordi & Co. (London) Ltd.* v. *Clayton & Waller Ltd.* (1930), [1928–1935] MacG. Cop. Cas. 154 (Ch.): taking eight bars, a fourth of the waiting motif in *Madame Butterfly*, may not infringe if "not the most distinctive or important part of that air."

295   Compare *Kipling* v. *Genatoson* (1920), [1917–1923] MacG. Cop. Cas. 203 (Ch.) with *Chappell & Co. Ltd.* v. *D.C. Thompson & Co. Ltd.* (1934), [1928–1935] MacG. Cop. Cas. 467 (Ch.).

296   See section G, "Owner's Rights," in this chapter.

297   *Tele–Direct*, above note 79; *Ancher, Mortlock, Murray & Wooley Pty. Ltd.* v. *Hooker Homes Ltd.*, [1971] 2 N.S.W.L.R. 278 (S.C.); *Nichols*, above note 252.

298   Compare the list in *U & R Tax Services Ltd.* v. *H & R Block Canada Inc.* (1995), 62 C.P.R. (3d) 257 at 268 (Fed. T.D.).

- Has the claimant's present or future ability to exploit her work been substantially affected?
- Is the user unfairly enriching himself at the author's expense? Has he saved himself much time, trouble, or expense by taking the features that make the claimant's work what it is?
- Do the two works compete for much of the same market? Is the market for the user's work one that ought fairly to belong to the author?

The more one answers these questions in the affirmative, the more likely one should find infringement. Since the variables differ from case to case, decisions on ostensibly similar facts may also — perhaps frustratingly — differ. The overall goal is to ensure that any decision furthers copyright as a means to encourage the production and dissemination of valuable creative work. At the same time, public access to and use of a work for socially desirable ends should not be unduly fettered. A balance must be struck between these two objectives.

c) Mediating Artistic Practice: Parody and Postmodernism

In deciding whether an activity infringes, courts should be careful not to interfere with fair artistic practices and trends. Substantiality can act as a rough mediator between what is and what is not acceptable. For example, parody could reasonably be given wide leeway when practised by writers, artists, and performers, except in the rare case where the parody is meant to, and does, substitute for its target. Purely commercial parodies could be more strictly controlled. So, for example, advertisers taking others' music for their jingles could be held to be taking a substantial part, even when they parody the music. Takings like these directly interfere with a composer's livelihood and the stream of income she can expect from having her work exploited.[299]

Other interferences seem less justifiable. Spoofs of trade-marks and labels that were found to be protected by copyright have been held to be infringements. A union was forbidden from caricaturing the St-Hubert rooster logo, even though this activity was part of a campaign designed to gain support for restaurant workers in a labour dispute with the mark owner. Similarly, a firm was stopped from marketing SCHLURPPES "tonic bubble bath," even though the product did not compete with tonic water

---

299   *Glyn v. Weston Feature Film Co.*, [1916] 1 Ch. 261; *Joy Music Ltd. v. Sunday Pictorial Newspapers (1920) Ltd.*, [1960] 2 Q.B. 60; *Campbell v. Acuff-Rose Music Inc.*, 114 S. Ct. 1164 (1994) (rap treatment of Roy Orbison's *Oh Pretty Woman*); compare *MCA Canada Ltd. (Ltée.) v. Gilbery & Hawke Advertising Agency Ltd.* (1976), 28 C.P.R. (2d) 52 (Fed. T.D.) (parody for jingle admittedly infringement).

and Schweppes lost no sales. Neither free speech nor free trading were found important enough interests to outweigh the court's desire to protect a trade-mark from having its value diluted. The strange thing is that trade-mark law may not have been violated by these acts; so copyright, as applied, has produced a result apparently at odds with trade-mark policy.[300] Even more dubious has been a U.S. court's decision to brand a whole post-modernist artistic practice — appropriating and recontextualizing previous artwork — as copyright infringement: postmodernism will go its own way whatever four New York judges say or do.[301] Courts as much as right-holders may need to be constantly reminded to "lighten up."

Unfortunately, many courts still work on the "rough practical test," frequently trotted out by claimants' lawyers, that "what is worth copying is prima facie worth protecting."[302] As a legal invitation, this is too crude to be overtly accepted. Taken literally, it begs all questions of copyrightability, infringement, and substantiality.[303] More often, however, the "test" operates covertly, directing action from the wings rather than taking centre stage. The upshot is that, in practice, people regularly seek permission to carry on arguably non-infringing activities because the cost of permission is usually less than the cost and inconvenience of going to court. But right-holders may refuse permission. When they do, the effect may be to eliminate a socially beneficial, or at least not socially harmful, practice. The uncertainties surrounding substantial infringement work very much to the advantage of powerful right-holders, and quite often to the disadvantage of the general community and the values of free expression.

10) Distributing and Importing Infringing Copies

Anyone can usually sell, resell, and rent lawfully acquired works and non-infringing copies without worrying about copyright.[304] But copy-

---

300 *Rôtisseries St-Hubert Ltée* v. *Syndicat des Travailleur(euses) de la Rôtisserie St-Hubert de Drummondville (CSN)* (1986), 17 C.P.R. (3d) 461 (Que. S.C.) [*St-Hubert*]; *Schweppes Ltd.* v. *Wellingtons Ltd.* (1983), [1984] F.S.R. 210 (Ch.). See section G(3), "Dilution," in chapter 4.

301 *Rogers,* above note 228.

302 *University of London,* above note 20 at 610.

303 *Ibcos Computers Ltd.* v. *Barclays Mercantile Highland Finance Ltd* . (1994), 28 I.P.R. 25 at 37 (Ch.); *National News Ltd.* v. *Copyright Agency Ltd.* (1996), 34 I.P.R. 53 at 71 (Austl. Fed. Ct.).

304 An exception is renting computer programs and sound recordings. See section G(7), "Rental," and section E(6), "Sound Recordings, Performances, Broadcasts," in this chapter.

right owners can control the distribution of infringing copies in Canada or unauthorized parallel imports. Someone who knows that a work infringes copyright, or knows that it would infringe had it been made in Canada, has to get the copyright owner's consent to deal with the work. Otherwise, he infringes if he does any of the following: sells or hires out the work; exposes it by way of trade, or offers it for sale or hire; distributes it for the purposes of trade or so as to affect the owner of the copyright prejudicially; by way of trade exhibits it in public; or imports it into Canada for sale or hire.[305] Indeed, these activities — as well as making an infringing work for sale or hire, possessing plates to make infringing copies, or performing works in public for private profit — are criminal acts that, on conviction after indictment, can attract penalties of up to a $1 million fine and/or five years jail.[306]

Two issues are pertinent to this discussion: parallel imports and the knowledge requirement.

a) Parallel Imports

The provision that a person who handles a work, knowing that it "would infringe copyright if it had been made within Canada," operates to prevent the import and commercial handling of unauthorized copies made outside Canada. Works made offshore without anyone's consent are obviously caught. Indeed, the Canadian owner or exclusive licensee who suspects that such goods are about to be imported can obtain a court order directing Customs to stop them at the border.[307] But the provision also strikes at goods legitimately made abroad that are imported into Canada. The idea is not to strike at the inadvertent or otherwise innocent importer. To be liable, the importer must know that the Canadian copyright owner would not have consented to the making of the works had they been made in Canada. [308]

These provisions work unevenly. Exclusive selling agents or distributors have been unable to use them because they typically have merely contractual rights that create no interest in copyright.[309] Canadian authors also have complained of the import of remaindered copies of their books, on which they may receive no royalty and which compete

---

305 *C Act*, above note 1, s. 27(4).
306 *C Act, ibid.*, ss. 41(1) & (2).
307 *C Act, ibid.*, s. 44.1.
308 *Clarke Irwin & Co.* v. *C. Cole & Co.* [1960] O.R. 117 (H.C.J.); *Fly by Nite Music Co.* v. *Record Wherehouse Ltd.*, [1975] F.C. 386 (T.D.).
309 *Maison du livre français de Montréal Inc.* v. *Institut littéraire du Qué. Ltée* (1957), 31 C.P.R. 69 (Que. S.C.).

with regularly priced local stock.[310] Bill C-32 proposes to remedy both these perceived faults by letting distributors with sole Canadian distribution rights prevent parallel imports and redistribution.[311] The bill does not, however, touch another pressing problem. Copyright in the trade-marks, labels, packaging, or even computer programs associated with goods (e.g., a computer chip that helps run a car or a microwave) has been used elsewhere to stop imports of the non-copyright goods themselves.[312] Similar strategies could be employed in Canada.

b) Knowledge

Whoever personally makes or authorizes the making of an infringing copy of a work infringes.[313] But, as already noted, those who deal (by sale, hire, import, etc.) with an infringing copy that they have not personally made infringe only if they know they are dealing with infringing copies. The ignorant, careless, or unsophisticated are spared. Claimants wanting to reach such dealers may need to inform the trade or a targeted dealer of their allegations and fully back them up, for proceedings issued before an innocent acquirer has had a reasonable time to investigate the allegations risk dismissal with costs. Turning a blind eye to the obvious can, however, amount to knowledge. A person is assumed to have "the ordinary understanding expected of persons in his line of business, unless by his or other evidence . . . [the court] is convinced otherwise."[314] Some say that knowledge only of the facts constituting infringement is enough and that an honest but mistaken belief that the goods do not infringe is irrelevant.[315] This comes close to equating constructive with actual knowledge. Bill C-32 would achieve this equation by extending liability to those who "should have known" that the copies were infringing.[316] Whether this looser standard, commonly applied as an "interpretation" of the *Act,* is legally justifiable is debatable.

---

310 *C Act*, above note 1, ss. 45(3)(d) & (5); *McClelland & Stewart Ltd.* v. *Coles Book Stores Ltd.* (1974), 7 O.R. (2d) 426 (H.C.J.) (Farley Mowat's *A Whale for the Killing*).

311 Bill C-32, above note 9, cls. 27.1 & 44.2, cl. 1(5) def. "exclusive distributor."

312 For example, *Frank & Hirsch (Pty.) Ltd.* v. *A. Roopanand Brothers (Pty.) Ltd.* (1993), 29 I.P.R. 465 (S. Afr. S.C., (A.D.)) (TDK blank audio tapes). Removal of the offending trade-mark or part, if possible, may avoid infringement.

313 There may, however, also be liability on other grounds — for example, vicarious liability. See section D(2), "Whom to Sue," in chapter 5.

314 *RCA Corp.* v. *Custom Cleared Sales Pty. Ltd.* (1978), 19 A.L.R. 123 at 126 (N.S.W.C.A.).

315 *Sillitoe,* above note 244.

316 Bill C-32, above note 9, cls. 27(2) & (3).

H. OWNER'S RIGHTS: SOUND RECORDINGS, PERFORMANCES, BROADCASTS

Copyright for sound recordings presently includes only first distribution, reproduction, and rental rights.[317] Bill C-32 proposes the addition of an authorization right. Record companies and makers connected to a *Rome Convention* country would also have public performance and telecommunication rights.[318] In addition, blank audio tape music royalties would be provided for Canadian record companies and individual makers. Entities from other states could have this right extended to them, based on reciprocity.[319]

Performers from WTO states have rights to fix their performance on a record, reproduction rights over records containing unauthorized fixations, telecommunication rights over their live performance, and authorization rights.[320] Bill C-32 proposes to add, for performers from *Rome Convention* states, rights of fixation, public performance, and telecommunication in respect of their live performances, as well as reproduction, rental, and authorization rights. A blank audio-tape music royalty is provided for Canadian performers and others, based on reciprocity.[321]

Bill C-32 proposes that broadcasters have rights to fix their transmissions, reproduction rights over unauthorized fixations, performance rights over television programs played in places where the public pays an entrance fee to view, a general authorization right, and a specific right to authorize simultaneous retransmission by other broadcasters.[322]

I. AUTHORS' MORAL RIGHTS

Authors have "moral rights" in respect of their works, quite apart from any copyright. The word "moral" is somewhat misleading. These rights are legally enforceable.[323] They are based on the idea that an author's

---

317   *C Act*, above note 1, s. 5(4).
318   For the content of these rights, see the corresponding headings under section G, "Owner's Rights: Literary, Dramatic, Musical, and Artistic Works," in this chapter.
319   Bill C-32, above note 9, cls. 18(1), 19(1), 27(5), & 81.
320   *C Act*, above note 1, s. 14.01.
321   Bill C-32, above note 9, cls. 15(1), 19(1), 27(5), & 81.
322   *Ibid.*, cl. 21. For the content of these rights, see the corresponding headings under section G, "Owner's Rights: Literary, Dramatic, Musical, and Artistic Works," in this chapter.
323   The term is a poor translation of *droits moraux*, roughly "personal" or "intellectual" rights.

work is an extension of the author and that any assault on it is as much an attack on the author as a physical assault. Parting with the copyright does not lessen the author's personal attachment to the work, and the author should have recourse against those who present the work differently from the way the author originally intended.[324]

1) General Features

The *Act* recognizes three rights: attribution, integrity, and association. Other analogous author interests are protected through common and civil law doctrines. The rights provided by the *Act* are intimately linked with copyright. They apply only to authors who have produced an original work protected by copyright, whether or not they still own the copyright.[325] The rights last as long as the copyright and descend to an author's estate. Otherwise, they are personal: they can be waived, but not assigned.[326] The usual schedule of remedies applies, but it is discretionary.[327]

Moral rights theory emanated from nineteenth-century Europe and became internationally entrenched in *Berne*'s 1928 revision. Canada legislated the *Berne* provision (art. 6[bis]) into the *Copyright Act* in 1931, later clarifying and expanding its operation in 1988. But moral rights were recognized even earlier in a 1915 *Criminal Code* amendment. This made it an offence either to change anything in a copyright-protected dramatic, operatic, or musical work that was to be publicly performed for profit or to suppress its title or authorship, unless the author or her legal representative consented. A filmmaker who took a play, changed its title, and suppressed the dramatist's name was successfully prosecuted in 1916.[328] This criminal provision was moved to the *Copyright Act* in 1921. Though still on the books, it has lain unused for at least the last half century.[329]

---

324 Moral rights of integrity may perhaps presently apply to sound recordings because they have a "deemed author" — the record producer. Under Bill C-32, above note 9, sound recordings have no "author" and so would have no moral rights; the same applies to performances and broadcasts.

325 See section E(1), "Author," and section C(1), "Originality," in this chapter.

326 *C Act*, above note 1, ss. 14.1, 14.2, 28.1, & 28.2.

327 For moral rights infringement the court "may" grant the author a remedy: *C Act*, *ibid.*, s. 34(1.1). Compare this wording with s. 34(1) for copyright infringement, where the owner is "entitled" to the stated remedies. See section D(3), "Remedy Selection," in chapter 5.

328 *Joubert* v. *Géracimo* (1916), 35 D.L.R. 683 (Que. C.A.).

329 *C Act*, above note 1, s. 43. The penalties for violation — maximum $250 or $500 fines, and two to four months' jail in addition for repeat offences — have not changed since 1921.

Authors' interests may also be protected through common and civil law doctrines. This protection was pointed out as long ago as 1911, when the Supreme Court forced a publisher to return the author's only copy of a rejected manuscript. One judge said:

> I cannot agree that the sale of a manuscript of a book is subject to the same rules as the sale of any other article of commerce, *e.g.*, paper, grain or lumber. The vendor of such things loses all dominion over them when once the contract is executed and the purchaser may deal with the thing which he has purchased as he chooses. It is his to keep, to alienate or to destroy. But it will not be contended that the publisher who bought the manuscript of "The Life of Gladstone," by Morley, or of Cromwell by the same author, might publish the manuscript, having paid the author his price, with such emendations or additions as might perchance suit his political or religious views and give them to the world as those of one of the foremost publicists of our day. Nor could the author be denied by the publisher the right to make corrections, in dates or otherwise, if such corrections were found to be necessary for historical accuracy; nor could the manuscript be published in the name of another. After the author has parted with his pecuniary interest in the manuscript, he retains a species of personal or moral right in the product of his brain.[330]

Sentiments like these may underpin authors' actions for passing-off, misappropriation of personality, or breach of contract when their interests are affected. Such claims, interestingly enough, have met with more success than assertions of the moral rights the *Act* provides. These rights and interests are now examined.

2) Attribution

The *Act* entitles an author to remain anonymous. It also entitles an author to be associated with the work by name or under a pseudonym, "where reasonable in the circumstances," when an act within copyright occurs (e.g., reproduction, translation, broadcast).[331]

The "reasonableness" qualification, introduced in 1988, has not been judicially discussed. It is presumably there for the sake of flexibility and to deter trivial complaints. For example, producing a music

---

330   *Morang & Co. v. Le Sueur* (1911), 45 S.C.R. 95 at 97–98, Fitzpatrick C.J.C., relying on civil law doctrine in an Ontario appeal.

331   *C Act*, above note 1, s. 14.1(1). The "reasonableness" qualification does not seem to apply to the right to remain anonymous.

video, an advertising campaign, or a complex computer program may involve inputs from many people. Demands for attribution could produce a list as long as that found at the end of a movie. The difficulties of deciding who did what and how it contributed to the final product may make it unreasonable for anybody to demand credit. This is certainly the way many advertising agencies and software companies proceed, preferring to stress their ownership rather than actual authorship. Presumably, too, the reasonableness qualification is what allows broadcasters not to mention composers or lyricists when playing records on air, while, perhaps paradoxically, often mentioning the names of the performers, who have no statutory moral rights.[332]

The qualification is unclear about whether it is supposed to reinforce or to undermine respect for contractual provisions that deal explicitly with credit. Suppose two people collaborate on a work, but only one is named co-author. In the absence of any agreement on the point, the omitted person is entitled to credit. A court may give damages for the past breach and order an appropriate credit line to be inserted. For example, if Martha thinks up a short story and takes it to John, a script doctor, to put into literary shape, Martha and John may technically be joint authors.[333] An appropriate credit line might be "by Martha and John" or, perhaps, *vice versa*. But if Martha's contribution is relatively more important, the credit line might better read "by Martha, with John."[334] Suppose, however, the contract said that John would get no credit. Would it be "reasonable in the circumstances" to enforce this agreement and perpetuate the lie that the work was a sole production? Or would it be more reasonable to refuse to enforce the provision and let the truth out? Since the *Act* specifically allows moral rights to be waived,[335] one suspects that contract may be allowed to trump truth.

3) Integrity

The right of integrity stops work from being "distorted, mutilated or otherwise modified," but only if this prejudices the author's honour or reputation.[336] Theoretically, then, the author may control the way her

---

332   Bill C-32 does not propose to change this position.
333   See section E(1)(c), "Joint Authors," in this chapter.
334   *Courtenay v. Polkosnik* (1983), 77 C.P.R. (2d) 140 at 144 (Ont. H.C.J.); compare
       Goulet v. Marchand (18 Sept. 1985), (Que. S.C.) [unreported]: part compiler of
       legal text entitled to co-author credit.
335   See section I(6), "Waiver," in this chapter.
336   *C Act,* above note 1, ss. 14.1(1) & 28.2(1).

work is presented, at least to some extent, though this control should not prevent reasonable adaptations and changes over time. So, for example, even "faithful" cinematic adaptations of a book rarely transpose the literary medium directly into a visual one; so long as the book's theme and spirit are fairly interpreted and presented, an author may not be able to complain if whole scenes and characters are omitted. Similarly, an artist's natural sensitivity should not interfere with the sort of experimentation that is the hallmark of much artistic progress. Where would parody and jazz be if authors could complain about the way a parodist or jazz musician handled their work? The reputation of both Leonardo da Vinci and the *Mona Lisa* remains intact, despite Marcel Duchamp's representation of her with an added moustache and goatee, and our understanding of art is enriched by the implications of Duchamp's iconoclasm.

Concerns like these may underlie the often sceptical reception with which moral rights are greeted in Canada. The scrawler of graffiti on a public sculpture may, on one view, be infringing the sculptor's moral rights. On another view, he may be exercising, however crudely, rights of free speech and comment. In any event, he is untraceable, and courts have not visited his delinquency on art owners, who have been held under no duty to preserve or restore inventory. Courts have even held that total destruction may not violate moral rights. Thus, when a town's clean-up crew dumped public sculptures in the local river after the works had deteriorated through vandalism and neglect, the Quebec courts dismissed the sculptors' claims against the town. The artists' reputation could hardly suffer from works that were out of sight and out of mind.[337] At the other extreme, a choreographer's claim that the ballet he composed could not be staged without his participation was also dismissed. Others could direct the work competently and not "every step or nuance of movement in every performance" need be duplicated. Near enough was good enough.[338] Against unpromising jurisprudence like this, a case where Michael Snow forced the Eaton Centre in downtown Toronto to remove Christmas decorations with which the centre's management had bedecked his Canada geese sculpture comes as somewhat of a surprise. The court there found that the work had indeed been distorted or modified to the prejudice of the artist's honour or reputation.[339]

---

337   *Gnass v. Cité d'Alma* (3 June 1977), (Que. C.A.) [unreported] [*Gnass*], discussed in D. Vaver, "Authors' Moral Rights in Canada" (1983) 14 I.I.C. 329 at 341ff.
338   *Patsalas v. National Ballet of Canada* (1986), 13 C.P.R. (3d) 522 at 528 (Ont. H.C.J.).
339   *Snow v. Eaton Centre Ltd.* (1982), 70 C.P.R. (2d) 105 (Ont. H.C.J.) [*Snow*].

Snow would have an even easier ride today because prejudice to an artist's honour or reputation is now "deemed to have occurred" whenever a painting, sculpture, or engraving is distorted, mutilated, or otherwise modified.[340] One trusts this "deeming" presents only a rebuttable presumption; otherwise, a modern-day da Vinci would have a clear claim against a follower of Duchamp who dared to interfere with even a print purchased from a museum gift shop. The *Act* also provides that merely changing a work's location or making good-faith efforts to preserve it is not automatically a distortion.[341] The right of owners of public artwork to relocate works to placate offended public sensibilities is therefore confirmed, at least if the new site still allows some public viewing. No attempt is made, however, to reconcile these provisions with the case earlier noted, in which public sculptures were relocated at the bottom of the local river.[342] Total destruction apparently continues to be less offensive than relocation to an obscure warehouse or handing the work back to the artist. The views of those who produced the now dismantled or crumbling sculptures of Lenin throughout Eastern Europe would be interesting on this point.

Proving prejudice to honour or reputation outside these "deemed" cases continues to be difficult. In *Snow*, the court said that considerable weight may be given to the artist's opinion if "reasonably arrived at."[343] But, more recently, "objective" evidence of prejudice has been insisted on. A novelist's moral rights claim that his work had been poorly anthologized by a copyright infringer was dismissed because the claimant's view was unsupported by expert opinion and his career had continued to flourish despite wide distribution of the repugnant work.[344] This approach may help stem some dubious claims — for example, where employers enlist their employees' moral rights as a tactic against competitors.[345] At the

---

340   *C Act*, above note 1, s. 28.2(2), introduced in R.S.C. 1988 (4th Supp.), c. 10, s. 6.

341   *C Act, ibid.*, s. 28.2(3).

342   *Gnass,* above note 337 at 338.

343   *Snow,* above note 339 at 106; see D. Vaver, "Snow v. The Eaton Centre: Wreaths on Sculpture Prove Accolade for Artists' Moral Rights" (1983) 8 Can. Bus. L.J. 81.

344   *Prise de Parole Inc.* v. *Guérin, Éditeur Ltée* (1995), 66 C.P.R. (3d) 257 at 266 (Fed. T.D.) (a copyright infringement claim, however, succeeded); similarly *Gnass,* above note 337, where the sculptors' defamation claim equally failed.

345   Nintendo tried this tactic in seeking to block *Game Genie,* a third-party cartridge that fitted a Nintendo computer and improved the way Nintendo videogames ran. The complaint of Nintendo's staff videogame designer that his artistic integrity had been compromised because of the new antics Super Mario and Donkey Kong were made to perform did not impress Canadian courts much: *Nintendo of America Inc.* v. *Camerica Corp.* (1991), 34 C.P.R. (3d) 193 (Fed. T.D.), aff'd (1991), 36 C.P.R. (3d) 352 (Fed. C.A.), refusing interlocutory relief.

same time, it may turn aside legitimate complaints from artists with well-established reputations: the da Vincis that even Duchamps cannot shake.

4) Association

The author may also control the use of the work "in association with a product, service, cause or institution." This right is part of the integrity right and so is infringed only if the use prejudices the author's honour or reputation.[346] An advertiser may therefore be unable to use a Gordon Lightfoot composition in a commercial, even if the copyright owner (typically the music publisher) agrees, unless Lightfoot also agrees. If he never appears in commercials, Lightfoot could argue that any use of his work in advertising is in itself offensive. That apart, whether Lightfoot has a right to refuse may depend on the commercial involved. His honour or his reputation could still be prejudiced if the music is badly presented, the lyrics are distorted, or the commercial is distasteful (e.g., for toilet cleaners rather than an anti-drug campaign).

5) Other Rights

The *Act* recognizes no other moral rights, although under *Berne* an author can prevent "derogatory action" in relation to her work beyond attribution, integrity, and association right infringements. The sort of derogatory action recognized in European states that take moral rights seriously may, however, also be recognized by the common or the civil law. For example, authors are said to have the right to create or to refuse to create a work; this right is reflected at common law in rules that invalidate unreasonable restraints on the right to work and that allow dilatory authors under contract to plead "writer's block" to specific performance (but not damages) actions brought by publishers.

In Europe, artists are also said to have a right to prevent excessive criticism of their work. This right may be vindicated in Canada through defamation law. European authors may also usually decide when or whether to make a work public. This feature is part of copyright in Canadian law — the first public distribution right.[347] Even the right, recognized in France, to withdraw a work from circulation or disavow it if

---

346   *C Act*, above note 1, ss. 14.1(1) & 28.2(1)(b).

347   *C Act*, *ibid.*, s. 3(1). Being a copyright, however, it can be exercised by the owner against an author's interests. This may happen when the copyright has been assigned or has first vested in someone other than the author (e.g., her employer). See also section G(1), "First Public Distribution," in this chapter.

it no longer represents the author's views may be recognized at common law. This author's right is rarely exercised in France because publishers can insist on being indemnified for the cost of existing stock. Common law courts could presumably develop a similar right subject to similar conditions. There is unfavourable old case law. For example, British poet laureate Robert Southey found he could not suppress distribution of a youthful poem he no longer believed in.[348] But is it really possible that a newspaper today could publish, with impunity, a letter to the editor, over the objections of a sender who has since found out that his facts are wrong and that the letter is defamatory?[349]

6) Waiver

One reason moral rights are more talked about than exercised in Canada is because the *Act* explicitly allows their waiver.[350] The waiver need not be in writing. It may even be implied, as when an engineer was held unable to complain about changes made in his design work for public safety reasons.[351]

Exploitation agreements often contain provisions under which authors expressly waive their moral rights in perpetuity. This practice has long been common, for example, in the motion picture industry; writers whose books, plays, or scripts are used for a film inevitably sign a standard form that lets the film company do what it likes with the material. The heirs of Victor Hugo cannot complain about Disney's animated version of *The Hunchback of Notre Dame* because the book is long out of copyright; but had Hugo been alive today he would have had no claim, either, because any contract he would have signed with a North American film company would have required him to waive all moral rights. Courts may sometimes restrict a waiver by construing it to cover only changes that do not prejudice the author's honour or reputation. But explicit language can presumably oust this qualification.[352] Otherwise, trying to invalidate such waivers is as difficult as avoiding any other contract provision for some abuse of power (fraud, misrepresentation, restraint of trade, unconscionability, etc.).

---

348   *Southey v. Sherwood* (1817), 2 Mer. 435, 35 E.R. 1006 (Ch.).

349   This act was unlikely even in the nineteenth century: *Davis v. Miller & Fairly* (1855), 17 D. 1166 (Ct. Sess., Scot.).

350   *C Act*, above note 1, s. 14.1(2). The waiver *prima facie* also benefits later copyright owners and licensees, but an assignment is not by itself a waiver: s. 14.1(4) & (3).

351   *John Maryon*, above note 61.

352   *Kerr*, above note 168.

7) Justification and Problems

How, then, can moral rights be theoretically justified? Metaphysical reasoning about the intimate link between an author and her work seems about as persuasive as attempts to base copyright protection on everyone's "natural" right to the fruits of his labour. A more plausible case for moral rights could draw on four sources:

- "Truth-in-marketing": Like trade-marks, moral rights help assure the public that the works it has come to associate with a particular author are indeed that author's genuine product.
- Social reward: Authors merit whatever reward (or lack of it) their work may bring, and that merit is in the work as they have issued it.
- Author empowerment: Moral rights give authors a bargaining chip which, given the greater power generally wielded by entrepreneurs, allows the former some say over the manner in which their work is later exploited.
- Cultural preservation: The public interest in a continuous record of its culture justifies giving authors some control over their works as a private right to be exercised for the public good.

In practice, however, there are enormous difficulties in enforcing moral rights in a digital era. They may be enough to cause the "moral" in "moral rights" to take on its more common meaning as an opposite of "legal," since moral suasion may come to replace legal enforceability on the Internet. How may an author stop a user from altering and redistributing work that has been downloaded from the Internet? How can he stop still later users altering it further? How can authorship in a composite work be traced and established? When practical problems like this combine with the scepticism with which North Americans treat moral rights, the threat to moral rights is clear.[353] By contrast, Europeans have tended to treat moral rights more reverentially. The notion of the Author as Romantic Genius may still linger there. Whether this respect will hold true much longer, except as a form of academic nostalgia, is an interesting question.

Meanwhile, how moral rights will play out in Canadian courts is uncertain. Take the problem of colourizing black-and-white movies.

---

353 A typical U.S. response to moral rights is to call them "elitist and despotic," "special-interest legislation . . . for the benefit of a minority who feel better knowing that the owner is not allowed to act in an uncultured way": for example, S.L. Carter, "Owning What Doesn't Exist" (1990) 13 Harv. J. L & Pub. Policy 99 at 100–1.

After initial hostility during the late 1980s from many film directors and actors, this practice has become so accepted in North America that a moral rights claim is almost inconceivable except against a totally incompetent adaptation. By contrast, in 1991 John Huston's heirs convinced France's highest court to stop a television screening of a colourized version of *The Asphalt Jungle*. Huston may have had no integrity right in the United States when the film was made, but the French court was willing to teach Americans a lesson in how to preserve a culture they did not recognize they had. The right of a film director and his estate to prevent modifications of his *oeuvre* which would prejudice his honour or reputation was affirmed.[354]

The reaction of Canadian courts to a case like Huston's would be interesting. Their overall record to date has, with few exceptions, shown little inclination to press moral rights liability much beyond what the common law or the civil law would have imposed anyway. Claims relying purely on the *Act* may therefore be risky propositions unless strong common or civil law support is also available.

J. USERS' RIGHTS: FREE USE

Fairly liberal exemptions to copyright are allowed by international law.[355] The *Act* provides some statutory exemptions, little changed since 1924. Others are imposed by common or civil law techniques. Principles of statutory interpretation, estoppel, waiver, implied licence, and public policy have all been invoked to prevent copyright laws from becoming "instruments of oppression and extortion."[356]

1) Specific Exemptions

The following narrowly focused exemptions apply to particular classes of work or activity.

354　Y. Gendreau, "The Continuing Saga of Colourization in France" (1993) 7 I.P.J. 340.

355　*Agreement on Trade-Related Aspects of Intellectual Property Rights, Including Trade in Counterfeit Goods*, (1994) 25 I.I.C. 209, art. 13 [*TRIPs*], generalizing from *Berne*, above note 2, art. 9(2), which applies only to the reproduction right.

356　*Canadian Assn. of Broadcasters* v. *Society of Composers, Authors & Music Publishers of Canada* (1994), 58 C.P.R. (3d) 190 at 196 (Fed. C.A.).

a) Artistic Work

Artists who no longer own their copyright may nevertheless continue to use preparatory material — for example, moulds, casts, sketches — from their earlier works for new projects if the main design of the earlier work is not repeated.[357]

Paintings, drawings, engravings, or photographs can also be made and published of certain works: architecture, sculpture, and works of artistic craftsmanship. A limitation for architecture is that the derivative work cannot itself be an architectural drawing or plan; for sculpture or works of artistic craftsmanship, the item must be permanently situated in a public place or building.[358] Presumably, this list includes works in a gallery's permanent collection, though not currently exhibited.

b) Musical Work

Music may be freely performed at any agricultural or agricultural-industrial exhibition or fair receiving a grant from a federal, provincial, or municipal authority, or held by its directors under such authority, but the performance must be "without motive of gain."[359] This exemption is rarely used, because a motive of gain has been found where any musician is paid to perform, or the music is designed to attract people to the event or to any special exhibition at the event.[360]

Music may also be performed by a church, college, school, or by a religious, charitable, or fraternal organization to further a religious, educational, or charitable object.[361] But putting on a function and applying the proceeds to a worthy object does not qualify: the performance must be a "participating factor in the [religious, educational, or] charitable object itself or in an activity incidental to it."[362]

A radio may be played anywhere without infringing public performance rights in music, but a licence is needed if it plays in a theatre ordinarily and regularly used for entertainment for which an admission charge is made.[363]

---

357 *C Act*, above note 1, s. 27(2)(b); *Franklin Mint Corp. v. National Wildlife Act Exchange Inc.*, 575 F.2d 62 (9th Cir. 1978); *McCrum v. Eisner* (1917), 87 L.J.Ch. 99.
358 *C Act, ibid.*, s. 27(2)(c).
359 *C Act, ibid.*, s. 27(2)(g).
360 *Western Fair*, above note 277.
361 *C Act*, above note 1, s. 27(3).
362 *C.A.P.A.C. v. Kiwanis Club of West Toronto*, [1953] 2 S.C.R. 111 at 115.
363 *C Act*, above note 1, s. 69(2); *Vigneux*, above note 259.

c) Newspapers

Newspapers may publish reports of addresses of "a political nature delivered at a public meeting,"[364] and also reports of public lectures, addresses, sermons, or speeches. The second class of report is, however, prohibited if a conspicuous notice prohibiting reports is kept at the main entrance of the building and, unless the building is being used for public worship, near the speaker.[365] Whether this prohibition can stand with the *Charter* guarantee of freedom of expression is doubtful. Reports, including those made in defiance of a prohibition, may nevertheless themselves have copyright.[366]

d) School Compilations

Short passages from literary works may be published in a collection intended for schools if the following conditions are met: the collection is composed mainly of non-copyright matter, the publication is described in the title and any advertising as intended for the use of schools, the literary works were not themselves published for the use of schools, the source from which the passages are taken is acknowledged, and no more than two passages from the same author are published by the same publisher within five years.[367] By contrast, a U.S. decision in 1996 allowed copy shops to produce course-packs for university classes, even though the materials contained substantial extracts from published literary works. The practice was initially treated as a fair use because the market for the works was said to be unaffected. Professors ordering the course-packs would not, the court said, have demanded that students acquire any book from which extracts had been made. However, on reargument, an 8:5 majority of the court reversed the earlier decision and held that such course-packs could be produced only with the copyright holder's permission and on payment of whatever fee the latter demanded.[368]

e) Computer Programs

The owner of a physical copy of a computer program can make a back-up copy if none is supplied. She may also make the program compatible

---

364   *C Act, ibid.*, s. 28.

365   *C Act, ibid.*, ss. 27(2)(e) & 28.02(2)(b).

366   See section C(1), "Originality," in this chapter.

367   *C Act*, above note 1, s. 27(2)(d).

368   *Princeton University Press* v. *Michigan Document Services*, 74 F.3d 1512 (6th Cir. 1996), rev'd 1996 Fed. App. 0357P (6th Cir. 1996), *en banc* [*Princeton*].

with her own computer. In either case, she must delete the copy or adaptation on ceasing to own the program.[369]

2) Copying Authorized by Legislation

Copying material under the *Cultural Property Export and Import Act*, *Access to Information Act*, federal and provincial *Privacy Acts*, and the *National Archives of Canada Act* is allowed.[370] Other legislation requiring or allowing copying may also implicitly exempt that act from infringing. For example, copying material from public registries may be allowed; this may also be true for material produced on discovery in litigation. The copying would have to be consistent with the reason for having the registry or the discovery in the first place. A manuscript that is produced on discovery may be copied for purposes relevant to the litigation, but cannot be distributed for sale.[371]

3) Repairs and Modifications

There may be a right at common law to repair, or to make spare parts designed to repair, products protected by copyright.[372] Authors' moral rights[373] may, however, need to be heeded to avoid changes that prejudice the author's honour or reputation.

The width of this right is ill defined and controversial. Presumably, public policy would allow repairs to avoid danger to the user or the public. Buyers may also be able to bring products up to the standard that a seller has expressly or impliedly promised but not met, even where the defect is not dangerous.[374] On the other hand, sellers have restricted rights to repair computer software by limiting the licence attached to the product, so that an unauthorized repairer who downloaded a program to diagnose an operating defect was found to infringe copyright.[375] Such attempts to withdraw or restrict repair rights need close scrutiny. There may be some ground to hold them void where

---

369   *C Act*, above note 1, ss. 27(2)(1) & (m).

370   *C Act, ibid.*, ss. 27(2)(h) to (k) & 28.02(2)(c)

371   *Home Office v. Harman*, [1981] Q.B. 534 at 558–59 (C.A.), aff'd on other grounds (1982), [1983] 1 A.C. 280 (H.L.).

372   *British Leyland Motor Corp. Ltd.* v. *Armstrong Patents Co. Ltd.*, [1986] A.C. 577 (H.L.).

373   See section I, "Authors' Moral Rights," in this chapter.

374   *John Maryon,* above note 61; compare *Saphena*, above note 183.

375   *MAI*, above note 236.

they collide with the public interest in having competition in the repair and aftermarket sectors.[376]

4) Imports

Imports of the following are allowed:

- up to two copies of any work published in a *WTO* state for the importer's own use;
- copies of any work for use by a federal or a provincial government department;
- copies required for any public library or institution of learning, before the work is printed or made in Canada; and
- any work lawfully printed in a *WTO* state and published for public circulation there.[377]

The Customs authorities have jurisdiction over these provisions, although enforcement is sporadic. Bill C-32 would extend the exemption to sound recordings, but tighten the provisions in other respects. For example, only one book could be imported for a library, archive, museum, or educational institution. Further copies would have to be obtained through the exclusive Canadian distributor.[378]

5) Public Interest

At common law, a person may have "good cause or excuse" to deal with material as a matter of public interest. Copying a judge's reasons for judgment (assuming these have copyright at all) has been suggested as acceptable for this reason.[379] Whistleblowers may also sometimes be excused from copying private documents and handing them over to a newspaper for publication. The exposure must first be found to be in the public interest — for example, if criminal or disgraceful conduct or matters affecting others' life or liberty is disclosed.[380] Merely making public information more accessible has, however, not been thought important enough to qualify as a good excuse for producing a low-priced abridgment. The *Charter* right of free expression was, perhaps

---

376 Compare section H(6), "Repairs and Modifications," in chapter 3.
377 *C Act*, above note 1, ss. 45(3) & (5).
378 Bill C-32, above note 9, cl. 45(1).
379 *British Columbia Jockey Club* v. *Standen* (1985), 8 C.P.R. (3d) 283 at 288 (B.C.C.A.).
380 *Lion Laboratories Ltd.* v. *Evans*, [1985] Q.B. 526 (C.A.) [*Lion*].

surprisingly, found irrelevant, even though the original material was produced under the aegis of the Canadian government, which claimed it wanted the material to have the widest public distribution.[381]

6) Fair Dealing

Anyone may deal fairly with any work for the purposes of private study, research, criticism, review, or newspaper summary. In the latter three cases, it is apparently mandatory for the source and the author's name, if given in the source, to be mentioned before the dealing can qualify as fair.[382] This rigid structure may be contrasted with U.S. law. There the "fair use" justification is worded expansively. The purposes — "criticism, comment, news reporting, teaching (including multiple copies for classroom use), scholarship, or research" — are non-exhaustive.[383] Nor is there any requirement to attribute source as a precondition of the use being fair. Still, the U.S. provision has not shielded a U.S. commercial copy shop from liability in producing university course-packs that contained substantial extracts from literary works. In Canada, a similar practice would have equal difficulty passing muster.[384]

The following passage from a U.K. case, where an ex-Scientologist successfully claimed fair dealing in a book critical of Scientology that contained long quotes from the church's teaching material, seems also to represent Canadian law:

> It is impossible to define what is "fair dealing." It must be a question of degree. You must consider first the number and extent of the quotations and extracts. Are they altogether too many and too long to be fair? Then you must consider the use made of them. If they are used as a basis for comment, criticism or review, that may be fair dealing. If they are used to convey the same information as the author, for a rival purpose, that may be unfair. Next, you must consider the proportions. To take long extracts and attach short comments may be unfair. But, short extracts and long comments may be fair. Other considerations

---

381   *James Lorimer,* above note 168.
382   *C Act,* above note 1, s. 27(2)(a) & (a.1). The analagous provisions relating to performers do not require attribution: *ibid.,* s. 28.02(2)(a).
383   *Copyright Act 1976,* above note 133, § 107.
384   Compare *Princeton,* above note 368 with *Laurier,* above note 8, where a criminal prosecution for infringement against an Ottawa copy shop failed; but the firm nevertheless took a reprography licence from CanCopy to avoid future problems.

may come to mind also. But, after all is said and done, it must be a matter of impression. As with fair comment in the law of libel, so with fair dealing in the law of copyright. The tribunal of fact must decide.[385]

This high level of uncertainty favours only those with deep pockets. Parliament has not only passed its responsibility to provide clear rules over to the courts but has let them regulate industries as "a matter of impression." The result has been that people have avoided going to law except as a last resort or to settle a principle: copyright is either ignored or negotiated around by private agreement. The following discussion of the jurisprudence may suggest why.

a) Factors to Consider
The following factors have been used to determine whether a dealing is fair: the purpose and character of the dealing; the nature of the source work; what and how much has been dealt with, compared with the source work as a whole; the effect of the dealing on the potential market for or value of the source work; whether the source work was available within a reasonable time at an ordinary commercial price; and any reasonable guidelines accepted by joint owner and user interests.

Some subsidiary general points have also been made, such as:

- One may deal fairly with even a whole work. How else can *haiku* or a photograph be sensibly criticized or reviewed? But the longer a work and the more taken, the less likely the dealing will be fair, as the owner's market is cut into by the new work.
- The dealing must be fair in relation to its purpose and medium. The fair amount copied for private study may be unfair if copied for criticism. Extracts, too long for a newspaper, may be found fair if used in a television news film.
- Dealings with unpublished material "leaked" in breach of confidence have had difficulty passing the test of fairness. Private sector leaks that further an important public interest, such as the due administration of justice, have been dealt with more leniently, but the treatment is far from uniform.[386]

---

385 *Hubbard v. Vosper*, [1972] 2 Q.B. 84 at 94 (C.A.) [*Hubbard*].

386 Compare *Fairfax*, above note 166, and *B.W. International Inc. v. Thomson Canada Ltd.* (1996), 137 D.L.R. (4th) 398 at 409–10 (Ont. Gen. Div.), rejecting fair dealing for leaked documents, with *Lion*, above note 380, accepting it so as to minimize convictions of innocent defendants.

- One can apparently deal fairly only for one's own purposes. A teacher may copy fairly for her own private study; her student may copy fairly for his private study; the student may, if the teacher's employee or agent (e.g., research assistant), copy for his teacher's purpose; but, otherwise, neither teacher nor student may copy for the other's purpose.
- Dealings for mixed purposes seem acceptable. I may criticize a work fairly, even if I mean also to educate, so long as the criticism is not a cover for another unallowed purpose.

A discussion follows of some general factors in light of these considerations.

i) Purpose of the Dealing

Fair dealing can occur only in respect of a closed set of purposes: newspaper summaries, criticism or review, research or private study.

Newspaper summaries Fair dealing for "newspaper summary" only is presently permitted. Bill C-32 would expand this permission to cover all media ("news reporting or news summary") and all subject matter (works, sound recordings, performances, etc.). There is a rigid requirement that the source and the author's (performer's, maker's, etc.) name must be mentioned before the dealing can qualify as fair.[387]

Criticism or review "Criticism" and "review" presumably involve analysing and judging merit or quality. "Review" may also include surveying past events or facts. The attempt to justify *Coles' Notes* study aids on these grounds failed, however, because criticism did not require as full a condensation of the source work as the *Notes* contained.[388] On the other hand, a British television program that criticized a film distributor's decision to stop exhibiting *Clockwork Orange* in the United Kingdom and included extracts totalling some 8 percent of the film was held to be dealing fairly.[389]

Parody and satire could qualify under this head as implicit fair criticisms of their target.[390] The apparently mandatory requirement that the source and the original authors must be mentioned might, however, rule out some otherwise qualifying material. As a policy matter, it would therefore be better that parody and satire not be held infringements in the first place.[391]

---

387 Bill C-32, above note 9, cl. 29.2.
388 *Sillitoe*, above note 244.
389 *Time Warner Entertainments Co.* v. *Channel Four Television Corp.* (1993), 28 I.P.R. 459 (C.A.).
390 The point was overlooked in *St-Hubert*, above note 300, holding a union liable for using caricatures of a firm's logo on stickers during a strike.
391 *C Act*, above note 1, s. 27(2)(a.1); see section G(9), "Substantial Infringement," in this chapter.

Research or private study "Research" in this context means investigating or closely studying a subject. "Study," on the other hand, involves applying oneself to acquire knowledge or learning, or examining and analysing a particular subject.[392] Although dealing for *private study* only is acceptable, this qualification does not apply to research. Thus, non-private or commercial research may qualify as fair dealing. This means that not only scholars and students may engage in reasonable discourse but private sector firms and workers should also be able to further their knowledge and research. Such activities become even more important to achieve national competitiveness in a global market. Firms may also be able to copy news or current affairs articles or programs — for example, to study public attitudes to their business.[393] However, in the United States, a corporation's research workers have not been allowed to copy journal articles for future reference where an efficient means of buying copyright clearances existed.[394]

Bill C-32 would clarify and exempt some of these activities. Non-profit educational institutions would be able to use material for tests and assignments, copy work onto blackboards or for overhead projection, perform work in class, tape news programs or commentaries off air for classroom use within the year, and tape other programs off air for thirty days' evaluation.[395] Non-profit libraries, archives, and museums would also be able to copy works to maintain and manage their collection, and copy specified material for people doing research or study.[396] A copy of a sound recording or work (but not film) could be made for a person with defective vision, but more than one copy would attract royalties fixed by the Copyright Board or agreement.[397]

---

392 *British Columbia (A.G.)* v. *Messier* (1984), 8 D.L.R. (4th) 306 at 309–10 (B.C.S.C.); see also G.A. Bloom & T.J. Denholm, "Research on the Internet: Is Access Copyright Infringement?" (1996) 12 Can. Intell. Prop. Rev. 337.

393 D. Vaver, "Clipping Services and Copyright" (1994) 8 I.P.J. 379 at 381–82.

394 *American Geophysical Union* v. *Texaco Inc.*, 37 F.3d 881 (2d Cir. 1994) [*Geophysical*]; compare D. Vaver, "Copyright inside the Law Library" (1995) 53 Advocate 355.

395 Bill C-32, above note 9, cls. 29.3–29.9. Tapes kept beyond these periods would be subject to a royalty set by the Copyright Board.

396 *Ibid.*, cls. 30.1 & 30.2.

397 *Ibid.*, cl. 32. Oddly, a large-print book could not be made, even if no such format was commercially available: *ibid.*, cls. 32(2) & (3). Nor is any provision made for the deaf: *ibid.*, cl. 1(5), def. "perceptual disability."

ii) Nature of the Work Taken From

Fair dealing applies to both published and unpublished work. Were it otherwise, plays could not be reviewed.[398] But fair dealing is harder to prove for unpublished documents unless, for example, they expose illegal or unethical practices. Biographers have had a particularly hard time. In the United States, for example, J.D. Salinger's biographer, Ian Hamilton, was forced into paraphrasing his subject's ideas after being enjoined from using direct quotes from Salinger's publicly archived correspondence.[399] Fair dealing is more likely for material with some public circulation (e.g., bulletins sent by a corporation to its stockholders) than for material where the interest in secrecy is higher (e.g., material produced on discovery).

iii) How Much and What Is Used

The amount and substantiality of the material taken from the source work is always relevant: Has the user taken more than reasonably necessary for the purpose? This criterion should be looked at broadly. The copying of very "substantial" extracts or even whole works can be fair, although the burden of justification gets higher the more is taken.[400] Guidelines settled by owner and user groups may also help if they sufficiently take account of the general public interest. Thus the Australian Parliament has deemed that copying one article from a periodical, or the greater of one chapter or 10 percent of a published edition, is fair dealing for research or study, without precluding other uses from qualifying.[401] A guideline like this may also be acceptable in Canada.

iv) How the Market for or Value of a Work Is Affected

It is always important to know what effect a use has on a work's present or reasonably expected future market. A use that substitutes for or competes with the copyright work is less likely to be held fair. A maker of instructional films had no trouble stopping buyers from making permanent copies for their convenience: it was being unfairly deprived of a sale or licence fee.[402] Owners may also be entitled to reserve future markets.

---

398 Public performance is technically not a publication: see section G(1), "First Public Distribution," in this chapter.
399 *Salinger v. Random House Inc.,* 811 F.2d 90 (2d Cir. 1987).
400 *Hubbard,* above note 385 at 98.
401 *Copyright Act,* 1968 (Austl.) No. 63, ss. 40(3) & 10(2).
402 *Tom Hopkins International Inc. (Tom Hopkins Champions Unlimited) v. Wall & Redekop Realty Ltd.* (1984), 1 C.P.R. (3d) 348 (B.C.S.C.), varied (*sub nom. Tom Hopkins International Inc. v. Wall & Redekop Realty Ltd.*) (1985), 6 C.P.R. (3d) 475 (C.A.).

Thus, a magazine publisher may stop its cartoons from being compiled into a thematic anthology: it may want to develop its own anthology later and so should be entitled to refuse to license a potentially harmful use.[403]

v) Easy Alternative Availability

Copyright owners can hardly complain of unwanted uses if their distribution or permission practices are unfair or inefficient. A U.S. court noted: "It is sensible that a particular unauthorized use should be considered 'more fair' when there is no ready market or means to pay for the use, while such an unauthorized use should be considered 'less fair' when there is a ready market or means to pay for the use."[404] This reasoning cannot, however, avoid the question whether payment is fairly due for particular uses in the first place.

b) Bill C-32

Bill C-32 would extend fair dealing on the same basis to sound recordings, performances, and broadcasts as it presently applies to works. Incidental non-deliberate inclusions of material would also be exempted: for example, a film documentary may not necessarily infringe just because a copyright logo appears in a shot.[405]

K. USERS' RIGHTS: PAYING USES

1) Music: Public Performance and Telecommunication

Someone wishing to perform a musical work in public or to communicate it to the public by telecommunication must obtain a licence from the Society of Composers, Authors and Music Publishers of Canada. SOCAN takes assignments of performance and telecommunication rights in musical works from composers and lyricists. It then issues blanket licences for its repertoire, which comprises virtually any piece of music still in copyright. The royalties received from licensing are distributed to composers, lyricists, and music publishers according to rules fixed by SOCAN's board. A 50 percent split of the royalties for original published music always goes to the publisher; the remaining 50 percent goes to the composer or composers. If lyricists are involved, the split is 25 percent to the composer(s) and 25 percent to the lyricist(s). Nothing seems to prevent private rearrangement of this division, even though

---

403   *Bradbury v. Hotten* (1872), L.R. 8 Ex. 1.
404   *Geophysical,* above note 394 at 898.
405   Bill C-32, above note 9, cl. 30.7.

SOCAN's rules try to discourage it. For example, a music publisher can buy the author's share of SOCAN royalties if the author goes bankrupt.[406] This practice suggests that a provision in the original publishing agreement, assigning the author's share of royalties to the publisher, may equally be held valid.

The fees SOCAN charges are fixed annually by the Copyright Board after hearing from SOCAN and considering any objections to the proposed tariff advertised in the *Canada Gazette*.[407] In 1994 SOCAN collected domestic fees of $66 million, of which $56 million came from radio and television, and $10 million came from licensing taverns, shopping centres, restaurants, halls, and the like. SOCAN also has affiliation agreements with foreign performing rights societies, and it similarly distributes monies received from foreign performances.

Bill C-32 would make public performance and telecommunication royalties payable also to record companies and performers (50 percent to each) whenever their commercially released records are played. A society organized on similar lines to SOCAN will likely administer the scheme, with the Copyright Board settling tariffs. Broadcasters would have to pay only $100 royalties on the first $1.25 million of advertising revenue. Beyond that, liability would be phased in gradually over five years, with a 20 percent incremental liability each year.[408]

2) Cable Retransmission

Since 1989 cable retransmitters of television and radio programming have paid royalties fixed by the Copyright Board for copyright material contained in distant broadcasts they retransmit. The Board sets a rate based on what willing sellers and buyers would have agreed to. This rate currently averages fifteen cents per subscriber per month. The lion's share of the $45 million per year this rate costs cable companies is distributed to collecting societies representing U.S. film and television companies (57 percent). Another roughly 13 percent goes to public television and non-U.S. foreign program producers, 12 percent to Canadian and U.S. networks, 10 percent to the baseball, hockey, and football leagues, and 3 percent to SOCAN.[409]

---

406   *Éditions MCC Ltée* v. *Assn. des Compositeurs, Auteurs & Éditeurs du Canada Ltée* (1987), 11 C.I.P.R. 322 (Que. S.C.).

407   *C Act*, above note 1, ss. 67–69.

408   Bill C-32, above note 9, cls. 19, 68 & 68.1.

409   *Royalties 1995–7*, above note 74, and *FWS*, above note 34. *Royalties 1995–7*, above note 74, sets out the 1995–7 television and radio tariffs. Performers are excluded: *C Act*, above note 1, s. 28.02(2)(d).

3) Collecting Societies

Other collecting societies based on the SOCAN model have formed to collect royalties for uses in circumstances where individual collection has proved either impossible or extremely costly to monitor and enforce. The collecting society seeks to reach agreements with users on royalties and related terms. Failing this, either party may apply to the Copyright Board.[410] Agreements filed with the Board within fifteen days of being concluded are insulated from attack under the *Competition Act*. The competition director may, however, ask the Board to examine any agreement thought to be against the public interest. No such request has been made to date.[411]

Operating under these provisions, the Canadian Musical Reproduction Rights Agency Ltd. (CMRRA) has licensed record producers to make sound recordings of the agency's repertoire at a standard negotiated rate. This rate presently is 5.9 cents per work per record, with an added 1.18 cents per minute for works longer than five minutes.[412] Similarly, the Canadian Reprography Collective (CanCopy) has concluded agreements with the federal government, universities, copy shops, and other institutions, providing for payment of royalties for photocopying from books.

Collecting societies would be given further roles by Bill C-32. For example, a blank audio-tape levy fixed by the Copyright Board would be administered by a collecting society representing eligible composers, lyricists, performers, and record companies.[413]

4) Unlocatable Owners

Copyright owners sometimes seem to disappear off the face of the earth, and efforts to locate them to obtain copyright permissions are unavailing. If the work is published, the Copyright Board can issue a non-exclusive licence to use the work in such cases. The Board has sometimes fixed an appropriate royalty to be paid to a collecting society. If the copyright owner does not collect the royalty within five years, the Board has authorized the society to apply the sum to general revenue. Bill C-32 would extend this right to license to most published matter having copyright.[414]

---

410   *C Act*, above note 1, s. 70.2.

411   *C Act, ibid.*, ss. 70.5 & 70.6.

412   Mechanical Licensing Agreement between CMRRA and CRIA (the Canadian Recording Industry Assn. Inc.), 1 October 1990, as am. 12 July 1991.

413   Bill C-32, above note 9, new Part VIII.

414   *C Act*, above note 1, s. 70.7; *Re Fritz (Licence to use English Language Instruction Video)* (1995), 62 C.P.R. (3d) 99 (Copyright Bd.); compare Bill C-32, *ibid.*, cl. 77.

FURTHER READINGS

Canadian

CANADIAN CONFERENCE OF THE ARTS, *Colloquium on the Collective Administration of Copyright*, Toronto, 31 October 1994 (Ottawa: Canadian Conference of the Arts, 1995)

CANADIAN INTELLECTUAL PROPERTY INSTITUTE, *Copyright in Transition: Enforcement, Fair Dealing and Digital Developments* (Ottawa: The Institute, 1994)

Copyright Reform: The Package, the Policy and the Politics, Insight/Globe & Mail Conference, Toronto, 30–31 May 1996

FOX, H.G., *The Canadian Law of Copyright and Industrial Designs*, 2d ed. (Toronto: Carswell, 1967)

HARRIS, L.E., *Canadian Copyright Law*, 2d ed. (Toronto: McGraw-Hill Ryerson, 1995)

HENDERSON, G.F., ed., *Copyright and Confidential Information Law in Canada* (Toronto: Carswell, 1994)

HOUSE OF COMMONS, STANDING COMMITTEE ON COMMUNICATIONS AND CULTURE, *Report of the Sub-Committee on the Revision of Copyright: A Charter of Rights for Creators* (Ottawa: Supply & Services, 1985)

HUGHES, R.T., *Copyright and Industrial Design* (Toronto: Butterworths, 1984) (regularly updated)

INFORMATION HIGHWAY ADVISORY COUNCIL, *Final Report of the Copyright Subcommittee: Copyright and the Information Highway* (Ottawa: The Council, 1995); council@ist.ca; debra.dgbt.doc.ca/pub/info-highway or http://debra.dgbt.doc.ca/info-highway/ih.html

INFORMATION HIGHWAY ADVISORY COUNCIL, *Final Report: Connection, Community Content: The Challenge of the Information Highway* (Ottawa: The Council, 1995); http://info.ic.gc.ca/info-highway/ih.html

MIKUS, J.-P., *Droit de l'édition et du commerce du livre* (Montreal: Thémis, 1996)

RICHARD, H., & CARRIÈRE, L., eds., *Canadian Copyright Act — Annotated*, 3 vols. (Toronto: Carswell, 1993) (updated periodically)

SOCIETY OF COMPOSERS, AUTHORS AND MUSIC PUBLISHERS OF CANADA (SOCAN), *SOCAN Facts: A Guide for Composers, Lyricists, Songwriters and Music Publishers* (1990), and *SOCAN Distribution Rules* (1994), available from SOCAN, 41 Valleybrook Drive, Don Mills, ON, M3B 2S6 (Tel. 1-800-55-SOCAN)

SOOKMAN, B.B., *Computer Law: Acquiring and Protecting Information Technology* (Toronto: Carswell, 1989) (updated periodically) c. 3

TAMARO, N., *The 1995 Annotated Copyright Act* (Toronto: Carswell, 1994), or N. Tamaro, *Loi sur le droit d'auteur: texte annoté*, 3d ed. (Toronto: Carswell, 1995)

TAWFIK, M.J., *The Secret of Transforming Art into Gold: Intellectual Property Issues in Canada–U.S. Relations.* Canadian-American Public Policy Paper No. 20 (Orono, Me.: Canadian-American Center, 1994)

VAVER, D., "Canada," in P.E. Geller & M.B. Nimmer, eds., *International Copyright Law & Practice* (New York: Matthew Bender, 1988) (updated annually)

VAVER, D., "Report on Moral Rights: Canada," in Association Littéraire et Artistique Internationale, *Le droit moral de l'auteur/The Moral Right of the Author*, Antwerp, 19–24 September 1993 (Paris: L'Association, 1994) at 207

Other

BRANSCOMB, A.W., *Who Owns Information? From Privacy to Public Access* (New York: Basic Books, 1994)

GOLDSTEIN, P., *Copyright: Principles, Law & Practice* (Boston: Little Brown, 1989)

GOLDSTEIN, P., *Copyright's Highway: From Gutenberg to the Celestial Jukebox* (New York: Hill & Wang, 1994)

GORDON W.J., et al., "Virtual Reality, Appropriation, and Property Rights in Art: A Roundtable Discussion" (1994) 13 Cardozo Arts & Ent. L.J. 89

GRAPHIC ARTISTS GUILD (U.S.), *Graphic Artists Guild Handbook: Pricing and Ethical Guidelines*, 8th ed. (New York: Graphics Artists Guild Inc., 1994)

KAPLAN, B., *An Unhurried View of Copyright* (New York: Columbia University Press, 1967)

KERNAN, A., *The Death of Literature* (New Haven, Conn.: Yale University Press, 1990), esp. cc. 4 and 5

LADDIE, H., P. PRESCOTT, & M. VITORIA, *The Modern Law of Copyright*, 2d ed. (Toronto: Butterworths, 1995)

LAHORE, J., *Intellectual Property in Australia: Copyright Law* (Sydney: Butterworths, 1988) (updated regularly)

NIMMER, M.B., & D. NIMMER, *Copyright* (New York: Matthew Bender, 1983) (updated annually)

PATRY, W.F., *The Fair Use Privilege in Copyright Law* (Washington, D.C.: Bureau of National Affairs, 1985)

PATTERSON, L.R., & S.W. LINDBERG, *The Nature of Copyright: A Law of Users' Rights* (Athens, Ga.: University of Georgia Press, 1991)

PHILLIPS, J.J., R. DURIE, & I. KARET, *Whale on Copyright*, 4th ed. (London: Sweet & Maxwell, 1993)

RICKETSON, S., *The Berne Convention for the Protection of Literary and Artistic Works: 1886–1986* (London: Centre for Commercial Law Studies, Queen Mary College, 1987)

SHERMAN, B., & A. STROWEL, eds., *Of Authors and Origins: Essays on Copyright Law* (Oxford: Clarendon Press, 1994)

SINACORE-GUINN, D., *Collective Administration of Copyright and Neighboring Rights*, (Boston: Little, Brown, 1993)

SKONE JAMES, E.P., *Copinger & Skone James on Copyright*, 13th ed. (London: Sweet & Maxwell, 1991)

U.S.A., *Report of the Working Group on Intellectual Property Rights: Intellectual Property and the National Information Infrastructure* (Washington, D.C.: Patent and Trademark Office, 1995) (Chair: U.S. Commissioner of Patents Bruce A. Lehman), iitf.doc.gov.

Historical

FEATHER, J., *Publishing, Piracy and Politics: An Historical Study of Copyright in Britain* (New York: Mansell, 1994)

PARKER, G.L., *The Beginnings of the Book Trade in Canada* (Toronto: University of Toronto Press, 1985)

PATTERSON, L.R., *Copyright in Historical Perspective* (Nashville: Vanderbilt University Press, 1968)

ROSE, M., *Authors and Owners: The Invention of Copyright* (Cambridge: Harvard University Press, 1993)

CHAPTER 3

PATENTS

A. INTRODUCTION

Patents for inventions are issued and protected solely under the *Patent Act*.[1] Intended to stimulate the creation and development of new technologies, they are granted to inventors of new, useful, and unobvious ideas with practical industrial application: new machines, products, processes, or improvements to existing technology. Without patents, ideas have little protection. As soon as a product implementing the new idea hits the market, anybody can copy it and compete with the original producer without incurring the initial costs of invention and product development. A patent gives its holder a lengthy breathing-space to enable the invention to be developed and marketed without competition except from non-infringing substitutes. The patentee can thus recoup its initial outlay plus recover a profit commensurate with the value the market puts on the invention.

---

1   R.S.C. 1985, c. P-4 [*P Act*]; in this chapter, called the "*Act*" [unless otherwise indicated, references are to the *Act* as amended]. The discussion deals mainly with patent applications made after the *Patent Rules, 1996* [*PR*] (the "*Rules*"), and the amendments to the *P* Act effected by the *Intellectual Property Law Improvement Act*, S.C. 1993, c. 15, took effect, namely, 1 October 1996. Previous applications and patents may be affected by transitional provisions that, for reasons of space, cannot be discussed here.

A patent is granted by the Patent Office (**PO**) and now generally lasts twenty years from the date of filing the application.[2] Its holder obtains an absolute monopoly: nobody may make, sell, or use the patented invention, even if he arrives at it independently without knowing of the earlier inventor or patent.[3] More than 25,000 applications are filed annually in Canada. In 1993–94, 14,000 patents were issued, and in 1994–95, 11,000. Annual maintenance fees (starting at $100 per year and rising progressively to $400 for each of the last five years) must be paid to the PO to keep the patent alive. More than 120,000 fees were paid in 1994–95, while 31,500 patents lapsed for non-payment. Sole inventors, small businesses, and universities usually pay half-rate.[4]

1) Trade Secret Protection for Ideas

Some protection can be granted at common law for ideas outside the patent system, through contracts and the breach of confidence action. Firms can erect a wall of secrecy around their operations to protect their trade secrets, potentially forever, against faithless employees, industrial spies, and co-venturers using trade secrets and other confidential information outside the purpose for which they were given it. Anything of potential economic value can be protected anywhere in the world. A trade secret confided in China and wrongly used in Canada may be protected if the Chinese confider sues in Canada. But common law protection is volatile. It can disappear despite the owner's best efforts. Someone may learn of the secret independently or may reverse-engineer it or the product that contains it; innocent buyers from an industrial spy may profit from their purchase and can end up destroying its value as a trade secret by publicizing it. Departing employees can also use information that has become part of their general skills and knowledge. The most the ex-employer can do is restrict the ex-employee by contract from

---

2   *P Act, ibid.,* s. 45; s. 2 def. "filing date"; for the filing date of an application made under the *Patent Cooperation Treaty,* 2 October 1989, Can. T.S. 1990 No. 22 [PCT], see section A(4), "International Patenting," in this chapter. The *Statute of Monopolies* (U.K.), 1624, 21 Jac. 1, c. 3, provided fourteen years protection from grant.

    The present monopoly period is effectively less than twenty years. Thus, monetary compensation for infringement is available only from when the specification is published, which may be as long as eighteen months after filing: *P Act, ibid.,* s. 55(2). Before 1989, patents lasted seventeen years from date of grant, which could be long after the date of application because of delays in the PO. Some delays were unavoidable. Others were deliberately caused by applicants intent on prolonging their monopoly.

3   *P Act, ibid.,* ss. 42 & 44.

4   *PR,* above note 1, s. 2, def. "small entity," Sch. II.

working in a particular field. Such restrictions are still vulnerable. They may, for example, not be enforced if they do not reasonably balance the employer's interests against the public interest in employee mobility, especially in times of economic instability and job insecurity.

2) Applying for a Patent

Patent drafting is an arcane art best left to professional patent agents. These agents are trained to make trifling advances look like Galilean leaps. In fact, a patent agent must be employed at least to handle the application after filing if anyone other than the inventor applies.[5] The application is anachronistically called a "Petition." This terminology dates back to the time when English patent applications were "humbly" made "To The Queen's Most Excellent Majesty." Until 1 October 1996 Canadian applications still contained vestiges of this ancient language, such as the final flourish that "Your Petitioner(s) therefore pray(s)" for a patent. These phrases, mercifully, have been eliminated.[6] The petition can be made by the inventor or by his assignee, guardian, or executor.[7] It comes with a patent "specification," comprising a "disclosure" detailing the invention and how it is carried out (often with drawings) and "claims" staking out the monopoly sought.

Timing is everything. The right to a patent depends on the claim date of the application, usually its filing date. An earlier inventor will lose out to one who arrives first at the PO with an application. If both arrive the same day, the timing is "deemed" a dead heat entitling both to patents.[8] The claim date may be even earlier if the Canadian application is filed within twelve months of an earlier filing in a *Paris Convention* or *WTO* state. The foreign filing date then becomes the Canadian claim date, bumping later local filings. Because applications are often rushed, technical defects are common but curable by amendment during PO proceedings or by filing a new application within twelve months. The second application can take the first's claim date if the same invention is retained. The PO will not allow major redelineations; and if by accident it does, the resulting patent can be invalid.[9]

---

5   *PR*, above note 1, s. 20(1).
6   *Ibid.*, Sch. I, Form 3.
7   *P Act*, above note 1, s. 27; s. 2 def. "legal representative."
8   *P Act*, *ibid.*, s. 27(1.5).
9   *P Act*, *ibid.*, s. 28.1; *Martin v. Scribal Pty. Ltd.* (1956), 95 C.L.R. 213 (P.C.) [*Martin*]; Canadian Intellectual Property Office, *Manual of Patent Office Practice*, §§ 7.01–7.06 [*MOPOP*] (Convention priority).

The rule is "one invention, one application." But inventions are like a many-faceted prism: multiple claims (sometimes running into the hundreds) covering all facets are allowed in the same patent. If more than one invention is disclosed, the PO can demand that the application be split into two or more "divisional" applications, each claiming only one invention.[10]

3) Proceedings in the Patent Office

For a patent to issue, the application must first be examined. The applicant has up to five years to request examination, so the market for the invention can be tested. It must meanwhile pay the usual annual maintenance fees.[11] If no timely request is ultimately made, the application is deemed abandoned. An application may also be withdrawn any time, but it becomes public eighteen months after filing. The application and its supporting documents are then laid open, and notice of the application appears in the *Canadian Patent Office Record*.[12] Examination was requested for more than 11,000 applications in 1994–95 — a two to three ratio in relation to the number of applications filed that year.

"Examination" means that a specialized examiner will check the specification against the technical documents in the PO's extensive library and decide whether a patent should be granted. Nobody can oppose the grant, although anyone who suspects that an application has been filed or sees the published application can "protest" the grant and send the PO material to use during examination. The interloper will not, however, be told of the PO's reaction.[13] The PO will then decide whether the applicant is "by law" entitled to a patent. Anything that would invalidate an issued patent bars the initial grant.[14] All aspects of patentability are checked: Is this an "invention"? Is it new, non-obvious, useful? Does the application fully disclose the invention? Do the claims fairly reflect the invention or are they too broad? All patent offices see their job as granting, not rejecting, patents, so an examiner's objections are directed to ensuring that a valid patent issues.

The applicant may overcome objections by argument or by amendment. If the examiner is satisfied, the application is allowed and a patent

---

10   *P Act*, *ibid.*, s. 36.
11   *PR*, above note 1, s. 96(1). Requests to examine a pre-1996 application can occur up to seven years after filing: *ibid.*, s. 150(1).
12   *P Act*, *ibid.*, s. 10.
13   *PR*, above note 1, s. 10.
14   *P Act*, above note 1, s. 40; *Martin*, above note 9.

issues, often stronger because of the interchange with the PO. If not satisfied, the examiner will reject the application, giving reasons. Rejection can be appealed to a Patent Appeal Board comprising senior PO examiners. The Board holds a hearing and recommends confirmation, reversal, or amendment of the examiner's decision to the Commissioner. The Commissioner only rarely disagrees with the Board's recommendation.

The PO can reject an application only if it is positively satisfied that the applicant is *not* by law entitled to a patent. No discretion is involved.[15] If judicial developments point to likely patentability, the PO may grant the application, leaving the courts to decide validity in contested litigation. An adverse PO decision is appealable directly to the Federal Court of Appeal and, ultimately, to the Supreme Court of Canada. The courts can substitute their views for the PO's and are not confined to the PO's grounds for rejection.[16] Although rarely interfering on technical questions, such as whether the invention works, courts have not hesitated to reverse longstanding PO practices or policies that have lacked a legal basis.

4) International Patenting

There is no such thing as an international patent. Patents are applied for country by country — an expensive proposition that involves much duplication among patent offices. Some attempts to avoid needless effort have occurred. Within much of Europe, for example, rules on patentability and infringement have been largely standardized; a single application to the European Patent Office in Munich can lead to patents being granted for those states the applicant has nominated. The Office can also revoke a wrongly granted patent, but the main tasks of adjudication fall to national courts.

A similar, but looser, model applies beyond Europe. The *Patent Cooperation Treaty* of 1970 sets up a simplified procedure for applicants wanting to obtain patents in several states. The *PCT* has been ratified by most industrialized countries, including Canada since 1990. So a Canadian national or resident may file an international application with the Canadian PO (the "receiving office"), designating the countries in which patents are sought. The Canadian filing date becomes the international filing date, and a copy of the application is sent to each desig-

15 *Monsanto Co.* v. *Canada (Commissioner of Patents)*, [1979] 2 S.C.R. 1108 [*Monsanto*].

16 *Pioneer Hi-Bred Ltd.* v. *Canada (Commissioner of Patents)*, [1989] 1 S.C.R. 1623 [*Pioneer*].

nated country and treated as a separate application there. Similarly, an application received in a foreign receiving office designating Canada is transmitted to the PO and treated as a local application. Although each country's substantive patent law must be complied with, member states accept a *PCT* application as complying with their procedural law. Search and examination reports can be obtained from International Searching and Preliminary Examination Authorities. For Canada, this is currently the European Patent Office rather than the U.S. Patent Office — perhaps surprisingly, since most Canadian patentees' first interest is the North American market. The search report may alert the applicant to potential problems, and the examination report can be filed with national offices as a non-binding aid on patentability.[17] The success of this procedure is witnessed by the fact that, in 1994–95, *PCT* applications made up 40 percent of the nearly 28,000 applications filed with the Canadian PO.

5) The Application Must Be Truthful

The petition for a patent must be truthful. The *Act* provides that even innocently made false "material allegation[s]" invalidate the patent.[18] But this provision applies only to false allegations in the petition. Misstatements in the disclosure or the claims are apparently irrelevant.[19] Moreover, courts have found few allegations "material." Suppose an applicant falsely alleges that she invented X, but gets a patent for less-than-X (which she did invent). Or suppose she says her employee Bloggs was the inventor, when employee Dingle really was. The allegations are all "immaterial," since the patent was issued to the right owner for the right invention.[20]

---

17   *MOPOP,* above note 9, § 22; *PR,* above note 1, ss. 50–66; G.O.S. Oyen, "The Canadian Patent Law Amendments of 1987" (1988) 4 I.P.J. 237 at 259ff; *Celltech Ltd. v. Canada (Commissioner of Patents)* (1993), 46 C.P.R. (3d) 424 (Fed. T.D.), aff'd (1994), 55 C.P.R. (3d) 59 (Fed. C.A.).

18   *P Act,* above note 1, s. 53(1); *Beloit Canada Ltée/Ltd. v. Valmet Oy* (1984), 78 C.P.R. (2d) 1 at 28–29 (Fed. T.D.), rev'd (1986), 8 C.P.R. (3d) 289 (Fed. C.A.) [*Beloit*].

19   A misstatement may make the patent invalid for other reasons — for example, if the misstatement does not properly disclose the invention or leads to its not working as promised. See sections C(3) and (4), "Usefulness" and "Contents of a Patent," and section G, "Invalidity" in this chapter.

20   *Procter & Gamble Co. v. Bristol-Myers Canada Ltd.* (1978), 39 C.P.R. (2d) 145 at 157, (Fed. T.D.), aff'd (1979), 42 C.P.R. (2d) 33 (Fed. C.A.); *Beloit,* above note 18 at 29–30 (T.D.).

A patent's specifications and drawings should contain only what is needed to describe, disclose, and exemplify the invention. Omissions or additions made wilfully "for the purpose of misleading" invalidate the patent.[21] Few patents collapse for this reason today since most applications are handled by professionals, who will not purposely mislead the PO.

This history should not, however, encourage too much complacency. Intellectual property rights may be vulnerable to the application of common law principles that traditionally took a dimmer view of even innocently false statements that materially contributed to the registration of a right.[22] The United States has a principle of "fraud on the Patent Office," where there has been deliberate or grossly negligent withholding of prior art or other pertinent information. This non-disclosure breaches a duty of good faith, imposed because of the *ex parte* character of the application process, and invalidates the patent even if it would have been issued had the truth been told.[23] Similar principles could equally be held applicable in Canada as a check on the integrity of the application process.

B. WHAT IS PROTECTED

1) Invention Defined

Any "art, process, machine, manufacture or composition of matter" or any new and useful "improvement" of one of these qualifies as a patentable "invention" in Canada if it is "new and useful."[24] This language (apart from the later addition of "process") goes back as far as pre-Confederation patent laws that borrowed from U.S. law.[25] The underlying aim is to protect ideas of "practical application in industry, trade or commerce."[26]

---

21 *P Act*, above note 1, s. 53(1).

22 For example, *Billings & Spencer Co. v. Canadian Billings & Spencer Ltd.* (1921), 20 Ex.C.R. 405 (design); *Prestige Group (Aust.) Pty. Ltd. v. Dart Industries Inc.* (1990), 19 I.P.R. 275 (Austl. Fed. Ct.) [*Prestige*]. Compare W.L. Hayhurst, "Grounds for Invalidating Patents" (1975) 18 C.P.R. (2d) 222 at 251–54.

23 See R.J. Goldman, "Evolution of the Inequitable Conduct Defense in Patent Litigation" (1993) 7 Harv. J.L. & Tech. 37.

24 *P Act*, above note 1, s. 2, def. "invention." The word "invention" also implies something not obvious: see section C(2), "Non-obviousness," in this chapter.

25 See also *The Patent Act of 1869*, S.C. 1869, c. 11, s. 6; compare *Patents Act*, 35 U.S.C. § 101 (1988) [*Patents Act, 1988*].

26 *MOPOP*, above note 9, § 16.03 (c).

This taxonomy of invention — something by definition unexpected or unforeseeable — is peculiarly a North American conceit. The United Kingdom never defined invention. Instead, the *Statute of Monopolies* of 1624 spoke of granting patents for "any manner of new manufactures," leaving the definition for judges to work out. Over time, they included within it methods of producing marketable products and other useful economic results.[27] European patent laws now define invention negatively by saying what is *not* considered patentable.[28]

Despite these methodological differences, what qualifies as patentable is remarkably similar worldwide. Historical exceptions sometimes lurk in corners; the Canadian ones derive largely from English law prior to the *European Patent Convention* of 1973. Over time the exceptions have become unstable, as perceptions about the boundaries between "pure" and "applied" science change, pressure mounts to make more material patentable, or ethical concerns about new technologies emerge. In the United States, reforms come as often from the courts (particularly the federal circuit in Washington, D.C., which handles all patent appeals) as from the Congress. U.S. courts say "anything under the sun that is made by man [*sic*]"[29] is patentable, and they often search for results that best advance U.S. economic policy. By contrast, Canadian judges are reluctant to extend the concept of invention beyond established precedent: it is Parliament's job, not the courts', to extend or contract patentability.[30]

2) Public Benefit Irrelevant

Inventions are patentable despite a lack of perceptible public benefit. Public benefit is supposedly measured by the market, not by the Patent Office or the courts.[31] Even concerns of legality or morality have, since 1994, been swept aside with the removal of the requirement that inventions must have no "illicit object in view."[32] A method for the better administra-

---

27   *National Research Development Corp.* v. *Australia (Commissioner of Patents)* (1959), 102 C.L.R. 252 (Austl. H.C.).

28   For example, *Patents Act 1977* (U.K.), 1977, c. 37, s. 1(2) [*Patents Act*]; *European Patent Convention*, 7 October 1973, as am. by Decision of the Administrative Council of the European Organisation of 21 December 1978, reprinted in *World Patent Law and Practice* (New York: Matthew Bender, 1996), art. 52 [*EPC*].

29   *Diamond* v. *Diehr*, 450 U.S. 173 at 182 (1981) [*Diamond*].

30   *Pioneer*, above note 16; compare *Wellcome Foundation Ltd. (Hitchings') Application*, [1983] F.S.R. 593 at 616 (N.Z.C.A.).

31   *Thompson & Co.* v. *American Braided Wire Co.* (1888), 6 R.P.C. 518 at 528 (H.L.).

32   *Patent Act*, R.S.C. 1985, c. P-4, s. 27(3), prior to amendment by *North American Free Trade Agreement Implementation Act*, S.C. 1993, c. 44, s. 192 [*NAFTA I A*].

tion of crack cocaine presumably would still be rejected as not being "useful"[33] — that is, against criminal law policy — but an invention with both legal and illegal uses (e.g., a deadlier handgun) would still be patentable.

The agnostic stance of Canadian patent law is not a necessary feature of it. The *Statute of Monopolies* of 1624 banned patents for inventions that were "mischievous to the state by raising prices of commodities at home, or hurt of trade, or generally inconvenient." The decision to patent could therefore take into account contemporary economic and social policies. Elizabethans, for example, feared the social disorder high unemployment might bring and so deemed it "inconvenient" to patent machines that would throw workers out of jobs. More recently, Commonwealth states that retain the *Statute of Monopolies'* criteria test the patentability of medical or surgical treatments[34] for public "inconvenience." And in Europe, inventions whose publication or exploitation would be "contrary to 'ordre public' or morality" are unpatentable.[35] Genetic engineering patents are currently under attack on this ground, although so far with little success.[36]

Testing inventions for their public benefit is not something the PO is now equipped to handle. A panel independent of the PO has been suggested to vet patent applications on the frontiers of knowledge for ethical concerns.[37] This appointment would give the public greater involvement in the decision to patent, and would acknowledge that the market alone cannot adequately judge public welfare.

3) Categories of Patentable Matter

What then qualifies as a "useful art, process, machine, manufacture or composition of matter" or an "improvement" of one of these? "Improvement" needs little comment. Most patents are not pioneers that open up a whole new field, but are for modest improvements to existing technology. Such patents give their holders no rights over any earlier patented invention they improve: neither patentee can use the other's invention without the other's licence.[38]

---

33   See section C(3), "Usefulness," in this chapter.

34   See section B(4)(e), "Medical or Surgical Treatments," in this chapter.

35   *EPC*, above note 28, art. 53(a).

36   See section B(3)(f), "Patenting Life," in this chapter.

37   Westminster Institute for Ethics and Human Values & McGill Centre for Medicine, Ethics and Law, *Ethical Issues Associated with the Patenting of Higher Life Forms,* (London, Ont., 1994) at 103ff.

38   *P Act*, above note 1, s. 32.

a) Art

In its narrow sense, an art is "an act or series of acts performed by some physical agent upon some physical object and producing in such object some change either of character or of condition."[39] This definition encompasses processes and methods. Art also more broadly connotes any applied learning or knowledge, including its resulting product. Known chemical compounds when applied to a new use have been patented as embodying a new art.[40]

The art must, however, be "useful." Written material and fine art are typically excluded because they fall under copyright. Professional arts and skills are similarly excluded because they are not traditionally (and should not be) bought and sold on the market. Methods of cross-examination, advocacy, or tax avoidance, building designs and land subdivision schemes, and medical or surgical treatments[41] cannot be patented by lawyers, architects, doctors, or anyone else. Were it otherwise, the professions would be hindered in exercising, sharing, and disclosing their skills in the best interests of their clients or patients.

b) Process

A process is a systematic series of interdependent actions or steps directed to some useful end. Often synonymous with "art," it excludes a machine, thing, or result. The process need not produce a marketable commodity so long as an economically useful result is achieved — for example, applying a selective herbicide to improve crop yields.

c) Machine

A machine may be an apparatus of interrelated parts (today often electronic) with separate functions. It may also be a mechanism or other device that modifies force or motion and that, by itself or combined with other elements, can achieve some useful end. Attempts to patent computer programs have sometimes come dressed up as claims to a new machine — a computer temporarily transformed by new software. The United States recently allowed a patent drafted in this fashion for a program, and similar Canadian applications have also sometimes slipped through.[42]

---

39   *Lawson v. Canada (Commissioner of Patents)* (1970), 62 C.P.R. 101 at 109 (Ex. Ct.) [*Lawson*].
40   *Shell Oil Co. v. Canada (Commissioner of Patents)*, [1982] 2 S.C.R. 536 [*Shell Oil*].
41   See section B(4)(e), "Medical or Surgical Treatments," in this chapter.
42   See section B(4)(d), "Computer Programs," in this chapter.

d) Manufacture and Composition of Matter

"Manufacture" connotes a product made manually or by an industrial process, by changing the character or condition of material objects. It therefore overlaps with "machine" and "composition of matter." "Composition of matter" connotes any composite article or substance — a solid, gas, fluid, or powder — produced from two or more substances. New molecules, purified substances, and even isolated microorganisms have been included in the United States.[43] The glide in law from inanimate to animate matter is, after all, short: only a couple of letters' difference.[44]

e) New Substances

New substances — that is, a manufacture or a composition of matter — raise interesting issues. The theoretical formula for a substance may be known, but a patent may still be issued to the first person to produce the substance. The claim may extend to homologues beyond the particular use discovered. For example, a researcher may make a new compound X, which she finds is good for killing crabgrass. She can patent X itself, not just X when used to kill crabgrass.[45] She may also patent all analogous substances. These analogues may run into the millions, so long as they can be "soundly" predicted, even without tests, to have similar herbicidal properties to X.[46] The later discovery by someone else that X or a homologue efficiently kills weeds other than crabgrass then may become a windfall for the patentee. Although this rule stops easy evasion of the invention, the result is problematic: Why should the patentee's limited prediction that X and its homologues can kill crabgrass entitle it morally to these substances for all uses?

One qualification should be noted. A patent may still be granted later for a non-obvious use of the patented substance. Neither patent can then be exploited for this new use without the concurrence of both patentees. On the first patent's expiry, the second patentee can still prevent the other patentee (and anyone else) from exploiting the substance within the claims of the second patent until it, too, has expired.[47]

---

43 *Re Bergstrom*, 427 F.2d 1394 (Ct. of Customs and Patent Appeals 1970).
44 See section B(3)(f), "Patenting Life," in this chapter.
45 *Marzone Chemicals Ltd.* v. *Eli Lilly & Co.* (1977), 37 C.P.R. (2d) 37 at 38 (Fed. C.A.) [*Marzone*].
46 *Monsanto*, above note 15.
47 *Shell Oil*, above note 40; *E.I. Du Pont de Nemours & Co. (Witsiepe's) Application*, [1982] F.S.R. 303 (H.L.) ("selection" patent).

f) Patenting Life

In 1980 the U.S. Supreme Court held that a genetically engineered bacterium that degraded crude oil was a patentable manufacture or composition of matter.[48] The Canadian PO followed suit in 1982, listing human-made items it thought were now patentable: "all micro-organisms, yeasts, moulds, fungi, bacteria, actinomycetes, unicellular algae, cell lines, viruses or protozoa; in fact . . . all new life forms which are produced *en masse* as chemical compounds are prepared, and are formed in such large numbers that any measurable quantity will possess uniform properties and characteristics."[49] Indeed, in the PO's view, higher life forms such as plants or animals were logically patentable: "If an inventor creates a new and unobvious insect which did not exist before (and thus is not a product of nature), and can recreate it uniformly and at will, and it is useful (for example to destroy the spruce bud worm), then it is every bit as much a new tool of man as a micro-organism."[50]

How far society wishes to encourage (let alone allow patents for) genetic engineering of plants, animals, humans, or animal and human parts is highly controversial. On the positive side are advantages such as improving human and animal life and gaining efficient agricultural yields. On the negative side are fears about reduced biodiversity, eugenics, suffering caused to sentient beings in experiments, the objectification of life, altering the balance of nature, and the general inappropriateness of humans playing God. Spectres of neocolonialism also surface when human cell-lines are developed from samples taken by researchers from Third World peoples. The end-product may become the subject of a patent owned and commercialized by governments and corporations in industrialized nations. This practice may raise bothersome questions. Did the subjects really know and consent to the commercialization of their body parts? Should they be excluded from any control or ownership over the resulting cell-lines? Are the benefits of exploitation appropriately shared? Have developed countries simply switched the form in which they exploit less-developed countries, from taking natural resources to taking genetic material?

Whether the Canadian PO became troubled by such questions is unclear. After its initial burst of enthusiasm, however, it decided to refuse a patent for a new hybrid soybean variety, produced only "accord-

---

48   *Diamond v. Chakrabarty*, 447 U.S. 303 (1980).
49   *Re Abitibi Co.* (1982), 62 C.P.R. (2d) 81 at 89 (Patent Appeal Bd. & Commissioner of Patents) [*Abitibi*]; *Re Application for Patent of Connaught Laboratories* (1982), 82 C.P.R. (2d) 32 (Patent Appeal Bd. & Commissioner of Patents).
50   *Abitibi, ibid.*, at 90.

ing to the laws of nature." In affirming, the Federal Court of Appeal went on to deny that hybrid plants were according to "common and ordinary meaning" a manufacture or composition. They were not "produced from raw materials" or "a combination of two or more substances united by chemical or mechanical means," except in a metaphorical sense.[51] This decision prompted the PO to turn 180 degrees and to refuse patents for higher life forms like plants and animals. The patent bar and the biotechnology industry, not unnaturally, took issue, arguing that no Canadian precedent definitively prevents the patenting of genetically engineered life forms. Until this challenge is resolved, the PO will continue to issue patents for processes for producing plants and animals if there is "significant technical intervention by man," but not for traditional biological breeding processes for producing plants and animals, since these are "essentially natural biological processes."[52]

By contrast, the U.S. Patent and Trademark Office in 1987 announced it would allow patents for "non-naturally occurring non-human multicellular living organisms, including animals." This arose in a case where a genetically altered oyster, designed for year-round eating, was thought to be patentable subject matter.[53] A flurry of activity then ensued around the so-called Harvard mouse. The rodent had been implanted by Harvard researchers with a cancer gene, and was useful as a standard tester for cancer cures in humans. The researchers obtained a U.S. patent in 1988. They failed, however, in 1995 in their attempt to obtain a Canadian patent, but this refusal is currently under appeal to the courts. A European patent application was initially successful, but it prompted a battle between pro-patent Eurocrats and a sceptical European Parliament, as well as proceedings by the Green Party to revoke the grant. Meanwhile, in the United States, although the National Institutes of Health in 1994 abandoned their attempt to patent the entire human genome,[54] more modest U.S. patents have been granted for recombinant animal and human DNA.

---

51 *Re Application for Patent of Pioneer Hi-Bred Ltd.* (1986), 11 C.P.R. (3d) 311 at 319–20 (Patent Appeal Bd. & Commissioner of Patents), [1987] 3 F.C. 8 at 13 (C.A.), aff'd on other grounds (*sub nom. Pioneer Hi-Bred Ltd. v. Canada (Commissioner of Patents)*), above note 16.

52 *MOPOP,* above note 9, § 16.05; *Re Application No. 079,973 (Now Patent No. 1,069,071)* (1979), 54 C.P.R. (2d) 124 (Patent Appeal Bd. & Commissioner of Patents).

53 *Re Allen,* 2 U.S.P.Q.2d 1425 (P.T.O. Bd. App. & Int. 1987); (1987), 1077 Official Gazette of the U.S. Patent and Trademark Office announced the new policy.

54 R.S. Eisenberg & R.P. Merges, *Opinion Letter as to the Patentability of Certain Inventions Associated with the Identification of Partial cDNA Sequences* (1995) 23 AIPLA Q.J. 1.

The controversy continues worldwide. In 1996 Papua New Guinea threatened to take the U.S. government before the International Court of Justice over a U.S. government-owned patent that claimed a human cell-line developed from blood taken from a Papua New Guinea tribesman in circumstances of dubious consent.

g) Plant Varieties

Concerns like those just discussed in respect of patenting life were not enough to prevent Canada from filling the gap in patent protection for plant life. This was done by passing the *Plant Breeders' Rights Act (PBR Act)* in 1990 and acceding the following year to the *International Convention for the Protection of New Varieties of Plants* of 1961. Administered by the Department of Agriculture, the *PBR Act* provides *WTO* members on registration with eighteen years' patent-like protection covering sale and propagation for sale of prescribed distinct new plant varieties — cultivars, clones, breeding lines, or hybrids that can be cultivated. The items prescribed so far are a mixed bag: African violet, alfalfa, apple, barley, bean, begonia, blueberry, canola/rape, cherry, chrysanthemum, clematis, corn, creeping red fescue, dianthus, flax, grapevine, impatiens, Kentucky bluegrass, lentil, maple, mustard, oats, peach, pear, pea, pelargonium, plum, poinsettia, potato, potentilla, raspberry, rose, soybean, spirea, strawberry, timothy, viburnum, wheat, and yew.[55] The PBR holder must pay annual maintenance fees and provide propagating material throughout the term of the right. The right does not prevent the development of different varieties from protected plants or the use of seeds taken from protected varieties.

The philosophy behind PBRs rejects the view that germplasm is the common heritage of mankind and thus unable to be privatized. The common heritage theory was originally supported by the less-developed nations that house most of the world's plant species. It was found to benefit them little in practice. Having let their germplasm leave their borders for nothing, they found the proprietary re-engineered seeds either unaffordable or irrelevant to their needs.[56] Consequently, the 1992 UN *Convention on Biological Diversity* simultaneously endorsed both national sovereignty over and worldwide access to genetic resources. How these contradictory concepts could stand together was left tantalizingly

---

55   *Plant Breeders' Rights Act*, S.C. 1990, c. 20, s. 2, defs. "new variety," "plant variety," and "prescribed"; s. 4; s. 6 [*PBR Act*]; *Plant Breeders' Rights Regulations*, SOR/91-594, Sched. I; D'Iorio & J.A. Erratt, "Plant Breeders' Rights — Practical Considerations" (1994) 11 Can. Intell. Prop. Rev. 277.

56   The seeds came typically bundled with compatible pesticides produced by the same petrochemical or pharmaceutical firm that owned the plant patent or PBR.

unclear. The *Convention*'s ambivalence over intellectual property's role was, however, only temporary. In 1994 *TRIPs* bound even developing states to move towards patent or PBR protection for plants.

The transition is not likely to be frictionless. A U.S. patent over all forms of genetically engineered cotton was eventually revoked after widespread opposition, but it has not stopped strategic patenting that privatizes and commercializes knowledge that some Third World nations to date have treated as free to all.[57] Many of the same objections raised against patenting life generally[58] have also been levelled against the extension of monopoly rights to plants and seeds.

h) Medicine and Food

After 1923, Canada issued patents only for new processes for making new medicines and foods, not for the products themselves. The patents were subject to compulsory licensing at low royalty rates, leading to a thriving generic drug industry. Under pressure from the U.S. pharmaceutical drug industry and its proxies in the U.S. government, this system was entirely dismantled between 1987 and 1993. Product patents for medicine and food are now granted, compulsory licensing is gone, and a Patented Medicine Prices Review Board monitors patented medicines for "excessive" prices.[59] The Board claims to have kept patented drug price increases close to the rate of inflation and to have restrained the opening price at which new patented drugs enter the market. For example, in 1994 and 1995 drug prices decreased slightly, despite an increase in the consumer price index. Overall prices are nevertheless higher than when compulsory licensing was in full swing, thus creating one more problem for Canada's embattled health care system.

4) Unpatentable Inventions

Some matters may be unpatentable.

---

57   Compare R.L. Margulies, "Protecting Biodiversity: Recognizing International Intellectual Property Rights in Plant Genetic Resources" (1993) 14 Mich. J. Int'l L. 322, with V. Shiva & R. Holla-Bhar, "Intellectual Piracy and the Neem Tree" (1993) 23 Ecologist 223.

58   See section B(3)(f), "Patenting Life," in this chapter.

59   *P Act*, above note 1, ss. 79–103; *Patented Medicines Regulations*, SOR/88–474; *ICN Pharmaceuticals Inc.* v. *Canada (Patented Medicine Prices Review Board)* (1996), 68 C.P.R. (3d) 417 (Fed. C.A.) [*ICN*].

a) Material under Other Intellectual Property Laws

Patenting should usually be denied where adequate protection exists under other intellectual property laws.[60] Semiconductor topographies are protectable under the *Integrated Circuit Topography Act*, plant varieties under the *PBR Act*, designs under the *Industrial Design Act*, trademarks under the *Trade-marks Act* and the law of passing-off, literary and artistic material under the *Copyright Act*. Why grant patents as well? Architectural or engineering plans and instructions for speech therapy and written directions for use — all protected by copyright — have therefore been refused patents.[61] But printed material serving a mechanical end may be patentable — for example, a method of printing a language to indicate stress and inflection, for scanning and encoding into a device for mechanical aural reproduction.[62]

b) Natural Phenomena, Scientific Principles, Abstract Theorems

A newly discovered natural law or phenomenon would include a new plant or animal found in the wild, a new mineral in the earth, or any other "product of nature." Other "discoveries" are equally unpatentable, such as "mere scientific principle or abstract theorem" or other purely mental operation.[63] Einstein could not patent the theory of relativity, nor could Newton the theory of gravity. Patents can, of course, be granted for a new practical application of the theory of gravity — for example, on an improved gravity pump.

c) Schemes, Plans, Business Methods

Many "sure-fire" schemes for winning money on lotteries or the racetrack have been invented, but none are patentable. Methods for aircraft pilots to handle the controls so as to reduce engine noise on takeoff are unpatentable: "as much outside the operation of any of the useful arts as would be a trainer's direction to a jockey in his control of a racehorse."[64] As in Europe,[65] systems for operating bank accounts or setting up trading markets for securities should also be unpatentable.

---

60   Compare section B(4)(d), "Computer Programs," in this chapter.

61   *Lawson*, above note 39; *Re Dixon Application No. 203* (1978), 60 C.P.R. (2d) 105 at 118 (Patent Appeal Bd. & Commissioner of Patents); *Wellcome Foundation Ltd.* v. *Australia (Commissioner of Patents)* (1980), 145 C.L.R. 520 (Austl. H.C.).

62   *Pitman's Application*, [1969] R.P.C. 646 at 649 (Patent Appeal Tribunal).

63   *P Act*, above note 1, s. 27(8); *Pioneer*, above note 16.

64   *Rolls-Royce Ltd.'s Application*, [1963] R.P.C. 251 at 255 (Patent Appeal Tribunal).

65   For example, *Patents Act*, above note 28, s. 1(2)(c), excluding "a scheme, rule or method for performing a mental act, playing a game or doing business . . . as such."

d) Computer Programs

Many countries are reluctant to grant patents for computer programs, fearing that technological progress in this volatile industry would be impeded. The Canadian PO has adopted this formal position since 1978. It does not matter theoretically whether the claim is phrased as a new method of programming computers or as an apparatus claim covering a newly programmed computer. Programs are effectively treated as algorithms — "a set of rules or processes for solving a problem in a finite number of steps" — and so fall under the prohibition against patenting abstract theorems.[66] A program may do sums faster than an unaided human, but that does not make doing sums patentable even if useful data result.[67] Patents are nevertheless allowed for a "computing apparatus programmed in a novel manner, where the patentable advance is in the apparatus itself," or for a "method or process carried out with a specific novel apparatus devised to implement a newly discovered idea."[68]

A 1981 U.S. decision allowed a patent for a rubber-curing process that depended on the computerized application of a known algorithm, and the Canadian PO has accepted this where a "real change in a tangible thing," not just the production of information, results.[69] Thus, a computerized method of controlling the operation of an industrial plant is patentable.[70] The United States has since allowed apparatus claims for *a general computer as modified by a new computer program*.[71] The Canadian PO has not to date formally changed its policy. Indeed, on 21 February 1995, in the wake of the new U.S. ruling, the Canadian PO issued the following guidelines, reaffirming its earlier position:

1. Unapplied mathematical formulae are considered equivalent to mere scientific principles or abstract theorems which are not patentable under section 27(3) of the Patent Act [now section 27(8)].

---

66 *Re Application No. 096,284* (1978), 52 C.P.R. (2d) 96 at 100 (Patent Appeal Bd. & Commissioner of Patents) [*096,284*]; see section B(4)(b), "Natural Phenomena, Scientific Principles, and Abstract Theorems," in this chapter.

67 *Schlumberger Canada Ltd.* v. *Canada (Commissioner of Patents)*, [1982] 1 F.C. 485 (C.A.); *Re Application for Patent No. 178,570* (1983), 2 C.P.R. (3d) 483 (Patent Appeal Bd. & Commissioner of Patents) [*178,570*].

68 *096,284*, above note 66 at 111–12.

69 *178,570*, above note 67, following *Diamond*, above note 29.

70 *Re Application for Patent of Tokyo Shibaura Electric Co.* (*sub nom. Re Application No. 241,635 for Patent by Tokyo Shibaura Electric Co.*) (1985), 7 C.P.R. (3d) 555 (Patent Appeal Bd. & Commissioner of Patents).

71 *Re Alappat*, 33 F.3d 1526 (Fed. Cir. 1994). See also U.S. Patent & Trademark Office, Request for Comments on Proposed Examination Guidelines for Computer-Implemented Inventions, 60 Fed. Reg. 28,778 (1995); *Fujitsu Ltd.'s Application*, [1996] R.P.C. 511 at 530–31 (Pat. Ct.) on U.K. practice.

2. The presence of a programmed general purpose computer or program for such computer does not lend patentability to, nor subtract patentability from, an apparatus or process.

3. It follows from 2. that new and useful processes incorporating a computer program, and apparatus incorporating a programmed computer, are directed to patentable subject matter if the computer-related matter has been integrated with another practical system that falls within an area which is traditionally patentable. This principle is illustrative of what types of computer-related applications may be patentable, and is not intended to exclude other computer-related applications from patentability.

Despite these guidelines, some patents the Canadian PO has granted for computer software may not be very different from those granted under the new U.S. policy. Whether this is desirable is debatable. It does indirectly what cannot be done directly: it simultaneously patents subject matter that may already be protected by copyright; and the fear that programming innovations may be impeded by broad blocking patents may come to be realized.

e) Medical or Surgical Treatments

Devices or drugs for treating human or animal illness are patentable. So are methods of testing not relating to any step of actual treatment or vital function of the body. But methods of treating living humans or animals by surgery or therapy are unpatentable. This is also true of methods of using medicine or similar substances to diagnose, prevent, or cure ailments in humans or animals.[72] Medical treatment should include any modification of organic function in humans or animals: methods to bond cuts and wounds and to reduce the urge to smoke have been ruled unpatentable.[73] Although purely cosmetic treatments, such as strengthening hair or nails, may escape the prohibition, those with an accompanying medical benefit — for example, cleaning teeth to make them both more attractive and also bacteria-free — remain unpatentable.[74]

---

72   *MOPOP*, above note 9, § 16.04(6); *Merck & Co. v. Apotex Inc.* (1994), 59 C.P.R. (3d) 133 (Fed. T.D.), aff'd on this point [1995] 2 F.C. 723 (C.A.).

73   *Tennessee Eastman Co. v. Canada (Commissioner of Patents)* (1970), 62 C.P.R. 117 (Ex. Ct.), aff'd [1974] S.C.R. 111; *Re Revici* (1981), 71 C.P.R. (2d) 285 (Patent Appeal Bd. & Commissioner of Patents); compare *Trade-marks Act*, R.S.C. 1985, c. T-13, s. 51(3), def. "pharmaceutical preparation."

74   *Imperial Chemical Industries Ltd. v. Canada (Commissioner of Patents)*, [1986] 3 F.C. 40 (C.A.).

The exception for medical treatment springs from ethical or emotional reasons based on a desire not to hamper the saving of life and the alleviation of suffering. Medicine is also a profession whose members should share their skills and should not foreclose others from applying them; an operating surgeon or prescribing physician should not have to worry about patent infringement.[75] Europe has a similar exception, but the United States and, more recently, Australia do not.[76] U.S. patents have been issued for the use of AZT to treat AIDS and for pure surgical methods like performing stitchless eye cataract surgery. The more medicine starts looking like a business, the greater becomes the pressure to allow patenting as for any other business.

C. CRITERIA FOR PATENTABILITY

To be patentable, every invention must be new, non-obvious, and useful.

1) Novelty

An invention need not be absolutely new in the sense that nobody anywhere ever thought of it or made it before — a criterion impossible to prove or disprove. Rather, it must be relatively new when compared with what was known in that art at the claim date. The claim is examined for this purpose: if its subject matter has been "disclosed" so as to have become "available to the public" anywhere in the world,[77] the invention is old and unpatentable.

This base of public knowledge is affected in two ways. First, an earlier Canadian application for the same invention — one previously filed or with priority based on an earlier foreign or local filing — becomes a disclosure from that priority date once the specification is published. An earlier application that remains secret because it is abandoned or withdrawn before being published is not a disclosure.

Second, the inventor has a one-year grace period during which he can disclose the invention before filing a Canadian application without this counting as public disclosure. This indulgence extends to the applicant for the patent (if different from the inventor) or someone obtaining knowledge of the invention directly or indirectly from either.[78] Other-

---

75 *Anaesthetic Supplies Pty. Ltd.* v. *Rescare Ltd.* (1994), 28 I.P.R. 383, (Austl. Fed. Ct.), dissent [*Rescare*].

76 *EPC*, above note 28, art. 52(4); *Rescare*, ibid.

77 *P Act*, above note 1, s. 2, def. "invention"; s. 28.2(1)(b).

78 *P Act*, *ibid.*, s. 28.2(1)(a); s. 2 def. "applicant."

wise, showing a single sample to a prospective customer to try to drum up trade would bar a patent. Unfortunately, the same indulgence is not recognized everywhere. The United States has a similar provision; but Europe allows only six months' grace, and then only for inventions shown at officially recognized international exhibitions or for disclosures that are an "evident abuse" of the inventor (e.g., breaking a confidentiality agreement).[79] The inventor who wants to patent outside Canada and the United States is better advised to file her patent application first and "show and tell" later.

a) What Is "Available to the Public"?

Information is disclosed if it is made publicly available without restriction. This disclosure may occur if the invention is shown off without any requirement of confidentiality, displayed in a public place, lectured on at a public conference, or even installed in one's house where guests can see it. But disclosures in a private document like an internal memo do not count. Nor do isolated private uses, idle gossip, experiments (especially abandoned or unsuccessful ones), or disclosures made under express or implied conditions of confidentiality.[80] Private information confined to a select group — for example, masonic rituals or aboriginal folklore — may therefore count as unavailable to the "public."

Still, disclosing the invention only once to one person can sometimes make it available to the public. The nineteenth century beau who impressed his intended by giving her a pair of corset steels he had invented, to replace those she complained were always breaking, thereby publicly disclosed his invention as surely as if he had put it in a shop window in the busiest part of town.[81] Today, a new part tucked deep in the bowels of an automobile engine may be publicly available the moment the first car is sold or given away. The seller or donor has, from then on, lost the power to prevent the buyer or others from detecting the new part and talking about it. Whether anyone in fact tried to do so is irrelevant.[82] This condition is not as harsh as might at first appear, since firms very often do get hold of early samples of their competitors' product precisely to see whether any new features in it are worth imitating.

---

79   *EPC*, above note 28, arts. 54(2) & 55; compare *Patents Act*, above note 28, s. 1(4).

80   *Minerals Separation North American Corp. v. Noranda Mines Ltd.*, [1947] Ex.C.R. 306, rev'd (1949), [1950] S.C.R. 36, aff'd (1952), 15 C.P.R. 133 (P.C.); *Procter & Gamble Co. v. Bristol-Myers Canada Ltd.* (1978), 39 C.P.R. (2d) 145 (Fed. T.D.), aff'd (1979), 42 C.P.R. (2d) 33 (Fed. C.A.).

81   *Egbert v. Lippmann*, 104 U.S. 333 (1881).

82   *Gibney v. Ford Motor Co. of Canada* (1967), 52 C.P.R. 140 (Ex. Ct.).

b) Prior Publication

Before 1989, only previous patents or printed publications could be used to show that an invention was old.[83] Now any disclosure that tells the public anywhere in the world about the invention qualifies: patents or anything else printed, written, oral, or even posted on the Internet. The disclosure has to be self-contained: making a mosaic of the prior art is not permitted. The invention is anticipated only if a skilled worker working on a problem would, on picking up the document, say, "By George, I've got it." So the information must give directions that, inevitably, would produce the claimed invention, or must for all practical purposes be equal to that in the patent.[84]

A double standard operates here. Courts give patents a non-literal "purposive" construction when they are testing for internal validity or trying to catch infringers.[85] When testing prior documents for novelty, however, they construe them narrowly. The documents are then subjected to "the closest scrutiny," and a "weighty burden" is placed on the challenger.[86] Sauce for the patent goose should perhaps also be sauce for the prior art gander. Prior documents should be examined purposively as a skilled reader would read them. This examination should cover obvious equivalents to described or claimed elements.

Nor does there seem to be any good reason why older, unexploited documents continue to be denigrated as mere paper anticipations, the "abandoned scrap heaps of dust-covered books which tell of hopes unrealized and flashes of genius quite forgotten."[87] This prejudice goes back to times of low literacy where prior publication understandably counted less than actual prior use.[88] It is no longer appropriate today, when much information is widely and instantly available, often electronically. Many ideas in written disclosures are ahead of their time or are not commercialized for other reasons. Yet many may have been scanned and their contents absorbed. If a disclosure in fact makes the invention publicly available, whether this occurred through an actual embodiment or a publication should be irrelevant. If one sale to one

---

83 *Patent Act*, R.S.C. 1985, c. P-4, s. 28(2), prior to amendment by R.S.C. 1985 (3d Supp.), c. 33, s. 10.

84 *Reeves Brothers Inc.* v. *Toronto Quilting & Embroidery Ltd.* (1978), 43 C.P.R. (2d) 145 at 157 (Fed. T.D.).

85 See section C(6)(a) "Purposive Construction Saves Claims," and section F(6), "Substantial Infringement," in this chapter.

86 *Diversified Products Corp.* v. *Tye-Sil Corp.* (1991), 35 C.P.R. (3d) 350 at 363 (Fed. C.A.).

87 *Eli Lilly & Co.* v. *Marzone Chemicals Ltd.* (1977), 37 C.P.R. (2d) 3 at 32 (Fed. T.D.), aff'd above note 45.

88 *Stead* v. *Anderson* (1847), 16 L.J.C.P. 250.

uninterested person is disclosure, so too should be one publication open to the view of many.

c) Undetectable Uses

Suppose a chemical in a sold compound cannot be detected through known means of analysis. Or suppose the product of a new process or a machine is sold, but the public cannot know the invention from the product itself. Is such an undetectable chemical or secret process or machine "disclosed" so as to have become available to the public?

U.K. case law before the *European Patent Convention* and U.S. case law would suggest it has been so disclosed. The leading pre-*EPC* U.K. case involved the sale of some batches of the antibiotic ampicillin. These batches, unknown even to the seller, contained some trihydrate form of the drug. The sales were held to prevent a rival from later patenting ampicillin trihydrate. By selling the product, the first maker put it out of its power to prevent trihydrate from being detected. Evidence that someone actually could or did detect it was irrelevant.[89] Similarly, sales of the output of a newly invented process or machine prevented a later patent for that process or machine. Nobody could have detected from the product sold that a new process or machine had been used, but this point was irrelevant.[90]

The U.S. and pre-*EPC* U.K. case law is distinguishable because the focus was on whether the invention was publicly used. It was also the focus in Canada before 1989, although the use had to make the invention "available to the public."[91] But now the question is whether there has been a public disclosure. This is not the same as use, but is there enough of a difference? Post-*EPC* U.K. courts have held so: under European law, the ampicillin case would be decided differently because European law, like the Canadian *Act*, denies novelty only where the invention was earlier made "available to the public." Had the ampicillin specification, however, disclosed a process resulting in ampicillin trihydrate, this would have made trihydrate available to the public, even if neither discloser nor the public knew it. As the later U.K. court put it:

---

89   *Bristol-Myers Co. (Johnson's) Application* (1973), [1975] R.P.C. 127 (H.L.).

90   *W.L. Gore & Associates Inc. v. Kimal Scientific Products Ltd.* (1987), [1988] R.P.C. 137 (Pat. Ct.). The corresponding U.S. patent was not invalidated because the court held that prior use bars only the inventor, not a third party, from a grant: *W.L. Gore & Associates Inc. v. Garlock Inc.*, 721 F.2d 1540 (Fed. Cir. 1983), criticized in D.S. Chisum, *Patents: A Treatise on the Law of Patentability, Validity, and Infringement* (New York: Matthew Bender, 1978), § 6.02[5][C].

91   *Patent Act*, R.S.C. 1985, c. P-4, ss. 27(1)(b)–(c) & 61(1)(a), prior to amendment by R.S.C. 1985 (3d Supp.), c. 33, s. 8 & s. 23.

"The Amazonian Indian who treats himself with powdered [chinchona] bark for fever is using quinine, even if he thinks that the reason why the treatment is effective is that the tree is favoured by the Gods."[92]

While Canadian courts may follow this reasoning, the result is doubtful patent policy. If a third party is commercially exploiting the invention at the claim date, a patent abridges its (till then) perfectly lawful business. Usually, too, what infringes a patent after grant should, if done previously, bar the grant. Since selling the output of a process or a machine generally infringes the process or the machine patent,[93] sales before the claim date should equally bar the grant. The policy is even stronger when the inventor is doing the exploiting, for to allow a patent then is to extend a monopoly for the period of secret exploitation. Inventors would be encouraged to put black boxes literally or figuratively around their invention to hide it from the public, and would patent only when they feared successful reverse-engineering. Why should the patent cake be so had and eaten?

d) Experimental Uses

For pragmatic reasons, judges have developed an exception for experiments reasonably necessary to perfect an invention or to test its merits or practical value, whether they are done by the inventor or by anyone else. Inventors may need to experiment to produce an accurate disclosure for the patent application. This work should not be prejudiced by the danger that like experiments, especially if unsuccessful and abandoned, by others will be treated as public disclosures barring a right to patent.[94] Experiments may not always involve limited public disclosure. For example, the best way to test a new method of highway construction may be to use it on a strip of highway and to see how it works under actual conditions. This experiment should not count as public disclosure, even if it runs for a season or two and is there for all to see.[95]

The receipt of money or other benefits may not prevent a use from being experimental, but the exception ceases once experimenting is no longer "reasonable and necessary" or the main purpose of the activity

---

92 *Merrell Dow Pharmaceuticals Inc. v. H.N. Norton & Co. Ltd.* (1995), [1996] R.P.C. 76 at 91 (H.L.).

93 See section H(8), "Existing Uses," and section F(2) and (4), "Owner's Rights," "Use" and "Imports," in this chapter; compare J.G. Colombo, "Reverse Engineering and Process Patents: When is the Process Disclosed?" (1991) 7 I.P.J. 85.

94 *Procter & Gamble Co. v. Calgon Interamerican Corp.* (1981), 56 C.P.R. (2d) 214 at 234 & 239 (Fed. T.D.).

95 *City of Elizabeth v. American Nicholson Pavement Co.*, 97 U.S. 126 (1878).

changes from experimental.[96] The first time a sailboard is tried out on a public beach may be an experiment, but once adjustments are made and the sailboard is used for the rest of the season, the experiment is over and the invention is publicly available. Anybody on the beach can now see how it works.[97]

2) Non-obviousness

Until very recently, the *Patent Act* did not expressly say that obvious inventions were unpatentable. Courts implied this criterion from the notion of "invention." Inventions implied inventive ingenuity, without which an advance was obvious; and patents are not granted for the obvious.

The *Act* is now explicit that the claimed invention must not, at its claim date, be obvious — "very plain" — to a person skilled in the relevant art or science. That person will be notionally apprised of all information publicly disclosed and available anywhere in the world before the claim date. Again, as for novelty, any disclosure by the inventor, applicant, or someone obtaining knowledge from either, for the year before the application was filed, does not count.[98] The test is objective: it does not matter that, to this inventor, her advance was momentous. Rather, the known public state of the art at the claim date is gathered and assessed as it would appear to a skilled worker in that field. The question becomes whether, to that notional person, the claimed invention would then have come directly and without difficulty. This notional worker has been called a "mythical creature (the man in the Clapham omnibus of patent law)," with "no scintilla of inventiveness or imagination; a paragon of deduction and dexterity, wholly devoid of intuition; a triumph of the left hemisphere over the right."[99]

Whether an advance is obvious as a matter of fact is supposed to present "a very difficult test to satisfy" because "[e]very invention is obvious after it has been made, and to no one more so than an expert in the field."[100] Generalizations like this are really reactions to a particular case and cannot be taken seriously. Many inventions seem amazing

---

96 *Canadian Patent Scaffolding Co.* v. *Delzotto Enterprises Ltd.* (1978), 42 C.P.R. (2d) 7 at 24 (Fed. T.D.), aff'd (1980), 47 C.P.R. (2d) 77 (Fed. C.A.).

97 *Windsurfing International Inc.* v. *Tabur Marine (G.B.) Ltd.* (1984), [1985] R.P.C. 59 (C.A.); compare *Windsurfing International Inc.* v. *Trilantic Corp.* (1985), 8 C.P.R. (3d) 241 (Fed. C.A.) [*Trilantic*].

98 *P Act*, above note 1, s. 28.3.

99 *Beloit*, above note 18 at 294.

100 *Ibid.* at 295 & 294.

years after they are made. Moreover, no data exist on the percentage of patents overall that may be obvious. PO screening weeds out egregious applications, but skilful patent drafting can sometimes slip the trite through. And when an obviousness issue finally hits a court, a judge with no science or engineering background may be so impressed by the wonders of technology that almost everything in the physical world will amaze — and so not be obvious — to him.

Realizing their technical limitations, courts (and even the PO) are often influenced by indirect evidence bearing on non-obviousness. For example, the problem the patentee worked on may have long been known and the path to its solution may have been littered with failures. The inventor, though highly qualified, may have experimented long and hard before hitting on the solution. The patented product may have been an instant success on the market, which therefore recognized the invention's value. (Of course, success becomes unimportant if the product differs significantly from the patent or if market success comes merely from clever marketing.) Disinterested experts may have praised the invention. Competitors may have accepted its validity by taking licences or by working around it. The more these factors abound and the longer validity stays unchallenged, the more the invention will be found unobvious.[101]

Take the case of a product that is made in a different material — for example, plastic instead of wood, metal, or glass. Most designers today would find the switch obvious, but sometimes more is needed to make the switch work. For example, in badminton, plastic shuttlecocks now replace the expensive feather-and-cork of yore. The change went beyond simply moulding a plastic feather and cork. There were major difficulties in replicating in plastic the flight characteristics of the feather-and-cork. The path to success was littered with failure. Unsurprisingly, the patent for the first successful shuttlecock was found unobvious.[102] By contrast, in another case, a designer was asked to turn his mind to new uses of "lazy-susan" turntables. He hit upon the idea of a portable tool caddy and made a prototype within two months. The result was later held obvious. Simplicity does not negate invention, but this idea and its execution, involving the adaptation of a commercially available article, would have occurred to "any skilled handy-man" and so was unpatentable.[103]

101 See R.L. Robbins, "Subtests of 'Nonobviousness': A Nontechnical Approach to Patent Validity" (1964) 112 U. Pa. L. Rev. 1169.

102 *Rosedale Associated Manufacturers Ltd.* v. *Carlton Tyre Saving Co. Ltd.*, [1960] R.P.C. 59 (C.A.).

103 *Rubbermaid (Canada) Ltd.* v. *Tucker Plastic Products Ltd.* (1972), 8 C.P.R. (2d) 6 at 15 (Fed. T.D.).

3) Usefulness

An invention must be "useful" to be patentable.[104] It must relate to the useful — not the fine or professional — arts, be directed to a practical use, and do the job the inventor claims for it.[105] It may still be uneconomic, unsafe, primitive, or commercially useless, but every new technology must start somewhere. Colour television began with crude pictures, yet the first patents enabled others to refine the invention into a commercial product. Some practical end must nonetheless be attained, or the result is merely an unpatentable discovery. A researcher producing a new compound has to show that it is something more than a scientific curiosity. Tests may have to be produced that point to some useful property — for example, as an analgesic.[106]

Inventions that do not work are useless and unpatentable. This restriction applies not only to perpetual motion machines, "death-rays," and other devices that defy the laws of physics — and which continue to turn up in patent offices — but also to drugs that turn out to be toxic or to manufacturing processes that manage to wreck the item they are supposed to produce.[107] But commercial success, or the fact that infringers actually use the invention, may suggest it is useful; for why would people spend time and money on rubbish?

4) The Contents of a Patent

A patent comprises two parts: the disclosure and the claims.[108]

a) Disclosure
In the disclosure, the applicant explains the story of her invention: what it is and how to put it to use. The various steps and the sequence of any process must be clearly set out. For a product, this means that the disclosure must show how to make and use it. For a new combination, the

---

104   *P Act*, above note 1, s. 2, def. "invention."
105   *Consolboard Inc. v. MacMillan Bloedel (Sask.) Ltd.*, [1981] 1 S.C.R. 504
       [*Consolboard*].
106   *Brenner v. Manson*, 383 U.S. 519 (1966); *Re Application No. 139,256* (1977), 51
       C.P.R. (2d) 95 (Patent Appeal Bd. & Commissioner of Patents). Compare *Visx Inc.
       v. Nidek Co.* (1995), 68 C.P.R. (3d) 272 (Fed. T.D.): a laser machine for eye
       surgery may cause mutations or tumours, but may still legally be "useful."
107   *Otta v. Canada (Commissioner of Patents)* (1979), 51 C.P.R. (2d) 134 (Fed. C.A.);
       X. v. Canada (Commissioner of Patents) (1981), 59 C.P.R. (2d) 7 (Fed. C.A.); *TRW
       Inc. v. Walbar of Canada Inc.* (1991), 39 C.P. R. (3d) 176 (Fed. C.A.).
108   *P Act*, above note 1, s. 34(1).

elements and the new result must be detailed. If a person skilled in the art can arrive at the same results only through chance or further long experiments, the disclosure is insufficient and the patent is void. A patentee may, for example, discover that culture grown from a new bacterial strain found in a Vancouver sewer has antibiotic properties. The strain may be fully described in the specification, but cannot be replicated without a sample being made available in a public depositary freely accessible to researchers. A sample must therefore be deposited, or the patent may be void for inadequate disclosure.[109]

b) Claims

In the claims, the applicant marks out the territory it wants to monopolize. Anything outside the fence is public domain: "what is not claimed is disclaimed." Typically, the claims start with the widest interpretation of what the invention is believed to be; then comes a series of ever more specific claims. Each claim is an independent grant of monopoly. One or more may be found invalid, without necessarily affecting the validity of any other.

One might expect that a competitor could, by looking at the claims, decide if an activity it proposes infringes. This, perhaps surprisingly, is not so. Next to interpreting patent claims, interpreting contracts is child's play. Predicting how a court at trial or on appeal will assess the technology and conflicting expert evidence on meaning and then figure out a claim's "true" meaning is close to soothsaying. Nor is the exercise always the neutral task courts say it is supposed to be: some courts cannot resist "construing" claims to catch "free-riders" or deliberate copiers.

The game for patentees, especially in highly competitive industries, is to reveal as little and to claim as much as possible. The less disclosed, the more that can be retained as competitive edge. The wider one claims, the tougher it is for imitators. But the specification must stay clear of the known and the obvious. It must demonstrate and claim only something over and above existing technology. Much patent drafting involves trying simultaneously to achieve these aims. Along the way several obstacles must be avoided, lest the claims or the whole patent end up invalid.

5) Reading a Patent

Patents are not drafted to be read and understood by the ordinary man, woman, or lawyer in the street, however well educated or interested. They are meant to be understood only by someone — or a team where

---

109   *P Act, ibid.*, s. 38.1(1); compare *Pioneer*, above note 16.

the invention crosses specialties — "skilled in the art or science to which . . . [the invention] appertains, or with which it is most closely connected."[110] Even then, the patent's meaning is ultimately a question of law, decided by a judge who usually is not skilled in any art or science, let alone the relevant one. Experts can say what the patent means to them or to a skilled reader, but judges are technically free to disregard their evidence.

To reach a decision, judges put themselves in the position of a reader skilled in the art who is reading the specification at its claim date. They must review the prior art to understand the approach that the reader would bring to the patent. The judge then applies principles of construction applicable to written documents generally, avoiding literalism where possible. So the patent is read as a whole against the context of what was generally known to those skilled in the art. The disclosure, the drawings, and the claims, being integral parts of the specification, must be read in the light of one another. If the specification uses technical terms in a particular way or provides a glossary, the same meanings should apply to the claims.

Oddly enough, the meaning or effect of the patent is apparently unaffected by any concessions or amendments made as the application wended its way through the PO: "the patentee and potential infringers are both bound by the terms of the patent as issued."[111] This rule is ripe for reconsideration. It reflects outmoded rules on construction of documents generally. Contracts are now interpreted against the history of their making; and in a trade-mark infringement case, the Supreme Court precluded a registrant from expanding the scope of its mark beyond what it had represented to the Trade-mark Office to obtain the registration.[112] This rule should apply equally to a patentee who submits an interpretation inconsistent with one it had earlier maintained before the PO.

In practice, courts rely heavily on expert evidence to help them understand how those skilled in the art would have understood the language of the patent at its claim date. Where the evidence conflicts, the judge selects the most likely meaning skilled readers would have adopted. However, if the experts agree, a judge who differs from them risks reversal for errror of law.[113] Extrinsic evidence like the inventor's

---

110   *P Act, ibid.*, s. 34(1)(b); *Consolboard*, above note 105.
111   *PLG Research Ltd. v. Jannock Steel Fabricating Co./Société de fabrication d'acier Jannock* (1991), 35 C.P.R. (3d) 344 at 349 (Fed. T.D.), aff'd (1992), 41 C.P.R. (3d) 492 (Fed. C.A.), rejecting the U.S. doctrine of "file wrapper" estoppel.
112   *S.C. Johnson & Son Ltd. v. Marketing International Ltd.* (1979), [1980] 1 S.C. R. 99.
113   *Dableh v. Ontario Hydro* (1996), 68 C.P.R. (3d) 129 (Fed. C.A.) [*Dableh*].

declarations of what she intended is excluded; *ex post facto* analyses like these, even if masquerading as the genuine thoughts of an objective person skilled in the art, are worthless.[114]

Ultimately, the disclosure should give skilled readers enough information for them to practise the invention with little difficulty when the patent period ends, and meanwhile to experiment with or to try to improve it. This is a major purpose of granting patents in the first place. If, at the end of the day, this purpose fails because of genuine doubts about what the disclosure reveals, the whole patent should be invalid. This is so if, for example, the drawings exemplifying the invention are so inaccurate that ordinary skilled workers in the art cannot make the invention following their directions.[115]

6) Claims Must Be Clear

The claims must set out the monopoly "distinctly and in explicit terms."[116] To readers of patents, this description sometimes sounds like a poor joke. Patent drafters seem congenitally unable to employ plain language, and they care even less about Flesch readability tests. Their credo is that of the British judge who derided any preference in claim drafting for monosyllables over polysyllables and for simple over complex sentences as a "retention of the kindergarten experience."[117] Others may sympathize with the Canadian judge who was faced with a patent for a simple mechanism to collect used toner from photocopiers. The leading claim consisted of one 178-word sentence with only six commas. Saying that claims like this one pass from "riddle to enigma," the judge pleaded with drafters to break claims up into shorter sentences. The Gettysburg Address was about as long as this claim: Why could drafters not emulate Lincoln?[118] But, having vented his spleen in a footnote, the judge still held the claim valid. Things are no different now. A judge at a recent interlocutory hearing was so befuddled with a claim (281 words, two commas) that she thought this "avalanche de mots" probably made the patent invalid; but after a nine-day trial another

---

114   *Nekoosa Packaging Corp.* v. *United Dominion Industries Ltd.* (sub nom. *Nekoosa Packaging Corp.* v. *AMCA International Ltd.*) (1994), 56 C.P.R. (3d) 470 (Fed. C.A.); *Merck & Co.* v. *Apotex Inc.*, [1995] 2 F.C. 723 (C.A.).
115   *Knight* v. *Argylls Ltd.* (1913), 30 R.P.C. 321 at 348 (C.A.).
116   *P Act*, above note 1, s. 31(2).
117   *Leonard's Application* (1965), [1966] R.P.C. 269 at 275 (Patent Appeal Tribunal).
118   *Xerox of Canada Ltd.* v. *I.B.M. Canada Ltd.* (1977), 33 C.P.R. 24 at 88, n. 14 (Fed. T.D.).

more sympathetic judge upheld the claim, while conceding it was no "literary masterpiece."[119]

The PO does encourage long sentences to be broken into sections, subsections, and paragraphs, but claims still proliferate into the hundreds despite the "one invention, one patent" rule. Both the PO and the courts, sympathetic towards technologies that are sometimes difficult to describe and to understand, have abdicated the field to the neurotic drafting practices of patent agents and lawyers. The problem is not confined to Canada. Patent drafting has drifted internationally into the sort of practices that in the past caused Charles Dickens to take up his pen. The result is that only another patent agent or lawyer can possibly parse, let alone interpret, a colleague's handiwork. Nothing will change until patent offices and courts everywhere start insisting that claims be readily comprehensible by actual (rather than notional) skilled persons, and not only after nine-day trials — upon pain of invalidity. Whether, however, this can come about without international action through bodies like the World Intellectual Property Organization, reinforced by national legislation, is debatable.

a) Purposive Construction Saves Claims

Drafting standards are certainly not improved by the principle that claims should be construed "purposively." Judges are reminded not to read patents too literally, with "the kind of meticulous verbal analysis in which lawyers are too often tempted by their training to indulge."[120] So a claim that covers the construction of "perpendicular" buildings could cover the leaning tower of Pisa, as infringers have found to their cost. If leaning the building a little does not affect how the invention works, then the claim, though literally saying "perpendicular," can purposively be construed to mean "more or less perpendicular" — and still be clear and distinct.[121]

This approach comes from a time when patentees and their agents were said to be "seldom skilled in the use of language."[122] It allows the brushing aside of technical objections so that specifications are con-

---

119   *Risi Stone Ltd.* v. *Groupe Permacon Inc.* (1990), 29 C.P.R. (3d) 243 at 247–48 (Fed. T.D.) (interlocutory); (1995), 65 C.P.R. (3d) 2 at 9 (Fed. T.D.) (trial).

120   *Catnic Components Ltd.* v. *Hill & Smith Ltd.* (1980), [1981] F.S.R. 60 at 65–66 (H.L.) [*Catnic*].

121   *Catnic, ibid.*, holding that "vertically" in a claim covering the back of a door lintel included backs with 8-degree slopes off the vertical. See section F(6), "Substantial Infringement," in this chapter.

122   *Ernest Scragg & Sons Ltd.* v. *Leesona Corp.*, [1964] Ex.C.R. 649 at 702 [*Scragg*].

strued "fairly, with a judicial anxiety to support a really useful invention if it can be supported on a reasonable construction of the patent."[123] This was how a claim for an electrocardiogram cream, "compatible with normal skin," comprising a "highly ionizable salt to provide good electrical conductivity," was saved. Some of the salts were toxic; so an infringer said the claim was void, as syntactically suggesting that any salt could produce a cream compatible with skin. Moreover, what salts qualified as "highly" ionizable? The Supreme Court called these objections "technicalities" and upheld the claim. A skilled chemist would automatically avoid any toxic salt without needing to be told. Syntax would not stand in the way. Scientists might also disagree on whether a salt qualified as "highly" ionizable, but why would anyone want to use a doubtful contender when thousands of known suitable salts were available?[124]

D. CORRECTING MISTAKES

In the rush to file early, applicants and their agents often make mistakes. The best time to correct is during examination of the application, before the patent is issued. The PO is quite liberal in allowing corrections then,[125] but amendments can be made even after the patent is issued. Unfortunately, form overwhelms substance. Instead of a single amendment procedure, there is a hotchpotch of badly drafted provisions, some dating to pre-Confederation: disclaimer, re-examination, reissue, correction of clerical errors, and judicial amendment. To be curable, the defect, which includes any produced by the inventor's agents, should be the result of a "mistake, accident or inadvertence, and without any wilful intent to defraud or mislead the public" (although this is not explicit for all the recourses).[126]

The procedures common to all intellectual property rights (correction of clerical errors and judicial amendment) are dealt with later.[127] Only those peculiar to patents are noted here: disclaimer, re-examination, and reissue.

---

123   *Hinks & Son v. Safety Lighting Co.* (1876), 4 Ch.D. 607 at 612, frequently approved in Canada.

124   *Burton Parsons Chemicals Inc.* v. *Hewlett-Packard (Can.) Ltd.*, [1976] 1 S.C.R. 555 [*Burton*].

125   For example, *PR*, above note 1, ss. 32(1) & 35.

126   *P Act*, above note 1, s. 48(1) (disclaimer), s. 47(1) (reissue), & s. 53(2); compare s. 53(1) (judicial amendment); *Burton*, above note 124.

127   See section C(3), "Expungement and Correction," in chapter 5.

1) Disclaimer

A specification may mistakenly claim more than the inventor invented or include someone else's invention. Newly found prior art may reveal the patent's overambition. The patentee can then disclaim the excess in writing and file the disclaimer with the PO, even during infringement proceedings or appeals. Whole claims, parts of claims, or parts of the disclosure may be disclaimed and will be read as part of the original specification — but without affecting pending litigation.[128]

Since the PO cannot apparently refuse to record a disclaimer,[129] it is up to the courts in contested litigation to inquire whether the *Act's* requirements were met: Was the specification too broad? Was the invention partly invented by someone else? Was the disclaimed material recorded through mistake, accident, or inadvertence? Was there no intent to defraud or mislead? If these preconditions do not exist, the disclaimer is void, but the original patent will wear the confessed defects like a scarlet letter.

2) Re-examination

A patentee (or anyone else) can ask the PO to re-examine its claims against newly discovered prior art that may affect the validity or the scope of the patent.[130] If a board of examiners decides that a "substantial new question" affecting patentability exists,[131] the patentee can present its views and propose amendments or new claims not expanding the monopoly. The board will, within twelve months, issue a certificate confirming, cancelling, amending, or adding to the claims. Cancellation operates retroactively, but amended or new claims are prospective only.[132]

---

128 *P Act*, above note 1, s. 48(4); *Canadian Celanese Ltd.* v. *BVD Co. Ltd.*, [1939] 1 All E.R. 410 (P.C.).

129 *P Act, ibid.*, s. 48; *Monsanto Co.* v. *Canada (Commissioner of Patents)*, [1976] 2 F.C. 476 (C.A.), modifying (1974), [1975] F.C. 197 (T.D.); *ICN*, above note 59.

130 A copy of the request is sent to patentee unless it initiated the procedure: *P Act, ibid.*, s. 48.1(3).

131 If no such question is found, the board can, without appeal or review, summarily terminate the proceeding: *P Act, ibid.*, s. 48.2(3). The same material can nevertheless be used in any later court challenge to the patent.

132 *P Act, ibid.*, ss. 48.3 to 48.5. The board's decision is appealable to the Federal Court of Appeal.

3) Reissue

A patent can be surrendered within four years of its date and the PO may reissue (or re-reissue) it for the balance of the term. This outcome may occur only if the original was mistakenly "defective or inoperative by reason of insufficient description and specification," or because the inventor mistakenly claimed more or less than was necessary. On reissue, identical claims date back to the original claim date. The surrender and amended claims, however, run only from the reissue date. This date can be outside the four-year period.[133]

The disclosure or claims may be rewritten to protect the invention as fully and as accurately as possible according to the inventor's original intent — however elusive that may be to divine.[134] Wholly invalid patents can be resurrected, at least if they have not since been declared invalid in impeachment proceedings. In one such case, the prosecution of a U.S. patent revealed faults in its Canadian counterpart. An application was made to impeach the Canadian patent. Since the patent had issued less than four years earlier, the patentee had the faults corrected through reissue before the impeachment action was heard. Newly found prior art was drafted around, and claims were added to protect the invention more fully. The first the challenger knew of these developments was when a suit was brought against it for infringing the reissued patent — which it lost.[135]

E. TITLE

1) Inventor

The petition should correctly name the inventor, for title to the invention can be derived only through him or her.[136] "Inventor" is not defined in the *Act*. Case law establishes that the inventor is whoever first independently thought of the invention and objectively manifested the idea. This manifestation may occur by the person communicating it to some-

---

133   *P Act, ibid.*, s. 47.
134   *Curl-master Manufacturing Co. v. Atlas Brush Ltd.*, [1967] S.C.R. 514; *Mobil Oil Corp. v. Hercules Canada Inc.* (1995), 63 C.P.R. (3d) 473 (Fed. C.A.) [*Hercules*].
135   *Burton*, above note 124, aff'g (1972), 7 C.P.R. (2d) 198 (Fed. T.D.).
136   But a misnomer may not invalidate a patent that is, in fact, granted to the right person. Suppose W1 and W2 are both employed by E, and W1 is the inventor or co-inventor with W2. A patent granted to E is valid even though W2 was named sole inventor. See section A(5), "The Application Must Be Truthful," in this chapter.

one else, writing it down, putting it into practice, or embodying it in a working model.[137] Keeping an idea in one's head does not make one an inventor, nor does taking it from some other person or a book.[138] The old British law that equated an inventor with whoever first imported a new technology into the country has long been abandoned. Since people in different parts of the world are often working on the same idea at the same time, two or more may very well qualify as inventors. The scientific community may give priority to one, but patent law gives priority to whoever first files for a patent.

The *Act* allows either the inventor or the assignee to apply for and obtain a patent, but an assignor to whom a patent is granted holds it in trust and must assign it to the assignee on demand. The true inventor or owner can also invalidate a patent issued to the wrong person or have it corrected to reflect the true title.[139] Even where the patent is valid despite a wrong attribution of inventorship,[140] the true inventor or inventors should be able to have this error corrected, so that the register may function as an accurate database of inventors as well as inventions.[141]

2) Joint Inventors

The *Act* does not define joint inventorship, yet most inventions today come from teamwork. Previously, courts tended to look for a single inventor. Where different people thought up different parts of a combination, the inventor was the person who thought of combining the parts. Today, team inventions are more likely to be treated as jointly invented or at least jointly owned by the team. Everyone who materially helped to create or to develop the idea, however big or small a role, can claim to be a co-inventor or a co-owner. This is especially so where there was a prior agreement to collaborate or where team members are named as co-authors of the publication disclosing the invention.[142]

---

137   *Christiani & Nielsen v. Rice*, [1930] S.C.R. 443, aff'd (*sub nom. Rice v. Christiani & Nielsen*) [1931] A.C. 770 (P.C); *Scragg*, above note 122.

138   *Muntz v. Foster* (1844), 2 Web. Pat. Cas. 96 (C.P.) [*Muntz*].

139   *P Act*, above note 1, s. 52; *Comstock Canada v. Electec Ltd.* (1991), 38 C.P.R. (3d) 29 (Fed. T.D.) [*Comstock*].

140   See note 20 above.

141   Compare section I(2), "Attribution," in chapter 2.

142   *Monsanto Co. v. Kamp*, 267 F. Supp. 818 (D.C. 1967); *Re CSIRO & Gilbert* (1995), 31 I.P.R. 67 (Austl. Patent Office).

Co-inventors can be added or deleted from an application with the PO's approval. A patent can be issued even if co-inventors refuse to join in applying or have disappeared from sight. On the other hand, someone who concurs in being named co-inventor will later find it difficult to claim that she was really the sole inventor.[143]

Co-inventorship or co-ownership may need rethinking in the light of new technologies. Suppose someone's body part is the source of an invention developed by researchers: Can the subject claim part ownership in any patent? Traditional patent principle says no: not even the owner of a stolen blank canvas on which a thief paints a masterpiece can claim copyright in the artwork. Yet the analogy is inexact for, without the starting material, the invention could not have been made at all. Excluding that person, without his or her consent, from the benefits of the invention may dampen the supply or enthusiasm of human research subjects. Charges of colonialism may also be unavoidable where the body parts came from a remote villager with limited understanding of the implications of the activity. Perhaps such subjects may not deserve to be called "co-inventors," but why not "co-owners"?[144]

3) Ownership: Employees

The inventor first owns the invention she made, but the federal *Act* says nothing about what happens when the inventor is an employee. This question is left to provincial law. Contracts of employment often provide that employees cannot reveal the firm's confidential information or trade secrets, and that the benefit of any inventions made on the job belongs to the employer. Such provisions, which make explicit what is anyway implicit, are enforceable if they are not unduly restrictive. Those that try to catch inventions made by ex-employees from ideas developed after they have quit employment may be void as unreasonable restraints of trade.

Where the contract says nothing about the ownership of inventions, a test like the one used in copyright law applies. The employer will own the employee's inventions where an employee is specifically hired to invent, innovate, or develop an invention, or even where he hands over an idea without thought of payment or under a contractual "suggestion box" policy that gives the invention to the employer. But not every

---

143   *P Act*, above note 1, ss. 31(1), (3); *Putti* v. *Gasparics* (1973), 13 C.P.R. (2d) 260 (B.C.S.C.).

144   Compare *Moore* v. *Regents of the University of California*, 793 P.2d 479 at 511–12 (Cal. S.C. 1990) (dissent).

invention made on the job belongs to the employer. Suppose a factory manager uses the workplace to improve the operation of a machine her employer owns. If not hired or paid to invent, the employee owns and can patent for herself any invention resulting from her experiments. The employer has no legal or moral claim to the fruits of employees' intellectual labour simply because it provided a propitious environment for invention or encouraged its employees' endeavours. The employer may use the particular improved machine without toll, but, unlike the position in the United States, cannot apply the improvement to other machines it owns or sells.[145]

The law favours employees who are open with their employers. Work done surreptitiously, using the employer's resources or information when the employee is in conflict of interest, raises suspicions of disloyalty and may lead courts to find that the employee has broken implied obligations of good faith owed to the employer and that any resulting invention belongs to the employer.

4) Ownership: Freelancers

Freelancers are treated less favourably in patent law than in copyright law. The *Copyright Act* is built round the image of the freelance author who earns her living from her copyrights and who may, without conflict of interest, recycle them for different clients. Where this is not so in fact — for example, where the author develops a business product for a firm to use as its own in its business — courts often realign the legal position to give the client ownership, or at least liberal rights of use.[146] By contrast, the *Patent Act* starts with no presumption favouring the commissioned freelance inventor. It leaves his rights to be worked out entirely by provincial law. The firm that calls in a consultant to help with a problem will usually own the benefit of any invention he develops as a solution. This is especially likely where the consultant is given access to the firm's trade secrets or confidential information, or is employed to put into practice an idea that the firm has already partly developed. The firm will then be entitled to patent the invention. This *prima facie* position may, however, be modified by express or implied agreement. For example, the parties' understanding may be that the freelancer will share in

---

145 For example, *Comstock*, above note 139 at 55–56; *Greater Glasgow Health Board's Application* (1995), [1996] R.P.C. 207 at 222 (Pat. Ct.). Compare section E(2), "Ownership: Employees," in chapter 2; Y. Gendreau, "La titularité des droits sur les logiciels créés par un employé" (1995) 12 Can. Intell. Prop. Rev. 147 at 153ff.

146 See section E(5), "Changing Ownership and Implying Rights of Use," in chapter 2.

gains made from exploiting the patent or may himself also license the patent on paying the patentee a reasonable royalty. Such an understanding can be given legal effect.[147]

5) Co-owners

Provincial law also governs the incidents of ownership, since the *Act* is silent on them. Without agreement, co-owners can work the patent themselves for their own account and may, except in Quebec,[148] also assign their interest without their co-owners' consent. But a co-owner is entitled to object to dealings that affect its right to exclude, such as adding another permitted user. An assignment to more than one assignee or a licence to someone else to use the patent is void without the co-owners' consent.[149] A co-owner can sue third parties for infringement, but should recover monetary remedies only according to its interest. Thus, a half-owner gets a whole injunction and delivery up, but only half the damages or profits.[150]

6) Government Inventions

Governments and Crown corporations can own and acquire patents just as the private sector may. The federal government also owns inventions made by federal employees within the scope of their duties. Included are inventions made with government equipment or financial aid, or "result[ing] from" or "connected with" the employee's duties or employment; these are effectively compulsory takings, since the government does not have to pay the inventor a cent.[151] The government can, however, make a discretionary award or waive its ownership rights. In practice, departmental heads act on the advice of an interdepartmental Public Servants Inventions Committee. Since 1993 there have been no ceilings on the amounts of an award, ostensibly to encourage inventiveness and teamwork in the public service.

---

147 For example, *Goddin & Rennie's Application* (1995), [1996] R.P.C. 141 (Ct. Sess., Scot.).

148 *Marchand* v. *Péloquin* (1978), 45 C.P.R. (2d) 48 (Que. C.A.).

149 *Forget* v. *Specialty Tools of Canada Inc.* (1995), 62 C.P.R. (3d) 537 (B.C.C.A.).

150 Compare *Massie & Renwick Ltd.* v. *Underwriters' Survey Bureau Ltd.*, [1940] S.C.R. 218 at 243 (copyright); see section E(1)(c), "Joint Authors," in chapter 2.

151 *Public Servants Inventions Act*, R.S.C. 1985, c. P-32, s. 3; *Public Servants Inventions Regulations*, C.R.C. 1978, c. 1332; *Mansfield* v. *M.N.R.* (1962), 23 Fox Pat. C. 19 at 29 (Tax Appeal Bd.).

Federal employees or federal Crown corporation employees who invent instruments or munitions of war are bound to secrecy if the Ministry of National Defence decides that the invention should be assigned to it. This will certainly occur with inventions vital to Canada's defence, where publication would prejudice public safety. The specification and eventual patent may be kept secret, but good faith infringers cannot be sued and can be licensed if secrecy is lifted. Less coercive procedures apply to inventions relating to the production, application, or use of atomic energy. These go to the Atomic Energy Control Board before being laid open or examined by the PO.[152]

F. OWNER'S RIGHTS

The patentee has the exclusive right of "making, constructing and using the invention and selling it to others to be used."[153] Anyone doing any of these acts in Canada without the patentee's consent infringes the patent.

Since the right affects people's liberty to trade, one might expect the words "making, constructing" and so on to be carefully delineated so that anything done outside them would be lawful, however adverse its economic impact on the patentee.[154] Instead, Canadian courts often resort to U.K. precedents on quite different language. Pre-1978 U.K. patents let patentees "enjoy the whole profit and advantage . . . accruing by reason of the said invention." Everyone else was, by the language appearing in the patent itself, excluded "either directly or indirectly" from using the invention without consent. Moreover, the patent itself urged that it be "construed in the most beneficial sense for the advantage of the patentee." All this encouraged U.K. courts to construe the monopoly expansively. Canadian courts followed suit, even though the Canadian *Act* lacked the U.K. language.[155] Even today some courts mimic old British *dicta* to the effect that any act that "interferes with the full enjoyment" of the monopoly infringes.[156] This approach may have made

---

152   *P Act*, above note 1, ss. 20–22.

153   *P Act, ibid.*, s. 42.

154   *Paper Converting Machine Co.* v. *Magna-Graphics Corp.*, 745 F.2d 11 (Fed. Cir. 1984); A. Benyamini, *Patent Infringement in the European Community* (Weinheim, Germany: VCH, 1993) at 60, on European patents.

155   For example, *Colonial Fastener Co. Ltd.* v. *Lightning Fastener Co. Ltd.*, [1937] S.C.R. 36 at 40–41 [*Colonial*].

156   *Wellcome Foundation Ltd.* v. *Apotex Inc.* (1991), 39 C.P.R. (3d) 289 at 315 (Fed. T.D.), aff'd (*sub nom. Apotex Inc.* v. *Wellcome Foundation Ltd.*) (1995), 60 C.P.R. (3d) 135 at 153 (Fed. C.A.) [*Wellcome* v. *Apotex*].

sense when courts in Canada were controlled by the Privy Council in Westminster. The mainly British judges who sat on this court looked at Canadian patent law through British eyes. Today it is better simply to read and apply the words of the Canadian *Act* directly, presumably in a "fair, large and liberal" way so as to make the monopoly meaningful.[157] Otherwise, applying British glosses on one set of words to interpret a different set of words in a Canadian statute is otiose. U.K. jurisprudence need not be ignored, but neither need it be slavishly followed.

1) General

There are obvious overlaps in the broad language of the patent grant: "making, constructing and using the invention and selling it to others to be used." For example, to build a patented machine is to "make" or "construct" it, and also to "use" the invention. The common thread is that the activity is usually for commercial purposes — to make a profit or to further the actor's business interests, for the "market place is the sole preserve of the patentee."[158] Only activities the patentee ought to control or profit from can be stopped. To import a patented product for tinkering, or to copy a patented invention for research or experiment, should be acceptable in principle because patents are there to encourage knowledge to be disseminated and built on — and not just by patentees. Inventors may conceive or give birth to new technologies, but they cannot control how their brainchildren develop. Things change, however, the moment experiment stops and preparation for marketing starts, for this is commercial exploitation within the patentee's right to profit from ("use") its invention.[159] The operation of these particular rights will be examined against this background.

2) Use

"Use" includes operating a patented machine, working a patented process for business reasons, or even doing acts preparatory to selling a patented product. Mere possession may not be use, but a business that possesses a patented product for trade may be presumed either to have used it or to intend to use it, unless it shows the contrary. A carrier who trans-

---

157   *Interpretation Act*, R.S.C. 1985, c. I-21, s. 12.
158   *Smith Kline & French Laboratories Ltd. v. N.Z. (A.G.)*, [1991] 2 N.Z.L.R. 560 at 566 (C.A.).
159   See section H, "Users' Rights: Free Use," in this chapter.

ports another's article can successfully rebut the presumption that it is using the article.[160]

"Use" applies both to patented products and processes, and also to their output. A patent that covers a zipper-making machine or method extends to zippers made by the machine or method. Each zipper sold without authority infringes the patent, even if the zippers themselves are unpatented.[161] This expansive doctrine applies, however, only if the patent plays an important part in production. Just because a patented hammer beats out some machine part does not mean that the patentee has any recourse against the finished product.[162]

Where the product obtained from a patented process is itself new, there is a presumption that the same product from elsewhere has been made by the patented process. A defendant infringes unless it shows that its process was non-infringing.[163] The presumption applies whether the product is or is not patentable, or if any product claim is invalid. Whether the product is the "same" is decided robustly. Chemical compounds may still be the same even if their purity levels differ.[164]

3) Sale

Selling the patented product or process at any level of distribution is a right reserved to the patentee. A buyer from the patentee or authorized licensee may resell or do what it likes with the product or process, unless a restriction was validly imposed and clearly brought to the buyer's notice at the time of sale.[165] Otherwise, each unauthorized sale is itself an infringement. Suppose a manufacturer, without the right-holder's consent, sells a patented product to a distributor, who sells it to a retailer, who in turn sells it to a consumer, who uses the product: each seller infringes, as does the consumer by using the product, whether or not the parties know they are infringing. Selling the patented article in kit-set form for the buyer to assemble is also infringement.[166] But merely offering or advertising the product for sale may be permitted, for, if noti-

---

160 *Pfizer Corp. v. Minister of Health*, [1965] 1 All E.R. 450 (H.L.)[*Pfizer*].

161 *Colonial*, above note 155.

162 *Wilderman v. F.W. Berk & Co.*, [1925] Ch. 116 [*Wilderman*]. See section F(5), "Imports of Products of Patented Machines or Processes," in this chapter.

163 *P Act*, above note 1, s. 55.1.

164 *Wellcome v. Apotex*, above note 156.

165 *Eli Lilly & Co. v. Apotex Inc.* (1996), 66 C.P.R. (3d) 329 at 343 (Fed. C.A.); *National Phonograph Co. of Australia Ltd. v. Menck*, [1911] A.C. 336 (P.C.) [*Menck*]; *Roussel Uclaf S.A. v. Hockley International Ltd.*, [1996] R.P.C. 441 (Pat. Ct.).

166 *Trilantic*, above note 97.

fied, the offeror could withdraw the product from sale.[167] A patentee who reasonably fears that the offeror would disregard a notice may nonetheless be entitled to a *quia timet* injunction.

The sale must be made in Canada. A U.S. company that took orders from Canadian buyers and sold free on board from a U.S. source was therefore held not to infringe a Canadian patent. The sales contract was concluded in the United States and the property in the goods passed there to the buyer, so no "sale" occurred in Canada.[168] Of course, the buyer may in such a case infringe on importing the goods into Canada for sale. This, however, did not affect the U.S. seller's liability.

4) Imports

The *Act* does not explicitly grant an exclusive right to "import," so importing for a permissible purpose like private experiment or research is presumably lawful.[169] *Quia timet* or anticipatory relief may nevertheless be available against importers who intend to sell or use an imported item that, if made in Canada, would have infringed a Canadian patent.[170] Imports for later sale or distribution may be infringing "uses" as soon as the goods enter the country. The importer need not know or suspect anything about the circumstances of the foreign manufacture, which indeed may be lawful there.[171]

A patentee who owns patents for the same invention in Canada and another country may be unable to stop imports from that country, unless a condition restricting export was imposed at source. But if the foreign patent is owned by someone else, importing for sale or use may infringe the local patentee's rights. Multinational corporations that want to divide up markets by territory tend to ensure that foreign patents are owned by foreign subsidiaries.[172]

---

167 *Minter v. Williams* (1834), 1 Web. Pat. Cas. 135 (K.B.).

168 *Domco Industries Ltd. v. Mannington Mills Inc.* (1990), 29 C.P.R. (3d) 481 at 496 (Fed. C.A.), leaving open the question whether concluding the contract of sale in Canada may itself be a "sale" within the prohibition.

169 See section H(1), "Experiments and Research," in this chapter.

170 *Lido Industrial Products Ltd. v. Teledyne Industries Inc.* (1981), 57 C.P.R. (2d) 29 at 38 (Fed. C.A.).

171 *Pfizer*, above note 160; compare *North American Free Trade Agreement*, 17 December 1992 (Ottawa: Supply and Services, 1993), art. 1709(5) [*NAFTA*], *Agreement on Trade-Related Aspects of Intellectual Property Rights, Including Trade in Counterfeit Goods*, (1994) 25 I.I.C. 209, art. 28(1) [*TRIPs*]. Compare section G(10), "Distributing and Importing Infringing Copies," in chapter 2.

172 Compare W.L. Hayhurst, "Intellectual Property as a Non-Tariff Barrier in Canada, with Particular Reference to 'Grey Goods' and 'Parallel Imports'" (1990) 31 C.P.R. (3d) 289.

5) Imports of Products of Patented Machines or Processes

Products made using a patented machine or process infringe the patent, whether the machine is situated locally or abroad. A patent for a machine or a method for making, say, nails or zippers is therefore infringed when those products, made abroad by the machine or method, are imported for sale into Canada.[173] But furniture fastened by offending nails or clothing containing the offending zippers may be imported without infringing. The role the patent played is probably incidental or comparatively "unimportant or trifling" in the production of the finished article.[174]

Complexities arise, however, where a final product undergoes multiple stages of production, each stage being separately patented to a different owner. Can any one owner sue an importer of the final or intermediate product so long as its process is important and not "merely incidental" to its making? It seems so, even if the other patentees are indifferent to the importation.[175] The same may apply to a product patent for an intermediate. An imported derivative may infringe if it is in the same field. For example, an intermediate for making antibiotics may be infringed if the derivative is a medicine, but not if it is a glue.[176]

Cases like this raise problems that are insoluble through semantics or logical deduction. On the one hand, some flexibility is necessary to prevent process or intermediate product patents from being easily evaded by importers of partly processed goods for local finishing. On the other hand , the holder of a subsidiary patent should not have substantially better remedies against imported products than it would if the product were made locally. This thought prompted a British court, even before European patent law was applied in the United Kingdom, to react coolly to the way British law had developed until then. Perhaps it would be better if imported products had to meet the standard test for substantial infringement: Was the import a mere variant of the product resulting from the patented process or the intermediate? If so, it infringed; if not, it could lawfully be imported for sale.[177]

---

173   *United Horse-Shoe & Nail Co. Ltd.* v. *Stewart* (1888), 13 App. Cas. 401 (H.L.); *Colonial*, above note 155; *Halocarbon (Ont). Ltd.* v. *Farbwerke Hoechst AG*, [1974] 2 F.C. 266 (T.D.), uncontested on appeal (*sub nom. Farbwerke Hoechst AG* v. *Halocarbon (Ont.) Ltd.*), [1979] 2 S.C.R. 929 [*Farbwerke*].

174   *Wilderman*, above note 162 at 127.

175   *Wellcome* v. *Apotex*, above note 156, following *Saccharin Corp. Ltd.* v. *Anglo-Continental Chemical Works*, [1901] 1 Ch. 414.

176   *Beecham Group Ltd.* v. *Bristol Laboratories Ltd.* (1977), [1978] R.P.C. 153 at 204 (H.L.) [*Beecham*]. The majority, however, left the point open.

177   *Beecham, ibid.* at 201, as interpreted in *Catnic*, above note 120 at 243.

A Canadian court might well adopt this last approach. It is similar to the rule found in Europe and in *TRIPs,* where only products obtained directly from a patented process infringe.[178] By contrast, the U.S. law of 1988 excepts only products that are "materially changed by subsequent processes" or that become "a trivial and nonessential component of another product."[179] A U.S. process patent for treating textiles could extend to imported dresses made from the textile, while a European patent probably would not. The U.S. rule is as much a product of U.S. economic policy as the European rule is based on what Europeans perceive as beneficial to their economy. What rule is appropriate for Canada is less clear. The path of caution may be to follow the European rule, since that presumably compensates the patentee fairly, while not unduly extending the monopoly. If a wider rule was warranted, Parliament could enact it.

6) Substantial Infringement

Assume that a prohibited act — making, selling, using, etc. — has occurred without a patentee's consent. We must still ask whether this happened in relation to a claim in the patent. Was a claimed product sold? Was a claimed process used?

This question may be easy to answer where the claims are crystal clear and the defendant's activity falls dead centre within them. More often the claims are opaque or the defendant's activity is off centre, sometimes even improving the patented invention. The patentee will then assert that the defendant substantially infringed by doing much the same thing in much the same way to achieve the same result.[180] Or, as it is sometimes put, did the defendant take the invention's "essence" or "pith and marrow"? If successful, the patentee gets not only the usual remedies for infringement but also the use of the defendant's improvements, at least if they are unpatented.

Whether a defendant has substantially infringed in this way used to be a question of fact and degree for the jury.[181] A number of factors,

---

178   *EPC*, above note 28, art. 64(2); *TRIPS*, above note 171, art. 28(1)(b).

179   *Patents Act*, 1988, above note 25, §§ 154 & 271(g).

180   *McPhar Engineering Co. v. Sharpe Instruments Ltd.* (1960), [1956–1960] Ex.C.R. 467, following *Graver Tank & Manufacturing Co. Inc. v. Linde Air Products Co.*, 339 U.S. 605 (1950).

181   This process continues to be U.S. law. Claim interpretation is a question of law for the judge; whether the defendant infringed, substantially or otherwise, is a question of fact for the jury: *Markman v. Westview Instruments Inc.*, 116 S.Ct. 1384 (1996); *Hilton-Davis Chemical Co. v. Warner-Jenkinson Co. Inc.*, 62 F.3d 1512 (Fed. Cir. 1995), cert. granted 116 S.Ct. 1014 (1996) [*Hilton-Davis*].

rather like those relevant to substantial infringement in copyright cases,[182] could be taken into account. The crucial difference, of course, was that patents had claims. From the late nineteenth century, the presence of claims started having more influence on findings of substantial infringement, especially as juries were removed from the scene. Judges tried, through legal tests, to bring order and structure out of the disorder and uncertainty of verdicts that may have depended as much on whether the defendant had or had not behaved decently as on what the patent was actually for. This movement had its zenith in 1981 when the House of Lords pronounced that substantial infringement depended solely on what the claims, properly construed, covered. The dichotomy between substantial and literal infringement was false: either there was infringement or there was not.[183] The supposed objectivity of semantics would replace the subjectivity that multifactor analysis too often entailed. With the better way now pointed out to them, Canadian and other Commonwealth courts dutifully adhered to the new faith.[184]

If certainty was the quest, semantics has proved a false grail. This result can best be understood through a simple, hypothetical example. Suppose there is a new recipe for making beef stew. The patentee claims a method that involves adding spices to the chopped meat and vegetables and then cooking the contents in a container in a standard oven for 2 hours at 150°C. An imitator who cooks for 2 hours 1 minute at 149°C clearly infringes. Nobody anywhere has difficulty dubbing this imitation a "colourable" difference or evasion, an "obvious mechanical equivalent," a "sharp practice," or even a "fraud on the patent," to quote just some of the vituperations in which judges have indulged. But suppose someone cooked the mixture for 1 hour at 225°C? Or used lamb instead of beef? Or omitted spices altogether? Or did all three in combination? Do any of these actions infringe?

Courts everywhere have struggled to explain whether and why this activity should or should not be an infringement. The results are inevitably inconsistent.[185] To see why, let us assume that the defendant followed our hypothetical patent precisely, except that she cooked the mixture for 1 hour at 225°C. Something like the following analytical framework may then be used to decide infringement:

---

182   See section G(9), "Substantial Infringement," in chapter 2.

183   *Catnic*, above note 120.

184   For example, *Hercules*, above note 134 at 488.

185   Compare A.M. Soobert, "Analyzing Infringement by Equivalents: A Proposal to Focus the Scope of International Patent Protection" (1996) 22 Rutgers Comp. & Tech. L.J. 189.

- First, isolate what the defendant did. Here she followed the patent, except for the variation of cooking the mixture 50 percent hotter for 50 percent of the time.
- Second, read the patent claim and ask: Do the defendant's acts fall literally within it? If yes, she infringes and that is the end of the case. The answer here, however, is no. Cooking for 1 hour at 225°C is clearly different from cooking for 2 hours at 150°C. So now:
- Does this difference "materially affect" how the invention works? If yes, the defendant does not infringe; if no, she may, depending on further analysis.

Here the difference probably does not materially affect how the invention works. The defendant does everything else the same: ingredients, equipment, heating, object of the exercise. Cooking at higher heats for shorter periods can, within limits, give the same result as cooking lower for longer. The defendant's method may be an improvement because the meal is prepared more quickly, but this feature does not matter: the same principle (tenderizing the meat, amalgamating and heating the ingredients to make an attractive dish) is used.

But this is only a probable answer. It is certainly arguable that reducing cooking time as dramatically as by half is a material difference. Much depends on the level of abstraction chosen. Does the patent cover a method simply of cooking, or of cooking at moderate heat? If the former, the difference between the patent and the impugned acts may be immaterial. If the latter, the difference may be very material. On questions like this, different courts have reached diametrically opposite results on the same patent.[186]

Let us accept for argument's sake that the defendant may have infringed. We must then ask two further questions:

- Would the lack of material difference be obvious to someone skilled in the art at the patent's claim date? If no, there is no infringement; if yes, there may be. Let us say yes, for argument's sake: a professional chef would likely know that cooking food hotter for a shorter time would yield the same result. So the final question must be asked.
- Did the patentee intend exact compliance with her claim to be an essential part of her invention? More precisely, would a skilled reader reading the claim in the context of the whole patent have understood

---

186   *Improver Corp.* v. *Remington Consumer Products Ltd.* (1989), [1990] F.S.R. 181 at 191–92 (Pat. Ct.) [*Improver* v. *Remington*]; *Improver Corp.* v. *Raymond Industrial Ltd.* (1989), [1990] F.S.R. 421 at 431–33 (H.K.S.C.).

the patentee was excluding immaterial differences? If yes, the defendant has not infringed; if no, she has.[187]

The virtuosity of this analytical method can only be admired. And yet, after all of it, we may still be unable to say definitively whether the defendant did or did not infringe our hypothetical cooking patent: any test that depends on divining what any inventor objectively intended to claim remains inherently uncertain. It is just a different sort of uncertainty; perhaps appeal courts find it easier to "correct" this supposed question of law than to work through an amorphous multifactor analysis that tries to balance the comparative merits of the particular patentee and defendant. Under the semantic analysis, whether the defendant knew of the patent or acted independently is irrelevant — although even now some courts cannot refrain from mentioning it as some sort of justification whenever they read a patent expansively. Bromides on construction — for example, we must construe patents in a way that is "neither benevolent nor harsh" but "reasonable and fair to both patentee and public"[188] — take us little further. Perhaps it is "reasonable and fair" to inquire whether the advance was a pioneering invention, producing a new result on new principles, or a mere improvement patent. The former may then be construed more benevolently than the latter, which may be tied down strictly to the particular method.[189]

Beyond this point, all seems indeterminate. That the patentee did not expressly say in its claim that cooking "substantially" or "approximately" for 2 hours at 150°C was covered is not in itself fatal, since a skilled reader supposedly can supply all the necessary adverbs. One is invited to speculate why immaterial variants might be excluded. Perhaps a skilled reader might conclude that the inventor did not know that heating temperatures could be radically increased with the same result. Perhaps the inventor might know that they could be increased, but deliberately confined herself to a narrow range lest stipulating more widely might make her invention old or obvious. Perhaps the inventor, for some reason unfathomable to the skilled reader (who is supposed to be unversed in patent law), deliberately chose to limit her claims, maybe to get a quicker and easier ride through the PO. The more plausible such

---

187   *Catnic*, above note 120 at 242–44, as explained in *Improver v. Remington, ibid.* at 189; *Wyeth-Ayerst Canada Inc. v. Canada (Minister of National Health & Welfare)* (1996), 67 C.P.R. (3d) 417 at 421–22 (Fed. T.D.).

188   *Consolboard*, above note 105 at 520; compare *Kastner v. Rizla Ltd.*, [1995] R.P.C. 585 at 593 (C.A.)

189   *Proctor v. Bennis* (1887), 36 Ch.D. 740 (C.A.).

speculations become, the more likely the claims may be "construed" to exclude immaterial differences.[190]

The goal of greater certainty has, therefore, not been attained. Courts end up reaching inconsistent results even on the same patent.[191] The foreign corporations that hold most Canadian patents are hardly perturbed, since uncertainty works for them when royalties in lieu of litigation are demanded. Local competitors pay up or try to steer clear of shifting perimeters of variable width.

A doctrine of substantial infringement may be a necessary safeguard against "sharp practice," as when 2 hours 1 minute heating time at 149°C is substituted for the claimed 2 hours at 150°C. This hardly justifies the present expansive and uncertain doctrine.[192] After all, patentees and their advisers write their own claims, invariably drafted as broadly as their invention. The document is often peppered with general language: "substantially" this and "approximately" that. Indeed, unchecked by a PO examiner, patentees might claim the moon and beyond. Mistaken underclaims have long been correctable through reissue, but then the rights of those who may have relied on the narrower grant are safeguarded. This protection is not achieved by the *ex post* "construction" courts put on claims years after the event at trial. Ultimately, a patentee who fails to write its claims "clearly and distinctly" (as the *Act* requires) to cover an activity has only itself and its advisers to blame. It should not ask a court's help to construe ("rewrite") claims *ex post facto* to cover something not earlier thought of or expressed.

G. INVALIDITY

Patents are invalid for "any fact or default which by this Act *or by law* renders the patent void."[193] The words "by this Act" have given little difficulty. They include explicit provisions that say non-compliance makes

---

190 *Eli Lilly & Co.* v. *O'Hara Manufacturing Ltd.* (1989), 26 C.P.R. (3d) 1 at 7 (Fed. C.A.); *Improver* v. *Remington*, above note 186 at 197; *Optical Coating Laboratory Inc.* v. *Pilkington P.E. Ltd.*, [1995] R.P.C. 145 at 158–59 (C.A.).

191 See the *Improver* cases, above note 186, where the same consumer device did not infringe a European patent in the United Kingdom and Hong Kong (for different reasons), but infringed in Germany and elsewhere in Europe, all courts supposedly applying the same test: *PLG Research Ltd.* v. *Ardon International Ltd.* (1994), [1995] F.S.R. 116 at 129–33 (C.A.).

192 Compare *Hilton-Davis*, above note 181.

193 *P Act*, above note 1, s. 59 [emphasis added].

a patent void: for example, where the petition contains an untrue "material allegation" or the specification is deliberately misleading.[194] Courts have also held that the *Act* implicitly renders the patent void for other defaults: for example, where there is no "invention" at all; where the invention is not new, properly disclosed, or useful; or where the claims are ambiguous or overbroad.

These examples do not exhaust the possibilities. The words "by law" emphasized above suggest there may be common law grounds for invalidity outside the *Act's* four corners.[195] The grounds are not raised much nowadays either because they are overlooked or because they overlap with grounds in the *Act* itself. A patent may be granted for an invention patented earlier ("double-patenting"). It may be granted for a broader and different invention than originally applied for. The grant may be tainted by lies in the application process which led to a favourable exercise of discretion. All these defaults may by law make a patent void, even though the *Act* says nothing about them.[196] The categories of invalidity "by law" may indeed not be closed. Any substantial and serious enough reason may do. Suppose, for example, that a microbiological invention can be worked only by using samples of the culture referred to in the patent. A patentee who does not make samples available for experiment when the specification is published has not given the public a key part of what a patent is granted for. This may be enough to avoid the patent, since the common law is "sufficiently flexible for the court to be able to formulate a new ground of repeal or revocation to meet a new situation."[197]

Complex arguments about interpretation or invalidity can theoretically be avoided by showing that a user is doing something that was not new at the claim date. Suppose the user can point to a piece of prior art — a patent, publication, or device — that discloses the same activity that the user is pursuing. Or suppose the user shows that its activity is just an obvious mechanical equivalent or improvement of the prior art. Logically, then, the user cannot be infringing. Either the patent sued on must be anticipated or obvious, or its claims do not cover the user's

---

194   *P Act, ibid.*, s. 53(1); see section A(5), "The Application Must Be Truthful," in this chapter.

195   W.L. Hayhurst, "Grounds for Invalidating Patents" (1975) 18 C.P.R. (2d) 222, provides an enlightening discussion.

196   *R. v. Mussary* (1738), 1 Web. Pat. Cas. 41 (K.B.); *Martin*, above note 9 at 222–23; *Prestige*, above note 22.

197   *Re American Cyanamid Co. (Dann's) Patent* (1970), [1971] R.P.C. 425 at 436 (H.L.).

activities. Whatever the reason, there can be no infringement. This way of running a case even has a name: the *Gillette* defence.[198] It supposedly saves costs, but few lawyers are brave enough to run it as their sole defence. One must be very sure of a holeproof basket before putting all one's eggs in it.

H. USERS' RIGHTS: FREE USE

Anyone can work an invalid patent. For valid patents, fairly liberal exemptions are, as for copyrights, allowed by international law.[199] Some exemptions in Canadian law are statutory.[200] Others arise from the limits judges have put on the words "make, use, construct," and so on, of the patent monopoly. As with copyrights, these exemptions let some "fair uses" occur, so the patent laws, like those of copyright, do not become "instruments of oppression and extortion."[201]

1) Experiments and Research

A major purpose of the patent law is to disclose technology for others to experiment with and build on, perhaps even themselves obtaining patents for advances in the art. Any use, manufacture, construction, or sale "solely" for experiments that "relate to the subject-matter of the patent" may be permitted.[202] A product may be made or a process may be used on a small scale if the defendant's purpose is to evaluate whether or how the invention works.[203] Acts beyond that, however, infringe. Thus, sales or purchases "on approval," where no payment is owed unless the product or process works, infringe.[204]

---

198 After *Gillette Safety Razor Co.* v. *Anglo-American Trading Co. Ltd.* (1913), 30 R.P.C. 465 at 480–81 (H.L.), where it was authoritatively expounded.

199 *NAFTA*, above note 171, art. 1709(6); *TRIPs*, above note 171, art. 30.

200 Including perhaps experiments and private non-commercial use, recognized in a backhand way in s. 55.2(6) of the *P Act*, above note 1, which says "[f]or greater certainty" that the specific exemption in s. 55.2(1) relating to obtaining official product approval "does not affect any exception" to a patent "that exists at law" for experiments and private non-commercial use.

201 *Canadian Assn. of Broadcasters* v. *Society of Composers, Authors & Music Publishers of Canada* (1994), 58 C.P.R. (3d) 190 at 196 (Fed. C.A.); *Micro Chemicals Ltd.* v. *Smith Kline & French Inter-American Corp.* (1971), [1972] S.C.R. 506 [*Micro*].

202 *P Act*, above note 1, s. 55.2(b). Compare *Patents Act*, above note 28, s. 60(5), (6).

203 *Muntz*, above note 138 at 101.

204 *Proctor* v. *Bayley* (1888), 6 R.P.C. 106 at 109 (Ch.), appeal dismissed (1889), 6 R.P.C. 538 (C.A.).

Experimental activities that, pre-patent, would not prevent its grant[205] are presumably also allowable post-patent. This does not, however, cover the full extent of the exemption. Experiments for "the gratification of scientific tastes, or for curiosity, or for amusement" may also be allowed.[206] So may experiments to test the patent, to see whether it may be improved, or even to see whether the user can make a quality commercial product according to the specification, if done in good faith and not to make money from the experiment.[207] Similarly, field tests to discover a product's unknown properties, to test a hypothesis, or to discover "whether something which is known to work in specific conditions, e.g. of soil or weather, will work in different conditions," are acceptable. Tests to demonstrate a product to a prospective customer are not.[208] *Quia timet* relief is available against the impending commercialization of an experimental use.[209]

2) Government Product Approval

Many products (e.g., medicine, chemicals, and explosives) cannot be made or sold without prior government approval for public safety or health reasons. It may be helpful or even necessary to use something patented to develop and submit information to solicit approval. The *Act* allows a patent to be employed for uses reasonably related to these purposes. The approval may be needed by federal, provincial, or foreign law (e.g., for exports from Canada) and can relate to any product, not just the one the patent is used for.[210] This exemption, however, applies only to products, not to methods or processes.

3) Stockpiling

Competitors are often impatient to work the invention as soon as the patent expires. They can buy or make the separate elements of a patented combination and ready it for assembly without infringing, but

---

205 See section C(1)(d), "Experimental Uses," in this chapter.
206 *Roche Products Ltd.* v. *Bolar Pharmaceutical Co. Inc.*, 733 F. 2d 858 at 862 (Fed. Cir. 1984).
207 *Micro*, above note 201. Compare *Integrated Circuit Topography Act*, S.C. 1990, c. 37, s. 6(2)(a) [*ICT Act*], allowing making or copying of topographies for research and analysis; *Dableh*, above note 113.
208 *Monsanto Co.* v. *Stauffer Chemical Co.*, [1985] R.P.C. 515 at 542 (C.A.); *Upjohn Co.* v. *T. Kerfoot & Co. Ltd.* (1987), [1988] F.S.R. 1 (Pat. Ct.).
209 *Cochlear Corp.* v. *Cosem Neurostim Ltée* (1995), 64 C.P.R. (3d) 10 (Fed. T.D.).
210 *P Act*, above note 1, s. 55.2(1).

they cannot make the product or machine and then stockpile it to be ready for sale or use the minute the patent expires. Making and selling are independent rights granted only to the patentee. Since patentees need time to market the invention after the patent application is filed, some think it only fair that competitors should be similarly handicapped when the patent expires, so the patentee benefits from as much of the twenty-year term as it can. Competitors who rush ahead can be enjoined.[211]

An exception exists for patented products (not processes) that fall within the government approval exemption.[212] Provided regulatory approval is required and sought, this material may be stockpiled for immediate sale once the patent expires.[213] This exemption, like the one for government approvals, was enacted in 1993 as part of the provisions that eliminated compulsory licensing for medicines. It provides that stockpiling must occur "during the applicable period provided for by the regulations."[214] This does not imply that the issue of regulations is a precondition to the operation of the exemption. The only regulations to date apply to patented medicines, so other material may apparently be stockpiled without constraint pending government approval.

The exemption is today regularly used by generic drug makers who can, during the patent period, apply for regulatory approval, with supporting samples, and stockpile the drug for sale once the patent expires. However, Health and Welfare Canada cannot issue a notice of compliance, allowing the drug to be sold, until the patent expires.[215] A generic drug maker may ask for earlier approval if it alleges that the patent is invalid or expired or if its proposed manufacture would not infringe. The patentee can stop an early notice, if the allegations are not "justified," by asking the Federal Court for an order of prohibition against Health and Welfare. The court proceedings should normally be decided within thirty months, so this is no substitute for the full-scale trial on infringement or validity that the parties can resort to in parallel proceedings. If the court agrees that the allegations are not justified, it will prohibit the immediate issue of the notice of compliance.

---

211 *Procter & Gamble Inc.* v. *Colgate-Palmolive Canada Inc.* (1995), 61 C.P.R. (3d) 160 (Fed. T.D.).

212 See section H(2), "Government Product Approval," in this chapter.

213 *P Act*, above note 1, s. 55.2(2).

214 *P Act, ibid.*

215 *P Act, ibid.*, s. 55.1(2)–(5); *Patented Medicines (Notice of Compliance) Regulations*, SOR/93–133, s. 7(1)–(2).

The system has engendered a raft of litigation seeking to test every possible loophole.[216] The decades-old enmity between proprietary and generic drug companies has found a new battlefield.

4) Private Non-commercial Use

Acts "done privately" either "on a non-commercial scale" or "for a non-commercial purpose" are apparently allowed.[217] This reflects a common law exemption, dating back to the nineteenth century, which permitted patents to be used not only for experiments but for private amusement or for making models.[218] Presumably, today, a parent could make a stroller for her child or children without worrying about patent infringement. Presumably, too, any private individual could act similarly to benefit herself, her family, and her immediate friends. But once word of her aptitude in making strollers got around and her private hobby started becoming a cottage industry supplying remoter friends and neighbours, her activities would come under the patent.

The exemption may also benefit some business activities. It contemplates that private acts, though done for a commercial purpose, may occur on a non-commercial scale and still be exempted. Whether businesses will be treated as generously as private individuals may, however, be doubted.[219] If a patented product imported by a private individual was allowed as a private non-commercial act,[220] it does not follow that a business could import a major piece of capital plant and claim exemption on the basis that buying one unit is acting on a non-commercial scale. Whether it could import the occasional piece of furniture for its office from an offshore mail-order house is equally doubtful. Viewed in isolation, the purchase is on a non-commercial scale, but, if many businesses bought like this, a local patentee could be seriously prejudiced. A court may welcome Parliament's recognition that businesses can, like individuals, sometimes be entitled to an exemption. It may, however,

---

216   *Eli Lilly & Co. v. Novopharm* (1995), 60 C.P.R. (3d) at 427–30 (Fed. T.D.), summarizes the principles to date.

217   *P Act*, above note 1, s. 55.2(6) (the French version is clearer than the English); similarly the *ICT Act*, above note 207, s. 6(2)(d). In Europe too, "[acts] done privately and for purposes which are not commercial" are exempt: compare *Patents Act*, above note 28, s. 60(5)(a).

218   *Jones v. Pearce* (1832), 1 Web. Pat. Cas. 122 at 125 (K.B.).

219   *P Act*, above note 1, section 55.2(6), refers to any exception "that exists at law" and is said to be inserted "[f]or greater certainty."

220   Contrary to *United Telephone Co. v. Sharples* (1885), 29 Ch.D. 164 [*Sharples*].

draw the line at the point where the user's activity deprives the patentee of a sale or licence fee that the patentee ought fairly to have.[221]

5) Education

A nineteenth-century English case holds that importing an infringing product to train the importer's potential employees or apprentices on its workings infringed the patent.[222] The training there was for the employer's business purposes, so the case leaves open whether uses for non-profit educational purposes infringe. Canadian courts could develop an exception covering educational uses, along the lines that the *Integrated Circuit Topography Act* provides for topographies. The *ICT Act* prohibits import or commercial exploitation, but making or copying the topography to teach others or oneself is allowed, even where the teaching is for profit.[223]

6) Repairs and Modifications

A patented article may be repaired, modified, or customized without infringement. Extensive repairs or changes that amount to reconstructing the article substantially, however, infringe the patentee's right to "make" or "construct" the invention.[224] Whether an activity is repair or modification, on the one hand, or reconstruction, on the other, is a factual issue that depends on what the patent claims, the nature of the patented article, and the character of the work done on it. Refilling a patented printer cartridge with toner and necessarily replacing any worn parts may be repair. Replacing the whole cartridge is not: "the office boy does [not] repair the water cooler when he replaces the empty water bottle with a new one."[225]

---

221   Compare topography rights, where private copying or making for non-commercial purposes is exempted, but importing or commercial exploitation is not: *ICT Act*, above note 207, ss. 6(2)(d) & 3(2).

222   *Sharples*, above note 220.

223   *ICT Act*, above note 207, ss. 6(2)(a) & 3(2).

224   *British Leyland Motor Corp. Ltd. v. Armstrong Patents Co. Ltd.*, [1986] A.C. 577 (H.L.).

225   *Canon Kabushiki Kaisha v. Green Cartridge Co. (Hong Kong) Ltd.*, [1995] F.S.R. 877 at 900 (H.K.S.C.), rev'd on other grounds (*sub nom. Green Cartridge Co. (Hong Kong) Ltd. v. Canon Kabushiki Kaisha*) (1996), 34 I.P.R. 614 at 630 (H.K.C.A.); *Solar Thomson Engineering Co. Ltd. v. Barton*, [1977] R.P.C. 537 at 555 (C.A.); *Hazel Grove (Superleague) Ltd. v. Euro-League Leisure Products Ltd.*, [1995] R.P.C. 529 at 540–41 (Pat. Co. Ct.). See also section D(2), "Whom to Sue," in chapter 5.

The public has a strong interest in saving scarce resources, in having a strong competitive aftermarket in reconditioning and reselling used goods and in providing unpatented replacement parts, and in counteracting strategies for built-in obsolescence that many manufacturers practise. This interest was recognized as far back as the 1930s, when automobile spark-plug manufacturers failed to close down an industry in reconditioning the plugs. The work was there labelled repair rather than reconstruction.[226] Perhaps the ultimate question is whether, in the light of the public interests noted, the patentee has been unfairly deprived of a sale.

It is an interesting question whether the patentee can stop or control repairs or changes short of reconstruction by restrictions notified to the buyer on the initial sale.[227] In the United States and Europe, patentees cannot control the aftermarket because their rights are exhausted in respect of a product on first sale, on which they get their full profit. Although this idea may apply in Canada in respect of trade-marked goods,[228] the pre-*EPC* British theory that a buyer's right to repair depends on an implied licence from the patentee has been followed for patents in Canada.[229] This practice suggests that Canadian patentees may indeed modify or eliminate the implied licence. No good reason (other than maximizing profits beyond what a U.S. or European patentee can earn) exists why Canadian patentees deserve this advantage. If this rule represents Canadian law, the only legal curbs on a patentee's power to control the aftermarket in these respects are the weak laws on anti-competitive practices and patent abuse.[230]

7) Visiting Ships, Aircraft, and Vehicles

A patent is not infringed if the invention is employed exclusively for the needs of a ship, vessel, aircraft, or land vehicle that enters Canada temporarily or accidentally, but goods cannot be manufactured on the craft for sale in or export from Canada.[231] The "needs" of the craft go beyond the bare necessities of navigation and should cover equipment adapted for the craft involved — for example, pipe-laying equipment for a pipe-

---

226 *A.C. Spark Plug Co. v. Canadian Spark Plug Service*, [1935] Ex.C.R. 57 [*A.C.*]. (trade-marks).

227 Buyers and sub-buyers are bound only by those restrictions brought to their attention at the time they acquire the patented material: *Menck*, above note 165.

228 *A.C.*, above note 226.

229 *Rucker Co. v. Gavel's Vulcanizing Ltd.* (1985), 7 C.P.R. (3d) 294 (Fed. T.D.).

230 See section I(2), "Abuse," in this chapter.

231 *P Act*, above note 1, s. 23.

laying ship. But if the ship starts using such equipment in Canadian waters, its presence here presumably will no longer qualify as "temporar[y] or accident[al]" and the exemption will not apply.[232]

8) Existing Uses

Suppose A makes or uses an invention B later patents. Had A's invention become publicly available, B's patent is invalid for lack of novelty.[233] But A may have kept its use out of the public eye. Can the use continue despite B's patent?

The answer is a qualified yes. As in many other systems, good-faith acquirers or independent inventors are personally protected in respect of acts done before a patent's claim date. If, before then, A "purchased, constructed or acquired" anything that later fell within a patent claim, A can keep using or selling the specific thing. A cannot, however, expand its use by "making" or "constructing" fresh examples.[234] If A built or bought a machine or used a process at the claim date, A can keep using it and using and selling its output despite the patent; but no further machine can be built if the patent claims a machine.[235] Goods are "purchased" or "acquired" where the buyer became their owner before the claim date. Goods then in an undeliverable state and (apparently) future or unascertained goods therefore infringe the patent, even though an agreement to buy was concluded before the claim date.[236]

The exemption protects good-faith acquirers, inventors, and investors against adverse claims. The idea is not to make lawful acts retrospectively unlawful. Nor does it seem right that A has to pay a patentee for teaching A something that A already knew and used. But the exemption has its rough edges. It has been applied to goods still outside Canada at the claim date, but not to offshore processes or their products. So while A can continue using a process worked in Canada and selling its output, the same does not apply to an offshore process. A cannot start

---

232 Benyamini, above note 154 at 283–86.

233 See section C(1), "Novelty," in this chapter.

234 *P Act*, above note 1, s. 56(1). The relevant date used to be when the specification was published (before 1989, when the patent first issued). Post-*NAFTA*, this date became the claim date. Pre-1994 patents are governed by the relevant pre-1994 law: ss. 56(2)–56(4), R.S.C. 1985, c. P-4, prior to amendment by *NAFTA* I A, above note 32.

235 *Libbey-Owens-Ford Glass Co.* v. *Ford Motor Co.*, [1969] 1 Ex.C.R. 529, aff'd [1970] S.C.R. 833.

236 *Merck & Co.* v. *Apotex Inc.*, [1995] 2 F.C. 723 (C.A.); compare *Barber* v. *Goldie Construction Co. Ltd.*, [1936] O.W.N. 384 (C.A.) (contract to built bridge exempt).

using a process in Canada even if **A** or anyone else worked it abroad before the claim date, and, apparently, **A** has to cease importing for use or sale products made by the process.[237]

I. USERS' RIGHTS: PAYING USE

1) Government Use

Before *NAFTA*, the *Patent Act* did not bind either the federal or the provincial governments. The federal government could use a patent whenever it wanted, but had to pay reasonable compensation as fixed by the Commissioner of Patents. This immunity disappeared in 1994. The federal and provincial governments are now bound by the *Act*.[238] To use a patent, they must usually first negotiate with the patentee. Only if this does not work can they then apply to the Commissioner for a non-exclusive right to use the invention domestically.[239] Negotiations can be skipped only for "public non-commercial" uses — for example, building a bridge where any tolls only amortize building and finance costs. Governments may even have to apply to the Commissioner for authority in cases of national emergency or extreme urgency;[240] but in real life it is hard to imagine a government sending its lawyers off to the PO before dealing with a life-threatening situation.

The patentee is entitled to "adequate" remuneration, as fixed by the Commissioner, presumably what sum a willing licensor and licensee would notionally have agreed for Canadian rights.[241] The licence will be tailored in scope and duration to the government's necessities, but can, on the patentee's request, be terminated when the government no longer needs it.[242]

2) Abuse

Patents in Canada have never been granted unconditionally. If a patentee abuses its rights, the patent can be compulsorily licensed to others at a reasonable royalty or, as a last resort, may be revoked. Patent abuses

---

237   *Farbwerke*, above note 173.

238   *P Act*, above note 1, s. 2.1.

239   *P Act*, *ibid.*, ss. 19(1), (2)(b) & (c); s. 19.1(1) & (6).

240   *P Act*, *ibid.*, s. 19.1(2).

241   *P Act*, *ibid.*, s. 19(4); *Re Pathfinder Camping Products Ltd.* (1982), 65 C.P.R. (2d) 119 (Commissioner of Patents).

242   *P Act*, *ibid.*, ss. 19(2)(a) &19(5).

may also violate the provisions of the *Competition Act* and can be stopped by the Competition Tribunal, or may sometimes even constitute torts against affected competitors.

Patentees have always fought the idea that they should somehow be accountable for how they choose to use or not use the "property" they have bought from the PO. Does the state tell landowners to work their land on pain of forfeiture or the imposition of a compulsory lease? Perhaps in some backward countries where the patent system is equally backward, but not Canada. Why should patentees be worse off than landowners? The obvious answer is that there is property and property. What is historically and socially acceptable for land may not be so for patents. Historically, patents from earliest times were granted to encourage new industry and to improve the community's quality of life through the availability of new technologies. Full disclosure by publishing the specification at the PO, though important, came only in the nineteenth century and, without practical deployment of the new technology, was but a modest benefit.

From Confederation until very recently — in fact until *NAFTA* — Canada's explicit policy was to encourage local manufacture of patented products. Until the 1930s the patentee could meet local demand through imports for a maximum of two years only. Local manufacture had to commence within that period, with a possibility of extension. Local licensing on reasonable terms became an option from the turn of the twentieth century. Non-compliance would invalidate the patent. Thus the Bell Telephone Co.'s telephone patent was revoked in 1885 when the minister of agriculture determined that local assembly of telephones from U.S.-made parts did not qualify as local manufacture.[243] The policy was refined in the patent revision of 1935. Failure to work or license a patent became one of a list of specified "abuse[s]" of patent rights, but revocation was now a last resort. The standard remedy was compulsory licensing at a reasonable royalty if the Commissioner of Patents found an abuse proved. Proceedings were initiated by any "interested" person (typically an intending competitor) or the attorney general of Canada, and the Commissioner's actions were appealable to the exchequer (now the federal) court.[244]

This is essentially the system in force today. It has been only moderately successful. The threat of intervention has not scared many patentees off. Proceedings have been prolonged and expensive; appeals are

---

243 *Re Bell Telephone Co.* (1885), 9 O.R. 339 (C.P.).
244 *The Patent Act*, 1935, S.C. 1935, ss. 65–70.

de rigueur; patentees, when alerted, often correct the abuse and retaliate against offending applicants. Of the fifty-three applicants who persisted between 1935 and 1970, only eleven got relief.[245] Today hardly anybody bothers trying: since *NAFTA,* patentees can manufacture abroad as they like and can meet local demand entirely through imports. A made-in-Canada for-Canada policy extant since Confederation has been completely reversed.[246] Only four things remain as abuses:

- failure to meet local demand for a patented article on reasonable terms;
- prejudice to an existing or future local trade or industry because a patentee is not granting licences on reasonable terms, and it is in the public interest to grant licences;
- unfair prejudice to local trade or industry because of conditions attached by a patentee;
- prejudice to the manufacture, use, or sale of unpatented materials used in a process or a process-dependent product patent occurring because, for instance, a patentee is compelling licensees to buy unpatented material from the patentee.[247]

Ironically, patentees probably have more to fear from U.S. law than from Canadian law, since U.S. courts have little compunction in applying U.S. anti-trust law extraterritorially. U.S. corporations, whose Canadian subsidiaries had used their patents to exclude competing imports into Canada, were enjoined from participating in this conspiracy to violate U.S. anti-trust law and were liable for treble damages to the injured competitor. Prohibitions on exports imposed on U.S. licensees may also be an abuse that prevents enforcement of the U.S. patent.[248]

---

245   Economic Council of Canada, *Report on Intellectual and Industrial Property* (Ottawa: Information Canada, 1971) at 67–68.

246   *Patent Act*, R.S.C. 1985, ss. 65(2)(a)–(b) & 65(4), as rep. by *NAFTA I A*, above note 32, s. 196.

247   *P Act*, above note 1, s. 68(2).

248   *Zenith Radio Corp.* v. *Hazeltine Research Inc.*, 395 U.S. 100 (1969).

FURTHER READINGS

Canadian

ALBERTA LAW REFORM INSTITUTION, *Trade Secrets* (Edmonton: The Institute, 1986)

BOCHNOVIC, J., *The Inventive Step: Its Evolution in Canada, the United Kingdom, and the United States* (Weinheim, Germany: Verlag Chemie, 1982), IIC Studies in International Property & Copyright Law No. 5

CANADIAN INTELLECTUAL PROPERTY OFFICE, *Manual of Patent Office Practice* (Hull: CIPO, 1 October 1996), available for downloading at http://info.ic.gc.ca/ic-data/marketplace/cipo/prod_ser/download/mopop/mopop-e.html

CRUCIBLE GROUP, THE, *People, Plants and Patents: The Impact of Intellectual Property on Biodiversity, Conservation, Trade, and Rural Society* (Ottawa: International Development Research Centre, 1994)

FOX, H.G., *The Canadian Law of Patents* (Toronto: Carswell, 1969)

HAYHURST, W.L., "Grounds for Invalidating Patents" (1975) 18 C.P.R. (2d) 222

HAYHURST, W.L., "Survey of Canadian Law: Industrial Property — Part I" (1983) 15 Ottawa L. Rev. 38

HENDERSON, G.F., ed., *Patent Law of Canada* (Toronto: Carswell, 1994)

HUGHES, R.T. & J.H. WOODLEY, *Patents* (Toronto: Butterworths, 1984) (updated annually)

HUGHES, R.T., ed., *Trade Secrets* (Toronto: Law Society of Upper Canada, 1990)

ROBERTS, R.J., "Technology Transfer Agreements and North American Competition Law" (1995) 9 I.P.J. 247

SOOKMAN, B.B., *Computer Law: Acquiring and Protecting Information Technology* (Toronto: Carswell, 1989) (updated periodically), c. 6

TAKACH, G.F., *Patents: A Canadian Compendium of Law and Practice* (Edmonton: Juriliber, 1993)

VAVER, D., "Civil Liability for Taking or Using Trade Secrets in Canada" (1981) 5 Can. Bus. L.J. 253

WESTMINSTER INSTITUTE FOR ETHICS AND HUMAN VALUES & MCGILL
  CENTRE FOR MEDICINE, ETHICS AND LAW, *Ethical Issues Associated
  with the Patenting of Higher Life Forms*, (London, Ont.: 12 Dec. 1994)

Other

BENYAMINI, A., *Patent Infringement in the European Community*
  (Weinheim, Germany: VCH, 1993), IIC Studies in Industrial
  Property & Copyright Law No. 13

CHISUM, D.S., *Patents* (New York: Matthew Bender, 1978) (updated
  annually)

DAM, K.W., "The Economic Underpinnings of Patent Law" (1994) 23 J.
  Legal Stud. 247

DEAN, R., *The Law of Trade Secrets* (Sydney: Law Book Co., 1990)

GILAT, D., *Experimental Use and Patents* (New York: VCH, 1995), IIC
  Studies in Industrial Property & Copyright Law No. 16

REID, W.V.C., *Biodiversity Prospecting: Using Genetic Resources for
  Sustainable Development* (Washington, D.C.: World Resources
  Institute, 1993)

VOGEL, F., & R. GRUNWALD, eds., *Patenting Human Genes and Living
  Organisms* (Berlin: Springer, 1994)

WHITE, T.A. BLANCO, *Patents for Inventions and the Protection of
  Industrial Designs*, 4th ed. (London: Stevens & Sons, 1974)

Historical

DUTTON, H.I., *The Patent System and Inventive Activity during the
  Industrial Revolution, 1750–1852* (Manchester: Manchester
  University Press, 1984)

HINDMARCH, W.M., *A Treatise on the Law relating to Patent Privileges for
  the Sole Use of Inventions* (London: Stevens, 1846)

MACLEOD, C., *Inventing the Industrial Revolution: The English Patent
  System, 1660–1800* (Cambridge: Cambridge University Press, 1988)

ROBINSON, W., *The Law of Patents for Useful Inventions*, 3 vols. (Boston:
  Little, Brown, 1890)

CHAPTER 4

TRADE-MARKS

Trade-marks and trade-names are protected both at common law and under the *Trade-marks Act*.[1] This chapter focuses on trade-mark protection under the *Act*, but also mentions available common law protection.

A. INTRODUCTION

Trade-marks are commonly classified as intellectual property, but there is nothing intellectual about them at all. Despite the blandishments of Madison Avenue and its Canadian counterparts, the law does not treat trade-mark production as intellectual. A mark may be a prosaic word or device. It may be thought of independently, or it may be someone else's idea. None of this matters. Nor do any rights to a mark flow from mere creation: the EXXON trade-mark was denied a copyright despite the enormous time and money proved to have been spent in selecting and securing it worldwide.[2] Only use or its surrogates — public recognition or an intention to use — create rights, and then not in the creator but in the person behind the use, intent, or creation of public recognition. Of course, later creativity may give rise to other rights — making a fancy

---

1 R.S.C. 1985, c. T-13 [*T Act*], including the *Trade-mark Regulations, 1995*, SOR/96-195 [*TR*]; in this chapter it is called the "*Act*."

2 *Exxon Corp.* v. *Exxon Insurance Consultants International Ltd.* (1981), [1982] Ch. 119 (C.A.). See section C(1), "Originality," in chapter 2.

design involving the word or producing a television commercial featuring it may attract copyright — but this is a separate issue.

Those uncomfortable with the "intellectual" epithet sometimes more aptly call these assets *industrial* property. This term signals their essentially commercial and profit-making character. But the *property* part of *industrial property* can still seriously mislead. True, trade-marks may be sold or licensed, pass in bankruptcy, or be "interests" under bulk sales laws; even innocent infringers can be enjoined. But they are not property in the full legal sense. An "owner" does not and should not have the right to exclude others from all or even most uses. The EXXON mark owner cannot stop the use of the word in this book or in other media. It cannot stop Shell saying its products are "cheaper than EXXON" (if they are). Nor has this property the stability associated with other property rights. Indeed, it is precisely when an owner starts treating its trade-marks as its property that it runs into trouble. Rights in EXXON may in law disappear if the mark is unused, if it is licensed without its owner controlling what products it is marked on, if it changes in character (e.g., from a manufacturer's mark to a distributor's mark), or if it becomes generic (perhaps "an exxon" to signify a massive marine pollution disaster?).[3]

Descriptively, therefore, trade-marks are not fully property; at common law, they cannot be saved from misappropriation or the ravages of some amorphous unfair competition. This has been a deliberate policy choice. The Supreme Court, for one, has cautioned against curtailing the "perceived benefits to the community from free and fair competition" by expanding the common law (particularly the passing-off action) beyond the protection of "the community from the consequential damage of unfair competition or . . . [trade]." But "unfair competition or trade" was no catch-all for any activity a judge thought distasteful: only misrepresentations that would likely cause public deception or confusion were covered.[4] Yet "misappropriation" and "unfair competition" continually crop up as magic solvents in legal and judicial discourse, whatever the Supreme Court says. Some judges have distinguished common law policy from that of the *Trade-marks Act*: the latter is there precisely "to prevent unfair competition and the misappropriation of intellectual property."[5] From this incantation it is seen as no leap

---

3   See section B(2)(b), "Distinctiveness," in this chapter.

4   *Consumer's Distributing Co. v. Seiko Time Canada Ltd.*, [1984] 1 S.C.R. 583, 10 D.L.R. (4th) 161 at 173, 175, 183, rev'g (1980), 29 O.R. (2d) 221 (H.C.J.), aff'd (1981), 34 O.R. (2d) 481 (C.A.) [*Seiko*].

5   *Lin Trading Co. v. CBM Kabushiki Kaisha*, [1987] 2 F.C. 352 at 357 (T.D.), aff'd on other grounds (1988), [1989] 1 F.C. 620 (C.A.) [*Lin*].

whatsoever to ban the parallel import of genuinely branded goods,[6] an activity the Supreme Court previously legitimated at common law[7] and one that the *Trade-marks Act* does not expressly prohibit.[8]

In fact, the *Trade-marks Act* does not, any more than the common law, set out "to prevent unfair competition and the misappropriation of intellectual property." The one explicit provision in the *Act* that did that was ruled unconstitutional by the Supreme Court in 1976.[9] Instead, the *Act* presupposes that effective national trade and commerce based largely on private enterprise depends on the regulation of a number of specific practices. Just as competition itself requires the balancing of interests between and among competitors and the public, so does an *Act* that regulates defined practices relating to branding. The Supreme Court said all this a half century ago when speaking of the *Act*'s predecessor (then grandly called the *Unfair Competition Act*). General Motors complained that another firm was using FROZENAIRE for the refrigerator it was selling and that buyers would confuse this brand of product for GM's FRIGID-AIRE. The Court said that "in fixing the limits of legislative protection the courts must balance the conflicting interests and avoid placing legitimate competition at an undue disadvantage in relation to language that is common to all."[10] GM's attempts to warn off the entire refrigerator trade from using any mark with a similar connotation to FRIGIDAIRE were also pointedly rebuffed: GM evidently "deems itself to have the equivalent of a copyright in the word mark and in each component; but that is not so; the trade mark monopoly is to protect the business of . . . [General Motors], not a proprietorship of the word itself."[11]

The same approach applies to today's *Trade-marks Act*, enacted just four years after the FRIGIDAIRE decision. The question, "What kind and degree of protection should be extended in this situation?" is not answered by overblown sentiments about "unfair competition" and misappropriation of "intellectual property." Protection both at common law and under the *Trade-marks Act* requires a careful balancing of com-

---

6   *Mattel Canada Ltd.* v. *GTS Acquisitions Ltd.* (1989), [1990] 1 F.C. 462 (T.D.) [*Mattel*], disapproved in *Smith & Nephew Inc.* v. *Glen Oak Inc.* (1996), 68 C.P.R. (3d) 153 (Fed. C.A.) [*Smith & Nephew*].

7   *Seiko*, above note 4.

8   This tendency was recently partly checked in *Smith & Nephew*, above note 6, denying the power of a registered trade-mark owner or licensee to halt parallel imports. See section G(2), "Imports," in this chapter.

9   *MacDonald* v. *Vapor Canada Ltd.* (1976), [1977] 2 S.C.R. 134 on s. 7(e) of the *T Act*, above note 1.

10 *General Motors Corp.* v. *Bellows*, [1949] S.C.R. 678 at 688 [*Bellows*].

11 *Ibid.* at 689.

peting interests, including the public's interests in free trade and discourse. Throwing "property" in the scales does not, as the Supreme Court pointed out in the FRIGIDAIRE case, help this process; indeed, it can wrongly skew it.

1) Contours of Trade-mark Law

Trade-marks exist to identify the trade source of products and services to potential customers. IVORY identifies a particular soap coming from a particular maker, although few buyers may know or even care who the maker is; when buying IVORY soap they are assumed simply to want assurance that its trade source is the same — or is controlled by the same entity — as before. Similarly, if they see a dishwashing liquid branded IVORY, they may assume it comes from the same trade source as IVORY soap and may wish to buy it because of their good experience with the soap.

Although this is the reductionist psychological model on which trade-mark law is built, in reality a trade-mark is more than the model implies. Not only does it provide the often visual equivalent of a sound-bite but it actually sells goods. Advertisers spend much money associating their marks with imagery designed to encourage impulse buying. Before seeing a COKE dispenser, one may not have been thirsty; but the sight of the mark actually arouses thirst and the host of satisfying imagery created by saturation advertising of the mark. Buying and using the product temporarily satisfies the craving — until one sees the mark again. Indeed, to consume COKE may really be to consume that mark rather than the drink. The mark serves to validate its consumer's position in society as a member of a privileged class: one who can afford the lifestyle the mark has come to symbolize.

The law of trade-marks and trade-names protects investment in these brand and corporate identities. Any enterprise that deliberately or unintentionally attracts custom by using a similar mark or name used by another firm may commit passing-off — a common law and statutory wrong[12] — and can be sued by the firm whose reputation has been ridden on. The firm may also register its trade-mark under the *Act* and can stop others from adopting similar marks for their product or service. A registration can last as long as the trade-mark — potentially forever —

---

12   *T Act*, above note 1, ss. 7(b)–(c). For differences between the statutory and common law actions, see W.L. Hayhurst, "What Is a Trade-mark? The Development of Trade-mark Law" in G.F. Henderson, ed., *Trade-marks Law of Canada* (Toronto: Carswell, 1993) 27 at 39–40.

but renewal fees (now $300) must be paid every fifteen years or the registration is expunged.[13] Registration gives additional benefits — for example, stronger nationwide protection and the option of using the federal court, with its greater intellectual property expertise and shorter backlogs. Unregistrable identifiers (e.g., scents) or even invalidly registered marks may still be protected at common law against passing-off. Registered and unregistered trade-marks therefore share a symbiotic relationship. The *Act* is set against and assumes an established regime of common and civil law protection for trade-marks and trade-names.

Trade-mark and trade-name laws are essentially facilitating. They allow firms to adopt and promote virtually any names, symbols, or designs — words like IVORY, designs like the crown for ROLEX watches, even colours like pink for a brand of insulation — as trade-marks for their products or services. Whether the degree of protection the law extends to trade-marks is warranted is another question. One may ask, for instance, why the aura deliberately created around many trade-marks should be legally supported through bans on unflattering allusions or connections. Defaming a person and defaming a thing are not moral or legal equivalents, however much trade-mark owners try to anthropomorphize their symbols. Seemingly trivial questions raise fundamental issues. For example, can ROLLS-ROYCE really not be used on any product at all (chicken feed?) without the car maker's consent? Should advertising like "the Rolls-Royce of chicken feed (or condoms)" or "as good as a ROLLS" really not be allowed? How far can a mark owner control brand use and perception where nobody is confused or misled? What is wrong with "free-riding" or implicitly debunking business symbols? Is it like flag desecration? Should the law concern itself with snob values or other irrational associations deliberately infused into some marks?[14] Trade-mark law pretends consistency with free speech and trade values, but is antithetical to them more often than is usually admitted. Some of these conflicts are noted in the discussion below.

2) Differences between Common Law and Statutory Protection

Trade-marks and trade-names are reasonably well protected at common law mainly through the passing-off action. There are, nevertheless, differences between passing-off protection and trade-mark registration

13   *T Act, ibid.*, s. 46.
14   See section G(3), "Dilution," in this chapter.

that make the latter advisable for most businesses that take their names and marks seriously.

Passing-off aims primarily to prevent the disruption of economic relations by misrepresentation. So proof is required of

- a reputation or goodwill acquired by the plaintiff in its business, name, mark, or other trading symbol;
- a misrepresentation by the defendant causing deception or confusion between the two enterprises;
- actual or likely damage to the plaintiff; and
- no reason of public policy to withhold a remedy.[15]

Registration, by contrast, aims to make trade symbols more like commodities and so increases both their intrinsic and their exchange value. A broad comparison of registration and passing-off protection reveals the following:

- Passing-off usually requires a symbol both to be used and to have gained a market reputation before protection can be claimed. By contrast, an application to register a mark can be filed well before use. Use must still be proved before registration, but no market reputation need normally be shown to derive from the use.
- Passing-off will protect a symbol only in the locality of its reputation. By contrast, a registration is usually Canada-wide. It can also be used as the basis for corresponding applications for similar protection in most other countries in the world.
- Passing-off requires proof that a defendant misrepresented its products, service, or business as, or connected with, the plaintiff's. It also requires proof of consequential injury to the claimant's relations with those who do business with it (i.e., its "goodwill").[16] A registration, by contrast, may protect the mark for the whole range of goods or services for which it is registered, without proof of damage. The registrant can also stop the use of different, but confusingly similar, marks for different businesses, even if the defendant prominently disclaims any connection between the two businesses.
- Passing-off requires the plaintiff to prove the existence and extent of its reputation each time an action is brought. By contrast, a registration is, until expunged, presumed valid for Canada for all the wares

---

15   *Ciba-Geigy Canada Ltd.* v. *Apotex Inc.*, [1992] 3 S.C.R. 120; *Erven Warnink BV* v. *J. Townend & Sons (Hull) Ltd.*, [1979] A.C. 731 at 748 (H.L.).

16   *Quia timet* relief is available to nip any proposed course of objectionable conduct in the bud.

and services for which it is registered. Protection continues, though the mark is little used or known.

- Passing-off does not prevent a mark's image from being diluted or tarnished. A misrepresentation of trade source must first still be shown, although this concept is sometimes stretched to breaking point. By contrast, a registration (controversially) directly protects a mark from any depreciation of its goodwill, even without any misrepresentation.[17]

Passing-off and registration can, nevertheless, work in tandem. Passing-off may still succeed where the plaintiff's registration is invalid. It is broader in some respects and more instantly adaptable to new situations than is the *Act*. For example, passing-off can also protect non-profit and public activity. Charities and even political candidates and parties — all dependent on reputation, public goodwill, and contributions — may be brought within the principle of protecting economic relations from injury or from misrepresentation.[18] The *Act* extends into the public and non-profit sector, but its presence there is more controversial. There are linguistic constraints on how far statutory construction can push the *Act* in new directions. There are also constitutional constraints. Too broad a reading of the *Act* may push a provision outside the "Trade and Commerce" power that underpins federal authority in this area.[19]

Other contrasts between passing-off and registration will be noted as the discussion proceeds. First, the process and requirements of registration are considered.

3) Applying for a Trade-mark

Before applying to register a trade-mark, one must first devise one. There are plenty of pitfalls. Descriptive, misdescriptive, generic words, names of people, and marks or symbols used by other enterprises or institutions should all be avoided. An arbitrary word — say, ELEPHANT for soap, rather than SUDSY — is often better, although SUDSY can grow to be a trade-mark if sales are big and enough money is spent promoting the brand.

After selection, it is usual to search the trade-marks register and corporations and business names registries and to get a preliminary report on what marks or names may conflict with the proposed mark. For ELEPHANT applied to soap, the search might include homophones or near

---

17   See section G(3), "Dilution," in this chapter.
18   Compare *Polsinelli v. Marzilli* (1987), 61 O.R. (2d) 799 (Div. Ct.).
19   See section B(5), "Constitutional Problems," in chapter 1.

homophones in English and French (ELLIEFANT, ELEFINT, OLIFON), marks with similar connotations (HIPPO, TRUNK, TRONC, SAFARI, maybe even TIGER and TIGRE), and design and label marks featuring elephants. The seriousness of any potential conflict is then assessed: Is there a reasonable likelihood of confusion[20] between the two marks? A decision on a future course of action must then be taken. It will partly depend on how much has already been invested in the chosen mark and its importance to the firm. Should the mark be changed a little or a lot? Should it be dropped altogether and some other mark adopted? Should some agreement be sought with the owners of any conflicting marks or names? Should the Registrar of Trade-marks be asked to expunge any inactive conflicting marks? Should an application be made to the Federal Court to expunge any marks thought to be invalid for any reason? Should one just go ahead and apply for registration anyway and see what the reaction of the Trade-marks Office is, and whether anyone comes out of the woodwork to oppose?

Once the decision to go forward is made, the application to register the trade-mark is made to the TMO. As with other intellectual property, it is foolish to start the application process without the help of a trade-mark agent or a specialized lawyer, for a host of technicalities has sprung up around what looks like a simple process. The application form must, of course, be correctly filled in. Even innocent errors can have serious consequences: the application may be rejected or any registration obtained may be invalidated, even years later. The application, accompanied by the $150 fee (another $200 is payable on registration), contains the following information:[21]

- The trade-mark sought should be stated or depicted. The exact mark that is used or proposed must be used. If the mark is simply a word or a combination of words, it should be shown in simple block capitals. The mark may, however, have design elements. It may be a word printed in fancy lettering, a label with graphic elements and letterpress, or a distinguishing guise like the COCA-COLA bottle.[22] If so, the mark should be applied for in this form and a drawing supplied. A further application or applications may be advisable to cover the dominant features of a design mark separately. Thus, separate registrations protect COCA-COLA as a word and also as presented in its fancy script.

---

20   See section G(4), "Confusion," in this chapter.
21   *T Act*, above note 1, s. 30.
22   See section B(1)(d), "Distinguishing Guise," in this chapter.

- A statement must appear in ordinary commercial terms of the specific wares or services for which the mark has been or will be used.[23]
- The basis of the applicant's title must be given. Has the applicant or its predecessor used the mark, or is it merely proposing to use it? Is the mark well known in Canada? Is the applicant basing its claim on a foreign registration in a *Paris Convention* or a *WTO* country?[24] More than one basis may be stated. Thus, the mark may be proposed to be used, and may also be the subject of a foreign registration. Or it may already have been used in Canada, and is also well known in Canada through its use abroad. Claiming two or more bases may be useful, for one may succeed where another fails. But the basis of proposed use should not be claimed where the mark has been used: these bases cannot be switched in mid-application, and the error can later prove fatal.[25]
- The date of first use or making known should be stated. The applicant can choose the earliest date it can support with evidence.
- For proposed marks,[26] the applicant must truthfully state who proposes to use the mark: the applicant itself, a licensee, or both.
- For certification marks,[27] particulars of the defined standard the mark is intended to indicate must be given. The applicant must also state it is not engaged in marketing wares or services such as those associated with the mark.
- A statement must be made that the applicant is satisfied it is entitled to use the mark in Canada.
- The applicant's address and a place for service in Canada must be given.

4) Proceedings in the Trade-marks Office

A TMO examiner checks the application for conformity with the *Act* and the *Regulations* and searches the register to confirm registrability and title. The applicant is notified of any objections and may meet them by argument, evidence, or amendment. Amendments can include disclaiming unregistrable material,[28] changing (but not extending) the statement of wares or services, inserting an earlier priority date, or even

---

23 The appendix to the Canadian Intellectual Property Office's *Trade Marks Examination Manual* gives guidance on acceptable and unacceptable statements.

24 See section F, "Title," in this chapter.

25 *TR*, above note 1, s. 31(d); *Manifatture Casucci di Caucci Ugo & C.S.a.s. v. Casucci Clothes Inc.* (1993), 52 C.P.R. (3d) 250 at 253 (T.M. Opp. Bd.).

26 See section B(1)(c), "Proposed Trade-mark," in this chapter.

27 See section B(1)(e), "Certification Mark," in this chapter.

28 See section C(4), "Disclaimer," in this chapter.

changing the mark itself — but not so as to "alter its distinctive charac-ter or affect its identity."[29] Ultimately, the applicant must satisfy the Registrar that (a) the application form complies with the *Act*, (b) nobody with a better title[30] has a pending application for a confusing mark, and (c) the mark applied for is registrable. This last element, reg-istrability, covers a wide field; namely, the mark must[31]

- be a *trade-mark*;
- not be *confusing* with a registered trade-mark;[32]
- not be a *generic mark* or other *generic symbol*;
- not be mistaken for an *official* or *prohibited mark*;
- not be *offensive*;
- not falsely suggest a *connection with a living or recently deceased indi-vidual*;
- not be a *name or surname*, unless *distinctiveness* is shown; and
- not be a *descriptive* or *deceptive mark*, unless *distinctiveness* is shown.

The examiner may, subject to appeal to the Federal Court, reject the application if not satisfied on any of the above, but usually gives the applicant the benefit of the doubt at this stage.[33] If not rejected, the application is then advertised in the *Trade-marks Journal* and the mark is registered if it is unopposed.[34] Registration of a proposed mark is post-poned until the applicant files a declaration that use of the mark has commenced. This must occur within three years of filing, or six months after the applicant is notified that the application is allowed.[35] About 16,000 marks are registered annually.

---

29   *T Act*, above note 1, s. 34; *TR*, above note 1, s. 31; *Magill v. Taco Bell Corp.* (1990), 31 C.P.R. (3d) 221 at 227 (T.M. Opp. Bd.).

30   See section F, "Title," in this chapter.

31   *T Act*, above note 1, ss. 12 &13. Italicized items are discussed further in this chapter.

32   The TMO sometimes sets aside its doubts on this score, lets the application be advertised, and then advises possibly affected registrants of the application.

33   *Canadian Parking Equipment Ltd. v. Canada (Registrar of Trade Marks)* (1990), 34 C.P.R. (3d) 154 at 160–61 (Fed. T.D.) [*Parking*].

34   *T Act*, above note 1, ss. 37 & 56; *Conde Nast Publications Inc. v. Gozlan Brothers Ltd.* (1980), 49 C.P.R. (2d) 250 (Fed. T.D.) [*Gozlan*]; *Molson Breweries v. Canada (Registrar of Trade Marks)* (1992), 41 C.P.R. (3d) 234 at 240 (Fed. T.D.) [*Molson*].

35   *T Act, ibid.*, ss. 40(2)–(3).

5) Opposition

Uncommonly for intellectual property, the trade-mark system has a formal procedure for opposing the grant of registration.[36] Oppositions are effectively mini-trials before a member of the Trade-marks Opposition Board. They are quite common and there is often a long backlog. The *Trade-marks Journal* is regularly scanned by trade-mark lawyers and agents with retainers to advise clients of any possibly troublesome application. Anybody with the inclination and money can oppose registration. The only requirements are a $250 fee and an accompanying detailed statement of opposition filed within two months of the *Journal* advertisement. The grounds for opposing are those for which the TMO initially checked the application (inaccurate application form, unregistrability of the mark) plus two more:

- the opponent has a better *title* than the applicant; and
- the mark lacks *distinctiveness*.[37]

Statements of opposition raising no "substantial issue for decision" can be struck out at this stage. Otherwise, a copy of the statement goes to the applicant, who files a counter-statement. Both parties then file affidavits or declarations, on which there may be cross-examination with leave and written argument in support of their case. The Board member then gives a decision on the papers or, if requested, after an oral hearing.

The applicant must satisfy the Board that the objections raised by the opponent have no substance: the examiner's earlier *ex parte* decision does not bind the Board.[38] Much of the case and evidence is considered as at the date of the Board's decision — typically many months, sometimes years after the initial filing. This can lead to a situation where registration may be barred because conflicting marks (including those of the opponent) have been registered during opposition proceedings.[39]

---

36   Registration of plant breeder rights (see section B(3)(g), "Plant Varieties," in chapter 3) also may be opposed: *Plant Breeders' Rights Act*, S.C. 1990, c. 20, s. 22.

37   *T Act*, above note 1, ss. 38; ss. 16 & 17 (entitlement to register); s. 2 def. "distinctive"; *TR*, above note 1, ss. 40–50. See also section F, "Title," and section B(2)(b), "Distinctiveness," in this chapter.

38   *Gozlan*, above note 34; *Molson*, above note 34.

39   *Simmons Ltd.* v. *A to Z Comfort Beddings Ltd.* (*sub nom. Park Avenue Furniture Corp.* v. *Wickes/Simmons Bedding Ltd.*) (1991), 37 C.P.R. (3d) 413 (Fed C.A.); *Canadian Olympic Assn.* v. *Olympus Optical Co.* (1991), 38 C.P.R. (3d) 1 (Fed. C.A.) [*Olympus*] (official mark).

The trend to judge registrability as at the date of the Board's decision is not, however, universal. It occurs where the mark is alleged to conflict with another registered mark or published official mark. But conflicting jurisprudence has resulted in different dates being treated as applying to different grounds of opposition. Thus, an applicant's title to a mark is judged as at the date the application was filed, but the mark's distinctiveness is tested as at the date the statement of opposition was filed.[40] Disparities like these provide an additional layer of complexity both for parties presenting evidence and for the Board member who deals with it. The various grounds of registrability and the evidence relating to them often intertwine. It is therefore easy to rely wrongly on an item of evidence that is relevant to one issue but is of little relevance or weight on another.

Cases are regularly won or lost on the nature and quality of the evidence and the extent to which the procedures laid out in the *Regulations* are closely observed. Board members rarely go outside the file or take judicial notice of much (including even registered trade-marks not formally evidenced). Decisions often go off on technical points of procedure, evidence, or burden of proof. Either party can appeal to the Federal Court. There, more evidence can be filed to try to change the complexion of the case. The Trial Division and Court of Appeal give due weight to the Board's judgment and experience, but will reverse decisions they think are wrong in law or fact, especially in the light of any additional evidence. The Supreme Court has not in recent years granted leave to appeal these decisions.

B. WHAT IS A TRADE-MARK?

Only indicia that qualify as a "trade-mark" are considered for registration. Not only do the TMO and the Opposition Board check, but if something that does not qualify slips by and does get registered, the registration is invalid and can be expunged.

1) Categories of Trade-mark

According to the *Act*, trade-marks fall into the following categories: (1) "classic" trade-marks, (2) service marks, (3) "proposed" trade-marks (either "classic" or service marks), (4) distinguishing guises, and (5) certification marks.

---

40   For example, *Clarco Communications Ltd.* v. *Sassy Publishers Inc.* (1994), 54 C.P.R. (3d) 418 at 430 (Fed. T.D.); *Merrill Lynch & Co.* v. *Bank of Montreal* (1993), 54 C.P.R. (3d) 473 at 477 (T.M. Opp. Bd.), aff'd (1996), 66 C.P.R. (3d) 150 (Fed. T.D.).

a) "Classic" Trade-mark

The most common trade-mark is the one that distinguishes one producer's product from another's. COCA-COLA is a familiar example. As a word or depicted in distinctive script, it distinguishes the product of the Coca-Cola Company and its franchisees from drinks made by other producers. The legal definition of a trade-mark is "a mark that is used by a person for the purpose of distinguishing or so as to distinguish wares. . . . manufactured, sold, leased, [or] hired . . . by him from those manufactured, sold, leased, [or] hired . . . by others."[41] Anyone in the chain of distribution can have its own trade-mark. FORD functions as a manufacturer's trade-mark for motor vehicles and parts manufactured by the Ford Motor Co. or its subsidiaries; LIFE BRAND functions as a distributor's or retailer's trade-mark for drugstore items sold by Shoppers Drug Mart; BUDGET functions as a lessor's or hirer's trade-mark for vehicles leased or hired by Budget Rent-A-Car. The definition makes clear that a mark either can be adopted intentionally as a trade-mark or may become one in practice without its user's intention or even knowledge.

b) Service Mark

This mark distinguishes services performed by one person from those performed by another.[42] Although long protectable at common law, service marks first became registrable in Canada only in 1954. MCDONALD'S is a service mark for restaurant services performed by McDonald's Corp., distinguishing those from other fast-food chains. MCDONALD'S may also possibly be registered as a classic trade-mark for various food products sold at the restaurants — for example, coffee in cups marked MCDONALD'S. Any activity benefiting others in Canada can qualify as a service. Financial and insurance services, repair, transportation, even services associated with retailing, including those of offshore mail-order houses and online information providers with Canadian subscribers, all potentially qualify.[43]

---

41   *T Act*, above note 1, s. 2, def. "trade-mark," para. (a).

42   *T Act*, *ibid.*, s. 2, def. "trade-mark," para. (a).

43   *Kraft Ltd.* v. *Canada (Registrar of Trade Marks)*, [1984] 2 F.C. 874 (T.D.) [*Kraft*];
     Riches, McKenzie & Herbert v. *Source Telecomputing Corp.* (1992), 46 C.P.R. (3d)
     563 at 564 (T.M. Opp. Bd.); *Société Nationale des Chemins de Fer Français SNCF* v.
     Venice-Simplon-Orient-Express Inc. (1995), 64 C.P.R. (3d) 87 at 91 (T.M. Opp. Bd.).
     See also A.F. Rush, "Internet Domain Name Protection: A Canadian Perspective"
     (1996) 11 I.P.J. 1.

This broad approach has caused the *Trade-marks Act* to become an informal (but effective) protection registry for the names of corporations, partnerships, and non-profit societies. So a sporting goods store called Run-Fast Sports Inc. can register RUN-FAST SPORTS as a mark for "retail sporting goods services" and acquire the power to block the use or registration of confusing names and marks. All Run-Fast must do is show it is using the indicia as a mark, not merely its trade name, and this requirement is modest enough. Displaying the mark in any distinctive graphics, together with a catchy slogan or statement of the services offered, separately from its trade name, will do.[44] There have been battles over trading names between (typically expansionist) firms that have and (typically local) firms that have not registered service marks under the *Act*. The former so far have had the upper hand, but the conflict is far from over.[45]

c) Proposed Trade-mark

The *Act* includes a "proposed trade-mark" as a separate category,[46] but it really is not. At common law, no trade-mark was usually protected without being both used and also acquiring a reputation from that use.[47] The *Act* changes this practice. An applicant can choose and apply to register a trade-mark before using it,[48] so long as the applicant proposes (i.e., intends) to use it as a trade-mark in Canada. The *Act* indeed seems to encourage such early applications. Priority is based on the application date, so that, unlike at common law, a proposed use trumps a later actual use.[49] If the mark is eventually rejected in the TMO, large resources will not have been expended on its promotion.

---

44   *Playboy Enterprises Inc.* v. *Germain* (1979), 43 C.P.R. (2d) 271 (Fed. C.A.); *Road Runner Trailer Manufacturing Ltd.* v. *Road Runner Trailer Co.* (1984), 1 C.P.R. (3d) 443 (Fed. T.D.); *Chanel* v. *Legacy International Inc.* (1994), 59 C.P.R. (3d) 386 (T.M. Opp. Bd.).

45   Compare *Reference Re Constitution Act, 1867, ss. 91 & 92* (1991), 80 D.L.R. (4th) 431 (Man. C.A.) on the collision between two Bricks.

46   *T Act*, above note 1, s. 2, defs. "trade-mark," para. (d), "proposed trade-mark."

47   Pre-launch publicity may, however, sometimes suffice for a passing-off action. So a competitor may not "spike the guns" of a firm that has advertised the launch of a new product by launching a competing product with a confusingly similar mark: *TV Guide Inc./TV Hebdo Inc.* v. *Publications La Semaine Inc.* (1984), 9 C.P.R. (3d) 368 (Que. S.C.).

48   Except if the application is for a distinguishing guise or a certification mark; see sections B(1)(d) and (e) in this chapter.

49   *T Act*, above note 1, s. 16(3). The proposed use must in turn become an actual use, before a registration can be granted: *ibid.*, s. 40.

d) Distinguishing Guise

The way goods are shaped, wrapped, or packaged can constitute a trade-mark, if the appearance is used to distinguish one trader's goods or services from another's. These marks are "distinguishing guises." They include distinctively shaped bottles (e.g., Coca-Cola's), containers, wares, and outer wrappers. The coloured coating of a medicinal tablet has, however, been excluded because it was thought to be part of the item itself, not a shape, wrapping, or container.[50]

There are some constraints. Distinguishing guises are registrable only after becoming distinctive through use. They cannot be certification marks.[51] They cannot "unreasonably . . . limit the development of any art or industry." Nor can they be proxies for patents or registered designs, since their utilitarian features remain open for use by all.[52] Indeed, "primarily or essentially" functional features like the PHILIPS shaver triple-head are unregistrable as guises or any other sort of trade-mark.[53]

Subject to analogous constraints, the tort of passing-off may also protect distinguishing guises. Thus, while its application for a distinguishing guise for its bottle was pending, Source Perrier stopped a competitor from marketing water in a look-alike Perrier bottle: confusion was likely even though the competitor's bottle was differently labelled.[54]

e) Certification Mark

Certification marks do not distinguish one producer from another. Indeed, a producer of goods such as those covered by the registration cannot directly own a certification mark.[55] Instead, the mark distinguishes products or services of a defined standard from others. The standard-

---

50   *Smith Kline & French Canada Ltd.* v. *Canada (Registrar of Trade Marks), (sub nom. Smith, Kline & French Canada Ltd.* v. *Registrar of Trade Marks (No.1))* [1987] 2 F.C. 628 (T.D.) [*Smith (No.1)*].

51   See section B(1)(e), "Certification Mark," in this chapter.

52   *T Act*, above note 1, s. 13; s. 2 (defs. "trade-mark," "distinguishing guise"); *Canada (Registrar of Trade Marks)* v. *Brewers Assn. of Canada*, [1982] 2 F.C. 622 (C.A.). [*Brewers*].

53   *Remington Rand Corp.* v. *Philips Electronics N.V.* (1995), 64 C.P.R. (3d) 467 at 476 (Fed. C.A.) [*Remington Rand*]. See sections B(2)(b)(iv) and (v), "Functional and Ornamental Features" and "Colour," in this chapter.

54   *Source Perrier SA* v. *Canada Dry Ltd.* (1982), 36 O.R. (2d) 695, at 700 (H.C.J.); compare *Reckitt & Colman Products Ltd.* v. *Borden Inc.*, [1990] 1 All E.R. 873 (H.L.).

55   *T Act*, above note 1, s. 23(1). Some differences are arbitrary: for example, no distinguishing guise or application based on proposed use is permitted: *Brewers*, above note 52; *Mister Transmission International Ltd.* v. *Canada (Registrar of Trade Marks)*, [1979] 1 F.C. 787 (T.D.) [*Mister Transmission*], criticized by W.L. Hayhurst, "Survey of Canadian Law: Industrial Property — Part I" (1983) 15 Ottawa L. Rev. 311 at 407, n. 968.

setter owns the mark and licenses those meeting the standard to use it. Certification marks have even been stretched to encompass franchising and merchandise licensing operations.[56] More typically, they cover appellations of origin for foods and wines (SWISS chocolate, STILTON cheese), seals of approval (the Canadian Standards Association's CSA APPROVED mark), and union labels certifying goods made by unionized labour.

Certification marks that have not become generic are also protectable by passing-off.[57] Producer groups long ago halted "Spanish champagne" from being imported into Britain. They also stopped British firms from participating in the mislabelling of spirits in South America as SCOTCH WHISKY.[58] But attempts to stop Ontario producers calling local sparkling wine "Canadian champagne" failed, since in North America "champagne" is now considered a generic term.[59]

2) Attributes of a Trade-mark

A trade-mark must be (1) a "mark," (2) distinctive or capable of becoming distinctive, and (3) "used" as a trade-mark.

a) Mark

The feature chosen must be a "mark." This presumably encompasses "any sign, or any combination of signs . . . including personal names, designs, letters, numerals, colors, figurative elements."[60] Slogans like "Let your fingers do the walking" for Tele-Direct's "yellow pages" directories have qualified. So have phone numbers.[61] The word "mark" may, however, suggest something visible and distinct from the product itself.[62] The sound pattern on a record company's audio-tapes has been

---

56   See, for example, *Mister Transmission, ibid.* This practice will likely decline now that registration for users of regular trade-marks has been abolished (in 1993). Certification marks were popular precisely because users did not need to be registered.

57   See also *T Act*, above note 1, s. 7(d).

58   *Bollinger v. Costa Brava Wine Co. Ltd.* (1959), [1960] Ch. 262; *John Walker & Sons Ltd. v. Henry Ost & Co.*, [1970] 2 All E.R. 106 (Ch.).

59   *Institut National des Appellations d'Origine des Vins et Eaux-de-Vie v. Andres Wines Ltd.* (1987), 60 O.R. (2d) 316 (H.C.J.), aff'd (1990), 74 O.R. (2d) 203 (C.A.). Compare section E, "Geographical Indications," in this chapter.

60   *North American Free Trade Agreement*, 12 December 1992 (Ottawa: Supply & Services, 1993), art. 1708(1) [*NAFTA*]. The *T Act*, above note 1, s. 2, def. "trade-mark," is silent on the meaning of "mark."

61   *Pizza Pizza Ltd. v. Canada (Registrar of Trade Marks)*, [1989] 3 F.C. 379 (C.A.).

62   *Insurance Corp. of British Columbia v. Canada (Registrar of Trade Marks)* (1979), [1980] 1 F.C. 669 (T.D.) [*Insurance*].

registered in Canada, but the validity of this registration is uncertain in the absence of any court decision. Whether the smell of a distinctive perfume or wine or the sound of a radio or television station's call sign is registrable is equally uncertain.[63]

The inconvenience of allowing trade-mark registrations for such indicia may be exemplified by Harley-Davidson's recent U.S. application to register the sound of its motorcycle engine as a trade-mark. Can Jay Leno's voice be far behind? Yet perhaps the Canadian legislation may need to be interpreted in a way that does not unfairly discriminate among classes of consumer. A visual mark cannot do its job for blind people. Admitting aural or olfactory indicia to registration would help ensure that the blind are not handicapped as consumers.

b) Distinctiveness

A trade-mark must either "actually" distinguish firm 1's products or services from firm 2's or be "adapted so to distinguish" them.[64] Some marks are born distinctive. They are "adapted to distinguish" because they have the capacity without use to be accepted as trade-marks. Invented words like KODAK, fancy designs, or arbitrary words like ELEPHANT for soap are examples. These marks are ideal candidates for applications based on proposed use.

Other marks are not so adapted to distinguish firm 1's products or services from firm 2's. They must work hard to become distinctive in fact. Thus, PERFECT or CANADIAN, being descriptive, is not initially "adapted" to distinguish between producers. Yet, by extended use and advertising over time, such marks can acquire distinctiveness — a secondary meaning "actually" distinguishing a single producer from others. They can then be registered. Even local distinctiveness may suffice. A mark distinctive only in Ottawa can be registered for the whole of Canada; its owner

---

63 Compare *Re Clarke*, 17 U.S.P.Q.2d 1238 (Trademark Trial & Appeal Bd. 1990), registering plumeria smell for sewing thread and embroidery yarn. An unregistrable mark might still be protected through an action for passing-off (sound or smell) or breach of copyright (sound).

64 *T Act*, above note 1, s. 2, def. "distinctive." Oddly enough, distinctiveness is mentioned only as a ground of opposition or invalidation: ss. 38(2)(d) and 18(1)(b). Inferentially, the TMO cannot reject a mark for non-distinctiveness before advertisement. But this is only partly true: some elements of distinctiveness are examined because, without them, a trade-mark cannot exist. For example, the TMO can register only trade-marks, and a trade-mark must be adapted to distinguish or must actually distinguish; moreover, descriptive, misdescriptive, and nominal marks are not registrable without proof of distinctiveness: s. 2 (def. "trade-mark," para. (a)), ss. 12(1)(a)–(b), & 12(2).

can block later marks that have acquired their own local distinctiveness, for the latter cannot now be distinctive in a part of Canada.[65]

Distinctiveness can come and go, but to stay alive a trade-mark must be distinctive whenever it is challenged. This may happen if it is opposed before registration or if, after registration, legal proceedings raising non-distinctiveness are started.[66] A non-distinctive trade-mark is a contradiction in terms. How non-distinctiveness comes about is irrelevant to the question of the mark's validity. What matters is the result, the mark's impact on its public.

i) Genericism

A trade-mark that becomes a product description falls into the language. It is no longer distinctive, hence it is no longer a trade-mark. "Gramophone" and "nylon" were both trade-marks once. Inadequate policing by their owners put them into the public domain in North America. THERMOS, on the other hand, was saved in the 1960s, even though most members of the public then used "thermos" to mean any vacuum flask. U.S. and Canadian courts decided that distinctiveness for a significant minority of consumers was enough to stave off expungement. Only the U.S. court followed the logic of this finding specifically to allow generic use of "thermos," with safeguards to protect the vulnerable minority. Competitors in the United States had to use "thermos" without a capital T, add their own brand name, and not use words like "original" or "genuine." The Canadian court thought competitors might also be able to use "thermos" legitimately for their products, but coyly refrained from offering any legal advice.[67]

ii) Multiple Use

A mark is not distinctive if it is used simultaneously in Canada by two (or more) firms. To customers of firm 1, the mark means firm 1's goods; to customers of firm 2, it means firm 2's. Since it distinguishes two firms' goods, it distinguishes neither from the other. Nobody can regis-

---

65   *Great Lakes Hotels Ltd.* v. *Noshery Ltd.*, [1968] 2 Ex.C.R. 622; *Clegg* v. *Matwel Industries Inc.* (1989), 28 C.P.R. (3d) 490 at 494–95 (T.M. Opp. Bd.). Compare section C(5), "Concurrent Registration," in this chapter.

66   *T Act*, above note 1, ss. 38(2)(d) & 18(1)(b); see section H, "Invalidity," in this chapter.

67   Compare *Aladdin Industries Inc.* v. *Canadian Thermos Products Ltd.*, [1969] 2 Ex.C.R. 80 [*Aladdin*] with *American Thermos Products Co.* v. *Aladdin Industries Inc.*, 207 F. Supp. 9 (D. Conn 1962), aff'd (*sub nom. King-Seeley Thermos Co.* v. *Aladdin Industries Inc.*), 321 F. 2d 377 (2d Cir. 1963).

ter in such a situation. If this situation arises after registration, the mark may become invalid if the registrant does nothing to stop the other firm's creation of a separate brand identity.[68] This may occur with marks that cause confusion,[69] not just identical marks. It may also occur where firms are under common control,[70] although a mark used by a licensee is now considered to be used by (and so distinctive of) the mark owner if the latter directly or indirectly controls the character or quality of the marked products.[71] Still, sloppy practices continue to cause non-distinctiveness. Bell Canada's registrations of WATS, CALLING CARD, and 900 SERVICE for telephone services were recently expunged because Bell had not exercised control over the way regional telephone companies used the marks Bell had licensed to them.[72]

iii)   Unadvertised Change of Product Origin

Trade-mark law usually cares little about changes in product or service quality: the mark owner's self-interest is supposed to take care of that. Buyers will eventually shy away from a brand whose quality is thought to have deteriorated. The public function of the mark as an attractor or repeller of custom is then fully vindicated. But some changes may make a trade-mark non-distinctive. This happened to the HEINTZMAN piano. When the manufacturer's Ontario plant closed, a successor to the Heintzman business started applying the mark to lower-quality pianos imported from Korea and the United States. The mark was expunged as non-distinctive because buyers continued to believe that HEINTZMAN still meant the high-quality Canadian product. A mark can legally change character — for example, from a manufacturer's to a distributor's mark or from having Canadian to having foreign associations — but steps must be taken to bring the mark's new message home to potential buyers to avoid their being confused.[73]

---

68   *Westwind Investments Ltd.* v. *Yannacoulias* (1990), 30 C.P.R. (3d) 231 (Fed. T.D.); *Laflamme Fourrures (Trois-Rivières) Inc.* v. *Laflamme Fourrures Inc.* (1986), 21 C.P.R. (3d) 265 (Fed. T.D.).

69   See section G(4), "Confusion," in this chapter.

70   *Ungine Aciers* v. *Canada (Registrar of Trade Marks)* (1978), [1979] 1 F.C. 237 (C.A.).

71   *T Act*, above note 1, s. 50(1); *S.C. Johnson & Son Ltd.* v. *Marketing International Ltd.* (1979), [1980] 1 S.C.R. 99 {*S.C. Johnson*].

72   *Unitel Communications Inc.* v. *Bell Canada* (1995), 61 C.P.R. (3d) 12 (Fed. T.D.) [*Unitel*].

73   *Heintzman* v. *751056 Ontario Ltd.* (1990), 34 C.P.R. (3d) 1 at 16-17 (Fed. T.D.) [*Heintzman*].

iv) Functional and Ornamental Features

Since trade-marks are not substitutes for patents or industrial designs, the holder of a patent or a registered design — valid, invalid, or since expired — is not encouraged to bolster this monopoly through a trade-mark on the same feature. So functional and ornamental features — elements that are integral to a product or that make it attractive — are not usually trade-marks. The question is whether the feature is "solely, primarily or essentially" ornamental or functional. If so, it is unregistrable. Such features have included things like a pattern on table glassware, a triple-head design for the blades of an electric shaver, and a stripe encircling a grain storage bin; in these cases, the market relied on trade-marks found elsewhere on the product to distinguish trade source.[74] On the other hand, ten Xs cross-stitched on jeans, though partly ornamental, was held to be a distinctive and effective trademark.[75] At bottom, only features that "unreasonably limit the development" of other trades should be denied protection. This is true of distinguishing guises[76] recognized by the *Act*. The same principle may apply by analogy to other trade-marks, too. If other traders can compete effectively using different designs, the mark should be upheld.

v) Colour

Colour can be, or be part of, a protectable trade-mark. The blue, white, and gold oblong Visa trade-mark for credit cards or the pink of Owens-Corning's insulation are well-known examples. Combinations of colour usually work better than a single colour because buyers may more readily recognize them as trade-marks and allow them to become distinctive. Prototypical colours for pills — white, yellow, green — while technically registrable, may be just too common to distinguish one owner's pills from another's in fact.[77] People might think these are the colour of the ingredients — as milk is white or beer is golden[78] — or they may think the colour is there to make the pill more attractive.

---

74 *W.J. Hughes & Sons "Corn Flower" Ltd.* v. *Morawiec* (1970), 62 C.P.R. 21 (Ex. Ct.); *Trail-Rite Flatdecks Ltd.* v. *Larcon International Inc.* (1988), 21 C.P.R. (3d) 403 at 408 (Sask. Q.B.); *Remington Rand*, above note 53.

75 *Santana Jeans Ltd.* v. *Manager Clothing Inc.* (1993), 52 C.P.R. (3d) 472 at 478 (Fed. T.D.).

76 See section B(1)(d), "Distinguishing Guise," in this chapter.

77 Compare *Smith, Kline & French Canada Ltd.* v. *Registrar of Trade Marks (No. 2)*, [1987] 2 F.C. 633 (T.D.) (pale green for Tagamet capable of being trade-mark) with *Smith Kline & French Laboratories Ltd.'s Cimetidine Trade Mark* (1988), [1991] R.P.C. 17 (Ch.) (held non-distinctive in United Kingdom in fact despite long use).

78 *John Labatt Ltd.* v. *Molson Cos. Ltd.* (1987), 19 C.P.R. (3d) 88 (Fed. C.A.) [*Labatt*].

Other times a particular colour may be competitively necessary: outboard motors may have to be black or white to match the full range of colours that boats come in. In such cases, distinctiveness should be rarely found: to grant one trader a monopoly in the colour may put other honest traders at a significant competitive disadvantage.[79]

This last point has not always been recognized. For example, pharmaceutical drug companies have sometimes persuaded courts that a patient who demands "the same again" means to receive not just a drug with the same active ingredients but the very same drug as before made by the same manufacturer.[80] This reductionist view of patient psychology suggests that good health policy and intellectual property law do not necessarily coincide, especially since trade-mark law allows the first maker itself to change ingredients without telling the public.

c) Use

Without "use" a trade-mark is nothing. It cannot be registered; if registered, it can be expunged. But "use" in law does not always coincide with "use" in ordinary speech. For example, a mark for services is used when displayed in performing or advertising them.[81] Not so for goods: there it must appear on the goods themselves or their packages, or must otherwise be notified at the time property in the goods is transferred or possession changes hands.[82] A mark for services is "used," but a mark for goods is not, in a television commercial.[83] Nor need a service mark involve a commercial transaction: those charities unable to acquire an official mark can register a regular service mark for their good works.[84] But a mark for goods must be used "in the normal course of trade." Token uses do not count, nor do promotional gifts, since nothing is exchanged for value.[85] Unsurprisingly, this practice causes applicants to try to juggle marks into the service category. BREADWINNERS for discount

---

79 *Qualitex Co.* v. *Jacobson Products Co.,* 115 S.Ct. 1300 at 1304 (1995).

80 *F. Hoffman-La-Roche & Co. AG* v. *DDSA Pharmaceuticals Ltd.,* [1972] R.P.C. 1 (C.A.) (green and black capsules for LIBRIUM tranquillizer); *Ciba-Geigy Canada Ltd.* v. *Apotex Inc.,* [1992] 3 S.C.R. 120 (LOPRESSOR pink and blue heart tablets); both passing-off cases, but the same applies to registered marks.

81 *T Act,* above note 1, s. 4(2).

82 *T Act, ibid.,* s. 4(1).

83 *Clairol International Corp.* v. *Thomas Supply & Equipment Co.,* [1968] 2 Ex.C.R. 552 [*Clairol*].

84 *Shapiro, Cohen, Andrews & Finlayson* v. *Fireman's Fund Insurance Co.* (1994), 54 C.P.R. (3d) 568 (T.M. Opp. Bd.) [*Shapiro*]. See section D(2) and (4) in this chapter.

85 *Sequa Chemicals Inc.* v. *United Color & Chemicals Ltd.* (1993), 53 C.P.R. (3d) 216 at 218 (Fed. C.A.).

coupons on groceries was accordingly registered as a service mark for "providing coupon programs pertaining to a line of food products."[86]

How and by whom the mark is used are equally important. Use must be as a trade-mark — to distinguish trader 1's product from trader 2's. A use by trader 1's licensee can distinguish trader 1's product from trader 2's, so long as trader 1 controls the character or quality of the licensee's product. Otherwise, the use may count as the licensee's and cause the mark to become non-distinctive of the licensor.[87]

i) Manufacturer versus Distributor

The question "Who is using whose mark?" often becomes acute in disputes between manufacturers and their distributors. Typically, a mark put on by the manufacturer continues to function as a manufacturer's mark: SONY means goods manufactured by Sony Corp., not distributed or selected by later sellers (including subsidiaries of Sony). The distributor's use is of the manufacturer's mark and for the manufacturer's benefit; the distributor acquires no rights and cannot register the mark.[88]

There are deviations from this prototype. Supermarkets order and sell goods under their house brands. The public understands the mark as the distributor's (the supermarket's), not the manufacturer's. Similarly, a manufacturer may allow its mark to be registered in its distributor's name, and the public may accept it as the distributor's mark. This arrangement may make sense where the manufacturer controls the distributor (e.g., its subsidiary company), but has proved disastrous for manufacturers when the distributor is at arm's length. If the distribution arrangement ends, the manufacturer may have to distribute its product under a completely different mark to avoid infringing its ex-distributor's registration.[89]

C. CRITERIA FOR REGISTRABILITY

Choosing a mark requires more than finding something distinctive that qualifies as a trade-mark. The mark must be registrable. Otherwise, the

---

86   *Kraft*, above note 43 at 875.

87   *T Act*, above note 1, s. 50(1).

88   *Lin*, above note 5; *Citrus Growers Assn. Ltd. v. William D. Branson Ltd.*, [1990] 1 F.C. 641 (T.D.); *Uniwell Corp. v. Uniwell North America Inc.* (1996), 66 C.P.R. (3d) 436 at 451–53 (Fed. T.D.).

89   *White Consolidated Industries Inc. v. Beam of Canada Inc.* (1991), 39 C.P.R. (3d) 94 (Fed. T.D.). See sections H(6) and (5), "Non-use," and "Abandonment," in this chapter.

TMO will reject it; and any registration, if wrongly made, is always vulnerable to being invalidated in court.[90] Various bars, from the absolute to the relative, must be avoided. This section considers (1) what makes marks "unregistrable," (2) how a disclaimer can sometimes overcome the objection, and (3) when concurrent registrations are possible.

1) Absolute Bars

The following trade-marks are absolutely barred from registration.

a) Marks Confusing with a Registered Trade-mark

A mark confusing with an existing registered trade-mark is not registrable. Before the TMO, the applicant carries the burden of showing "no reasonable likelihood" of confusion.[91] Sometimes buying up the confusing marks or having them expunged for non-use or other ground of invalidity removes this objection.

b) Generic Marks

A mark cannot be "the name *in any language* of any of the wares or services" for which it is used or proposed.[92] So *airplane, avion, aeroplano,* and *Flugzeug* cannot be registered for aircraft. How many speakers of the language there are in Canada is irrelevant: importers or exporters from any country should not be inhibited from using whatever language they wish to denote a product or service. Nor does it matter that the applicant first coined the name: good practice requires product innovators to coin both a generic name (for others to use) and a trade-mark (for their own use). The prohibition goes further than the common law, which accepts a foreign generic word as distinctive if it was not commonly recognized as such — even if few people in Canada actually know the language or the word.

"Shredded wheat" provides an example of avoidable pitfalls. Nabisco's predecessor, which had patents covering the manufacturing process, started selling "Shredded Wheat" at the end of the nineteenth century. Trade-mark registrations for SHREDDED WHEAT were eventually sought or obtained in Canada, the United States, and the United Kingdom. When the patents expired, Kellogg became a competitor and was immediately sued for infringement and passing-off. The litigation col-

---

90   *T Act*, above note 1, ss. 37(1), 38(2), & 18(1)(a).
91   *T Act, ibid.*, s. 12(1)(d); *Gozlan*, above note 34. See section G(4), "Confusion," in this chapter.
92   *T Act, ibid.*, s. 12(1)(c) [emphasis added].

lapsed when Kellogg successfully moved to ensure that registrations for SHREDDED WHEAT were refused or invalidated in major markets.[93] Had Nabisco systematically promoted its product as "SHREDDED WHEAT™ biscuits" — denoting it as a "biscuit" while staking out "shredded wheat" as a trade-mark — the words may perhaps in time have become distinctive of a particular producer rather than a particular product. As it was, Nabisco itself used "shredded wheat" in its packaging and advertising to denote the product. The public came to understand the words this way. Other traders could equally use them to denote the product if they differentiated it from the original. This Kellogg did when it entered the market, adding its own distinctive marks and adopting different packaging.

c) Other Generic Symbols

A mark that, in ordinary good-faith commercial usage, has become recognized in Canada as designating the kind, quality, quantity, value, place of origin, or date of production of any product or service is unregistrable for wares or services of the same general class. Denominations of plant varieties under the *Plant Breeders' Rights Act* also come into this category. Any similar mark or name that would likely be mistaken for these indicators also cannot be used or registered.[94] Thus XXX is unregistrable for beer since it is generally recognized as an indicator of strength. Prohibited indicia in these categories may be part of a registered mark if they are used non-deceptively and made subject to an appropriate disclaimer.[95] So BABY DUCK CANADIAN CHAMPAGNE was registered for Canadian champagne, once CANADIAN CHAMPAGNE was disclaimed.[96]

d) Wine and Spirit Appellations

Marks for wines or spirits cannot include protected geographical indications listed by the Registrar, if the wine or spirit does not come from that area.[97] At first sight, this means that the BABY DUCK CANADIAN CHAM-

---

93   *Canadian Shredded Wheat Co. v. Kellogg Co. of Canada*, [1938] 1 All E.R. 618 (P.C.), further proceedings [1939] S.C.R. 329; *Kellogg Co. v. National Biscuit Co.*, 305 U.S. 111 (1938); *Shredded Wheat Co. Ltd. v. Kellogg Co. of Great Britain Ltd.* (1939), 57 R.P.C. 137 (H.L.).

94   *T Act*, above note 1, ss. 12(1)(e), 10, & 10.1.

95   See section C(4), "Disclaimer," in this chapter.

96   *Caves Jordan & Ste-Michelle Ltée v. Andres Wines Ltd.* (1985), 6 C.I.P.R. 49 (Fed. T.D.) [*Caves Jordan*].

97   *T Act*, above note 1, s. 12(1)(g)–(h); ss. 11.11–11.2. See section E, "Geographical Indications," in this chapter.

PAGNE mark would not have been saved by a disclaimer and that the use of the word "champagne" may have been banned. However, the list of geographical indications, established in 1996 as a *TRIPs* obligation, presently allows the use of Champagne, as well as other terms commonly used in the Canadian liquor trade.[98]

e) Marks Similar to Official Marks

No mark the same as or very like an official mark can be used as a trade-mark or otherwise in business, except with its owner's consent.[99] These marks include royal arms and crests, flags, and marks adopted by public authorities — for example, Olympic marks and university emblems.

f) Offensive Marks

A "scandalous, obscene or immoral" word or device cannot be used as a trade-mark or otherwise.[100] A fair amount should be tolerated, since commercial expression is protected under section 2(b) of the *Canadian Charter of Rights and Freedoms*. MISS NUDE UNIVERSE for beauty pageants and associated merchandise was unobjectionable on this count: however distasteful nude (or other) beauty contests may be to many, the mark itself was not scandalous to the public at large.[101]

g) Suggested Connection with Individuals

Anything falsely suggesting a connection with any living person (including a portrait or signature) cannot be used or registered without his or her consent. Nor may the portrait or signature of anyone who died less than thirty years ago be similarly used without the estate's consent.[102] These provisions effectively create rights, exercisable without proof of injury or damage, in an individual's personality or other features by which he or she may be recognized.[103] For portraits and signatures, the right passes to the estate and lasts thirty years after death. The individual must, however, have a significant public reputation throughout Canada. Quebec artist Niska and European fashion designer Jean Cacherel failed to prevent registration of NISKA and CACHEREL for cloth-

---

98   *T Act, ibid.*, ss. 11.18(3)–(4).

99   *T Act, ibid.*, ss. 12(1)(e) & s. 9. See Section D, "Official Marks," in this chapter.

100   *T Act, ibid.*, ss. 12(1)(e) & 9(1)(j).

101   *Miss Universe Inc. v. Bohne* (1991), 36 C.P.R. (3d) 76 at 82–83 (T.M. Opp. Bd.), aff'd (*sub nom. Miss Universe Inc. v. Bohna*) [1992] 3 F.C. 682 (T.D.), rev'd on other grounds (1994), [1995] 1 F.C. 614 (C.A.).

102   *T Act,* above note 1, ss. 12(1)(e), 9(1)(k), (l), & 9(2).

103   *Carson v. Reynolds,* [1980] 2 F.C. 685 (T.D.) [*Carson*]; *Insurance,* above note 62.

ing; a reputation in Quebec or Europe is not necessarily a Canada-wide reputation.[104] Johnny Carson and Philippe de Rothschild were acknowledged to be more recognizable: HERE'S JOHNNY could not be registered for portable toilets, and a Toronto cigar shop could not call itself "Rothschild at Yorkville."[105]

By contrast, the common law can, through torts of passing-off and misappropriation of personality, grant journeymen and Wayne Gretzkys alike a right to market their personalities: their name, voice, likeness, and other recognizable characteristics. This right has been extended by some provinces — British Columbia, Manitoba, Newfoundland, Quebec, and Saskatchewan — to everyone, famous or not, as an element of personal privacy and dignity. A photograph of simple citizen Jane Doe cannot end up in a foot-powder advertisement without her consent, although a photograph of her foot could if she was not recognizable from it. Similarly, a celebrity may not complain of the use of his image in the news media or biographies.[106] In the United States, this right has gone so far as to cover advertising that simply evokes a celebrity's image. Vanna White, the hostess of the television game show *Wheel of Fortune*, successfully claimed that her rights were infringed by a print advertisement that depicted a robot that was recognizable as an imitation of White going about her business on the show.[107]

2) Relative Bars

Some marks may, though initially unregistrable, be registered on proof of distinctiveness in fact.[108] The mark's initial meaning is then replaced in buyers' minds by a secondary meaning acquired through intensive sales and advertising, linking the mark with its user's goods or services.

---

104   *Bousquet v. Barmish Inc.* (1991), 37 C.P.R. (3d) 516 at 524 (Fed. T.D.), aff'd (1993), 46 C.P.R. (3d) 510 (Fed. C.A.); *Lortie v. Standard Knitting Ltd.* (1991), 35 C.P.R. (3d) 175 at 179–81 (T.M. Opp. Bd.)

105   *Carson*, above note 103; *Baron Philippe de Rothschild SA v. Casa de Habana Inc.* (1987), 19 C.P.R. (3d) 114 (Ontario H.C.J.). Carson won similar litigation in the United States: *Carson v. Here's Johnny Portable Toilets Inc.*, 698 F.2d 281 (6th Cir. 1983).

106   *Joseph v. Daniels* (1986), 11 C.P.R. (3d) 544 (B.C.S.C.); *Bogajewicz v. Sony of Canada Ltd.* (1995), 63 C.P.R. (3d) 458 (Que. S.C.); *Gould Estate v. Stoddart Publishing Co.*, [1996] O.J. No. 3288 (Gen. Div.) (QL) [*Gould*].

107   *White v. Samsung Electronics America Inc.*, 971 F.2d 1395 (9th Cir. 1992), application for re-hearing denied, 989 F.2d 1512 (9th Cir. 1993). See section C(2)(a), "Names and Surnames," in this chapter.

108   See section B(2)(b), "Distinctiveness," in this chapter.

The registration may be limited to the product, service, and territory in which distinctiveness is shown. So the exclusive right to a mark distinctive only in Vancouver may be limited to that city.[109] An application based on proposed use in such a case will therefore fail; only one based on actual use and acquired distinctiveness has any prospect of success.

At common law, any mark was capable in law of becoming distinctive. CAMEL HAIR for belting was found to have acquired a secondary meaning of belting made by a particular producer, even though the product was (unbeknownst to most) made of camel hair. No rival could then call its belting CAMEL HAIR, whether or not its product was made of camel hair, since the public would believe that the goods were produced by the first maker. Rivals could, however, discreetly advertise their belting as made of camel hair if the promotion did not suggest any trade connection with the CAMEL HAIR™ product.[110]

A stricter standard was required for registration before 1954, and even more recently (1994) in the United Kingdom. Some marks were thought incapable in law of ever becoming distinctive, and no trader was denied the right to use laudatory words like "super," "standard," "perfect," or "perfection." But the *Act* has returned to the common law standard. PERFECTION itself is registered for dairy products, and CANADIAN failed to be registered for beer only because Molson failed to discharge the "very heavy" onus of proving distinctiveness for it.[111] The system's operation depends on that distinctiveness being convincingly proved, since the *Act* provides even honest traders with a narrow set of defences — much narrower than at common law, where no misrepresentation means no liability.[112]

Marks falling under this relative bar are (1) names and surnames, (2) descriptive marks, and (3) deceptive marks.

a) Names and Surnames

A word that is "primarily merely" the name or surname of a living person or one who died less than thirty years ago is *prima facie* unregistrable because it is often not distinctive.[113] MCDONALD for goods may not

---

109 *T Act*, above note 1, ss. 12(2) & 32; *Home Juice Co.* v. *Orange Maison Ltée*, [1968] 1 Ex.C.R. 313 at 318, conceded on appeal [1970] S.C.R. 942 [*Home Juice*].

110 *Frank Reddaway & Co. Ltd.* v. *George Banham & Co. Ltd.*, [1896] A.C. 199 (H.L.).

111 *Perfection Foods Ltd.* v. *Chocolat Perfection Inc.* (1991), 35 C.P.R. (3d) 185 (T.M. Opp. Bd.); *Molson Cos.* v. *Carling Breweries Ltd.* (1988), 19 C.P.R. (3d) 129 (Fed. C.A.).

112 See sections I and H, "Users' Rights," and "Invalidity," in this chapter.

113 *T Act*, above note 1, s. 12(1)(a).

distinguish one McDonald's goods from another McDonald's. It also seems unfair to give the first Ronald McDonald to use his name as a mark a monopoly running against all other Ronald McDonalds (perhaps from the same extended family) wanting to go into a similar business. But the unfairness diminishes once the market recognizes RONALD McDONALD as distinguishing a particular producer (whatever his or her real name); for a second Ronald McDonald would then cause market confusion in adopting that name for similar goods or services. At common law, this could be passing-off, although the law once said that personal names could be used honestly as trade-names — everyone's birthright, even if some confusion resulted.[114] The distinction probably no longer holds,[115] especially today when use as a trade-name very easily slips into use as a service mark.[116] The public are accustomed to people of similar names trading in different businesses. One trade-name may become more famous than another, but that should not give its owner the right to close others down or obstruct new entrants who wish to use the same name for their business. It is more pertinent to ask the following questions:

• Is it a fair business decision for the second entrant to use his name in the type of business he is carrying on? So Ronald McDonald, MD, can hardly stop another Ronald McDonald, MD, from practising medicine under his name.

• Is the way the second entrant uses the name reasonably designed to minimize deception and confusion? If so, some confusion may have to be tolerated lest personal names be monopolized simply on the basis of priority of use.[117]

Two very different questions are asked, however, when registrability is in issue. First, is the word (or words) in fact someone's name or surname? If not, nobody's patrimony is being usurped and the mark is unobjectionable. RONALD McDONALD is initially barred even if arbitrarily chosen or coined: people of that name exist somewhere in the world, as a check of telephone directories reveals. But a coined or fictitious name,

---

114 *Hurlbut Co. v. Hurlbut Shoe Co.*, [1925] S.C.R. 141 [*Hurlbut*].

115 *Boswell-Wilkie Circus (Pty.) Ltd. v. Brian Boswell Circus (Pty.) Ltd.* (1983), [1985] F.S.R. 434 (S.Afr. S.C. Prov. Div.), modified (1985), [1986] F.S.R. 479 (S. Afr. S.C. (A.D.)).

116 See section B(2)(c), "Use," in this chapter.

117 *Joseph E. Seagram & Sons Ltd. v. Seagram Real Estate Ltd.* (1990), 33 C.P.R. (3d) 454 (Fed. T.D.) [*Seagram*]; *Bell Insurance Agencies Ltd. v. Bell & Cross Insurance Agency Ltd.* (1983), 72 C.P.R. (2d) 46 (Man. Q.B.).

not shown to be someone's real name (SCARLETT O'HARA, OLIVER TWIST), may be acceptable.[118] So, too, may a name with added descriptive matter, since the mark is then not predominantly just a name: for example, O'HARA CONTOURS or McDONALD EXTRA.[119]

The second question is more difficult: Would a potential buyer immediately respond to the word by thinking its primary meaning is merely a name or a surname? Again this depends on the evidence presented. The average bibliophile would be primarily impressed by COLES for books as a surname rather than by its rare meaning of cabbages (as in cole slaw).[120] Drinkers might react differently to ELDER for beverages, an uncommon name with other meanings (tree, older person, senior officeholder); it is registrable since its surname significance does not predominate over other meanings.[121] Oddly enough, obviously foreign words like GALANOS for toiletries or NISHI for electronics are judged by the perceptions of the notional Canadian "of ordinary intelligence and education in English or French," who would not recognize these words as Spanish or Japanese surnames.[122] This standard wrongly discounts the reaction of significant linguistic populations in Canada who may be target markets for the products in question.

b) Descriptive Marks

A mark "clearly" (i.e., plainly or self-evidently) descriptive as "depicted, written or sounded" in English or French of "the character or quality" of its wares or services "or of their place of origin" is *prima facie* not registrable. Nor is one clearly descriptive of "the conditions" of production of the wares or services or "the persons employed in their production."[123] These bans do not apply to suggestive marks, and much material slips by in this category. The trade-marks register is full of oddities caused by decisions which are said to turn largely on their own facts, but which as a body close the door to very few marks indeed. Consider the following:

---

118   *Gerhard Horn Investments Ltd.* v. *Canada (Registrar of Trade Marks)*, [1983] 2 F.C. 878 (T.D.).

119   *Hawick Knitwear Manufacturers Assn.* v. *W. Howick Ltd.* (1972), 9 C.P.R. (2d) 93 (T.M. Opp. Bd.).

120   *Canada (Registrar of Trade Marks)* v. *Coles Book Stores Ltd.* (1972), [1974] S.C.R. 438.

121   *Elder's Beverages (1975) Ltd.* v. *Canada (Registrar of Trade Marks)*, [1979] 2 F.C. 735 (T.D.).

122   *Galanos* v. *Canada (Registrar of Trade Marks)* (1982), 69 C.P.R. (2d) 144 at 155 (Fed. T.D.); *Nishi* v. *Robert Morse Appliances Ltd.* (1990), 34 C.P.R. (3d) 161 at 167 (Fed. T.D.); compare *ROC International* v. *Rocbel Holdings Ltd.* (1994), 53 C.P.R. (3d) 109 at 112–13 (T.M. Opp. Bd.).

123   *T Act*, above note 1, s. 12(1)(b).

i) Character or Quality

Only matter material to the composition of a product is "clearly descriptive" of it. KOLD ONE therefore is acceptable for beer but GOLDEN is not, because apparently goldness is, but coldness is not, intrinsic to beer.[124] But DOCTORS for thermometers, PIPEFITTERS for wrenches,[125] and general laudatory words like PERFECT and PERFECTION are all *prima facie* prohibited, as traders should not be hindered in associating this language with their products.

In practice, this ban is a weakling. True, the Supreme Court once asserted that ellipses can be clearly descriptive: so OFF! for insect repellant was unregistrable because of its common use in conjunction with other words for all sorts of products that eliminated nuisances.[126] But the implications of this decision are largely ignored today. How else does one explain registrations like FROM PATIENCE COMES PERFECTION for alcohol, repetitions like PIZZA PIZZA for pizza, and "Franglais" like LE JUICE for juices — all said to be merely "suggestive," not clearly descriptive, of their wares?[127] Manipulating what the mark is registered for also helps. So, for example, a mark descriptive of goods may not be descriptive of services. AUTOMATIC PARKING DEVICES OF CANADA was said to be not descriptive of the business of providing servicing and services for such equipment, the judge even calling the combination of words "unusual"![128] Yet the collocation is obvious enough and may hinder later traders honestly wanting to use other similar obvious collocations for goods as well as services. Very little is left unregistrable if decisions like this are taken seriously.

ii) Geographic Marks

The ban on marks clearly descriptive of "the place of origin" of their associated goods or services *prima facie* bars geographic names and their variants: for example, TORONTO, TORONTONIAN, TORONTO'S. The right to indicate where a firm's output comes from should be free for all. If any protection is warranted, the most appropriate form seems to be a certi-

---

124   *Provenzano v. Canada (Registrar of Trade Marks)* (1977), 37 C.P.R. (2d) 189 (Fed. T.D.), aff'd (1978), 40 C.P.R. (2d) 288 (Fed. C.A.); *Labatt*, above note 78.

125   *Lubrication Engineers Inc. v. Canadian Council of Professional Engineers*, [1992] 2 F.C. 329 (C.A.) [*Lubrication Engineers*].

126   *S.C. Johnson*, above note 71.

127   *Perfection Foods Ltd. v. Hiram Walker & Sons Ltd.* (1988), 21 C.P.R. (3d) 136 (T.M. Opp. Bd.); *Pizza Pizza Ltd. v. Canada (Registrar of Trade Marks)* (1982), 67 C.P.R. (2d) 202 (Fed. T.D.) [*Pizza*]; *Coca-Cola Co. v. Cliffstar Corp.* (1993), 49 C.P.R. (3d) 358 (T.M. Opp. Bd.). See section C(4), "Disclaimer," in this chapter.

128   *Parking*, above note 33 at 160.

fication mark or a geographical indication.[129] This would typically be held by a governmental authority or a producers' association, and the ban on descriptive appellations would not apply. Thus, SWISS for chocolate was appropriately registered as a certification mark by a Swiss chocolate makers' association.[130] Still, many marks connoting geographic origin have been privatized at common law or registered by individual traders. This has created obstacles for later entrants. Thus, the registration of OKANAGAN CELLARS for wine prevented another winery from registering OKANAGAN VINEYARDS, even on disclaiming the word OKANAGAN.[131] The wisdom of allowing either to register is debatable, for the registration would hinder all wine makers of the region from sharing in the reputation they helped to create for the Okanagan as a wine-producing area.

The registrability of a geographic mark often seems to boil down to asking how ignorant the average Canadian is about the geography of Canada or any other country. Would this exemplar of ignorance's first impression — or at least, one hopes, the impression of a significant section of the Canadian community — be to recognize the mark as describing a place of origin? VICTORIA and probably RADIUM pass this test, but FARAH (a village in Afghanistan) probably does not. Even VICTORIA and RADIUM are problematic because both have equally significant non-geographic meanings. Whether they would be recognized as places of origin may depend on the product or service they are used for. On first impression, VICTORIA for retirement planning services or RADIUM for mineral water may denote a place of origin, whereas VICTORIA or RADIUM for automobiles may well not.

One then asks: Would the average Canadian buyer immediately think the product or service came from or was associated with that place? LABRADOR and AMAZON immediately denote places of origin, but most would assume that LABRADOR for bananas or AMAZON for snowsuits were arbitrary marks not denoting the product's place of origin. Nor are marks merely suggestive of origin banned. The TMO has claimed that the average Canadian might think that CÔTE D'AZUR for toiletries suggests French provenance, but apparently would not believe that the

---

129   See section B(1)(e), "Certification Mark," and section E, "Geographical Indications," in this chapter.

130   *Sanna Inc. v. Chocosuisse Union des Fabricants Suisses de Chocolat* (1986), 14 C.P.R. (3d) 139 (T.M. Opp. Bd.); *T Act*, above note 1, s. 25.

131   *Calona Wines Ltd. v. Okanagan Vineyards Ltd.* (1988), 20 C.P.R. (3d) 573 (T.M. Opp. Bd.) [*Calona*]; compare *American Waltham Watch Co. v. U.S. Watch Co.*, 53 N.E. 141 (Mass. S.C. 1899).

goods came from the Côte d'Azur.[132] Where he might think they did come from was not explored.

c) Deceptive Marks

Marks that would deceive people into making false buying decisions do the very opposite of what marks are meant to achieve: hence the prohibition of marks "deceptively misdescriptive" of character, quality, origin, and so on. SHAMMI for gloves with no chamois or LIVER DINNER for cat food without much liver are obviously unregistrable.[133] One might have thought the CÔTE D'AZUR mark would have been held deceptive, but it was not.

This inconsistency suggests that the prohibition has not been treated very seriously. Laudatory marks like PERFECTION or PREMIER have been said not to be deceptively misdescriptive, even if the product they come with is second rate, because buyers are considered to be hardened against this sort of puffery. And once again, suggestive marks — those whose lie is more veiled and may operate subconsciously — escape criticism more readily. For example, should the use of German-sounding names for wines — such as HOCHTALER — be allowed for Canadian wines that have few characteristics associated with German wines (other than wetness), and need not be made by anyone having the slightest connection with Germany or German wine-making methods? Should WINSTON'S CHOICE be allowed for whisky because it only suggests it was the particular liquor Winston Churchill drank, even where the drink is a Canadian rye Churchill never heard of? These petty lies are not enough to deny registrability,[134] but this laxity only encourages resources to be spent on yet further ingenious ways of taking advantage of buyer credulity.

3) Foreign Registered Marks

One object of the *Paris Convention* was to make trade-marks validly registered in one country easily transportable to others, with whatever

---

132 *Avon Canada Ltd. v. Ethier International Inc.* (1990), 34 C.P.R. (2d) 410 (T.M. Opp. Bd.).

133 *T Act*, above note 1, s. 12(1)(b); *Canada (Deputy A.G.) v. Biggs Laboratories (Can.) Ltd.* (1964), 25 Fox Pat. C. 174 (Ex. Ct); *General Foods Ltd. v. Ralston Purina Co.* (1975), 20 C.P.R. (2d) 236 at 238 (T.M. Opp. Bd.).

134 *Stabilisierungsfonds für Wein v. Andres Wines Ltd.* (1985), 5 C.P.R. (3d) 256 (T.M. Opp. Bd.); *Scotch Whisky Assn. v. Mark Anthony Group Inc.* (1990), 31 C.P.R. (3d) 55 at 60 (T. M. Opp. Bd.).

minor changes were thought necessary to make the mark acceptable to local markets. On proof of the foreign registration, a *Convention* application (which now includes applications from WTO members) is vetted on slightly different, theoretically less rigorous, registrability criteria from regular applications.[135] In fact, Canada's standard registrability criteria are now so lax that few marks fare better claiming *Convention* benefit. The *Convention* applicant must still show its title;[136] the mark must not be confusing with a Canadian registered mark; it cannot falsely suggest a connection with a living individual; it cannot be mistaken for an official mark; it cannot be offensive (in the sense of "contrary to morality or public order"); and it cannot be "of such a nature as to deceive the public." Objections that a mark is generic, descriptive, or misdescriptive, though not directly available, can be made indirectly; for a mark must not be "without distinctive character" having regard to its use abroad and all the circumstances, and so must have some distinctiveness.[137] So BARRIER BAG for bags to package food and LUBRICATION ENGINEERS for lubricants were denied registration as either standard or *Convention* marks, since both were "clearly descriptive" and so "without distinctive character." Only cogent evidence of distinctiveness from extensive use overcomes such objections.[138]

4) Disclaimer

A trade-mark may be distinctive as a whole but may comprise elements that individually are unregistrable. So SUPER KODAK may be registrable as a whole, but SUPER by itself would not be. Since registration might suggest some entitlement to monopolize SUPER by itself, the TMO regularly requires a disclaimer of the exclusive right to use it and other descriptive words, names, surnames, and generic words.[139] The disclaimed matter is still part of the mark and is considered when judging confusion and infringement. Over time, it may even acquire distinctiveness, and a fresh application for registration without a disclaimer may succeed.

---

135 *T Act*, above note 1, ss. 14 & 31. Applicants often claim both ordinary registrability and *Convention* benefit — just in case one basis fails.

136 See section F, "Title," in this chapter.

137 *T Act, ibid.*, s. 14(1). If opposed, the *Convention* mark also must overcome a general distinctiveness challenge: s. 38(2)(d). See section B(2)(b), "Distinctiveness," in this chapter.

138 *W.R. Grace & Co. v. Union Carbide Corp.* (1987), 14 C.P.R. (3d) 337 (Fed. C.A.); *Lubrication Engineers,* above note 125.

139 *T Act*, above note 1, s. 35. See section C(2)(b), "Descriptive Marks," in this chapter.

Disclaimers are not accepted for deceptively misdescriptive matter, official marks, or offensive marks. These marks must be dropped altogether if the application is to proceed.[140] Similarly, if nothing distinctive remains after the disclaimer, there is nothing to register and the application will be rejected. THE CANADIAN JEWISH REVIEW in Hebraic-style lettering was thus denied registration for periodicals because, after the words were disclaimed, nothing remained.[141] On the other hand, PIZZA PIZZA was registered for pizza, with "pizza" disclaimed; the registration then covered only the duplicated words and gave no monopoly over "pizza" used separately.[142]

5) Concurrent Registration

Two identical or confusingly similar marks cannot coexist on the register for the same class of goods or services. There are three exceptions:

- One entity may register and hold a set of otherwise confusingly similar associated marks — for example, McDonald's Corp.'s EGG McMUFFIN, McSUNDAE, McCHEESE, McFEAST — but the marks can be transferred only as a block.[143]
- The registration of some marks may be limited to the territory where they have become distinctive.[144] An identical mark may then become distinctive and registrable for another territory. This exception applies to descriptive and misdescriptive marks, names and surnames.[145]
- Firm 1 may have used a confusingly similar mark or name in good faith before the registrant firm 2 filed its application. Firm 1 can then use the mark concurrently in a defined territory if the Federal Court considers this use is not "contrary to the public interest" — for instance, if there is no public confusion in firm 1's territory, or perhaps if firm 2 does not plan to expand there. Unfortunately, to be eligible for the order, firm 1 must first prove that title to the mark has become unchallengeable. This means firm 1 must wait five years after registration before applying to the Court.[146]

---

140   *Caves Jordan*, above note 96; *Lake Ontario Cement Ltd.* v. *Canada (Registrar of Trade Marks)* (1976), 31 C.P.R. (2d) 103 (Fed. T.D.). Compare section C(1)(c), "Other Generic Symbols," in this chapter.
141   *Canada Jewish Review Ltd.* v. *Canada (Registrar of Trade Marks)* (1961), 37 C.P.R. 89 (Ex. Ct.).
142   *Pizza*, above note 127.
143   *T Act*, above note 1, s. 15.
144   *T Act, ibid.*, s. 32 (Registrar); *Home Juice*, above note 109 (court imposes limitation).
145   See section C(2), "Relative Bars," in this chapter.
146   *T Act, ibid.*, s. 21; *Kayser-Roth Canada (1969) Ltd.* v. *Fascination Lingerie Inc.*, [1971] F.C. 84 (T.D.). See section H(4), "Inferior Title," in this chapter.

D. OFFICIAL MARKS

Various bodies and authorities can use identifying marks and symbols that cannot be adopted by anyone else in connection with a business, as trade-marks or otherwise, without prior consent. Neither the exact mark nor one so similar as to be likely mistaken for it can be adopted.[147] Though technically not trade-marks, many of these official marks in practice function much the same way. Protection for some is automatic. For others, the Registrar of Trade-marks must first post a notice in the *Trade-marks Journal*. Others still must have that notice preceded by one given to the World Intellectual Property Organization bureau in Geneva.

1) Marks Automatically Protected

The following marks and symbols are automatically protected:[148]

- The arms, crests, and standards of the royal family or anything suggesting royal, vice-regal, or governmental patronage, approval, or authority.
- The Red Cross and its emblem, the Red Crescent, Red Lion, and Sun emblems, and the international civil defence sign (an equilateral blue triangle on an orange ground).
- The national flags of *Paris Convention* or *WTO* countries.
- The United Nations, and its official seal or emblem.
- The Royal Canadian Mounted Police, any combination of letters relating to the RCMP, and any pictorial representation of a uniformed RCMP member.

2) Marks Protected after Public Notice

The following marks are protected once the Registrar of Trade-marks, at the adopter's request, gives public notice that a mark or symbol has been adopted and used:[149]

- The arms, crests, and flags of Canada, its provinces, and municipalities.
- Other armorial bearings formally granted by the Governor General and publicly notified by the Registrar at the former's request,

---

147 *T Act, ibid.*, ss. 9(1) & 9(2)(a).
148 *T Act, ibid.*, s.9(1)(a)–(d), (f)–(h.1), (i.2), (m), & (o).
149 *T Act, ibid.*, ss. 9(1)(e), (n.1), & (n).

although a use that will not likely mislead the public into connecting the user with the bearer is allowed.[150]

- A university's badges, crests, emblems, and marks.
- Badges, crests, emblems, and marks adopted and used by the Canadian Armed Forces.
- Badges, crests, emblems, and marks adopted and used as an official mark by any Canadian "public authority" for its wares and services. Anybody operating for the public benefit and subject to significant government control or financing may qualify under this head. Many groups have taken advantage of these provisions, from the Canadian Olympic Association and Expo 86 Corporation to charities like the WWF — World Wide Fund for Nature and more localized charities.[151]

3) Foreign Official Marks

The following symbols are banned, once they are listed with the World Intellectual Property Organization bureau in Geneva and once the list is publicly notified by the Registrar of Trade-marks in the *Trade-marks Journal*:[152]

- National, territorial, or civic arms, crests, and emblems of *Paris Convention* and *WTO* countries, and their territorial or civic flags.
- Official signs or hallmarks indicating control or warranty adopted by such countries. These indicia are, however, allowed on products that are not the same as or similar to those for which the indicia were adopted. A silver hallmark, assuming it has no copyright, may be used on a T-shirt.[153]
- Armorial bearings, flags, emblems, or name abbreviations of an international intergovernmental organization (e.g., UNESCO, GATT, IMF).

4) Exploitation and Protection

The owners of these marks and symbols may themselves exploit them, as universities do when they sell T-shirts and other knick-knacks with the university's crest on them. They may license others, as the RCMP

---

150   *T Act, ibid.*, s. 9(2)(b)(ii).

151   *Canada (Registrar of Trade Marks) v. Canadian Olympic Assn.* (1982), [1983] 1 F.C. 672 (C.A.); *British Columbia v. Mihaljevic* (1989), 26 C.P.R. (3d) 184 (B.C.S.C.), aff'd (1991), 36 C.P.R. (3d) 445 (B.C.C.A.); *WWF — World Wide Fund for Nature v. Incaha Inc.* (1995), 61 C.P.R. (3d) 413 (T.M. Opp. Bd.).

152   *T Act*, above note 1, s. 9(1)(i), (i.1), & (i.3).

153   *T Act, ibid.*, s. 9(2)(b)(i).

has done to market its official marks and emblems for royalties.[154] The owners may also prevent the registration of the same or very similar marks, and they can sue and stop infringements without needing to prove injury or damage.[155]

Although official marks are convenient for their owners, the scheme regulating them is not well integrated with that for regular trade-marks. More institutions have taken advantage of it than was originally contemplated; its effect on existing users is not well thought out; and no reason exists why many official mark owners should not seek registration as those in the private commercial sector do. The way the Canadian Olympic Association protects an ever-expanding range of OLYMPIC marks and symbols gives a glimpse of the system in action. The COA typically has the Registrar of Trade-marks notify through the *Trade-marks Journal* the COA's adoption of the marks. The Registrar does not check for conflicts with any registered mark, nor can the COA's action be opposed. The COA's rights, once publicly notified, are apparently perpetual against all goods and services, not merely competing or confusingly similar product lines.[156] There is no procedure for removing unused or undistinctive marks.

The COA can, moreover, easily oppose the registration of regular trade-marks it finds objectionable. Marks that are the same or that sound or look very like an official mark are unregistrable. Even if it has no official mark yet, the COA can stop a pending registration simply by filing an opposition, immediately adopting and using a conflicting mark, getting the mark publicly notified for the first time, and informing the Opposition Board any time before it gives its decision on the opposition.[157] The few existing uses that can avoid infringement have their rights frozen at the date the COA mark appears in the *Trade-marks Journal*. For example, OLYMPIAN for typeface fonts was allowed to continue as an unregistered mark, but could not be registered once the COA's OLYMPIAN official mark had been publicly notified.[158] Similarly, the *Guinness Book of Olympic Records* could not be packaged with Konica film and be marketed as the Konica Guinness Book of Olympic Records.[159]

---

154 L. Carrière, "La Protection des noms, marques et signes de la Gendarmerie royale du Canada" (1996) 8 C. Prop. Intell. 281.

155 *Carson*, above note 103.

156 *Canadian Olympic Assn. v. Allied Corp. (sub nom. Allied Corp. v. Canada Olympic Assn. — Assn. Olympique Canadienne)* (1989), [1990] 1 F.C. 769 (C.A.) [*Allied*].

157 *Olympus*, above note 39.

158 *Allied*, above note 156.

159 *Canadian Olympic Assn. v. Konica Canada Inc.* (1991), [1992] 1 F.C. 797 (C.A.).

All this protection no doubt preserves the integrity of Olympic marks between games. It allows the COA to mount effective licensing programs whenever the games are held in Canada. The COA can also act as proxy for foreign committees to stop unauthorized uses when the games are held abroad. The financing of the games, especially since 1984 in Los Angeles, has moved from the public to the private sector and to a heavy reliance on corporate sponsorship. In this light, perhaps the COA can make a persuasive case for having such extensive rights.[160] Whether all the other charitable institutions that have obtained official marks for little used symbols can make similar cases with equal force is more doubtful.

E. GEOGRAPHICAL INDICATIONS

At the insistence of European countries (particularly France) with established appellations of origin for better-class wines and food, *TRIPs* contains a set of provisions designed to extend worldwide protection for appellations of origin. In Canada, the existing system of certification marks[161] takes care of much of this obligation. *TRIPs*, however, required special protection for appellations relating to wines and spirits. Accordingly, Canada introduced a system in 1996 to protect "geographical indication[s]" for wines and spirits, as an alternative to certification marks.

The new system creates a hybrid somewhere between an official mark and a regular trade-mark. It prohibits the adoption or use as a trade-mark or otherwise of any "protected" geographical indication for a wine or spirit not originating in that area. The TMO keeps a list of these indications. Listing is preceded by a notice published by the Minister of Industry in the *Canada Gazette,* giving particulars of the geographical indication and the body responsible for it. An opposition may be filed in the TMO on the sole ground that "the indication is not a geographical indication." It must be one that

(a) identifies the wine or spirit as originating in the territory of a WTO Member, or a region or locality of that territory, where a quality, reputation or other characteristic of the wine or spirit is essentially attributable to its geographical origin, and

---

160   The COA has even garnered some judicial sympathy for the need to spread its "tentacles of trade mark protection . . . far and wide": see *Canadian Olympic Assn.* v. *Gym & Tonic Ltd.* (1988), 19 C.P.R. (3d) 98 at 102 (Fed. T.D.).

161   See section B(1)(e), "Certification Mark," in this chapter.

(*b*) except in the case of an indication identifying a wine or spirit originating in Canada, is protected by the laws applicable to that WTO
Member.[162]

The *TRIPs* provisions from which this definition comes are obviously a rough-and-ready compromise, and their ambiguities have been
transported into local law. What, for example, is the word "identifies"
in paragraph (a) in the definition of "geographical indication" supposed
to mean? In its country of origin, "Beaujolais" is certainly an appellation
of origin that identifies a style of wine coming from the Beaujolais
region in France. But suppose there is a wine grown and made in Canada called "Canadian Beaujolais." Many customers may then understand "beaujolais" to mean any red quaffing wine designed for early
drinking. Must a geographical indication, to qualify as such, merely
identify the wine in its country of origin, or must it also in fact so identify the product to consumers in Canada? If the indication is now
generic in Canada, is it registrable?

A later provision specifically allows the adoption, use, or trade-mark
registration of any indication "identical with a term customary in common language in Canada as the common name for the wine or spirit."
This provision suggests that such a customary term could indeed be
listed. Why else would the exemption be needed?[163] So, if beaujolais was
indeed generic in Canada, a mark such as FIZZY BEAUJOLAIS for a mixture
of Canadian red wine and carbonated water might be registrable, even if
Beaujolais itself were listed as a geographical indication.[164]

Other important exemptions exist:

- Customary grape variety names may continue. So may the use of
  some specific words. Some of these are unsurprising: Champagne,
  Port, Sherry, Chablis, Burgundy, Rhine, Sauterne, Claret, Grappa,
  Ouzo. Others come as more of a surprise: Bordeaux, Chianti, Malaga,

---

162 *T Act*, above note 1, s. 2, def. "geographical indication"; ss. 11.11–11.15.

163 *T Act, ibid.*, s. 11.18(2)(a), tracking *Agreement on Trade-Related Aspects of
Intellectual Property Rights, Including Trade in Counterfeit Goods*, (1994) 25 I.I.C.
209, art. 24.6 [*TRIPs*]; *Re Crosfield & Sons Ltd.'s Application* (1909), [1910] 1
Ch. 130 (C.A.).

164 Compare *Institut National des Appellations d'Origine* v. *Vintners International Co.*,
958 F.2d 1574 (Fed. Cir. 1992), allowing registration of CHABLIS WITH A TWIST for
"California White Wine With Natural Citrus," despite the objection of French
Chablis producers. See also J. Chen, "A Sober Second Look at Appellations of
Origin: How the United States Will Crash France's Wine and Cheese Party"
(1996) 5 Minn. J. Global Trade 29 at 50–58.

Marsala, Médoc, Sambuca, Curaçao. Items may be added or deleted by order-in-council.[165]

- Canadian businesses may continue with any geographical indication used for at least ten years before 15 April 1994, or for any shorter period if the use is "in good faith."[166]
- Unauthorized uses or even trademark registrations of a listed indication may continue unless (a) enforcement proceedings are taken within five years of the mark's becoming generally known or registered, and (b) the unauthorized user knew the word was protected when adopting or first using it.[167]

These exemptions parallel those in *TRIPs,* but the countries of Europe clearly hope they will be only temporary. *TRIPs* requires states to negotiate towards increased protection for these appellations. It may be that Canadian producers and importers will eventually have to phase out currently exempted uses and transform Canadian champagnes or ports into "sparkling" or "fortified" wines instead, since *TRIPs* disapproves of expressions like "imitation sherry," "port style," and "champagne type."[168] Whether this means that Spain may have to agree to reconsider its attitude towards fishing off the Canadian coast, in return for Canada's agreement to ban the use of "sherry" for Sherry-like wines, is an interesting speculation.

F. TITLE

Having chosen a mark, can the adopter rightly call it "mine own"? Title does not come from inventing or selecting a registrable mark. It comes instead from

- use[169] of the mark,
- making it well known[170] in Canada, or
- filing an application to register a proposed mark.[171]

---

165   *T Act*, above note 1, s. 11.18.
166   *T Act, ibid.*, s. 11.17.
167   *T Act, ibid.*, s. 11.19.
168   *TRIPs*, above note 163, arts. 23(1) & 24.
169   See section B(2)(c), "Use," in this chapter.
170   See section F(1), "Well-known Mark," in this chapter.
171   Even earlier filing dates can be claimed by persons or corporations from a *Paris Convention* or *WTO* state: the filing date of a corresponding application in that state if the Canadian application is filed within six months: *T Act*, above note 1, s. 34(1). See section B(1)(c), "Proposed Trade-mark," in this chapter.

Whoever first does one of these acts has title to the mark. But this *prima facie* title can be upset. Anyone who earlier used, applied for, or made a reputation for the same mark anywhere in Canada can stop the registration. So may anyone in Canada who did the same with a confusing trade-mark, or who earlier used a confusing trade-name (the name under which a corporation, partnership, or individual does business).[172] The TMO initially checks only for better title based on the same or a confusing registered trade-mark or pending application. In opposition proceedings, or if the registration is later challenged, any claim of better title is examined. This includes claims based on earlier confusing trade-names, as well as on confusing registered and unregistered trade-marks.

There are some qualifications. Marks or names abandoned by the date the application was advertised are irrelevant.[173] So are trade-names not in active use: mere adoption, registration, or incorporation creates no title in them.[174] Most important, challenges can be mounted only by the claimant with the better title. Nobody can oppose or invalidate a registration by saying a third party's title is better than that of the applicant or registrant.[175] And a successful challenger cannot just take over the mark or application: it must file its own application and see how this in turn survives the rigours of TMO procedure.[176] Once a trade-mark has been registered for five years, the registrant's title is challengeable only on limited grounds.[177]

Evidence that fails to prove a better title may prevent registration on other grounds. For example, a famous mark may be unregistrable in Canada because its owner cannot meet the strict requirements of a well-known mark.[178] Still, if many Canadians do know of the foreign mark, it cannot be distinctive in Canada of anyone other than the foreign mark owner. So the foreign owner may not be positively entitled to register the mark, but may successfully oppose or invalidate registration on the ground of this lack of distinctiveness.[179]

---

172   *T Act, ibid.*, ss. 16(1) to (3), subss. (a) to (c); s. 2, def. "trade-name." The standard test for confusion applies: See section G(4), "Confusion," in this chapter.

173   *T Act, ibid.*, s. 16(5).

174   *Optagest Canada Inc.* v. *Services Optométriques Inc. S.O.L.* (1991), 37 C.P.R. (3d) 28 at 32 (Fed. T.D.).

175   *T Act*, above note 1, s. 17(1).

176   *Royal Doulton Tableware Ltd.* v. *Cassidy's Ltd./Cassidy's Lteé* (1984), [1986] 1 F.C. 357 (T.D.) [*Royal Doulton*].

177   See section H(4), "Inferior Title," in this chapter.

178   See section F(1), "Well-Known Mark," in this chapter.

179   *Andres Wines Ltd.* v. *E. & J. Gallo Winery* (1975), [1976] 2 F.C. 3 (C.A.) [*Gallo*]. See section B(2)(b), "Distinctiveness," in this chapter.

1) Well-Known Mark

Making a mark well known in Canada can give its owner title only under strict conditions:[180]

- The mark must have been "used" in a *Paris Convention* or *WTO* country in the Canadian sense of "use."[181]
- The mark must have become "well" known in Canada in a significant section of the country so as to have had an impact on a substantial number of Canadians.[182] A substantial part of a major province should do. The suggestion that Windsor, Ontario, might not qualify under this test seems doubtful.[183] Local use in Windsor is enough to create national rights for a trade-mark. Why should this not be equally true if the mark becomes well known there?
- The mark's fame must have arisen through advertisements in print media circulating in Canada or in radio or television broadcasts ordinarily received in Canada. Knowledge gained through word of mouth, from cruising the Internet, or from programs available only on cable is insufficient: none of this qualifies as broadcasting. Advertising in small readership magazines or the occasional spot on a U.S. border station whose signal spills over into Canada may not make the mark "well" known to Canadian dealers or users. Something close to saturation advertising in widely circulating magazines or on border stations with a substantial Canadian audience is required.[184]

G. OWNER'S RIGHTS

A trade-mark owner's rights may be infringed by (1) an exact imitation, (2) imports, (3) dilution, or (4) confusion.

1) Exact Imitation

The registrant's rights are obviously infringed where another person uses, without permission, the exact mark on the exact goods or services

---

180   *T Act*, above note 1, s. 5.
181   See section B(2)(c), "Use," in this chapter.
182   *Valle's Steak House v. Tessier* (1980), 49 C.P.R. (2d) 218 (Fed. T.D.).
183   *Robert C. Wian Enterprises Inc. v. Mady* (1965), 46 C.P.R. 147 (Ex. Ct.).
184   *Gallo*, above note 179. Local distribution of wares also makes a mark well known (s. 5(a)), but this will usually amount to an actual use entitling the user to registration on that basis anyway. Compare section G(4)(b)(v), "Confusion: Marks in Different Territory," in this chapter.

for which the first trade-mark is registered. A defendant who imports or sells fake ROLEX watches, innocently or otherwise, infringes the ROLEX mark registered for watches; indeed, the watches can be stopped at the border. The registrant need show nothing about the market for ROLEX watches or customer perceptions to get relief. Nor is it a defence that the watches were priced so cheaply that no customers would be fooled into thinking they were getting a genuine ROLEX.[185]

There is no infringement under this head if no "use" in the technical sense occurs. A registrant who complains that its mark has been used generically in the news media — for example, "thermos" in lower case rather than THERMOS® — cannot insist that the media change their ways: the media themselves are not using the mark, since "use" for goods occurs only at point of sale or on change of possession of the goods.[186] Accurate uses of the mark to indicate trade source — "GRUNGE brand watch: nearly as good but cheaper than ROLEX" — may also be permitted under this head. ROLEX, as used in this slogan, does distinguish the watches of the Rolex Watch Co. from others including GRUNGE, and does not imply any business association between ROLEX and GRUNGE. This practice may, however, amount to an actionable dilution of ROLEX as a trade-mark.[187]

2) Imports

Whether the parallel importer of genuine branded goods is "accurately" using the mark is a thorny question. The common law does not forbid such imports unless the seller passes itself off as an authorized distributor or suggests that the goods have attributes they in fact lack, such as an international warranty.[188] Where a local registered trade-mark is involved, however, interlocutory injunctions have sometimes been granted against parallel imports. Multinational firms may thus preserve local distribution networks and pricing practices free of foreign intra-brand competition.[189] This seems unjustifiable where the trade-mark is owned in Canada by the same legal corporation that had it affixed

---

185 *T Act*, above note 1, ss. 19 & 53.1.

186 See section B(2)(c), "Use," in this chapter.

187 *Clairol*, above note 83. See section G(3), "Dilution," in this chapter.

188 *Seiko*, above note 4.

189 For example, *Remington Rand Ltd.* v. *Transworld Metal Co.*, [1960] Ex.C.R. 463. Compare W.L. Hayhurst, "Intellectual Property as a Non-Tariff Barrier in Canada, with Particular Reference to 'Grey Goods' and 'Parallel Imports'" (1990) 31 C.P.R. (3d) 289 at 306–13.

abroad, for the mark then continues accurately to designate the trade source. It seems equally unjustifiable where the brand is a global brand used by a multinational's various subsidiaries, for the multinational firm effectively approves of the mark's use by any subsidiary that puts the branded goods into commerce. The Federal Court of Appeal recently took this view when it refused to let a mark owner or its licensee halt parallel imports of genuinely branded goods.[190]

More problematic is the case of the Canadian distributor that holds the mark with the foreign owner's consent and consistently emphasizes only the Canadian connection. The strongest case is where the products differ. Heinz Canada could bar imports of Heinz U.S. ketchup into Canada because it asserted that the Canadian product came mainly from Canadian-grown tomatoes and was formulated for local tastes.[191] Results like this, however, encourage undesirable strategic behaviour. Products may be formulated differently and product get-up may be kept similar precisely to prevent parallel imports. Multinationals can promote brands internationally and suggest identity of trade source, while simultaneously claiming in national courts that the brand is in fact locally produced by a different trade source. Trade-mark law should not support such strategies where steps can be taken to prevent buyer confusion. Thus, there seems no valid policy reason why Heinz U.S. ketchup should not be allowed to circulate in Canada, so long as consumers are aware that it differs from the Heinz Canada product. At common law the parallel importer would have to point this distinction out, but the Heinz multinational enterprise could equally be held responsible for clarifying a confusion of its own making.

3) Dilution

A mark may be used non-confusingly, but in a way that may tarnish its image or reduce its drawing power. Suppose ROLEX is marked on condoms; or a sign is put up beside a ROLEX watch display: "Buy GRUNGE watches: cheaper but as good as ROLEX"; or an insect repellant is adver-

---

190   *Smith & Nephew*, above note 6, following *Revlon v. Cripps & Lee Ltd.*, [1980] F.S.R. 85 (C.A.), and overruling *Mattel*, above note 6. A specific provision, dating back from the days of compulsory patent licensing, also prohibits drug companies from using the *Trade-marks Act* to prevent parallel imports, by the strategy of having marks held by an affiliate: *T Act*, above note 1, s. 51.

191   *H.J. Heinz Co. of Canada v. Edan Foods Sales Inc.* (1991), 35 C.P.R. (3d) 213 (Fed. T.D.), "perhaps open to question," according to *Smith & Nephew*, above note 6.

tised under the slogan "Where there's life, there's bugs," to spoof the Budweiser slogan "Where there's life, there's Bud." In none of these cases is confusion likely. Nobody would likely think the Rolex Watch Co. had started making condoms, nor that there was a trade association between it and GRUNGE, nor that Budweiser had moved into the insect repellant business.[192] Still, trade-mark owners would like to stop such uses. The value of their mark often depends on the affective associations built around it by advertising. Why should others free ride on or diminish this value?

This idea is reflected in section 22(1) of the *Act*: no one can "use" a registered trade-mark "in a manner that is likely to have the effect of depreciating the value of the goodwill attaching thereto."[193] The reputation of a trade-mark, its persuasive effect or snob value, built up by advertising, is said to be part of its goodwill. The value of this goodwill can depreciate "through reduction of the esteem in which the mark itself is held or through the direct persuasion and enticing of customers who could otherwise be expected to buy or continue to buy goods bearing the trade mark."[194] Section 22(1) thus steps in where confusion fails to tread, halting parodies and even some comparative advertising. Thus the PERRIER mark owner stopped the use of PIERRE EH! on bottled water to spoof some now forgotten antic of then prime minister Pierre Trudeau.[195] In the leading case, Clairol moved to stop the use of its marks on comparison charts found on REVLON hair-rinse packages. The charts showed which REVLON product most approximated a MISS CLAIROL or HAIR COLOR BATH product. Revlon's advertising was perfectly acceptable at common law: no false or misleading claims were made, nor were Clairol's products smeared. Yet the court enjoined Revlon and said Clairol was also entitled to monetary relief.[196]

---

192 Some courts have, however, stretched confusion and passing-off to encompass such cases: *Chemical Corp. of America* v. *Anheuser-Busch Inc.*, 306 F.2d 433 (5th Cir. 1962); *Mutual of Omaha Insurance Co.* v. *Novak*, 836 F.2d 297 (8th Cir. 1987) ("Mutant of Omaha" T-shirt enjoined, over dissent).

193 *T Act*, above note 1, s. 22(1). See W.L. Hayhurst, "Unauthorized Use of Another's Mark in Canada: Fair Use or Actionable?" (1985) 75 T.M.R. 1 at 13–18.

194 *Clairol*, above note 83 at 573.

195 *Source Perrier S.A.* v. *Fira-Less Marketing Co.*, [1983] 2 F.C. 18 (T.D.).

196 *Clairol*, above note 83; compare *Johnson & Johnson Inc.* v. *Bristol-Myers Squibb Canada Inc.* (1995), 62 C.P.R. (3d) 347 (Ont. Gen. Div.) (EXCEDRIN vs. TYLENOL). On comparative advertising using geographical indications, see *T Act*, above note 1, s. 11.16(2)–(3), and section E, "Geographical Indications," in this chapter.

The court in *Clairol* insisted that only "uses" in the technical trade-mark sense can dilute a mark.[197] This restriction at least allows consumer magazines to criticize products, and unions to caricature the marks of firms they are striking, without fear of trade-mark consequences. But this interpretation of section 22(1) also means that

- A trade-mark associated with goods is not legally "used" when appearing in promotional fliers or the broadcast media. In law, the mark is "used" only at point of sale or change of possession of the goods: that is, on the goods themselves or their packaging, on stands where the goods are shelved, or perhaps in in-store catalogues. So Revlon, though forbidden to put CLAIROL marks on its product packaging, could carry them in comparative advertising in fliers or on television.
- Comparative advertising carrying a mark associated with services is nevertheless not allowed because it technically qualifies as "use." This exclusion gives mark owners one more reason to dream up some service they can associate with their goods and register a mark for it.
- The "Where there's life, there's bugs" spoof of the Budweiser slogan mentioned earlier would be unobjectionable on two grounds: (a) the spoof is a different mark from the registered mark "Where there's life, there's Bud"; and (b) the spoof is used for a different product from that for which the latter slogan was registered (insect repellant, not beer). Section 22(1) applies only to a defendant's use of the trade-mark as registered, and then only if applied to the same product or service.

The policy underlying these results is not readily explicable. Some courts have tried to rationalize it by applying the ban on comparative advertising only where a defendant falsely implies some connection between the two businesses.[198] But a serious question about section 22(1)'s meaning exists, enough to enable trade-mark owners to harass competitors by threatening to seek, and sometimes even managing to obtain, interlocutory injunctions.[199]

---

197   *Syntex Inc. v. Apotex Inc.* (1984), 1 C.P.R. (3d) 145 (Fed. C.A.) and *Rôtisseries St-Hubert Ltée v. Syndicat des Travailleur(euses) de la Rôtisserie St-Hubert de Drummondville (CSN)* (1986), 17 C.P.R. (3d) 461 (Que. S.C.) hold similarly. See section B(2)(c), "Use," in this chapter.

198   *Nintendo of America Inc. v. Camerica Corp.* (1991), 34 C.P.R. (3d) 193 at 205–6 (Fed. T.D.), aff'd on other grounds (1991), 36 C.P.R. (3d) 352 (Fed. C.A.); *Future Shop Ltd. v. A & B Sound Ltd.* (1994), 55 C.P.R. (3d) 182 at 187 (B.C.S.C.).

199   For example, *Purolator Courier Ltd. — Courrier Purolator Ltée v. Mayne Nickless Transport Inc. (sub nom. Purolator Courier Ltd. v. Mayne Nickless Transport Inc.)* (1990), 33 C.P.R. (3d) 391 (Fed. T.D.).

This reservation suggests that section 22(1)'s interpretation needs reconsideration in at least two respects. First, the arbitrary distinction between service and goods marks suggests that "use" is not employed entirely in its technical sense. Second, "depreciation of goodwill" seems to be wrongly equated with any diversion of custom or lack of respect shown to a trade-mark.

Confining section 22(1) to cases where a common connection is falsely suggested may be one way to save the provision from another threat: that of being an unreasonable and unjustifiable limit on the guarantee of commercial free expression under section 2(b) of the *Canadian Charter of Rights and Freedoms*. Otherwise, this provision may well be held invalid as inconsistent with the *Charter*. There should be few mourners at this funeral. Neither *NAFTA* nor *TRIPs* requires anti-dilution measures. The broad concept of confusion[200] adequately protects trade-mark owners' interests. The intrusion on the right of others to advertise and accurately employ trade-marks that section 22(1) creates seems, moreover, quite disproportionate to whatever remaining legitimate interests trade-mark owners may conjure up.[201]

4) Confusion

Suppose a different mark from ROLEX for watches is used on the same wares or services: say, NOLEX on watches. Or the same mark is used for different wares (ROLEX computers) or as a trade-name ("Rolex Cameras Ltd."). Whether or not this use is permissible depends on whether the defendant's mark or name is likely to be confusing with the plaintiff's mark. In addition, the plaintiff must prove that the defendant was selling, distributing, or advertising wares or services in association with it.[202]

Likelihood of confusion is trade-mark law's doctrine of substantial infringement.[203] It is the instrument through which the competing interests of users of similar marks and names are adjusted and defined. Its legal component, defined comprehensively in the *Act*, applies to infringement and statutory passing-off, and is used to decide initial registrablity and title as well.[204] Marks are confusing if their use in the same

---

200   See section G(4), "Confusion," in this chapter.

201   Compare *Irwin Toy Ltd. v. Quebec (A.G.)*, [1989] 1 S.C.R. 927.

202   *T Act*, above note 1, s. 20(1).

203   Compare sections G(9) and F(6), "Substantial Infringement," in chapters 2 and 3.

204   For statutory passing-off, see *T Act,* above note 1, s. 7(b). A trade-mark's registrability (see section C in this chapter) depends on its likely lack of confusion with an existing registered mark (see section C(1), "Absolute Bars," in this chapter); priority of title (see section F, "Title," in this chapter) depends on the likely lack of confusion with an earlier trade-mark or trade-name.

area would likely lead — not necessarily has led — to the inference that the goods or services associated with them are "manufactured, sold, leased, hired or performed by the same person." The goods or services need not be of the "same general class." These principles also apply, *mutatis mutandis*, to alleged confusion between trade-marks and trade-names.[205] Whether this inference of common trade source is likely involves "a judicial determination of a practical question of fact."[206]

a) Factors to Consider

A decision on whether or not likely confusion exists requires "all the surrounding circumstances" to be examined, including:

(*a*) the inherent distinctiveness of the trade-marks or trade-names and the extent to which they have become known;

(*b*) the length of time the trade-marks or trade-names have been in use;

(*c*) the nature of the wares, services, or business;

(*d*) the nature of the trade; and

(*e*) the degree of resemblance between the trade-marks or trade-names in appearance or sound or in the ideas suggested by them.[207]

This section of the *Act* provides a non-exhaustive checklist against which to review the evidence. The plaintiff's "dream case" looks like this: its own earlier mark is inherently distinctive, well known, used for a long time on goods or services purchased by unsophisticated customers in a hurry, where the result of a mistake may be disastrous (e.g., getting the wrong prescription drug). On the other side, the defendant's later mark is identical, proposed to be used on identical wares or services sold through the same trade channels, and deliberately adopted with knowledge of the plaintiff's mark.

Real life is fuzzier because some of the above factors are usually missing and the courts weigh factors differently from case to case. But the closer a plaintiff's case resembles the dream case, the more likely it will succeed. The mental picture many judges start off with is like some bad Western version of the dream case. On one side is the hero, the successful business that has heavily invested in creating and rearing its mark. On the other side is the stranger who rides into town, the villainous "free-rider" trying to "cash in" on or steal away the mark. The villain has to convince the court that appearances are deceiving and that

---

205   *T Act, ibid.*, ss. 6(2)–(4).

206   *Benson & Hedges (Canada) Ltd.* v. *St. Regis Tobacco Corp.* (1968), [1969] S.C.R. 192 at 199.

207   *T Act*, above note 1, s. 6(5).

he does not merit the villain label: "Fear not, judge, the hero's mark will still be safe even if I use my mark. Please do not concoct a vision of widespread public confusion just to protect the hero's business. There's room for both of us in this town."

This struggle between competing visions of how a marketplace should function is rarely glimpsed from beneath the welter of legalese in which judgments tend to be wrapped. The hallmark of the case law on confusion seems itself to be confusion.

b) Recurrent Themes

Since confusion supposedly is a factual question, the result reached in one case does not determine that of another. Some themes nonetheless constantly recur.

i) Similarity of Marks

In practice, the last statutory factor noted above — "the degree of resemblance between the trade-marks or trade-names in appearance or sound or in the ideas suggested by them" — is the one with which most analyses should start. If CATERPILLAR and MERCEDES do not resemble each other at all, everything else is pretty irrelevant. The other statutory factors become significant only once the marks are identical or very similar. But similarity can come in various guises: appearance, sound, or the ideas both marks suggest. ROLEX and NOLEX, as words, suggest no particular idea, but they look and sound so similar that even careful folk may confuse them.[208] And if ROLEX is registered as a word without any design features, making NOLEX look different from the way the ROLEX mark is usually presented in block capitals — for example, writing it in script or adding swirls and flourishes — is irrelevant in an infringement action. At common law, the two marks are compared as actually used to see whether the second misrepresents itself as the first; in infringement proceedings, the registration of ROLEX as a word gives its owner the exclusive right to use in any fair and normal way it chooses, including the right to present it in calligraphic form. If the two words may be confused however they appear, there is infringement even if the trade-mark has never been used in that form.[209]

As to ideas, SMOOTHIES for candy may not look or sound much like SMARTIES, and their dictionary meanings may differ, but the idea both

---

208 Compare *Gigi Inc. v. Bigi (Can.) Ltd.* (1988), 21 C.P.R. (3d) 439 (Fed. T.D.): BIGI does not infringe GIGI for women's clothing.

209 *Mr. Submarine Ltd. v. Amandista Investments Ltd.* (1987), [1988] 3 F.C. 91 (C.A.) [*Mr. Submarine*].

suggest has been found close enough for buyers to believe the trade source of the two candies is likely the same.[210] Even marks that look and sound entirely different may share a common confusing idea: for example, MOONSHINE for detergents may be objectionable over SUNLIGHT for the same goods.

ii) Standards of Comparison

Some standard shibboleths are trotted out from case to case:

- The marks must be compared without considering what steps the second user took or might take to avoid confusion. Putting "no connection between my firm and mark X" up in lights beside one's mark is irrelevant. The question is not: Does or will the defendant run its business non-confusingly?[211] Second users face a more rigorous test: Is there likely confusion between the two marks, however their owners might run their businesses in the ordinary course?
- The marks must be considered as a whole, including any disclaimed portions.[212]
- The relevant reaction is that of the average buyer with reasonable apprehension and eyesight, not a "moron in a hurry." Still, the fact that buyers often have an imperfect recollection of the first mark is taken into account to give the registrant broad protection.
- The presence or absence of evidence of actual confusion is very relevant, especially where the marks or names have operated alongside each other for some time. But likely confusion is often found without instances of actual confusion, typically where one or both of the marks have not been used, but also even when they have.
- One must look at similarities between the symbols and not be beguiled by their dissimilarities.
- Other trade-marks on the register may also be looked at, for example, to see whether practical coexistence is possible.
- A properly conducted survey or other expert evidence on likely buyer confusion may be admitted in evidence and, indeed, is often preferred to the unbecoming spectacle of actual live confused and unconfused buyers parading through a courtroom. In practice, judges

---

210 *Rowntree Co. v. Paulin Chambers Co.* (1967), [1968] S.C.R. 134.

211 This question would, however, be a critical issue in a passing-off action. Any means of minimizing confusion is then relevant. A prominent disavowal that the two businesses are connected may even work if buyers will likely notice and understand it: *Associated Newspapers Plc. v. Insert Media Ltd.*, [1991] 1 W.L.R. 571 at 578–79 (C.A.).

212 See section C(4), "Disclaimer," in this chapter.

tend to put themselves mentally in the position of the typical buyer faced with the conflicting marks. The resulting judgment often seems influenced by how the judge thinks she would have reacted in the buyer's situation.

iii) Inherent Distinctiveness

Marks can be ranged on a spectrum from "very strong" to "very weak." The trade-marks register often signals the mark's location. The presence there of many similar marks suggests that the mark is weak and that minor differences may serve to distinguish it. By contrast, stronger marks are rewarded with wider and stronger protection. KODAK, a coined word of no recognizable meaning, is more broadly protected than STYLE for shampoo: practically, this means that HI-KODAK for cycles would likely infringe KODAK for optical equipment, whereas HI-STYLE would likely not infringe STYLE even for identical wares.[213] But exercise can make the weak strong and successful. MCDONALD'S (a common surname and thus initially weak) is more broadly protected now than earlier in its history because of extensive advertising and high sales. Even the MC prefix has sometimes been protected because of McDonald's promotion of a "McLanguage" that it has striven (perhaps vainly) to preserve as its own. So registrations of MCPUPPETS, MCSAURUS and MCBEAN to others were either refused or strictly limited to goods or services unconnected with food or publications; and in the United States, an infringement suit succeeded against a motel chain calling itself MCSLEEP INN.[214]

Still, a strong/weak spectrum analysis hardly is determinative. KODIAK looks and sounds very like KODAK. Yet in Canada KODIAK has very different associations from KODAK. Indeed, it is registered to a firm other than the Eastman Kodak Co. for goods like boots and liquor, remote from cameras and optical equipment.

iv) Circumstances of Sale

More sophisticated or expert buyers in a specialized market are less likely to be misled by similar marks than are ordinary members of the public, but even experts may be confused when the marks are very similar. Price and other circumstances of purchase are relevant. A pair of

---

213 *La Maur Inc. v. Prodon Industries Ltd.,* [1971] S.C.R. 973.

214 *McDonald's Corp. v. Clem Saila Inc.* (1989), 24 C.P.R. (3d) 400 (T.M. Opp. Bd.) (McPUPPETS); *McDonald's Corp. v. Rodden* (1993), 50 C.P.R. (3d) 557 (T.M. Opp. Bd.) (MCSAURUS); *McDonald's Corp. v. Coffee Hut Stores Ltd.* (1996), 68 C.P.R. (3d) 168 (Fed. C.A.) (MCBEAN); *Quality Inns International Inc. v. McDonald's Corp.,* 695 F. Supp. 198 (D. Md. 1988) (MCSLEEP INN).

marks on beer cans may confuse, but the same marks may not when they are used on big-ticket items. People are typically less careful buying beer in a bar or a self-service liquor store — and so are more likely to be unwittingly confused — than when they are buying cars or computers, where comparison shopping is the norm. One reason for finding FROZENAIRE non-confusing with FRIGIDAIRE was that "refrigerators are not hurriedly picked off a shelf; they represent a substantial purchase and to each transaction some degree of attention and consideration . . . [is] given."[215]

v) Marks in Different Territory

Registration gives Canada-wide protection. One must postulate the use of both marks side by side "in the same area,"[216] whether or not this is true or even likely. A use in Vancouver may infringe a registered mark that has been used only in Toronto and for which no westward expansion is planned. The question is whether the coincident use of the registered mark and the Vancouver mark or trade-name, were it to occur, would likely lead prospective purchasers or users to infer that the goods came from or were associated with the same trade source.[217]

Common law protection is less extensive, but covers not only the territory where the mark or name is used but also wherever the mark or name is well known to the public. Firms or marks with a Canada-wide or international reputation may therefore, in principle, have Canada-wide protection even though they do no business in Canada and plan none. A U.S. pest control firm stopped an Ontario pest control firm from deliberately adopting the U.S. firm's distinctive name: Ontarians had used the U.S. firm's services in the United States and might deal with the local firm in the belief it was an affiliate.[218] Similarly, a Vancouver restaurant could not use the name of a Hong Kong restaurant well known to many Vancouverites who would wrongly believe the two were connected.[219] The key is to establish possible harm to goodwill (e.g., loss of control over the business the indicia symbolize) flowing from the mistaken belief of a significant number of local people that they are dealing with the well-known firm or its products.

---

215   *Bellows*, above note 10 at 692.
216   *T Act*, above note 1, s. 6(2).
217   *Monsieur Silencieux Ltd.* v. *Clinique de Silencieux du Saguenay Inc.* (1972), 6 C.P.R. (2d) 23 at 26 (Fed. C.A.); *Mr. Submarine*, above note 209 at 12. Compare section C(5), "Concurrent Registration," in this chapter.
218   *Orkin Exterminating Co.* v. *Pestco Co. of Canada* (1985), 50 O.R. (2d) 726 (C.A.).
219   *Coin Stars Ltd.* v. *K.K. Court Chili & Pepper Restaurant Ltd.* (1990), 33 C.P.R. (3d) 186 (B.C.S.C.).

vi) Marks in Different Business

Identical marks or names may co-exist in different, yet quite similar, lines of business without confusion. Confusion is still a question of fact, although it may in law exist even where businesses are not "of the same general class."[220] A mark may be so well known that its repute "spills over" into other businesses, and buyers seeing the mark will infer a common trade source. A famous mark like ROLLS-ROYCE cannot be used on watches or clothing without the car maker's consent: people may infer Rolls-Royce had gone into that line of business, or at least had approved or licensed the use of its mark there. Some even say such marks cannot be used in any line of business, however remote, but this is special pleading. Whether ROLLS-ROYCE on chicken feed is in fact confusing with ROLLS-ROYCE for automobiles is just that, a question of fact, not law, to be judged with no presumption either way.

Less famous marks — particularly those associated with or distributed through the popular media — also benefit from a broad ROLLS-ROYCE–like notion of confusion. *Vogue* magazine has successfully opposed the registration of VOGUE for costume jewellery and photo albums. Since the magazine also peddles dress patterns and includes fashion photos, its readers might easily assume that the publisher had branched out into making jewellery or photo albums — or at least into approving, licensing, or sponsoring their making by other firms.[221] Similarly, SUNLIFE for fruit juice was enjoined by the owner of SUNLIFE for insurance services.[222] The Toronto Maple Leafs also stopped the registration for bubblegum of LEAF superimposed on a maple leaf, since children buying snacks at the Toronto rink might assume the club was behind the bubblegum sales as well.[223] But only reasonably predictable diversifications should be assumed. Speculative claims that a business might go into any line of business should be repelled as just dressed-up claims to a perpetual copyright.[224]

The court in the *Sun Life* case also found that the defendant had committed the wrong of passing-off by misrepresenting a trade connec-

---

220 *T Act*, above note 1, s. 6(2).

221 *Gozlan*, above note 34; *Conde Nast Publications Inc.* v. *Gottfried Importing Co.* (1990), 31 C.P.R. (3d) 26 (T.M. Opp. Bd.).

222 *Sun Life Assurance Co. of Canada* v. *Sunlife Juice Ltd.* (1988), 65 O.R. (2d) 496 (H.C.J.).

223 *Leaf Confections Ltd.* v. *Maple Leaf Gardens Ltd.* (1986), 12 C.P.R. (3d) 511 (T.D.), aff'd (*sub nom. Maple Leaf Gardens Ltd.* v. *Leaf Confections Ltd.*) (1988), 19 C.P.R. (3d) 331 (Fed. C.A.).

224 *Seagram*, above note 117 at 467–68.

tion between its business and the plaintiff's. The defendant had initially adopted the SUNLIFE mark in the same format as that used by the insurer, and seemed intent on trading on the fame of the insurer's mark. The court seemed equally intent on stopping this identification. As is true of registered marks, a shared "common field of activity" is not a precondition for passing-off: whether the two businesses would likely be confused is a question of fact.[225] The court found confusion to be likely in the *Sun Life* case. Had the mark been initially adopted innocently in a different format, and had SUNLIFE not been treated as a famous mark akin to ROLLS-ROYCE, a finding of confusion would have been less plausible, for few sane buyers could have possibly believed that the insurance company had moved into or was somehow connected with the fruit juice business.

vii) Character Merchandising

Character merchandising has benefited from the broad approach taken under the previous heading. *Crocodile Dundee*'s film distributor successfully opposed registration of those words as a mark for clothing: film-goers, being familiar with merchandising spinoffs, would assume that the clothing was licensed by the film company. A passing-off action against the same applicant also succeeded in provincial court.[226] Products associated with films or shows have been protected as well. In Australia, the producers of *The Simpsons* stopped a brewery from marketing DUFF beer, a fictitious brand favoured by the Homer Simpson character in the show. Even parodies may be prevented: CARE BEARS frightened off an application for SCARED BEARS for overlapping wares.[227] But SCARED BEARS was registered for business activity remote from where CARE BEARS' owner had until then taken or licensed the characters. And a character's reputation may fade over time. Thus PINK PANTHER for beauty products was, perhaps surprisingly, found registrable over the protest of the *Pink Panther* film distributor, because no evidence of recent use or licensing — hence repute — of the mark for Canada was

---

225 *Falconbridge Nickel Mines Ltd.* v. *Falconbridge Land Development Co.* (1974), 15 C.P.R. (2d) 213 at 220 (B.C.S.C.).

226 *Paramount Pictures Corp.* v. *Howley* (1992), 43 C.P.R. (3d) 551 (T.M. Opp. Bd.), finding non-distinctiveness; *Paramount Pictures Corp.* v. *Howley* (1991), 5 O.R. (3d) 573 (Gen Div.). See also *Tribune Media Services Inc.* v. *Enterprises PVN Enterprises Inc.* (1995), 64 C.P.R. (3d) 113 (T.M. Opp. Bd.) (DICK TRACY).

227 *Twentieth Century Fox Film Corp.* v. *South Australian Brewing Co. Ltd.* (1996), 34 I.P.R. 225 (Austl. Fed. Ct.); *Those Characters from Cleveland Inc.* v. *Clem Saila Inc.* (1990), 31 C.P.R. (3d) 69 at 74–75 (T.M. Opp. Bd.)

produced before the TMO. It was only on appeal when further evidence was led establishing continuous Canadian use and repute for the film character mark, that registration was finally denied.[228]

H. INVALIDITY

A registration can be invalidated on several grounds.

1) Initial Unregistrability

A mark unregistrable at the date of registration is invalid and may be expunged.[229] The older the registration, the more convincing the evidence need be, for the old saw "time heals all" animates many judges faced with challenges to a successful long-standing mark.[230] This attitude is especially true where a challenger knew of the registration for years, but did nothing.[231]

Some marks require evidence of distinctiveness before they can be registered.[232] These marks may have been registered without that evidence being proffered, especially if registration was unopposed. If the mark was in fact distinctive when registered, the fact that the TMO failed to insist on this evidence — for example, that it wrongly thought the mark was not descriptive — is not a ground of invalidation.[233]

2) Misrepresentation

Applicants owe the TMO a duty of good faith, especially in *ex parte* phases of TMO procedure. An innocent misrepresentation to the TMO may therefore result in invalidity, even though the *Act* does not explicitly include such a ground. Historically, only "material" misrepresenta-

---

228 *United Artists Pictures Inc. v. Pink Panther Beauty Corp.* (1996), 67 C.P.R. (3d) 216 (Fed. T.D.), rev'g (1990), 34 C.P.R. (3d) 135 (T.M. Opp. Bd.).

229 *T Act*, above note 1, s. 18(1)(a). See section C, "Criteria for Registrability," in this chapter.

230 For example, *Aladdin*, above note 67 at 109–10, refusing to expunge on "scanty" evidence a registration that had "stood unchallenged for more than half a century."

231 *Anheuser-Busch Inc. v. Carling O'Keefe Breweries of Canada Ltd.* (1986), 10 C.P.R. (3d) 433 at 446–48 (Fed. C.A.), finding laches and acquiescence.

232 See section C(2), "Relative Bars," in this chapter.

233 *T Act*, above note 1, s. 18(2); *Piattelli v. A. Gold & Sons Ltd.* (1991), 35 C.P.R. (3d) 377 at 383 (Fed. T.D.).

tions, causing a registration that would not otherwise have been made, have proved fatal. A registration made on an innocently false declaration that a proposed trade-mark was now in use has been invalidated.[234] Invalidation may be possible on wider grounds. Suppose a deliberate or very careless error did not cause the registration, but induced the TMO to exercise its discretion in the applicant's favour during the proceedings. Why should an applicant benefit from this error, especially where there was nobody around to formally oppose the request for indulgence?[235]

3) Lack of Distinctiveness

A registration is invalid if the mark is non-distinctive at the time proceedings bringing the validity of the registration into question are commenced.[236] The focus is therefore on the post-registration history of the mark. A mark owner who lets its mark's trade source message become muddied for any reason risks invalidity. Common faults are allowing others to use a mark without controlling the associated product or service, or switching the status of the mark (e.g., from a manufacturer's mark to a distributor's mark) without informing buyers of the mark's new meaning. But a mark lost can be regained if initially omitted steps are taken later. So long as the public knows of the new meaning by the time expungement proceedings are begun, and that meaning squares with what the register reveals, the registration will be secure. For example, THERMOS at one time probably meant any vacuum flask, not just those put out under the aegis of Canadian Thermos Products Ltd.; but its owner eventually woke up to the danger and took steps to resurrect the word as a mark. By the time a competitor filed proceedings to invalidate the registration, the mark had become distinctive enough for the court to allow the registration to continue.[237]

Even a mark that when registered was not then in fact distinctive may possibly be vulnerable. True, non-distinctiveness is technically separate from unregistrability: it can be raised in the TMO as a ground of objection as such only in opposition proceedings.[238] But the TMO may reject applications for features that do not qualify as a "trade-

---

234 *Unitel*, above note 72; compare *Billings & Spencer Co. v. Canadian Billings & Spencer Ltd.* (1921), 20 Ex.C.R. 405 (designs).
235 Compare section A(5), "The Application Must Be Truthful," in chapter 3.
236 *T Act*, above note 1, s. 18(1)(b).
237 *Aladdin*, above note 67; see section B(2)(b)(i), "Genericism," in this chapter.
238 *T Act*, above note 1, s. 38(2)(d); compare s. 37(1).

mark," even though the *Act* does not specify this ground as one of initial objection.[239] A mark not used "for the purpose of distinguishing or so as to distinguish" one producer's goods or services from another's is no "trade-mark" at all. It may therefore not be fit subject matter for registration in the first place.[240]

4) Inferior Title

A registration may be invalid if the applicant lacks title to the mark. This defect is not uncommon: for example, a use may have been localized and distant from the registrant's, and the TMO proceeding may have gone unopposed. Invalidation for lack of title is, however, subject to some qualifications.[241] Challenges can be mounted only by the person with better title. Even then, the registration cannot be challenged after five years unless the challenger proves the mark was adopted with knowledge that the challenger had (a) previously used or made well known a confusing trade-mark, or (b) earlier used a confusing trade-name.[242]

Who initiates the proceeding — the challenger for expungement, the registrant for infringement — is irrelevant so long as the proceeding is filed before the five years are up. This cut-off is a form of prescription affecting substantive rights. A case started within time may be heard outside the five years without affecting either party's rights. Extensions of time or other indulgences may, however, become less likely as time slips by and the prejudice to the registrant increases.[243]

5) Abandonment

The registration of an abandoned mark is no longer valid and may be expunged by the court.[244] Abandonment requires non-use and an intention to abandon. Non-use by itself may merely imply that the owner has temporarily stock-piled or parked the mark for later use. A formal act

---

239 Compare *Smith (No. 1)*, above note 50; *Unitel*, above note 72.

240 *T Act*, above note 1, s. 2, def. "trade-mark." See section B(2)(b), "Distinctiveness," in this chapter.

241 *T Act*, *ibid.*, s. 18(1); s. 17.

242 *T Act*, *ibid.*, s. 17(2). See section F, "Title," in this chapter. Other grounds of invalidity — unregistrability, non-distinctiveness, abandonment — are not affected by this five-year rule.

243 *Hiram-Walker-Consumer's Home Ltd.* v. *Consumer's Distributing Co.* (1981), 58 C.P.R. (2d) 49 at 51–52 (Fed. T.D.).

244 *T Act*, above note 1, s. 18(1)(c).

such as voluntarily applying to the TMO to cancel the registration,[245] or circumstantial evidence such as a long period of non-use, coupled with a passive acceptance of widespread infringement, may prove abandonment.[246] This possibility is equally true at common law. However, a firm that stops trading may still, at common law, have a residual goodwill in its name. Nobody else can simply pick up that name for its own business.[247] This rule helps avert consumer confusion, and also enables receivers and trustees in bankruptcy to have an asset they can sell for the benefit of creditors.

6) Non-use

A mark unused for at least three years can be summarily struck off the register. This power is entrusted to the Registrar of Trade-marks, who can initiate action at any time. Normally, however, the Registrar waits for a written request (accompanied by a $150 fee) asking that the registered owner be required to file a declaration or affidavit showing (a) that the mark was in use within the last three years or (b) "special circumstances" excusing the absence of use.[248]

The procedure is there to prune "dead wood" off the register. The registrant need not have abandoned the mark; no use and no excuse is enough for the mark to be summarily expunged. The procedure is often resorted to when an applicant finds conflicting marks on the register or has such marks cited against it in opposition. Registrants also conduct periodic sweeps of the register to clear off marks that threaten the distinctiveness or the strength of their own marks. Since anyone at all can file requests, law firms or trade-mark agents often do so on behalf of clients and become nominal parties while preserving the clients' anonymity.

There need not be heavy use, so long as there is some. Even a single genuine transaction may be enough. An affidavit by the mark owner exhibiting photographs and invoices that show the fact and nature of the use usually suffices.[249] Sometimes marks are redesigned to respond to changing times and fashions; although the mark as used is technically not

---

245   *T Act, ibid.*, s. 41(1)(b).

246   D. Vaver, "Summary Expungement of Registered Trade Marks on the Ground of Non-Use" (1983) 21 Osgoode Hall L.J. 17 at 19 ["Summary"].

247   *Ad-Lib Club Ltd. v. Granville*, [1971] 2 All E.R. 300 (Ch.).

248   *T Act*, above note 1, s. 45; Vaver, "Summary," above note 246. See section B(2)(c), "Use," in this chapter.

249   *Mantha & Associés/Associates v. Central Transport Inc.* (1995), 64 C.P.R. (3d) 354 (Fed. C.A.); *Shapiro*, above note 84.

the mark as registered, courts have equated the two where the mark retains its dominant features and the differences do not confuse unwary buyers.[250] Otherwise, not many excuses for non-use are accepted. The court will consider how long the mark has not been used, whether this arose from circumstances outside the owner's control, and whether the owner intends shortly to resume use. A decision not to use because of industry recession has even failed as a "special circumstance";[251] but this approach may need reconsideration, since *TRIPs* allows obstacles "arising independently of the will" of the mark owner to be excuses for non-use.[252]

The person making the request has standing to be heard by the Registrar and to appeal to the Federal Court. Appeals are in fact quite common and have sometimes turned the summary procedure into a mini-trial, complete with procedural motions, fresh evidence, and cross-examination.[253]

7) Consequences of Invalidity

Expungement does not necessarily mean that the mark is now free to be used by anyone. The ex-registrant may still have some rights against others, including the expunger. For example, a ten-year-old registration may be invalid for initial unregistrability ten years ago, but the owner may since then have acquired a reputation in the mark, protectable by a passing-off action. Similarly, a reputation gained since the invalid registration may entitle the owner, even immediately after expungement, to reapply to register the same mark. The mark may have been unregistrable then, but it may be registrable now. The TMO will then consider the new application on its merits. Attempts to short-circuit this process by persuading the Federal Court to maintain the registration or amend it to reflect current realities are therefore usually unsuccessful. The court prefers this task to be performed by the TMO, which will deal with the application in the regular way. This procedure gives those who may not have been parties before the court a chance to oppose registration.[254]

---

250 *Promafil Canada Ltée* v. *Munsingwear Inc.* (1992), 44 C.P.R. (3d) 59 at 71–72 (Fed. C.A.).

251 *Canada (Registrar of Trade Marks)* v. *Harris Knitting Mills Ltd.* (1985), 4 C.P.R. (3d) 488 (Fed. C.A.); *Lander Co. Canada* v. *Alex E. MacRae & Co.* (1993), 46 C.P.R. (3d) 417 at 421 (Fed. T.D.).

252 *TRIPs*, above note 163, art. 19(1). Import restrictions or other government requirements are instanced.

253 *Meredith & Finlayson* v. *Canada (Registrar of Trade Marks)* (1990), 33 C.P.R. (3d) 396 (Fed. T.D.).

254 *Royal Doulton*, above note 176.

I. USERS' RIGHTS

A registrant obviously cannot complain of any acts that are not infringements under the *Act*. Users may also act as they wish in relation to an invalidly registered mark, so long as there is no passing-off.[255] International law also allows quite broad leeway for specific exemptions to trade-mark infringement.[256] Canada has, however, not expanded on the limited range of permissible activities listed in the 1953 *Act*.

1) Specific Exemptions: Consistent with the *Charter*?

The concluding words of section 20(1) of the *Act* specifically exempt the following:

> (a) any *bona fide* use of . . . [a person's] personal name as a trade-name, or
>
> (b) any *bona fide* use, other than as a trade-mark,
>   (i) of the geographical name of his place of business, or
>   (ii) of any accurate description of the character or quality of his wares or services,
>
> *in such a manner as is not likely to have the effect of depreciating the value of the goodwill attaching to the trade-mark.* [Emphasis added.]

This provision may limit the freedom of commercial expression guaranteed by section 2(b) of the *Canadian Charter of Rights and Freedoms*.[257] If so, would it qualify as a reasonable limit "demonstrably justifi[able] in a free and democratic society" under section 1 of the *Charter*?[258] The closing words (italicized above) are the same as those found in section 22(1) of the *Act*, and the same weaknesses that may make section 22(1) constitutionally infirm apply similarly to the closing italicized language in s. 20(1) ("in such a manner . . . trade-mark"). This should not affect registrants much. They are already well protected by the law of passing-off, which applies even where an exempted activity does not infringe a registration, and by the way the exemptions, as well as the notion of confusion,[259] have to date been interpreted in their favour. Indeed, some interpretations of the exemptions may overlook the obvious point that

---

255 Compare section H(7), "Consequences of Invalidity," in this chapter.
256 *TRIPs*, above note 163, art. 17.
257 *Canadian Charter of Rights and Freedoms*, Part I of the *Constitution Act, 1982*, being Schedule B to the *Canada Act 1982* (U.K.), 1982, c. 11, s. 1.
258 See section G(3), "Dilution," in this chapter.
259 See section G(4), "Confusion," in this chapter.

sections 20(1)(a) and (b) apply only after infringement under sections 19 or 20(1) has been found. This suggests that the exemptions should apply even where some confusion nevertheless remains. Registrants that choose descriptive and geographic marks or names as trade-marks cannot expect to be protected as fully as those that opted for inherently distinctive marks in the first place.[260]

2) Personal Names

Under section 20(1)(a), echoing the common law, *bona fide* use of a "personal name" as a trade-name is permitted. Different members of a family may trade separately under similar business names, another member may use the surname as a trade-mark, and each may still preserve their own distinct identity in the eyes of the public.[261] How far someone can use his name in other cases depends on the strength of the mark and the way the second entrant chooses to use his name. Presumably someone born Ronald Ebenezer Mcdonald cannot now open a hamburger bar under the name "Ronald Mcdonald" or through a company called "Ronald Mcdonald Ltd." This restriction holds true for similar acts by a Ronald Macdonald. These uses would not be held *bona fide* — that is, honest and in good faith — were McDonald's Corp. to sue for infringement of its RONALD MCDONALD mark. But business names like "Ronald Ebenezer McDonald [Ltd.]" or "R.E. McDonald Foods [Ltd.]" should be acceptable under section 20(1)(a). The use may not be *bona fide* only if the second entrant did something else to suggest a connection with MCDONALD'S restaurants. A purpose like this might well lead to an order that the defendant switch to some completely different trade-name. It may be everybody's birthright to use his or her own name in business, but not deliberately to cause likely business confusion.[262]

3) Accurate Descriptions

Traders may *bona fide* and accurately describe the character of their wares or services, but again this common law right as reflected in section 20(1)(b)(ii) is severely limited, quite apart from the "[no] depreciat[ion] of goodwill" requirement. The need to avoid "use . . . as a trade-mark" is difficult to comply with. Paolo Gucci, a breakaway scion

---

260   See section B(2)(b), "Distinctiveness," in this chapter.

261   *Heintzman*, above note 73 at 14–15.

262   Compare *Hurlbut*, above note 114. See section C(2)(a), "Names and Surnames," in this chapter.

of the well-known Gucci family, could not mark furniture as "Designed by Paolo Gucci" because this was to use the registered mark GUCCI as a trade-mark.[263] A philologically constricted view has also been taken on what constitutes an "accurate description." A luggage shop could not call itself "La Bagagerie Willy" because LA BAGAGERIE was a registered mark and because *bagagerie* in "accurate" French meant luggage as contents, not container.[264] Yet some dictionaries did show the latter meaning, before it was deleted on representations made by the mark owner. The inference that *bagagerie* may have meant "container" to some was discounted by the court, which preferred an "accurate" meaning the mark owner had contrived to bring about.

4) Geographical Names

As noted earlier, OKANAGAN VINEYARDS (with OKANAGAN disclaimed) was denied registration over the registered mark OKANAGAN CELLARS.[265] Presumably, section 20(1)(b)(i) allows Okanagan Vineyards still to indicate on the labels of its wines that its business is located in the Okanagan Valley and that its wines were made there, if this is true and an acceptable commercial custom. The requirement of *bona fides* seems to protect the registrant adequately against any untoward practices.

5) Resales, Repairs, and Modifications

A person buying genuinely trade-marked goods in ordinary commerce may usually resell them without complaint from the person who affixed the mark. The mark continues to tell the truth about the trade source of the goods, whether they are sold new or used.[266] The goods may also be repaired and resold without infringement. Concealing the fact they are repaired or second-hand may, however, amount to dilution[267] or passing-off.

A distinction is made between repair and reconstruction. Goods that are reconstructed or substantially modified may no longer rightfully proclaim a connection with the trade-mark owner, and the mark

---

263   *Guccio Gucci Sp.A. v. Meubles Renel Inc. (sub nom. Meubles Domani's v. Guccio Gucci Sp.A.* (1992), 43 C.P.R. (3d) 372 (Fed. C.A.).

264   *Bagagerie S.A. v. Bagagerie Willy Ltée* (1992), 45 C.P.R. (3d) 503 (Fed. C.A.).

265   *Calona*, above note 131; see section C(2)(b)(ii), "Geographic Marks," in this chapter.

266   Compare section G(2), "Imports," in this chapter.

267   See section G(3), "Dilution," in this chapter.

may have to be deleted.[268] This decision depends on the trade involved. For example, car manufacturers have long tolerated third party modification or rebuilding of vehicles carrying their original nameplates. This indulgence is largely voluntary and may end if a particular practice impairs the mark's image or vehicle safety. Rolls-Royce can object to the placing of its distinctive grille or flying lady emblem on a VW bug's front end as an infringement or dilution of its trade-mark, even where the proverbial "moron in a hurry" would scarcely be confused.[269] On the other hand, the sale in Australia of used LEVI jeans was found not to infringe the registered LEVI mark, even though the jeans had been stone-washed, bleached, dyed, patched with decorations or transformed from full-length to shorts. The fact that the jeans' quality or durability had changed did not matter. Once new LEVIs had been sold to a retail buyer, the registrant's power to control how its mark was used was exhausted. The mark owner could only prevent resellers from using marks confusing with LEVI, or passing off altered or used goods as unaltered or unused. Passing-off might be avoided through prominent labels that indicated that the jeans were used and had been altered without the registrant's consent.[270]

FURTHER READINGS

Canadian

CANADIAN TRADE MARKS OFFICE, *Trade Marks Examination Manual* (updated periodically)

CONSUMER & CORPORATE AFFAIRS CANADA, *Working Paper on Trade Marks Law Revision* (Ottawa: Information Canada, 1974)

FOX, H.G., *Canadian Law of Trade Marks and Unfair Competition*, 3d ed. (Toronto: Carswell, 1972)

HAYHURST, W.L., "Survey of Canadian Law: Industrial Property — Part II" (1983) 15 Ottawa L. Rev. 311

HENDERSON , G.F., ed., *Trade-marks Law of Canada* (Toronto: Carswell, 1993)

---

268   *A.C. Spark Plug Co.* v. *Canadian Spark Plug Service,* [1935] Ex.C.R. 57.
269   See section H(6), "Repairs and Modifications," in chapter 3.
270   *Wingate Marketing Pty. Ltd.* v. *Levi Strauss & Co.* (1994), 121 A.L.R. 191 (Austl. Fed. Ct.).

HOWELL, R.G., "The Common Law Appropriation of Personality Tort" (1986) 2 I.P.J. 149

HUGHES, R.T., & T. POLSON ASHTON, *Hughes on Trade Marks* (Toronto: Butterworths, 1984) (updated regularly)

INSIGHT EDUCATIONAL SERVICES, *Trade Mark Oppositions Practice* (Toronto: Insight Press, 1992)

RICHARD, H.G., et al., eds., *Canadian Trade-Marks Act Annotated* (Don Mills, Ont.: R. de Boo, 1989) (updated regularly)

VAVER, D., "What's Mine Is Not Yours: Commercial Appropriation of Personality under the Privacy Acts of British Columbia, Manitoba and Saskatchewan" (1981) 15 U.B.C. L. Rev. 241

Other

AMERICAN LAW INSTITUTE, *Restatement of the Law: Unfair Competition* (ALI Pubs., 1995)

BROWN, R., "Advertising and the Public Interest: Legal Protection of Trade Symbols" (1948) 57 Yale L.J. 1165

LANDES, W., & R. POSNER, "Trade-mark Law: An Economic Perspective" (1987) 30 J.L. & Econ. 265

MCCARTHY, J.T., *Trademarks and Unfair Competition*, 2d ed. (Rochester, N.Y.: Lawyers Co-operative Publishing Co., 1984)

SCHECHTER, F., "The Rational Basis of Trademark Protection" (1927) 40 Harv. L. Rev. 813

SHANAHAN, D.R., *Australian Law of Trade Marks and Passing Off*, 2d ed. (Sydney: Law Book Co., 1990)

WHITE, T.A., & R. JACOB, *Kerly's Law of Trade Marks and Trade Names*, 11th ed. (London: Sweet & Maxwell, 1986)

CHAPTER 5

MANAGEMENT AND ENFORCEMENT

A. INTRODUCTION

The statutory intellectual property regimes have been deliberately organized to facilitate a free national and international market in rights. The rights can, subject to the occasional minor irritation from competition laws, be bought and sold in combination. They may usually be split up horizontally and vertically — by territory, time, market, and so on — and dealt with accordingly. The maximum extraction of rents is thus assured. The right-holder may also transfer or license some rights while retaining others. So the copyright owner of a book may assign the German translation right for Germany and may license the dramatization right for ten years to someone else, while retaining all other rights. The main obligations on the right-holder are to pay periodic maintenance fees for some rights (e.g., patents), to renew others periodically (e.g., registered trade-marks), and to record title in national intellectual property registries so that a rough database of who holds what in the intellectual property world is provided to buyers, users, and (theoretically) the general public.

The framework is flexible enough to accommodate changes in practice that respond to new distribution and communication methods. The Internet, for example, provides opportunities for freelance authors to deal directly with users without the intervention of middlemen like publishers, record companies, or art dealers. In this milieu, speedy standard licences may become more common than signed transfers of rights.

B. ASSIGNMENTS AND LICENCES

1) Interpretation

What is assigned or licensed is a matter of negotiation, and the ordinary principles of contract interpretation apply to the result. Interpretation is not necessarily a neutral exercise. In copyright and patents, for example, European judges often take a pro-author or pro-inventor stance, construing grants strictly against the grantee and leaving new uses under the control of the grantor (often the author or inventor). Some Canadian courts are similarly inclined,[1] but the occasional swallow does not necessarily make a summer. For example, media distributors with an eye towards electronic delivery and future means of exploitation may ask freelancers to sign contracts that contain a clause transferring "all now or hereafter existing rights of every kind and character whatsoever pertaining to said work, whether or not such rights are now known, recognized or contemplated for all purposes whatsoever" to the distributor. Will Canadian courts "construe" this in a limited way, or will they hold it to mean that the grantor has relinquished all control over the work forever in favour of the distributor?[2]

Traditional contract principles may allow courts to take some account of how freelancers are often economically dependent on media distributors and so are placed in an inferior bargaining power when dealing with them. There may also be room for manoeuvre if the contract is entered irregularly — for example, if reasonable steps were not taken to bring onerous boilerplate to the other party's attention before the contract was concluded. This principle may invalidate the typical "shrink-wrap" licence found in a pre-packaged computer program.[3] But, in the end, an agreement a transferor had ample time to read or get legal advice on before signing will usually be enforced. Avoidance is likely only where there was misrepresentation, fraud, undue influence, unreasonable restraint of trade, unconscionability, or a breach of trust. Only a union or the occasional persistent author with a deep pocket and a finely honed sense of grievance is likely to pursue cases like these.

---

1   For example, *Bishop* v. *Stevens*, [1990] 2 S.C.R. 467 [*Bishop*] (copyright) and *Comstock Canada* v. *Electec Ltd.* (1991), 38 C.P.R. (3d) 29 at 51ff (Fed. T.D.) [*Comstock*] (patents and designs).

2   For example, *Muller* v. *Walt Disney Productions Inc.*, 871 F. Supp. 678 (D.N.Y. 1994).

3   Compare *North American Systemshops Ltd.* v. *King* (1989), 97 A.R. 46 at 51 (Q.B.) (unenforceable), with *ProCD Inc.* v. *Zeidenberg*, 86 F.3d 1447 (7th Cir. 1996) (enforceable).

2) Assignments

The main constraints on free disposability derive from the character of the particular right involved. For example, some copyrights revert to their author's estate twenty-five years after death notwithstanding any assignments.[4] Other rights are personal; for example, authors' moral rights[5] cannot be assigned or licensed, but may be waived or asserted by the author's estate for the duration of the copyright. Provincial legislation preventing misappropriation of personality — the individual's right to control his or her name, voice, or image from being used in advertising — also typically creates a personal right that terminates on the individual's death. Rights in trade secrets and confidential information also are partly rooted in the impulse to protect privacy and personal confidences. Such rights may pass in bankruptcy, but may not be fully transferable: How does the transferor of an idea "deprive" herself of it, short of lobotomy? Trade secrets are nevertheless in practice often "assigned" or "licensed." In law, this may mean only that the transferor promises not to use or resell the idea, or not to sue the "licensee" for committing what would otherwise be a wrong.

a) Trade-marks

The most significant practical constraints on disposability probably apply to registered or unregistered trade-marks. Provisions in the *Trade-marks Act* suggesting that such marks can be freely assigned or licensed are a trap.[6] The provision may be literally true, but the implication that the assignee, licensor, or licensee can then act freely with the "property" is assuredly false. To survive, a trade-mark must maintain distinctiveness:[7] it must continue accurately to distinguish one producer from another. The mark a famous artist puts on her works to indicate authorship may be practically unassignable, for nobody else may be able to use it without deceiving the public. The common law right preventing misappropriation of personality, although recently said to be a property right,[8] may similarly be limited.

Territorially limited assignments, if acted upon, are also suspect: the use of the same mark by different people in different parts of the country

---

4   See section F (2), "Reversion," in chapter 2.
5   See section I in chapter 2.
6   *Trade-marks Act*, R.S.C. 1989, c. T-13, ss. 48–50 [*T Act*].
7   See section B(2)(b), "Distinctiveness," in chapter 4.
8   *Gould Estate* v. *Stoddart Publishing Co.*, [1996] O.J. No. 3288 (Gen. Div.) [*Gould*].

makes it non-distinctive of any one person in Canada and so invalid. Even where the whole interest in the mark is assigned, the assignee must use the mark to convey the same message as before or tell the market of any change. A failure in this respect caused the HEINTZMAN mark for pianos to be lost: the assignee applied the mark to Korean and U.S.-made pianos while buyers still thought they were getting the well-known higher-quality instrument formerly made in Ontario. The mark may have survived had the public immediately been told that henceforth it meant goods, wherever made, selected by the assignee.[9]

b) Formalities

Most assignments should be in writing; and, indeed, writing may be mandatory to effect a legal (as distinct from an equitable) assignment.[10] Writing requirements usually are designed to increase certainty and to protect the imprudent, hasty, or naive; but informal writings may suffice if there are no suspicious circumstances. A simple receipt for money received for "five original card designs inclusive of all copyrights" was held validly to assign the copyright in the designs, which were orally identified.[11] A signed writing delivered electronically should also be valid today. The sender's name, put at the end of the message at the instigation of the sender, should be as valid as an illiterate person's "X," if the intention that it operate as a signature is clear.[12]

The writing may operate as an assignment of intellectual property even if intellectual property is not specifically mentioned, so long as an intention to assign it can be discerned or proved. Loose generalities, such as transferring all "property" in a physical asset, should be avoided, since this may not encompass associated intellectual property. A sale of all a firm's business assets and goodwill should usually, however, pass all its intellectual property.[13] Existing rights of action should

---

9   *Heintzman v. 751056 Ontario Ltd.* (1990), 34 C.P.R. (3d) 1 at 16–17 (Fed. T.D.).

10 For example, *Copyright Act*, R.S.C. 1985, c. C-42, s. 13(4) [*C Act*]; *Patent Act*, R.S.C. 1985, c. P-4, s. 50 (1) [*P Act*]; *Industrial Design Act*, R.S.C. 1985, c. I-9, s. 13(1) [*ID Act*]; compare *White Consolidated Industries Inc. v. Beam of Canada Inc.* (1991), 39 C.P.R. (3d) 94 at 116 (Fed. T.D.) (writing not needed to assign trademarks). Compare section B(4), "Equitable Assignments and Licences," in this chapter.

11 *E.W. Savory Ltd. v. World of Golf Ltd.*, [1914] 2 Ch. 566 at 568 and 573–74.

12 *Interpretation Act*, R.S.C. 1985, c. I-21, s. 35(1): "'Writing', *or any term of like import, includes words . . .* represented or reproduced by any mode of representing or reproducing words in visible form" [emphasis added].

13 *Massie & Renwick Ltd. v. Underwriters' Survey Bureau Ltd.*, [1940] S.C.R. 218; compare *Webb & Knapp (Can.) Ltd., v. Edmonton (City)*, [1970] S.C.R. 588.

also pass, if the parties so intend, with an assignment of the property associated with the action, although some doubtful case law claims this transfer is impossible at common law.[14] An assignor cannot later contest the validity of any assignment; so back-dating is permissible, although it may not create rights against non-parties.[15]

3) Licences

An assignment changes ownership in the right from assignor to assignee. By contrast, a licence is just a consent, permission, or clearance (the terms are all interchangeable) to use intellectual property on the terms specified by the licensor; the licensor remains the owner. A licence may be quite informal and even implied. Posting material, without any stated restrictions, on an electronic bulletin board may, for example, imply a licence to users to download and make a hard copy of it at least for their private use. Licences are usually personal to the licensee unless transfer or sublicensing is clearly permitted or implied from the circumstances.[16]

Regrettably, people often speak loosely of "selling rights" without clarifying (or perhaps knowing) whether a licence or an assignment is meant. So documents referring to licensors and licensees can end up being construed as assignments, and *vice versa*: the labels the parties use are not conclusive.[17]

a) Exclusive, Sole, and Non-exclusive Licences
Licences can be exclusive, sole, or non-exclusive. An exclusive licence gives the licensee the power to exercise a right to the exclusion of all

---

14 *Union Carbide Canada Ltd.* v. *Trans-Canadian Feeds Ltd. (No. 1)* (1967), 49 C.P.R. 7 (Ex. Ct.). Compare *Fredrickson* v. *Insurance Corp. of British Columbia* (1986), 28 D.L.R. (4th) 414 at 423–424 (B.C.C.A.); Bill C-32, *An Act to Amend the Copyright Act*, 2d Sess., 35th Parl., 1996, introducing cl. 13(6) into the *Copyright Act* [Bill C-32]; *United Artists Pictures Inc.* v. *Pink Panther Beauty Corp.* (1996), 67 C.P.R. (3d) 216 at 222–24 (Fed. T.D.) (assignment of registered trade-marks passed right to continue opposition to an application to register).

15 *Star-Kist Foods Inc.* v. *Canada (Registrar of Trade Marks)* (1988), 20 C.P.R. (3d) 46 at 50 (Fed. C.A.); *Cheerio Toys & Games Ltd.* v. *Dubiner*, [1966] S.C.R. 206 [*Cheerio*].

16 For an unsuccessful attempt to circumnavigate a "no sublicensing" clause, see *Eli Lilly & Co.* v. *Apotex Inc.* (1996), 66 C.P.R. (3d) 329 (Fed. C.A.). See also M.B. Eisen, "Copyright and the World Wide Web" (1996) 12 Can. Intell. Prop. Rev. 405.

17 *Messager* v. *British Broadcasting Co.*, [1928] 1 K.B. 660 (C.A.), aff'd (1928), [1929] A.C. 151 (H.L.).

others including the licensor: it is as close to an assignment as a lease of land is to an outright conveyance of the fee simple. For copyrights, patents, and industrial designs, it should be in writing.[18] A sole licence means that the licensee is the only licensee appointed, but does not preclude the licensor from competing with the licensee. A non-exclusive licence implies that other licensees may be appointed to compete with one another and the licensor. The typical permission to download that is found or implied on the Internet likely falls into this last category.

An exclusive distributor will not, however, be an intellectual property licensee unless it is authorized to do an act within the owner's rights. So a distributor authorized to sell patented and copyright goods is a licensee under the patent, but not under the copyright; for a patent holder has, but a copyright holder has not, the sole right to sell patented goods. The distributor may be a copyright licensee if, for example, it is authorized to reproduce the protected material even for limited purposes such as promotion.[19]

Unfortunately, the terminology of exclusive, sole, and non-exclusive is not always used consistently, and parties can create hybrid relationships. In any event, whenever a claimant sues for infringement, it must prove that the defendant had no licence or consent to do the acts complained of.[20]

b) Right to Sue

At common law, all licences — from a simple oral copyright permission to quote extracts from a book, to a comprehensive written exclusive licence covering a complex technology — are treated alike in one respect. Being mere permissions, they are usually thought to convey no proprietary interest in the right and so give the licensee no power to sue for infringement.[21] The position is largely reversed by statute, but with little rhyme or reason. What is common is that, except for copyright, the owner should usually be joined in litigation as co-plaintiff or co-defendant to avoid double jeopardy. The need for joinder also emphasizes that a licensee's rights are derivative and so are subject to any defence the infringer has against the owner.

---

18   *C Act*, above note 10, s. 13(4) (see also Bill C-32, above note 14, cl. 2(7) & 13 (7));
     P Act, above note 10, ss. 50(2) & (3); *ID Act*, above note 10, ss. 13(2)–(3).

19   *Bouchet v. Kyriacopoulos* (1964), 45 C.P.R. 265 at 278 (Ex. Ct.), aff'd (*sub nom.*
     Kyriacopoulos v. Bouchet) (1966), 33 Fox Pat. C. 119 (S.C.C), finding (unusually)
     an implied right to this effect; compare *Avel Pty. Ltd. v. Multicoin Amusements Pty.
     Ltd.* (1990), 171 C.L.R. 88 at 103–4 (Austl. H.C.) [*Avel*].

20   *Avel, ibid.* at 94–95 and 119–20.

21   *Domco Industries Ltd. v. Armstrong Cork Canada Ltd.*, [1982] 1 S.C.R. 907.

Patent, plant breeder's right, and integrated circuit topography licensees are treated best: exclusive, non-exclusive, or even implied licensees can all sue.[22] An exclusive or non-exclusive trade-mark licensee may also sue, except to halt parallel imports of its licensor's products; the licensor should usually be given two months' notice to decide whether or not itself to sue, but only the owner (not the infringer) can complain of any failure to give due notice.[23] However, only the exclusive licensee of an industrial design can sue.[24] This is also true of copyrights, except the language allowing suits by the "grant[ee of] . . . an interest in the [copy]right by licence" in the *Copyright Act* may include suits by irrevocable non-exclusive licensees who have invested time and money in exploiting the right.[25]

The right to sue for infringement does not extend to agents who handle rights on behalf of an owner, nor usually to distributors.[26] Bill C-32 would, however, allow sole Canadian book distributors the right to prevent unauthorized imports and distribution.[27]

c) Duration and Estoppel

Licences may be given for free or for consideration. A gratuitous licence may be withdrawn at any time, even if it has a stated expiry date, although reasonable notice is usual. Inequitable revocations should also be preventable, for example, where the grantee has reasonably relied on the consent continuing.[28] Contractual licences may be withdrawn only if the contract expressly or impliedly allows, if the contract is avoided

---

22   For example, *P Act*, above note 10, s. 55; *Signalisation de Montréal Inc. v. Services de Béton Universels Ltée* (1992), [1993] 1 F.C. 341 (C.A.), allowing the buyer of a patented machine to sue for infringement.

23   *T Act*, above note 7, s. 50(3); *Tonka Corp. v. Toronto Sun Publishing Corp.* (1990), 35 C.P.R. (3d) 24 (Fed. T.D.); *Smith & Nephew Inc. v. Glen Oak Inc.* (1996), 68 C.P.R. (3d) 153 at 167 (Fed. C.A.).

24   *ID Act*, above note 10, s. 15.

25   *C Act*, above note 10, s. 13(4) & s. 36; *Ashton-Potter Ltd. v. White Rose Nurseries Ltd.*, [1972] F.C. 689 (T.D.), rev'd on other grounds (*sub nom. White Rose Nurseries v. Ashton-Potter Ltd.*) [1972] F.C. 1442 (C.A.). D. Vaver, "The Exclusive Licence in Copyright" (1995) 9 I.P.J. 163 at 189ff.

26   *Bishop*, above note 1; *955105 Ontario Inc. v. Video 99* (1993), 48 C.P.R. (3d) 204 (Ont. Gen. Div.). The distributor may, however, sometimes be a licensee: see section B(3)(a), "Exclusive, Sole, and Non-exclusive Licences," in this chapter.

27   See section G(10)(a), "Parallel Imports," in chapter 2.

28   *Dorling v. Honnor Marine Ltd.* (1963), [1964] Ch. 560 at 567–68, undisputed on appeal (1964), [1965] Ch. 1 at 13 (C.A.); *Computermate Products (Aust.) Pty. Ltd. v. Ozi-Soft Pty. Ltd.* (1988), 12 I.P.R. 487 (Austl. Fed. Ct.); compare *Katz v. Cytrynbaum* (1983), 2 D.L.R. (4th) 52 at 57 (B.C.C.A.).

for some vitiating factor (e.g., misrepresentation, undue influence, unconscionability), or if the contract is discharged for repudiation or serious breach.

Licences silent on duration usually last until the expiry of the right, presumably the last right, if more than one is licensed. The parties may, however, still be entitled to terminate on reasonable notice, depending on how the licence contract is construed. The ex-licensee must then respect the right on termination of the licence. Sometimes when a long-term licence covering confidential information expires, a licensee who has started up a new business on the faith of the licence may use the information after the licence has run its course; but this depends on what the contract says or implies or the nature of the relationship between the parties.[29]

A licensee must abide the licence during its term despite the expiry, initial invalidity, or later invalidation of any intellectual property rights.[30] This rule of "licensee estoppel," drawn from feudal property law, is hardly self-evident when applied to intellectual property. In the United States, a patent licensee can stop paying royalties if the right is found invalid and can itself challenge the validity of the patent.[31] The most a Canadian licensee can do is to contest validity once the licence expires, or if the licensee is sued for infringement.

4) Equitable Assignments and Licences

It is sometimes thought that an oral contract gives the assignee or licensee no rights if the statute requires writing. This is not true. Intellectual property laws are passed in the context of mature existing systems of law, including principles of equity. These principles continue to apply, unless they are plainly inconsistent with the right involved. For example, to hold and exercise a trade-mark in trust may cause the mark to lose distinctiveness and become invalid.[32] But can it be true that a person who bought, paid for, and acted on an intellectual property right

---

29 *Chicago Blower Corp. v. 141209 Canada Ltd.* (1990), 30 C.P.R. (3d) 18 at 54–55 (Man. Q.B.); *Cadbury Schweppes Inc. v. FBI Foods Ltd.*, (1996), 69 C.P.R. (3d) 22 (B.C.C.A.) [*Cadbury Schweppes*].

30 For example, *Culzean Inventions Ltd. v. Midwestern Broom Co.* (1984), 82 C.P.R. (2d) 175 at 194 (Sask. Q.B.).

31 *Lear Inc. v. Adkins*, 395 U.S. 653 (1969).

32 *Laflamme Fourrures (Trois-Rivières) Inc. v. Laflamme Fourrures Inc.* (1986), 21 C.P.R. (3d) 265 at 274 (Fed. T.D.). See section B(2)(b), "Distinctiveness," in chapter 4.

gets nothing — except a right to a refund — simply because the seller refused to sign a writing?[33] Equitable principles have operated even further in trying to make sense of bargains that are not inherently unfair, but do not precisely comply with the formalities of the *Acts*. For example, copyright in a non-existent work cannot in law be assigned, any more than one can transfer property in non-existent land or goods. Parties who agree to transfer such copyright are, however, treated in equity as promising to assign the future copyright once the work is created. At that point, the promisee becomes the equitable assignee and beneficial owner of the copyright, and the promisor is the equitable assignor with a bare legal title.[34] The assignee should therefore be able to have its interest perfected by a court order that either compels the assignor to put the assignment in writing or authorizes the registrar of the court to sign a writing binding the assignor.

An equitable title is still less than a legal one. For example, the legal owner may divest the equitable owner's interest by a transfer to a *bona fide* buyer without notice. The equitable owner can then sue the assignor only for restitution or breach of contract. And an equitable owner may obtain only interlocutory, not final, relief without joining the legal owner or producing a legal assignment.[35] This last point has not always been recognized — for example, by the court that disqualified an oral exclusive copyright licensee from even being a co-plaintiff in an infringement action.[36] Decisions like this one require reconsideration.

C. REGISTRATION AND EXPUNGEMENT

A copyright arises once a work is created; a trade-mark or trade-name is protected once it is used and gets known; confidential information is protected once it is produced and guarded. But other rights — patents, designs, registered trade-marks, PBR and ICT rights — exist only when they are first granted or registered by the Canadian Intellectual Property

---

33 *Western Front Ltd.* v. *Vestron*, [1987] F.S.R. 66 at 76–78 (Ch.). The buyer should get a refund anyway if the sale occurred in suspicious circumstances — for example, if the seller was tricked or hurried into a transaction that he or she would not have entered on reflection. Equity does not support sharp dealing.

34 *Performing Right Society Ltd.* v. *London Theatre of Varieties Ltd.* (1923), [1924] A.C. 1 at 13 (H.L.) [*London Theatre*]; *C Act*, above note 10, s. 63.

35 *London Theatre*, ibid. at 14 and 35.

36 *Jeffrey Rogers Knitwear Productions Ltd.* v. *R.D. International Style Collections Ltd.* (1986), 19 C.P.R. (3d) 217 (Fed. T.D.).

Office and continue until they are expunged by the CIPO or by federal court order. Trade-marks, however, can continue to be protected under provincial law, irrespective of registration or expungement under the *Trade-marks Act*. Moreover, copyright registration is optional. The copyright is affected only if the entry is expunged on the ground of a finding that there is no Canadian copyright in an item: for example, if the work is unoriginal or the copyright has been abandoned.[37]

1) Failure to Register

The registers usually indicate initial title, changes of title, and (except for trade-marks) the existence of exclusive licences. A failure to record changes differs in seriousness among rights. A discrepancy between the actual and the registered title for a trade-mark may result in the mark lacking distinctiveness:[38] the message on the register is not the one conveyed in the market. Elsewhere, a plaintiff may be able to prove its actual title, whatever the register reveals, because the register and any CIPO certificates are only presumptive evidence.

a) Priorities

What effect registration or non-registration has on priorities usually turns on provincial law. Explicit federal priority provisions exist only for patents, copyrights, and PBRs. The provisions are rather simplistic when compared, for example, with the priority schemes that most provinces have adopted for secured transactions — and then the federal provisions differ from one other. For patents, assignments and registrable licences take priority in order of registration: an unregistered grantee is subordinate to a later registered grantee. For copyright and PBR rights, the same applies, except a later registered grantee has priority only where it takes the right for valuable consideration without actual notice. A PBR registration must occur within thirty days. No times are provided for the other rights.[39] Transactions that mortgage or charge interests in these rights to secure a debt may, presumably, also fall within their scope.

The two courts that have to date dealt with the *Patent* and *Copyright Act* provisions seem not to have thought much of either. The first court allowed only later non-fraudulent patent registrants to take priority,

---

37 See chapter 2.
38 See section B(2)(b), "Distinctiveness," in chapter 4.
39 *C Act*, above note 10, s. 57(2); *P Act*, above note 10, s. 51; *Plant Breeders' Rights Act*, S.C. 1990, c. 20, s. 31(3) [*PBR Act*]; *Plant Breeders' Rights Regulations*, SOR/91-594, s. 12.

while the second seemed to subordinate the whole copyright scheme to provincial law.[40] Careful practitioners accordingly may have to register security documents over patents, copyrights, and PBRs both provincially and federally, and hope for the best.

2) Presumption of Validity

The existence of a registered right is usually proved by producing the CIPO certificate evidencing the right or a certified copy of the register entry. A presumption of validity covering all aspects then applies. For patents, this means that the invention is presumed to be new, useful, non-obvious, adequately disclosed, and properly claimed, and that the persons noted on the register hold the interests stated there.[41] Challengers must plead and prove their case on the usual balance of probabilities standard. Once evidence is introduced, the presumption disappears and the question is simply whether the evidence is sufficient to discharge the onus of proof.[42] Borderline cases tend to favour the right-holder. For example, judges in patent cases often speak of their "anxiety" to protect genuine inventions when a patent's validity is put in issue.[43]

a) Copyrights

Certain presumptions apply even to unregistered copyrights. The work is presumed to be protected; its author is presumed to be the owner; the author is presumed to be whoever is so named on a work; the publisher is presumed to be the owner of an anonymous or pseudonymous works; and a film's maker is presumed to be whoever is so named on it.[44] For registered copyrights, however, the particulars on the register and the certificate of registration oust these presumptions.[45]

---

40   *Colpitts v. Sherwood*, [1927] 3 D.L.R. 7 at 13 (Alta. C.A.) (patents); *Poolman v. Eiffel Productions S.A.* (1991), 35 C.P.R. (3d) 384 at 392 (Fed. T.D.) (copyrights).

41   For example, *P Act*, above note 10, s. 43(2); *A. Pellerin et Fils Ltée v. Enterprises Denis Darveau Inc.* (1994), 59 C.P.R. (3d) 511 at 515 (Fed. T.D.) (patents); *Silverson v. Neon Products Ltd.* (1978), 39 C.P.R. (2d) 234 at 238-39 (B.C.S.C.) (copyright).

42   *Diversified Products Corp. v. Tye-Sil Corp.* (1991), 35 C.P.R. (3d) 350 at 359 (Fed. C.A.).

43   For example, *Kramer v. Lawn Furniture Inc.* (1974), 13 C.P.R. (2d) 231 at 233 (Fed. T.D.).

44   *C Act*, above note 10, ss. 34(3) & (4).

45   *Ibid.*, s. 53; *Circle Film Enterprises Inc. v. Canadian Broadcasting Corp.*, [1959] S.C.R. 602.

3) Expungement and Correction

A registration that is initially invalid or that has since become invalid can be expunged. What constitutes invalidity for patents or trade-marks was noted in chapters 3 and 4. This section looks more generally at what can be corrected or expunged across all the registers, and who can do it: the CIPO or the federal court.

a) General

The statutes provide a bewildering array of devices to correct mistakes. Take the *Patent Act*: one error in a patent is correctable through five different procedures! The Federal Court can vary or expunge the registration ("void the patent," as the *Act* unattractively calls it); the patentee can itself correct some errors;[46] it can also apply to the Patent Office to correct some as "clerical error[s]" and others through reissue or re-examination.[47] The idea that a patent for a genuine invention should not be lost on a technicality is translated into procedures that themselves bristle with technicalities. Meanwhile the Patent Office's attempts at rationalization have been partly foiled by the courts — which have said that patentees can risk choosing whatever procedure suits them[48] — and the critical question of how third-party rights are affected is not dealt with comprehensively. One may, of course, turn to ancient English practice, which might disallow an amendment unless the applicant accepted a condition to ensure third-party rights, including those in pending litigation, were not affected.[49] A modern technology code should not, however, have to be administered by resorting to 150-year-old precedents.

b) CIPO Powers to Correct Clerical Errors

The CIPO usually has power to correct a "clerical error" in any document recorded in the office. This does not mean that errors arising from ignorance of fact or law can be corrected. The power relates instead to mistakes made in the mechanical process of writing or transcribing. Typical errors are dropped "nots," or sometimes even whole lines. It does not matter who makes the error: the owner, its agents, or the CIPO

---

46   See section D(1), "Disclaimer," in chapter 3.
47   See sections D(2) and (3), "Re-examination" and "Reissue," in chapter 3.
48   *Monsanto Co.* v. *Canada (Commissioner of Patents)* (1974), [1975] F.C. 197 (T.D.), rev'd [1976] 2 F.C. 476 (C.A.); *Bayer AG* v. *Canada (Commissioner of Patents)* (1980), [1981] 1 F.C. 656 (T.D.) [*Bayer*].
49   *Re Nickels' Patent* (1841), 1 Web. Pat. Cas. 656 at 663–664 (Ch.) [*Nickels'*].

itself.[50] So the old English patent that a dozing Patent Office clerk wrote out as "covering" instead of "*recovering*" fabric was duly corrected.[51] Since the error usually does not invalidate the right, the CIPO's power to correct may presumably be exercised retroactively. This is not, however, a general power to post-date, ante-date, or extend times; a power like this may have to be found elsewhere in the legislation.[52]

The CIPO's discretion to correct must be exercised judicially. Inexcusable delay may be a bar, but the CIPO cannot apparently refuse to correct merely because it thinks another remedy may be more appropriate.[53] Quite major and unobvious mistakes have been corrected even if these caused the expansion of the initial monopoly.[54] Perhaps this correction is acceptable where the mistake was the CIPO's, or where terms can be imposed to ensure that the owner gets no unfair advantage from correction. A point like this is explicitly made under the *PBR Act*, where the CIPO can impose terms and correct only if this is "in the interests of the due administration of this Act and is not prejudicial to the interests of justice."[55] Whether this is implicit in respect of other registers is unclear. It would obviously be better if such a power were spelt out, rather than having to be left to implication.

c) Federal Court Powers

The registers ought continuously to reflect the current picture of the rights and their holders. They do not, of course, since neither the CIPO nor the courts are entitled to conduct any systematic investigations of validity of their own accord. Rectification is typically sought in counterclaims in infringement proceedings or in independent proceedings. Provincial courts can declare registrations invalid between the parties and

---

50 *Bayer*, above note 48; *Re Maere's Application*, [1962] R.P.C. 182 at 185 (U.K. Patent Office); compare *Integrated Circuit Topography Act*, S.C. 1990, c. 37, s. 19(4) ("typographical or clerical error") [*ICT Act*].

51 *Nickels'*, above note 49.

52 *P Act*, above note 10, s. 8; *C Act*, above note 10, s. 61; *ID Act*, above note 10, s. 20; *Trade-marks Regulations*, SOR/96-195, s. 33 (see also *T Act*, above note 6, s. 41(1)); *PBR Act*, above note 39, s. 66(1)(a) (also "error in translation"); *ICT Act*, above note 50, s. 19(4) (also "typographical error"). Compare *Celltech Ltd. v. Canada (Commissioner of Patents)* (1993), 46 C.P.R. (3d) 424 (Fed T.D.), aff'd (1994), 55 C.P.R. (3d) 59 (Fed. C.A.).

53 *Bayer*, above note 48; *Re Sandoz Ltd.'s Application* (1989), 15 I.P.R. 229 at 236 (Austl. Commissioner of Patents).

54 *Bayer, ibid.*; compare *Eagle Iron Works v. McLanahan Corp.*, 429 F.2d 1375 at 1383 (3d Cir. 1970).

55 *PBR Act*, above note 39, ss. 66(1)–(2).

dismiss infringement claims accordingly on any ground that would lead to expungement, but the Federal Court alone can formally expunge for invalidity or amend the register to make it "accurately express or define" these rights.[56] Only then will other users be free of the risk of infringement.

Not everyone has standing to apply to correct the register. The government of course may apply, through the CIPO or the Attorney General, depending on the statute. So may any "aggrieved" or "interested" persons, presumably meaning anyone "affected or [who] reasonably apprehends that he may be affected by any entry in the register."[57] And once there is an application, the court can even expunge or amend on grounds not raised before it or the CIPO: for parties may be loath to raise points that may come back to haunt them in other cases, or may even be legally barred from challenging validity.[58] This judicial spontaneity rarely occurs in practice because of the risk of injustice in dealing with points the parties have not addressed by argument or evidence.[59]

i) Grounds of Invalidity and Correction

What constitutes invalidity varies among rights. At one end of the spectrum, the grounds for invalidating PBRs are exhaustively listed.[60] Further along, the grounds for invalidating trade-marks, though also listed, have effectively been added to by the courts.[61] At the other end of the spectrum is the formula for patent invalidity: "any fact or default which by this Act *or by law* renders the patent void." These grounds may

---

56   For example, *ICT Act,* above note 50, s. 24(1). The *ID Act,* above note 10, s. 22(1), is more narrowly drawn and raises a question whether jurisdiction exists to expunge for post-registration events: compare *Bayer Co. v. American Druggists' Syndicate Ltd.*, [1924] S.C.R. 558 with *General Electric Co. v. General Electric Co. Ltd.*, [1972] 2 All E.R. 507 (H.L.).

57   This is how "interested person" is defined in s. 2 of the *T Act,* above note 6 (see also s. 57(1)). This statutory definition seems effectively to summarize the jurisprudence on what constitutes an "aggrieved" or "interested" person in the absence of a definition: compare *P Act,* above note 10, s. 60(1); *ID Act,* above note 10, s. 22(2); *ICT Act,* above note 50, s. 24(3).

58   See sections B(3) and B(3)(c), "Licences" and "Duration and Estoppel," in this chapter; *Cheerio,* above note 15.

59   Compare *Natural Colour Kinematograph Co. Ltd. (in Liq.) v. Bioschemes Ltd.* (1915), 32 R.P.C. 256 (H.L.) with *Imperial Oil Ltd. v. Lubrizol Corp.* (1996), 67 C.P.R. (3d) 1 at 11 (Fed. C.A.) [*Imperial Oil*].

60   *PBR Act,* above note 39, s. 44(3) (failure of subject matter, prior use, or failure to maintain deposits of propagating material).

61   *T Act,* above note 7, s. 18(1); *Unitel Communications Inc. v. Bell Canada* (1995), 61 C.P.R. (3d) 12 at 51–54 (Fed. T.D.) [*Unitel*].

include an unclosed category of common law grounds of invalidity beyond those the *Act* makes explicit or implicit.[62]

Expungement is the standard remedy for registrations that are initially invalid or that have since become invalid. Registrations that infringe earlier registrations or result from a material misrepresentation may also be expunged.[63] Rightful owners can be substituted for interlopers if the initial application was otherwise in order,[64] and even modest changes to the right itself can be made. Thus the court can redraw the contours of design registrations in "non-essential" particulars, and add or strike details in patent specifications or drawings that are unintentionally too cryptic or verbose.[65] This power is, however, rarely exercised.

Although the court's powers are at least as wide as the CIPO's,[66] it has shied away from becoming a parallel forum. Thus, whether a defective patent should or should not be amended may be better decided according to established Patent Office practice than in an *ad hoc* decision in a hotly contested infringement action.[67] For similar reasons, the court has not switched trade-mark owners or amended trade-mark registrations. The Trade-mark Office can better deal with issues of title, registrability, and third-party rights on an application to re-register. Where, however, an issue has been fully ventilated in court — for example, whether a mark was used and who used it first — the court may make a declaration to avoid relitigation of the point before the TMO.[68]

---

62 *P Act*, above note 10, s. 59 [emphasis added]; see chapter 3 and section H, "Invalidity," in chapter 4.

63 *Unitel*, above note 61; *Billings & Spencer Co.* v. *Canadian Billings & Spencer Ltd.* (1921), 20 Ex.C.R. 405; *Findlay* v. *Ottawa Furnace & Foundry Co.* (1902), 7 Ex.C.R. 338 at 349. This depends on the nature of the right. For example, a patent may validly be granted for an improvement on another patented product, even though the working of one patent within the other's claims may infringe the latter.

64 *Gold* v. *Downs* (1988), 19 C.P.R. (3d) 292 (Fed. T.D.); *Geodesic Constructions Pty. Ltd.* v. *Gaston* (1976), 16 S.A.S.R. 453 at 469 (S.C.); *Comstock*, above note 1. The court cannot act before registration: *Cellcor Corp.* v. *Kotacka* (1976), [1977] 1 F.C. 227 (C.A.).

65 *ID Act*, above note 10, s. 23(1); *P Act*, above note 10, s.53(2).

66 *Lightning Fastener Co.* v. *Canadian Goodrich Co.*, [1932] S.C.R. 189 at 195–96.

67 See *Electrolytic Zinc Process Co.* v. *French's Complex Ore Reduction Co.*, [1930] S.C.R 462; compare *B.V.D. Co. Ltd.* v. *Canadian Celanese Ltd.*, [1937] S.C.R. 221, aff'd (*sub nom. Canadian Celanese Ltd.* v. *B.V.D. Co.*) [1939] 1 All E.R. 410 (P.C.).

68 *Royal Doulton Tableware Ltd.* v. *Cassidy's Ltd./Ltée* (1984), [1986] 1 F.C. 357 (T.D.); *Pitney Bowes Inc.* v. *Canada (Registrar of Trade Marks)* (1993), 49 C.P.R. (3d) 5 (Fed. T.D.).

D. ENFORCEMENT

Most intellectual property disputes settle without going to court. The incentives for settlement or informal dispute resolution are high because infringement litigation can quickly become prohibitively expensive. Alternative dispute resolution through mediation or arbitration is also possible, but as yet uncommon.

If litigation is pursued, trials are often bifurcated: liability is tried first, and the question of remedy is then litigated only if the claimant has been successful on liability. Infringements attract the usual remedies. Those most commonly sought are final injunctions, interlocutory injunctions, damages, accounts of profits, and delivery up.[69] These remedies are now discussed. A paragraph on limitation periods then concludes this section.

1) Court Selection

Litigation may be brought in either the provincial courts or the Trial Division of the Federal Court, depending on the right infringed. For infringement of a registered federal right or copyright, the plaintiff can usually choose between the provincial or the Federal Court; both have concurrent jurisdiction. The Federal Court is sometimes preferred because its judges are more experienced in this litigation, the case can often be more quickly heard and appealed, and the Federal Court's orders are enforceable Canada-wide. It is the only forum if amendment or invalidation of a federal register is sought.

The Federal Court, however, lacks jurisdiction over disputes involving provincial law. Suppose a licensee is not paying royalties or a party to an agreement settling an intellectual property dispute does not observe its terms. Since the dispute is merely over whether a contract has been broken, the Federal Court cannot hear it.[70] The court may, however, decide contractual points incidentally to an infringement action. If, for example, a defendant pleads that an infringement is permitted by its contract with the claimant, the court has jurisdiction to interpret the contract to determine if there has indeed been an infringement.[71] However, no claim in tort, unless arising from a valid federal

---

69   Claimants sometimes seek declarations, and of course always want their costs and pre- and post-judgment interest. These remedies are not discussed here.

70   *Sabol v. Haljan* (1982), 36 A.R. 109 (C.A.).

71   *Titan Linkabit Corp.* v. *S.E.E. See Electronic Engineering Inc.* (1993), 44 C.P.R. (3d) 469 (Fed. T.D.).

statute,[72] can be attached to an infringement claim. It is therefore quite possible for two sets of litigation over the same matter to be pending, one in a provincial court, the other in the Federal Court. There may even be two infringement actions started. For example, a threatened party may start an action seeking a declaration of non-infringement from a provincial court, and the right-holder may respond by bringing its own infringement action in Federal Court. One or other court may then stay the case before it, if the issues and relief sought are essentially the same; otherwise both cases may proceed.

2) Whom to Sue

The *Copyright Act* extends liability beyond direct infringers to those who "authorize" infringement.[73] Otherwise, intellectual property legislation is typically silent on precisely who can be implicated. General common law principles of complicity and vicarious responsibility should apply. Those who directly participate in a wrong, therefore, are as liable as the main actor. Principals, partners, and employers may be jointly and severally liable for infringements committed by their agents, co-partners, and employees acting in the scope of their authority or employment. Parent corporations should not automatically be liable for their subsidiaries' acts unless these acts are done as agents. Nor may directors, officers, and managers be liable for a corporation's wrongs, unless they formed the corporation to infringe, or directly ordered, authorized, or procured infringement. Not preventing an infringement within one's power to control, or not fulfilling one's duties to the corporation, apparently does not in itself attract liability.[74]

Those who merely "contribute" to infringement may not themselves be infringers.[75] Sellers of videocassette recorders may not be responsible for the unlawful copying of tapes by buyers. Similarly, suppliers of chem-

---

72 For example, a claim for statutory passing-off under s. 7(b) or (c) of the *T Act*, above note 6.

73 *C Act*, above note 10, s. 3(1); see chapter 2.

74 *Reading & Bates Construction Co. v. Baker Energy Resources Corp.* (1986), 13 C.P.R. (3d) 410 (Fed. T.D.); *Mentmore Manufacturing Co. v. National Merchandise Manufacturing Co.* (1978), 40 C.P.R. (2d) 164 (Fed. C.A.) (patents); *C. Evans & Sons Ltd. v. Spritebrand Ltd.*, [1985] 2 All E.R. 415 (C.A.) and *King v. Milpurrurru* (1996), 34 I.P.R. 11 at 35 (Austl. Fed. Ct.) (copyright); *Halocarbon (Ont.) Ltd. v. Farbwerke Hoechst AG*, [1974] 2 F.C. 266 (T.D.), aff'd (*sub nom. Farbwerke Hoechst AG v. Halocarbon (Ont.) Ltd.*), [1979] 2 S.C.R. 929 (parent & subsidiary).

75 Compare *Hatton v. Copeland-Chatterton Co.* (1906), 10 Ex.C.R. 224, aff'd (1906), 37 S.C.R. 651.

icals for use in process patents or of parts for incorporation in a patented product or combination may not be responsible if a buyer uses the items to infringe.[76] On the other hand, providers of online bulletin board services may perhaps be liable for infringing material posted by subscribers. The possible hardship such a rule may entail, especially for non-profit operators, has led to the suggestion that liability should exist only if the operator knew or should have known that posted material infringed copyright and had not acted reasonably to limit potential abuses.[77]

It is not only the new technology that is threatening traditional rules of immunity. Courts themselves have sometimes chosen to extend liability incrementally. So a seller who supplies all the parts of a combination patent for the buyer to assemble may infringe either directly or jointly with the buyer if a common design to infringe is proved.[78] Whether such a common design between **A** and **B** can readily be inferred merely because **A** deliberately persuades or induces **B** to infringe is more doubtful. This comes close to insinuating the common law tort of inducement into an intellectual property statute by renaming it "joint infringement." If it is *ultra vires* to use provincial tort law to bolster a federal right, doing so indirectly should fare no better. Arguments that the persuader is acting immorally and deserves condemnation can be met by the rejoinder that intellectual property rights "are derived from statute and not from the Ten Commandments" and that it is for Parliament, not "the clergy or the judiciary," to define those rights.[79]

Defendants must therefore be selected with care. Strategies like taking out newspaper ads warning off the trade, or sending letters or copies of threatening correspondence to retailers and wholesalers, should be avoided. If the right later proves invalid, the plaintiff may itself be sued

---

76   *Slater Steel Industries Ltd.* v. *R. Payer Co.* (1968), 55 C.P.R. 61 at 70–83 (Ex. Ct.); *CBS Songs Ltd.* v. *Amstrad Consumer Electronics*, [1988] A.C. 1013 (H.L.) [*CBS*].

77   Information Highway Advisory Council, *Final Report: Connection, Community Content: The Challenge of the Information Highway* (Ottawa: The Council, 1995) at 120; *R.* v. *M.* (*J.P.*) (1996), 67 C.P.R. (3d) 152 (N.S.C.A.): computer bulletin board operator, knowingly making infringing copies of computer software available to selected users, held guilty of "distribut[ing]" them to the copyright owner's prejudice: *C Act*, above note 10, s. 42(1)(c). Compare J. Ginsburg, "Putting Cars on the 'Information Superhighway': Authors, Exploiters, and Copyright in Cyberspace" (1995) 95 Colum. L. Rev. 1466 at 1492ff; *Religious Technology Centre* v. *Netcom On-Line Communications Services Inc.*, 33 I.P.R. 132 (D. Cal. 1995).

78   *Windsurfing International Inc.* v. *Trilantic Corp.* (1985), 8 C.P.R. (3d) 241 (Fed. C.A.).

79   *CBS*, above note 76 at 1057; similarly, *Compo Co.* v. *Blue Crest Music Inc.* (1979), [1980] 1 S.C.R. 357 at 372–73.

for the wrong of injurious falsehood and may have to pay damages for business disruptions. At common law, the plaintiff is liable only if it knew its right was invalid or otherwise acted inexcusably. Knowledge or dishonesty need not be proved where a federal right is shown to be invalid and the injured party relies on section 7(a) of the *Trade-marks Act*; this provision requires only proof of injury to business caused by a competitor's false or misleading statement.[80]

3) Remedy Selection

There is a trend in the general law towards synthesizing common law and equitable remedies and making the combined schedule available to all wrongs, while keeping things flexible so as to be able to do justice in the individual case. This trend should apply equally to intellectual property law. Perhaps courts should usually award the claimant's remedy of choice if he is otherwise entitled to it, but some courts appear more interested in awarding whatever remedy the court thinks most appropriate in the circumstances. This may occur partly through the application of equitable considerations. Innocent infringers, particularly those who change their position after long delay by the right-holder, may be let off entirely, may have to pay only damages (no injunction or account), or may be enjoined but pay no money to the claimant.[81] Particular intellectual property statutes may encourage even greater flexibility. Thus the court is given a very broad remedial discretion for moral rights infringements and trade-mark dilution.[82] Language like that in the *Trade-marks Act* — the court "may make any order that it considers appropriate in the circumstances" — may also prompt judges to tailor relief more precisely to the circumstances of each case instead of mechanically granting whatever a claimant wants.[83] This approach may deserve to be endorsed more widely.

---

80 *S. & S. Industries Inc.* v. *Rowell,* [1966] S.C.R. 419, on *T Act,* above note 6, s. 7(a), and the common law; compare *M & I Door Systems Ltd.* v. *Indoco Industrial Door Co.* (1989), 25 C.P.R. (3d) 477 (Fed. T.D.); *Safematic Inc.* v. *Sensodec Oy* (1988), 21 C.P.R. (3d) 12 (Fed. T.D.).

81 *Habib Bank Ltd.* v. *Habib Bank AG Zurich,* [1981] 2 All E.R. 650 (C.A.); *Seager* v. *Copydex Ltd.,* [1967] 2 All E.R. 415 (C.A.) [*Seager*]; *Champion Spark Plug Co.* v. *Sanders,* 331 U.S. 125 (1947).

82 *C Act,* above note 10, s. 34(1.1); *T Act,* above note 6, s. 22(2); compare *Clairol International Corp.* v. *Thomas Supply & Equipment Co.,* [1968] 2 Ex.C.R. 552 at 577.

83 *T Act, ibid.,* s. 53.2. See, for example, *Gray Rocks Inn Ltd.* v. *Snowy Eagle Ski Club Inc.* (1971), 3 C.P.R. (2d) 9 at 26 (Fed. T.D.) (trade-marks); *Omark Industries Inc.* v. *Sabre Saw Chain (1963) Ltd.* (1976), 28 C.P.R. (2d) 119 at 140–41 (Fed T.D.) (patents).

4) Final Injunction

An intellectual property right-holder has, by statute, a sole or exclusive right, which makes the injunction an appropriate remedy unless it is barred by statute[84] or by some equitable reason such as acquiescence, lack of clean hands, or unconscionability. A breach of common law or provincial statutory rights — for example, passing-off, misappropriation of personality, breach of confidence — can similarly be enjoined. Injunctions have issued even against unknown defendants — for example, street vendors selling fake ROLEX watches on the run.[85]

Although injunctions are discretionary, the Federal Court of Appeal once said that only the claimant's conduct can bar relief and the fact that no loss is suffered is irrelevant. To refuse an injunction otherwise is "tantamount to the imposition of a compulsory licence . . . [in] the absence of legislative authority."[86] The court accordingly granted the federal government an injunction against an unauthorized abridgment infringing copyright. This holding, to the extent that it fetters the equitable discretion, should be treated with caution. Thus, injunctions have been refused in breach of confidence cases where a good-faith confidant had expended money in ignorance of the confider's rights, but the claimant could recover the market value of the secret as damages.[87] Similarly in the US, damages instead of an injunction were suggested in a case where videorecorder manufacturers were said to be abetting copyright infringement by home-tapers.[88] More recently, damages instead of injunctions in copyright infringement cases have been encouraged as one way to minimize incursions on free speech.[89] This flexibility seems preferable to the restrictive approach suggested by the Federal Court of Appeal.

---

84   For example, a building should not be halted in mid-construction, even if it infringes copyright: *C Act,* above note 10, s. 40(1).

85   *Montres Rolex S.A. v. Balshin* (1992), [1993] 1 F.C. 236 (C.A.).

86   *R. v. James Lorimer & Co.,* [1984] 1 F.C. 1065 at 1073 (C.A.).

87   *Seager,* above note 81; D. Vaver, "What Is a Trade Secret?" in R. Hughes, ed., *Trade Secrets* (Toronto: Law Society of Upper Canada, 1990) 1 at 37–39.

88   *Universal City Studios v. Sony Corp.,* 659 F.2d 963 at 976 (9th Cir. 1981), rev'd 5:4 on liability (*sub nom. Sony Corp. of America v. Universal City Studios Inc.*), 464 U.S. 417 (1984), the dissenters agreeing with the lower court on remedy, at 499–500.

89   P.N. Leval, "*Campbell v. Acuff-Rose*: Justice Souter's Rescue of Fair Use" (1994) 13 Cardozo Arts & Ent. L.J. 19 at 23–26.

5) Interlocutory Injunction

Quickly seeking interlocutory relief is almost *de rigueur* in intellectual property cases. Delay may, after all, defeat an application, even if the claimant otherwise seems to have a good case. Many parties also settle or are loath to go to trial (sometimes years later) for a final adjudication of their rights, especially if the court has indicated a tentative view on the parties' respective merits. Intellectual property cases have in fact largely figured in settling the principles for interlocutory relief for the whole range of disputes throughout the Commonwealth. The original *Anton Piller* injunction — a pre-trial order allowing seizure of infringing material that a defendant might otherwise hide — involved breach of copyright and confidence.[90] And *American Cyanamid Co. v. Ethicon Ltd.*,[91] settling when interlocutory injunctions should be granted, was a U.K. patent case, where an injunction was issued to prevent a defendant from commencing to market surgical sutures. The House of Lords, concerned that interlocutory hearings were turning into full-scale trials on incomplete evidence, instructed judges merely to satisfy themselves that there was a "serious question to be tried" or that the applicant had a "real prospect of succeeding in . . . [its] claim for a permanent injunction at the trial".[92]

The Supreme Court of Canada has recently endorsed this approach: judges should not ask whether a *prima facie* case was made out, but must deal with applications "on the basis of common sense and an extremely limited review of the case on the merits."[93] Once past that threshold, the applicant faces two major hurdles. First, it must show it would suffer injury that cannot be adequately compensated in damages ("irreparable harm"). Second, the balance of convenience must favour an injunction. This means the court must consider which party would suffer more from the grant or refusal of an injunction, and how third parties might be affected (i.e., the public interest). Ultimately, the overall equities should be reviewed without the strait-jacket of any set formula, including, it seems, any imposed by *American Cyanamid* itself.

---

90 *Anton Piller KG v. Manufacturing Processes Ltd.*, [1976] Ch. 55 (C.A.), followed in *Nintendo of America Inc. v. Coinex Video Games Inc.* (1982), [1983] 3 F.C. 189 (C.A.).

91 [1975] A.C. 396 (H.L.) [*American Cyanamid*].

92 *Ibid.* at 407–8.

93 *RJR-MacDonald Inc. v. Canada (A.G.)*, [1994] 1 S.C.R. 311 at 348 (*Charter* challenge to legislation restricting tobacco advertising).

A British court recently made this point forcefully in an intellectual property case involving allegations of misappropriation of computer software. The claimant's allegations were only weakly supported by evidence. The court thought *American Cyanamid* did not preclude taking into account the claimant's likely merits as an important factor. Courts should not try to resolve difficult issues of fact or law on interlocutory applications, but they should be able to assess the relative strengths of each party's case as it appears from any credible evidence then produced. This helps parties reach settlements and reduces litigation costs. The court summarized its views on interlocutory injunction as follows:

1. The grant of an interlocutory injunction is a matter of discretion and depends on all the facts of the case.
2. There are no fixed rules as to when an injunction should or should not be granted. The relief must be kept flexible.
3. Because of the practice adopted on the hearing of applications for interlocutory relief, the court should rarely attempt to resolve complex issues of disputed fact or law.
4. Major factors the court can bear in mind are (a) the extent to which damages are likely to be an adequate remedy for each party and the ability of the other party to pay, (b) the balance of convenience, (c) the maintenance of the status quo, (d) any clear view the court may reach as to the relative strength of the parties' cases.[94]

Whether these views will ultimately prevail in the United Kingdom, or how they may affect Canadian courts, remains to be seen. Meanwhile, it is clear that there is no presumption for or against interlocutory injunctions in intellectual property cases or any particular class of them.[95] For example, a pre-*American Cyanamid* practice developed of not granting injunctions for recently issued patents where validity was challenged, but it no longer holds. The prospect held out by *American Cyanamid* that interlocutory hearings would become much quicker and cheaper has not, however, fully materialized. Each party still tries to stack the balance of convenience in its favour with kilos of evidence, as if physical and legal weight were equations; and each now argues that some nuance in *American Cyanamid* or the reams of jurisprudence applying it favours it more than the other party. *American Cyanamid* is thus honoured more in letter than in spirit.

---

94   *Series 5 Software Ltd.* v. *Clarke*, [1996] F.S.R. 273 at 286 (Ch.) [*Series 5*].
95   See *Turbo Resources Ltd.* v. *Petro-Canada Inc.*, [1989] F.C. 451 (C.A.), summarizing principles and refusing a trade-marks injunction; compare *826129 Ontario Inc.* v. *Sony Kabushiki Kaisha* (1995), 65 C.P.R. (3d) 171 (Fed. T.D.), granting an injunction.

It is worth recalling that the *American Cyanamid* trial judge, after dealing with the threshold question, exercised his discretion, with the House of Lords' approval, in less than two paragraphs to dispose of the case in the applicant's favour:

> The defendants, as already stated, are not yet on the market and so have no business in these sutures which will be brought to a stop; no factory will be closed down; and no workpeople be thrown out of work. The plaintiffs, on the other hand, have a substantial and growing market; and . . . I see no reason why the defendants should be allowed . . . to jump the gun and establish themselves in the market before the trial. If they were allowed to do, it would not only disrupt the plaintiff's existing and future business, but might well mean that the plaintiffs, even if they succeeded at the trial, as a commercial matter could not in practice ask for a permanent injunction.
>
> . . . [O]nce doctors and patients have got used to the defendants' product on the market in the period prior to the trial, it would be, as a commercial matter, hardly possible for the plaintiffs, even if successful, by the grant of an injunction at the trial to deprive the public of it. . . .[96]

Judges today could do worse than emulate this brevity. The attempt earlier noted to reorientate the law,[97] if generally accepted, should not be taken as an encouragement to return to the days of trying (and appealing) cases twice: once on an interlocutory injunction application, and a second time at the final trial on the merits.

6) Damages

Damages for infringement track those for tort generally. The claimant should receive monetary compensation (general and aggravated damages) restoring it to the position in which it would have been had the infringement never occurred. The claimant's present economic position is compared with that hypothetical state; the difference — excluding reasonably avoidable and "remote" losses (i.e., those not flowing naturally and directly from the wrong) — is what the infringer owes.[98] But every case will have its own peculiarities. The object is to compensate

---

96 *American Cyanamid Co. v. Ethicon Ltd.* (1973), [1975] R.P.C. 513 at 520 (Ch.), aff'd above note 91 at 409–10.

97 *Series 5*, above note 94.

98 *Colonial Fastener Co. Ltd. v. Lightning Fastener Co Ltd.*, [1937] S.C.R. 36 at 41 [*Colonial*]; *General Tire & Rubber Co. v. Firestone Tyre & Rubber Co. Ltd.*, [1975] 2 All E.R. 173 (H.L.) [*General Tire*].

this claimant — not some other claimant, who could have lost more or less from the same infringement — for the particular wrong and, if appropriate, to award punitive damages against egregiously bad infringers.[99]

Every infringement is a separate wrong. So a patent covers rights to make, use, or sell the invention. Each unit made infringes, each unit further sold or used infringes again, and the patentee should technically get compensation for each wrong. A sense of proportion must, however, be retained, and double or overlapping recovery should be avoided. Some complaints are trivial and deserve no award: overcompensation is as much a vice as undercompensation.

The following are some guidelines to assess damages.

a) Lost Sales

If a right-holder's business is selling the protected products, it can obviously recover its lost net profit on sales the infringer took from it by selling competing products. The infringer cannot escape by proving it could have sold a non-infringing substitute. A publisher once sold a school anthology containing a major section of a novel without obtaining copyright clearance. It had to compensate both the author for lost royalties and a rival publisher, who owned the copyright, for the latter's profit on sales lost from the competition.[100] An infringer may also undercut prices because it does not have the claimant's start-up cost (e.g., research, development, and market creation). A claimant reducing prices to meet this competition can also recover for its lost margin and any general business decline — for example, if the infringer produces an inferior product that makes the market turn against the claimant's product as well.[101] Claimants have even recovered for losses outside the monopoly — for example, for unpatented products like lost service contracts and spare parts sales associated with the sale of a patented product lost to an infringer.[102] Such awards are understandable when the infringer made similar gains, but are less acceptable where it did not, for the monopoly then is effectively extended beyond the grant.

---

99 See section D(6)(e), "Infringer's Knowledge or Innocence," in this chapter.

100 *Prise de Parole Inc.* v. *Guérin, Éditeur Ltée* (1995), 66 C.P.R. (3d) 257 (Fed. T.D.) [*Prise*].

101 *Lam Inc.* v. *Johns-Manville Corp.*, 718 F.2d 1056 (Fed. Cir. 1983); *Catnic Components Ltd.* v. *Hill & Smith Ltd.*, [1983] F.S.R. 512 at 528–30 (Pat. Ct.).

102 *Gerber Garment Technology Inc.* v. *Lectra Systems Ltd.*, [1995] R.P.C. 383 (Pat. Ct.).

b) Reasonable Royalty

What if the right-holder could never have made the infringer's sales — for example, they would have gone to other competitors, or the infringer created a new market? The right-holder is then entitled to damages based on a reasonable licence fee. For right-holders in the licensing business — for example, copyright collecting societies or research labs — this is the actual royalty fee they would have charged the defendant for a licence. If the right-holder never licenses (e.g., a manufacturer using a secret process), then a notional reasonable royalty fee may be set: what a willing licensor and licensee in the shoes of the particular parties would have negotiated under existing market conditions. The factors real-life negotiators, acting reasonably with a view to reaching an agreement, would use in that line of business are then taken into account: for example, comparable fees for comparable licences anywhere, the infringer's savings and profits, any admissions by either party of the figure it would be willing to accept as a royalty.[103]

The onus is on the claimant to provide a reasonable basis for the court to act on. But the reasonable royalty formula is ultimately a device to prevent unjust enrichment: the infringer is treated like the car thief, who has to pay the owner a reasonable rental for the time the owner was deprived of her property, even if the owner had put the car in storage for the winter. Neither party can avoid a calculation on this basis by saying that, in the real world, they would never have entered into licence negotiations with the other or would have settled only for other-worldly rates.

c) Intangible Losses

Infringements may sometimes cause right-holders intangible losses. For example, someone who puts up a building infringing an architect's plans may deprive the architect of the reputation that would have come her way from news of the building (placards on the site, etc.). Damages for copyright infringement may compensate for this lost credit.[104] Sometimes, too, damages can cover embarrassment and distress, as when a national newspaper publishes a private photograph without copyright clearance.[105]

---

103 *Colonial Fastener Co. Ltd.* v. *Lightning Fastener Co.* Ltd., [1936] Ex.C.R. 1, aff'd above note 98; *General Tire*, above note 98; *Georgia-Pacific Corp.* v. *U.S. Plywood-Champion Papers Inc.*, 318 F. Supp. 1116 (D.N.Y. 1970), modified 446 F.2d 295 (2d Cir. 1971).

104 *Kaffka* v. *Mountain Side Developments Ltd.* (1982), 62 C.P.R. (2d) 157 at 163 (B.C.S.C.). This loss may also infringe moral rights or amount to passing-off, and should be similarly compensable.

105 *Williams* v. *Settle*, [1960] 2 All E.R. 806 (C.A.).

d) Apportioning Damages

An infringer who takes one chapter from a ten-chapter book should pay damages only on the loss caused by taking that chapter. Exceptionally, this may be like taking the whole book: a newspaper that publishes the juiciest chapter in a biography might so satiate the market that demand for the book on general release might be much less, even zero. More often, the loss would be less. One might start with the proportion of pages taken in relation to the whole book and then increase or lower this rate depending on the importance of the chapter, the cost to the infringer of substitutes, the infringer's profit on the enterprise, and the likely effect on the copyright owner's own sales or future licensing efforts.

This approach may not always be appropriate. For example, an infringer may so interweave the right-holder's work with its own as to make separation impossible. Other times a refusal to apportion is less justified. Thus, where a finished article infringes a patent on a part or a process, courts have awarded the patentee its entire lost profits on the finished article. So the patentee of a type of baseboard for children's beds recovered the profits it had lost on selling whole beds from a competing infringer. Similarly, a patentee of a zipper-making machine and method recovered its lost profits on selling zippers.[106] This principle presumably stops at the point an airplane seller tries to recover lost profits on sales, simply because it holds a patent on the screws with which the plane is fastened.

The reluctance to apportion does not appear when an infringer's profits are assessed on an account of profits.[107] So profits were apportioned where an infringing trade-mark only contributed to product sales, where a film owed its success more to its cast and staging than to the copyright play it infringed, and where a patented section of a machine was not a "driving force" in the sales of the whole machine.[108] This approach should apply equally to damages. A claimant should not avoid apportionment simply by switching remedies, for then a punitive element creeps into an award in cases where punitive damages would not directly be awardable.

---

106   *Feldstein* v. *McFarlane Gendron Manufacturing Co.* (1966), [1967] 1 Ex.C.R. 378 at 386; *Colonial*, above note 103; compare *Stovin-Bradford* v. *Volpoint Properties Ltd.*, [1971] 1 Ch. 1007 at 1016 (C.A.) (copyright).

107   See section D(7), "Account of Profits," in this chapter.

108   *Dubiner* v. *Cheerio Toys & Games Ltd.*, [1966] 2 Ex.C.R. 801 [*Dubiner*]; *Sheldon* v. *Metro Goldwyn Pictures Corp.*, 106 F.2d 45 (2d Cir. 1939), aff'd 309 U.S. 390 (1940); *Beloit Canada Ltée/Ltd.* v. *Valmet Oy* (1995), 61 C.P.R. (3d) 271 at 279 (Fed. C.A.) [*Beloit*].

e) Infringer's Knowledge or Innocence

The main object of damages is to compensate the victim, but it is not the only object. Punitive damages can be awarded, as for any civil wrong, against a deliberate infringer who has behaved in a particularly appalling manner. The publishing company which did not bother to get copyright clearance for an anthology it published and which then, denying any infringement until just before trial, cavalierly continued to sell the book over the copyright owner's complaints, had punitive damages of $20,000 awarded against it.[109] This is well within the ordinary range of punitive damages presently being awarded in Canada: usually from $5000 to $50,000. The highest award so far is $15 million against Imperial Oil Ltd. for its allegedly "callous disregard" of an interlocutory injunction in a patent infringement case. The Federal Court of Appeal set the award aside, partly because the trial judge had not yet assessed compensation (damages or an account of profits) and so could not know whether an additional punitive award was warranted to further mark the court's disapproval of the defendant's conduct. The Court of Appeal nevertheless did not appear shocked by the size of the award made. Indeed, it indicated that on retrial the sum could be more or less than $15 million: "It depends on what figures would be required to deter [Imperial Oil] and others, in all the circumstances of this case."[110] Awards like this one are intended to mark society's disapproval of egregious conduct, to deter its repetition, and generally to teach the world that infringement does not pay. Deliberate conduct that does not warrant a punitive award may indirectly cause compensatory damages to be awarded rather more liberally than otherwise.

What then of the innocent infringer, which does not know that its acts constitute infringement? Innocence is usually irrelevant to liability[111] or to the grant of an injunction. Monetary relief may, however, sometimes be withheld — for example, for moral rights infringements and trade-mark dilution, where awards are specifically made discretionary.[112] No monetary remedy is also available against the infringer of an

---

109   *Prise*, above note 100. The copyright owner and author got $10,000 each, on top of substantial compensatory damages.

110   *Imperial Oil*, above note 59, at 22.

111   But some knowledge or intent is necessary for secondary copyright infringement by importers and distributors: *C Act*, above note 10, s. 27(4). As to trade secrets, see section D(6)(f), "Special Cases," in this chapter.

112   *C Act, ibid.*, s. 34(1.1); *T Act*, above note 6, s. 22(2). See section I, "Authors' Moral Rights," in chapter 2, and section G(3), "Dilution," in chapter 4.

unregistered copyright who "was not aware and had no reasonable ground for suspecting that copyright subsisted in the work."[113] But only the occasional Candide or cryptomnesiac may qualify for this state of grace, for everyone is supposed to assume that anything arguably under the *Copyright Act*'s scope is probably protected, and ignorance of fact or law is no excuse.[114] No monetary remedy is similarly available to an industrial design infringer who "was not aware, and had no reasonable grounds to suspect, that the design was registered"; but an encircled "D" with the design owner's name marked on most goods automatically removes the defence.[115] The design infringer must in other cases still act prudently; innocence may be pleaded by someone who markets an independently produced design, but less plausibly by someone who copies a design without legal advice or a designs register search.[116]

f) Special Cases

Special rules on damages assessment apply to particular rights. For example, a patentee may recover "reasonable compensation" for infringements occurring between the time its specification is published and the date of grant. "Reasonable compensation" would not include punitive damages. Whether an account of profits is encompassed is not clear, but an award on this basis seems possible. True, the account strips the defendant of its gains, but the remedy may still be considered as a form of compensation for an injured plaintiff.[117] Copyright holders also have special remedies. Presently, infringing copies are deemed to belong absolutely to the copyright owner, who may take proceedings to have them handed over or to recover damages equivalent to their full market value if sold. The copyright owner of a drawing engraved without authority onto a gold medallion is made the owner of the medallion and is entitled to its full price if the article is sold.[118] Continuing criticism of this punitive result has led to a proposal to eliminate this remedy and to

---

113   *C Act, ibid.*, s. 39.
114   *Bulman Group Ltd.* v. *"One Write" Accounting Systems Ltd.*, [1982] 2 F.C. 327 (T.D.); *Slumber-Magic Adjustable Bed Co.* v. *Sleep-King Adjustable Bed Co.* (1985), 3 C.P.R. (2d) 81 (B.C.S.C.). On cryptomnesia, see section G(2)(b), "Subconscious Copying," in chapter 2.
115   *ID Act*, above note 10, ss. 17(1)–(2).
116   *John Khalil Khawam* v. *K. Chellaram & Sons (Nigeria) Ltd.*, [1964] 1 All E.R. 945 at 947 (P.C.).
117   *P Act*, above note 10, s. 57(2). Compare *Imperial Oil*, above note 59, at 21.
118   *Infabrics Ltd.* v. *Jaytex Ltd.* (1981), [1982] A.C. 1 (H.L.).

substitute a right, drawn from U.S. law, to elect damages of between $500 and $20,000 for all infringements involved in an action.[119]

For trade secrets, courts have developed a flexible regime by analogy to copyright and patent cases. Sometimes information is treated like stolen property: patentable ideas are then assessed at the sum a patent may have fetched, while simpler ideas are assessed at the rate a consultant would have charged. Other times, only the value of the headstart the information gave the acquirer or the diminished value of the information as an asset is assessed. An acquirer's innocence or change of position may also reduce or extinguish liability. Once any damages award is paid, the information may sometimes continue to be used without further liability.[120]

7) Account of Profits

An infringer sometimes profits more than the right-holder loses from an infringement. The latter may then find it convenient to elect to recover the infringer's net gain. This remedy, called an "account of profits," prevents unjust enrichment and deters infringement. This remedy has recently resurged in Canada because (1) it is available even where the claimant can prove no loss; (2) the infringer, instead of the right-holder, has to lay open its books of account and prove what charges against revenue are proper to produce a net profit figure;[121] and (3) the claimant can usually recover compound prejudgment interest at prime rate on those profits.[122] However, there are limitations.

---

119   Bill C-32, above note 14, cls. 38.1(1)–(3). Collecting societies are proposed to be given a separate right to elect between three and ten times any unpaid royalties: *ibid.*, cl. 38(4). For background and critique, compare J. Berryman, "Copyright Remedies: An Ever Tightening Noose" with Canadian Music Publishers Assn., "A Case for Statutory Damages in Canadian Copyright Law" by G. Henley in *Copyright Reform: The Package, the Policy and the Politics*, Insight/*Globe & Mail* Conference, Toronto, 30–31 May 1996.

120   D. Vaver, "Civil Liability for Taking or Using Trade Secrets in Canada" (1981) 5 Can. Bus. L.J. 253 at 288–91; Vaver, "What Is a Trade Secret?" above note 87 at 36–39; *Valeo Vision S.A. v. Flexible Lamps Ltd.*, [1995] R.P.C. 205 at 227–28 (Ch.); *Cadbury Schweppes*, above note 29 (headstart damages plus injunction).

121   *C Act*, above note 10, s. 35(2), restates equity practice.

122   *Reading & Bates Construction Co. v. Baker Energy Resources Corp.* (1994), [1995] 1 F.C. 483 (C.A.). Generally, see C.L. Kirby, "Accounting of Profits: The Canadian Experience" (1993) 7 I.P.J. 263; M. Gronow, "Restitution for Breach of Confidence" (1996) 10 I.P.J. 219.

- An account typically substitutes for damages. Only exceptionally can a plaintiff have both,[123] and then double-counting must be avoided: the plaintiff should not recover both its lost profit and the defendant's net gain on the same unit. A right-holder may also recover multiple accounts of profits against multiple infringers in respect of the same goods, or an account against one and damages against another.[124] Where an account and damages are alternative remedies (as in patent and trade-mark cases), a claimant must choose between them and cannot simply ask for whichever may turn out the better for it. The court may, however, order the defendant to produce sufficient data about its profits so that the claimant may exercise an informed choice.[125]

- The court can deny an account in its discretion — for example, if the infringer did not know it was infringing or made no profits, or the claimant delayed long before suing or was less than candid in presenting its evidence at trial.[126]

- Determining what the infringer gained from the infringement can be controversial. The old story that no movie ever makes a profit — at least for any writer or actor foolish enough to contract for a percentage of the "net"[127] — is not confined to Hollywood and films. Sometimes sales profits have to be apportioned because the infringement was not the main reason for sales.[128] Other times, deductions are disputed. Thus Canadian courts have often disallowed fixed overheads,

---

123 Both remedies are awardable for copyright infringement: *C Act*, above note 10, s. 35(1); Bill C-32, above note 14, cl. 35(1).

124 *Ray Plastics Ltd. v. Canadian Tire Corp.* (1995), 62 C.P.R.(3d) 247 (Ont. Gen. Div.); *Catnic Components Ltd. v. C. Evans & Co. (Builders Merchants) Ltd.*, [1983] F.S.R. 401 at 423 (Pat. Ct.).

125 *AlliedSignal Inc. v. Du Pont Canada Inc.* (1995), 61 C.P.R. (3d) 417 at 444–45 (Fed. C.A.); *Island Records Ltd. v. Tring International Plc.*, [1995] 3 All E.R. 444 (Ch.); *Tang Man Sit v. Capacious Investments Ltd.* (1995), [1996] 2 W.L.R. 192 (P.C.); *Colbeam Palmer Ltd. v. Stock Affiliates Pty. Ltd.* (1968), 122 C.L.R. 125 (Austl. H.C.).

126 *Consolboard Inc. v. MacMillan Bloedel (Sask.) Ltd.*, [1981] 1 S.C.R. 504, aff'g (1978), 39 C.P.R. (2d) 191 at 220-22 (Fed. T.D.); *Globe-Union Inc. v. Varta Batteries Ltd.* (1981), 57 C.P.R. (2d) 254 at 257–58 (Fed. T.D.), aff'd on this point (*sub nom. Johnson Controls Inc. v. Varta Batteries Ltd.*) (1983), 80 C.P.R. (2d) 1 at 22 (Fed. C.A.).

127 See P. O'Donnell & D. McDougal, *Fatal Subtraction: The Inside Story of Buchwald v. Paramount* (New York: Doubleday, 1992).

128 See section D(6)(d), "Apportioning Damages," in this chapter.

but this has rightly been condemned elsewhere as punitive on infringers. Any overhead, fixed or variable, that assists the infringement should in principle be deductible.[129]

The problem with this remedy is less its theory than the cost of working it out. Experts may have to analyse infringers' books, and hearings can run into weeks as infringers demonstrate their unease at competitors' nosing around their confidential information. Over a century ago a British judge said of this remedy:

> [T]he difficulty of finding out how much profit is attributable to any one source is extremely great — so great that accounts in that form very seldom result in anything satisfactory to anybody. The litigation is enormous, the expense is great, and the time consumed is out of all proportion to the advantage ultimately attained; so much so that in partnership cases I confess I never knew an account in that form worked out with satisfaction to anybody. I believe in almost every case people get tired of it and get disgusted. Therefore, although the law is that a Patentee has a right to elect which course he will take, as a matter of business he would generally be inclined to take an inquiry as to damages, rather than launch upon an inquiry as to profits.[130]

The Canadian judge who, taking an account of profits in a patent case, heard seventeen interlocutory motions before sitting twenty-two days to hear the accounting evidence and legal argument would no doubt concur.[131]

8) Delivery Up

A right-holder who obtains an injunction against infringement is usually entitled to an ancillary order requiring the infringer to deliver up any infringing goods in its possession. This removes temptation and makes injunctive relief fully effective. The goods do not, however, belong to the right-holder. The order commonly allows infringers the option of destroying the goods on oath.[132] The court should make the least disruptive order that protects the claimant's rights. Where goods carry

---

129 *Dart Industries Inc. v. Decor Corp. Pty. Ltd.* (1993), 179 C.L.R. 101 (Austl. H.C.), disapproving *Teledyne Industries Inc. v. Lido Industrial Products Ltd.* (1982), 68 C.P.R. (2d) 204 (Fed. T.D.).

130 *Siddell v. Vickers* (1892), 9 R.P.C. 152 at 163 (C.A.).

131 *Beloit Canada Ltd. v. Valmet Oy* (1994), 55 C.P.R. (3d) 433 at 435 (Fed. T.D.), rev'd (1995), above note 108.

132 *Dubiner*, above note 108.

infringing trade-marks, the appropriate order may be to have the offending labels delivered up and any deceptive markings obliterated from goods left in the defendant's possession. Similarly, no order to deliver up a machine that infringes a patent should be made if removing a part can make the machine non-infringing.[133]

Two qualifications should be noted. First, a constructive trust may be imposed to avoid unjust enrichment, for example, where property has been acquired by using information confidentially entrusted to the acquirer. The defendant may have to hand over the property or its gross proceeds to the claimant.[134] Second, copies that infringe copyright are presently deemed to be owned by the copyright owner, who can therefore have them delivered up as its own property. Bill C-32 proposes to replace this provision by one allowing pre-judgment seizure and orders for destruction of the copies on application by any interested party.[135]

9) Limitation Period

Litigation to recover relief for infringement must be started within three years for copyright and moral rights, industrial designs, and ICT rights. Trade-marks and PBR limitations are governed by the provincial law where the infringement occurred — typically three years in Quebec and as long as six years in the common law provinces. The common law periods usually start running from when the claimant should, with reasonable diligence, have discovered the material facts on which the wrong was based.[136]

---

133   *Baxter Travenol Laboratories of Canada Ltd.* v. *Cutter (Can.) Ltd.* (1983), 68 C.P.R. (2d) 179 (Fed. C.A.).

134   *LAC Minerals Ltd.* v. *International Corona Resources Ltd.*, [1989] 2 S.C.R. 574. See also section E(1)(c), "Joint Authors," in chapter 2.

135   *C Act*, above note 10, s. 38; compare Bill C-32, above note 14, cl. 38.

136   D. Vaver, "Limitations in Intellectual Property: 'The Time Is Out of Joint'" (1994) 73 Can. Bar Rev. 451.

FURTHER READINGS

BROWN, R.S., "Civil Remedies for Intellectual Property Invasions: Themes and Variations" (1992) 55 L. & Contemp. Probs. 45

CAIRNS, D.J.A., *The Remedies for Trademark Infringement* (Toronto: Carswell, 1988)

HAYHURST, W.L., "Grounds for Invalidating Patents" (1975) 18 C.P.R. (2d) 222

HENDERSON, G.F., "Problems Involved in the Assignment of Patents and Patent Rights" (1966) 60 C.P.R. 237

KLIPPERT, G.B., *Unjust Enrichment* (Toronto: Butterworths, 1983)

MADDAUGH, P.D., & J.D. MCCAMUS, *The Law of Restitution* (Aurora: Canada Law Book, 1990)

PATERSON, R.K., "Directors' Liability for Infringements" (1985) 1 I.P.J. 369

PURI, K., "*Anton Piller* Relief — Palatable in Europe?" (1995) 8 I.P.J. 347

SHARPE, R.J., *Injunctions and Specific Performance*, 2d ed. (Aurora: Canada Law Book, 1993)

SISSI, R. EL, "Security Interests in Copyright" (1995) 10 I.P.J. 35

VAVER, D., "Civil Liability for Taking or Using Trade Secrets in Canada" (1981) 5 Can. Bus. L.J. 253

WADDAMS, S.J., *The Law of Damages*, 2d ed. (Aurora: Canada Law Book, 1991)

WILKOF, N.J., *Trade Mark Licensing* (London: Sweet & Maxwell, 1995)

CONCLUSION

Intellectual property law as a whole seems ripe for wholesale reconsideration, both nationally and internationally. One might start with its fundamental premise: that the system of rights it establishes enhances the goals of desirable innovation, creativity, and the widest distribution of ideas, information, products, and technology in the most efficient and, generally, best way. This premise is of course empirically unprovable, even if all agree on what "best way" means. It assumes that throwing a private property right around every activity with potential value in exchange and creating a market in such rights ultimately benefits not only the right-holders but also, in equal or at least reasonable measure, the communities of which they form part. It further assumes that this best of all possible worlds can exist only if the property/market model is the sole mechanism to achieve the stated goals, and that no other system — even one that includes the model as one component — could be devised that would benefit the community more.

In fact, intellectual property already functions within a mixed system of public and private sector policies that affect cultural and economic behaviour. These policies include tax incentives, government contracts, direct subsidies and charitable contributions to arts, regional development funding, honours and prizes, and social rewards for generally approved activities. The idea that intellectual property should dominate discourse, to the reduction or elimination of all else, is simply one ideology. It cannot be true of all times and places. It is not true of Canada today. Whether it should be is a different question.

Even if intellectual property law is accepted as the best method of stimulating high levels of innovation and social progress, the way it operates in Canada hardly achieves these goals or seems compatible with the aspirations of a modern liberal democracy. The laws are poorly drafted and poorly integrated with one another, and cannot be understood except by specialized lawyers. However much the rhetoric of inventors, creators, and innovators is employed, the *Acts* seem more designed by big business for big business. Smaller operations and the general public are left to the side as passive viewers — to be affected, but not themselves to affect anything.

The rights can also be fiendishly expensive to enforce. A few years ago a doyen of the intellectual property bar pointed with apparent pride to the fact that Canadian patent litigation was five to ten times cheaper than its U.S. counterparts. Still, bills in the hundreds of thousands of dollars were "reasonably common," although it was "very rare" for fees and disbursements to exceed $1 million.[1] Presumably *Beloit Canada Ltée v. Valmet Oy* was one of those very rare cases, "almost Dickensian in its length and complexity," according to the judges hearing yet another appeal concerning it.[2] By early 1995 the litigation had run up $2.1 million in accountants' fees alone to ascertain that the defendants owed the patentee some $3.6 million for infringing (a sum later increased by compound interest apparently spanning a decade and a half). The lawyers' bills were not likely trumped by those of the accountants. After two decades of litigation, the plaintiff was presumably left with something more than a place in Canadian legal history.

Intellectual property litigation has been said to be "by and large . . . the most technical both in terms of the factual subject matter and the law itself," even when compared to tax, constitutional, and competition law cases.[3] Factual complexity may be largely unavoidable, although less "technical" law could reduce the range and hence the expense of factual inquiries. It is important, however, to understand what is meant by "technical" in this context. The laws are certainly hard to read and understand; but, even when explained, the results they produce hardly

---

1   Consumer & Corporate Affairs Canada, *Intellectual Property: Litigation, Legislation & Education: A Study of the Canadian Intellectual Property and Litigation System* by G. F. Henderson (Ottawa: Supply & Services, 1991) at 17.

2   *Beloit Canada Ltée v. Valmet Oy* (1995), 61 C.P.R. (3d) 271 at 274 (Fed. C.A.), rev'g in part (*sub nom. Beloit Canada Ltd. v. Valmet Oy*) (1994), 55 C.P.R. (3d) 433 at 435 (Fed. T.D.), where the trial judge speaks unenthusiastically of his experience presiding over the remedy phase of the case.

3   Henderson, above note 1.

square with the way many ordinary, law-abiding citizens think and act. To tell these people, as copyright owners periodically do, that it is unlawful to record radio or television broadcasts without first obtaining clearance from umpteen right-holders is to invite disbelieving stares. This is but one example of the lack of a comprehensible and coherent moral centre which makes much of intellectual property law so "technical" and unpersuasive.

We can now review some of these "technicalities."

A. DRAFTING STANDARDS

A degree of mystique and uncertainty in the part of intellectual property law regulated by the common law may be thought tolerable because of the much-vaunted benefits flowing from the common law's adaptability and capacity for growth. Mysticism and uncertainty should not, however, be a feature of laws passed by Parliament. Yet anyone reading intellectual property statutes for the first time is struck by their complexity and tortuousness. These are not "user-friendly" laws, even for lawyers. The *Integrated Circuit Topography Act* is the least objectionable, but it is the newest, shortest, and least used law.

The *Trade-marks Act* is probably the best of the various statutes, considering the amount of traffic it carries. And so it should be, drafted as it was under the watchful eye of Harold Fox, Canada's leading intellectual property lawyer of the day. Still, it has a certain old-world quaintness about it. Product marks are marks for "wares"; product get-up is called a "distinguishing guise"; and the *Act*'s main point — letting someone apply to register a trade-mark — comes half way through the *Act* (at section 30) after a bewildering set of definition sections and other provisions retailing what is legal and what is not. And then the "simple" application to register bristles with problems only a specialist could know about. The general practitioner, let alone the do-it-yourselfer, who handles a trade-mark application or opposition very quickly gets out of his depth. Everything seems simple, but the simplicity is deceptive, for anyone taking the *Act* at face value is sure to come to grief.

Whether the *Copyright Act* or the *Patent Act* qualifies as the least user-friendly law of all is a close call. The *Copyright Act*'s British progenitor, passed in 1710, was, according to its preamble, "for the encouragement of learned men to compose and write useful books." Most such men and women would be stumped were they to try to read today's *Copyright Act*, with or without Bill C-32. Almost anything written, drawn, recorded, or published in some way virtually anywhere in the world has copyright in Canada: yet that simple thought takes pages and pages of labyrinthine provisions to express.

The *Patent Act* is supposed to regulate and encourage cutting-edge ideas and technology, and some of it is of recent vintage — for example, the part regulating patented medicine prices. Yet, overall, the *Patent Act* is the most antique and obscure of the statutes in language and structure. Some provisions and procedures date back to the mid-nineteenth century. Basic questions such as invalidity are left to inference and to an open-ended stream of common law stretching back to the seventeenth century. User rights are poorly spelt out. The very scope of the monopoly is still defined by glossing cryptic language according to British jurisprudence that the British themselves no longer follow!

These internal deficiencies are magnified by inconsistencies among the statutes. Inconsistency is undesirable intrinsically, as well as practically, for much technology crosses rights. A single piece of computer technology may involve patents, trade-marks, copyrights, integrated circuit topography rights, and industrial design rights — quite apart from common law rights. Purely technical issues relating to the creation or transfer of rights should not depend arbitrarily on what right is involved. Two examples will suffice: registration and limitation. All the statutes have registries for recording title, yet the provisions for registration and expungement differ only because they were drafted at different times by different hands. These discrepancies encourage a search for subtle differences even where they do not and should not exist. Meanwhile, basic issues like priorities between competing transfers are either left completely to provincial law or (as for patents, copyrights, and plant breeders' rights) differ among themselves and leave relationships with provincial priority laws unsettled. This is not good enough for the amount of traffic the registries carry: about 100,000 new entries, 60 percent representing changes of title, are recorded every year.

As for limitations, the time limits differ arbitrarily among rights; the basic drafting of the limitation provisions is not standard; and, even where two provisions do read the same in the English, the French version reads differently.[4] Two rights (registered trade-marks and plant breeders' rights) have no limitation provision at all; in these areas, one or more provincial limitation laws will apply, but only after a conflicts-of-law analysis to determine which will apply.[5]

---

4   *Patent Act*, R.S.C. 1985, c. P-4, s. 55.01; *Industrial Design Act*, R.S.C. 1985, c. I-9, s. 18.

5   D. Vaver, "Limitations in Intellectual Property: 'The Time Is Out of Joint'" (1994) 73 Can. Bar Rev. 451.

Intellectual property laws, then, barely comply with the basic precept of the Rule of Law that laws must be written clearly and comprehensibly for those whose conduct is regulated and affected by them — businesses and the general public alike, not just lawyers or a small specialized clique of them. Unclear, inconsistent, and archaic laws impose deadweight costs on the economy, to say nothing of the frustration of those whose conduct they aim to guide.

The idea of a single technology code covering all intellectual property rights has often been floated. It is desirable if for no other reason than to standardize stock provisions such as acquisition and transfer of rights, remedies, administration, registries, limitations, and even application forms and procedures among rights.

B. COPYRIGHT

The idea that copyright should protect, and so encourage, the whole gamut of creative endeavour sounds good in principle, but even before the impact of the digital revolution was felt, copyright policy had sunk into incoherence. The law is supposed to reward workers in the fields of art, literature, music, and drama, yet employers, repackagers, and distributors frequently make much more from the system than do the toilers in the field. It is supposed to stimulate the production of work that would not otherwise have been produced at all or as well, yet much routine material is protected: trivial correspondence, private diaries, simple logos (amply protected by trade-mark and passing-off laws), and even the doodlings of toddlers. It is supposed to encourage the dissemination of local culture. Yet, on one hand, this goal is thwarted by international regulations like *Berne, NAFTA,* and *TRIPs,* which require foreign material to be as freely disseminated and fully protected as local material, while, on the other hand, much of the traditional culture of Canada's aboriginal peoples is left unprotected. It is supposed to protect products that are in fact cultural, yet how computer programs (essentially electronic machine parts) or business and legal forms — classed alongside novels and poetry as original literary works — qualify as culture, except in some trivial sense, has never been explained and, indeed, is unexplainable.

Digital technologies have thrown copyright's anomalies into starker relief. More fundamentally, they have thrown into question whether copyright can or should exist in the digital world. After all, copyright is premised on the initial production of a tangible original work, which is then exploited either through mass marketing of copies, public performance, or broadcast. Unauthorized intrusions into this market are usually relatively quick and easy to detect and to close down through the use of civil or criminal sanctions. But as existing works are digitized, with or without authorization, or new works are made available solely in digital format, copyright becomes powerless to cope with the manipulation and movement of intangible electronic streams. Detection and enforcement become difficult, sometimes impossible, and rights that appear on the books are ignored in practice. Access to music, art, literature, and other material in digital form has given users the power to modify these works or data at will, replicate them almost infinitely, and transmit them anywhere in the world to others, who in turn have the same capabilities; and power, once given, will inevitably be used. In this world, every user is a potential re/author and re/distributor of material made available electronically to her. In this world, the only way in which an initial provider of a work or information can practically profit from its investment may be through reliance on shared ethical understandings, encryption technology, and good marketing (e.g., the provision of services like help lines and regular updates to which users wish to subscribe).

Whether or in what way copyright will ultimately cope in this new order is far from clear. Business and governments alike still seem committed to preserving copyright, and recent efforts have gone towards trying to strengthen the system, tightening copyright owners' control over electronic activity, adapting copyright rules to achieve that goal, and shrinking the scope of the public domain. Whether these efforts amount to overkill is a legitimate issue. The present criminal and proposed civil sanctions seem draconian, especially in the context of a law that is often uncertain and ill-attuned to the daily habits of many people. The sanctions include criminal penalties of up to $1 million. fines and/ or 5 years' jail, and proposed statutory damages of up to $20,000 which do not have to correlate with the copyright holder's actual loss. Added to other available remedies, they impose liabilities on infringers more extensive than those for the meanest patent infringer, environmental polluter, or trespasser to land.[6] What makes copyright infringers more morally culpable than them?

---

6   Bill C-32's proposed scheme has been called "one of the most complex and some would say draconian remedial structures in the common law world": J. Berryman, "Copyright Remedies: An Ever Tightening Noose," in *Copyright Reform: The Package, the Policy and the Politics*, Insight/*Globe & Mail* Conference, Toronto, 30–31 May 1996, at 19. Alan Young has also questioned why the criminal law should apply to vindicate essentially private rights: "Catching Copyright Criminals: *R. v. Miles of Music Ltd.*" (1990) 5 I.P.J. 257 at 273.

C. PATENTS

The patent system is also under strain, but less so from the digital revolution that is affecting copyright. Though overtly designed to further economic welfare, the patent system often has difficulty getting respect from those who deal in economic welfare: economists. Even supporters may turn out lukewarm: they see "nothing better" to enable small producers or independent inventors to reap their reward, but freely admit that it is "almost impossible to conceive of any existing social institution so faulty in so many ways."[7] An independent study conducted in 1958 on the U.S. patent system came to this "disappointingly inconclusive conclusion":

> None of the empirical evidence at our disposal and none of the theoretical arguments presented either confirms or confutes the belief that the patent system has promoted the progress of the technical arts and the productivity of the economy. . . .
>
> If one does not know whether a system "as a whole" (in contrast to certain features of it) is good or bad, the safest "policy conclusion" is to "muddle through" — either with it, if one has long lived with it, or without it, if one has lived without it. If we did not have a patent system, it would be irresponsible, on the basis of our present knowledge of its economic consequences, to recommend instituting one. But since we have had a patent system for a long time, it would be irresponsible, on the basis of our present knowledge, to recommend abolishing it. This last statement refers to a country such as the United States of America — not to a small country and not a predominantly nonindustrial country, where a different weight of argument might well suggest another conclusion.[8]

It was precisely the fear that the rapidly industrializing countries of Asia might continue to harbour only lukewarm enthusiasm for a system monopolized largely by foreign multinational corporations that led the

---

7   J. Jewkes, D. Sawers & R. Stillerman, *The Sources of Invention*, 2d ed. (New York: W.W. Norton, 1969) at 188; compare S.N.S. Cheung, "Property Rights and Invention" (1986) 8 Research in Law & Economics 5, summarizing other views.

8   U.S. Senate, Subcommittee on Patents, Trademarks and Copyrights, *An Economic Review of the Patent System* (Study No. 15) by F. Machlup (U.S.: Comm. Print, 1958), 79–80; similarly, E.T. Penrose, *The Economics of the International Patent System* (Baltimore: Johns Hopkins, 1951) at 40; compare A.S. Oddi, "Un-Unified Economic Theories of Patents — The Not-Quite-Holy Grail" (1996) 71 Notre Dame L. Rev. 267.

industrialized nations, in which these corporations were headquartered, to campaign successfully for the entrenchment of the high levels of intellectual property protection and national treatment that the *TRIPs* agreement of 1994 eventually contained. This movement continues apace at the international level under the aegis of the World Intellectual Property Organization.

Even on the assumption that the patent system is the best means of achieving a high rate of desirable technological process, it is shot through with inconsistencies at every point. One may start with patentability itself. The system is unconcerned with any relative need for a particular invention. The new knick-knack and the most socially useful idea are treated equally: no greater incentive for one is provided over the other. On the other hand, demarcations are made between "basic" and "applied" research, and then between what is and what is not obvious. Basic research and "pure" theory are winnowed out as unpatentable, though central to other later "inventions." For the theorist comes perhaps praise and a prize; for the applied scientist and his employer, the patent. Nor is the patent hard to get: almost any new gadget or way of doing things can surmount the obstacle of non-obviousness: "the slightest differences between the invention and the prior art" may be enough, "particularly in the hands of a skilled patent agent."[9] Validity is of course not guaranteed, but firms often find it cheaper to become licensees than to incur the costs and uncertainties of litigating validity; the public bears the cost through higher priced goods and services. Standards of patentability could of course be raised, but the courts cannot be relied to do so. One court that unilaterally tried to raise standards by applying an economic model of obviousness — would the advance have occurred soon anyway without the incentive of a patent? — was firmly rebuffed on review: the usual saws were trotted out to uphold the technological marvels achieved by the interaction of a ball, groove, and spring in a socket wrench.[10]

A major benefit of the system is supposedly the requirement for early public disclosure of the invention, but this advantage works only erratically. Firms can decide not to patent and can hide their technology by relying on trade-secret law instead; only when competitors themselves might patent or reverse-engineer will the firm show interest in

---

9 F. Farfan, "What Should the General Practitioner Know about Patents, Anyway?", in *Intellectual Property for the General Practitioner* (Toronto: Canadian Bar Association-Ontario, 1988) at 4 [emphasis omitted].

10 *Roberts v. Sears Roebuck & Co.*, 723 F.2d 1324 (7th Cir. 1983) (*en banc*), rev'g 697 F.2d 796 (7th Cir. 1983).

patenting. Then the incentive is to disclose either too little or too much: too little, so the best means of working the invention can be withheld from competitors or developed after the application is filed; too much, so the cost of analysing what is important works out higher than the cost of buying a licence that sorts the wheat from the chaff.

The very scope of a patent is left uncertain. The *Patent Act* has left courts to develop a doctrine of "substantial infringement" to catch activity that, at first sight, does not fall within a patent's claims. With no jury to explain matters to, courts have produced a complicated analysis that promises certainty, but fails to deliver. Parliament is, however, more to blame than the courts. The legislature should decide how wide a monopoly a Canadian patent should have and not leave the question over to judges, who have, predictably, provided a mish-mash concocted from British and U.S. ingredients. This question of "law" is really a question of economic and social policy. The approach other states have taken is relevant but not controlling. A U.S. judge recently pointed out that the analytical complexity of the law of substantial infringement

> arises because technologic growth benefits not only from the activities of the originators, but also from those who improve, enlarge, and challenge. The larger public interest requires setting the optimum balance between the purpose of supporting the inventor, in the national interest, and the purpose of supporting improvement and competition, also in the national interest.[11]

Judges cannot be expected to create laws "in the national interest" out of the narrowly focused evidence and arguments of particular legal disputes. Only legislatures are competent to do this, after considering the wider array of factors relevant to public policy-making.

D. TRADE-MARKS

The trade-mark system too is due for overhaul. One may start with examination. In practice, few marks prove unregistrable — probably just enough for examiners to claim a justification for their own existence. The courts have meanwhile told the TMO not to waste time initially by examining applications too closely anyway.[12] Why then have an examination

---

11   *Hilton-Davis Chemical Co. v. Warner-Jenkinson Co. Inc.*, 62 F.3d 1512 at 1531–32 (Fed. Cir. 1995), Newman J. (concurring).

12   For example, *Canadian Parking Equipment Ltd. v. Canada (Registrar of Trade Marks)* (1990), 34 C.P.R. (3d) 154 at 160–61 (Fed. T.D.).

system at all? Many marks — that is, "official" marks — are already registered without examination; might this not be made to apply to all marks, as happens in some civil law systems, and with copyrights in the Copyright Office?[13] Registrations could then be challenged either in infringement or in post-registration opposition proceedings, so resources would be shifted into scrutinizing only contentious marks. What seems indefensible is the present hybrid system, under which a mark adopted by a goose preservation society can be registered on demand, while a mark adopted by a goose supplier will be examined, possibly opposed, and will still be liable to invalidation after registration. Sauce for the goose supplier should be sauce for the goose preserver too.

Policies appropriate when the *Act* was enacted in 1953 look less compelling when they are revisited four decades later, partly because the jurisprudence has developed unexpectedly. Who would have thought, for example, that the introduction of the service mark concept in 1953 would have turned the *Act* into a nationwide business names registry? The *Canadian Charter of Rights and Freedoms* has also changed how the *Act* is perceived. Thus, the prohibition on depreciating a trade-mark's goodwill,[14] which has hindered comparative advertising for the last quarter of a century, now looks decidedly at odds with the constitutional protection the Supreme Court has thrown around commercial speech over the last decade.

These features, though perhaps not fully foreseen initially, are nonetheless consistent with the big-business bias of the *Act*. The prototypical mark envisaged is one associated with a nationwide business; as a result, Canada's mass marketers, multinational offshoots, and local businesses with visions of expansion or franchising are warmly embraced. But the *Act* appears indifferent to the problems of many small to medium-size businesses with only local or regional aspirations, although these businesses today are as much, if not more, a mainstay of the Canadian economy. The Manitoban company that would be quite content with trade-mark protection coincident with the scope of its local customer base is, instead, encouraged to acquire Canada-wide rights. It can then harass or extract tribute from businesses in Victoria or Halifax which may have operated honestly for years without confusion and whose only mistake was not to get a registration or have lawyers constantly scanning the *Trade-marks Journal*. Even if the Manitoban company does acquire imperialist ambitions that eventually conflict

---

13   No attempt should, of course, be made to emulate the remainder of the present defective scheme that applies to official marks. See section D, "Official Marks," in chapter 4.

14   See section G(3), "Dilution," and section I, "Users' Rights," in chapter 4.

with an established local enterprise in Vancouver, why should its decision to expand automatically cut off the right of the Vancouver business to retain the goodwill associated with its own symbols?

The *Act*'s bias against concurrent or regional registrations may have suited the monolithic aspirations of the "sea-to-shining-sea" often multinational business model of the 1950s. One may query its appropriateness to the economy of the twenty-first century, where the small or localized business needs as much encouragement as the large. One possible solution may be to devise a more flexible system, under which enterprises obtain a national registration that, after five years, might be recontoured to the firm's actual customer base. The registration could be regularly reviewed, perhaps every five years or on application by the registrant or anyone else. Registrations would then more closely match the area of likely customer confusion, instead of stretching to points where the registrant can demonstrate no interest other than opportunism.

E. SOCIAL CONTROL

If one feature stands out about intellectual property law, it is how much the law affects the public, but how little the public affects it — indeed, how little the law lets the public affect it. Intellectual property law is a social construct that shuns social participation, let alone control. Few Jane and John Does turn up at legislative hearings when revision or amendment of the law is contemplated; they are certainly not present at the international meetings where global intellectual property standards are set. The registries of the Canadian Intellectual Property Office are open to the general public, but are rarely consulted by it. Trials involving intellectual property matters are by a judge alone, without a jury. The *Acts* justify themselves by how they benefit the public, but the justifications are long on assertion, short on proof. Beneath the veneer, one finds an infrastructure inhospitable to public entry. Any do-it-yourselfer trying to obtain a right (other than copyright, which is automatic) is sure to come to grief even if he assiduously tries to follow the relevant *Act* and *Regulations*.

The substance of the law is no more embracing. The tone is well set by the British judge who, admitting that the "public interest" could override a copyright, indicated how atrophied this "public" interest is: "[T]here is a world of difference between what is in the public interest and what is of interest to the public," he said, with no trace of embarrassment.[15] This approach permeates intellectual property generally.

---

15   *Lion Laboratories Ltd.* v. *Evans,* [1985] Q.B. 526 at 553 (C.A.).

Patents cannot be refused even where they are shown to have no public benefit, and the language in which they are drafted is accessible only to someone skilled in the art — not to a lay person, however highly educated. Trade-mark litigants scrap over who can bring their particular brand of truth before the public; the occasional lay person who testifies at a trial about how she is or is not confused will not readily repeat the experience after the public mocking she will receive from an experienced cross-examiner.

If intellectual property rights really do benefit the public, any member of the public should be able to oppose grants that may not operate in the public interest, or have those that are not so operating expunged. Anyone can challenge the grant of a European patent before the European Patent Office, and a study on the ethical issues involved in patenting life forms has proposed a similar scheme for Canada.[16] In Canada, however, only someone "interested" or "aggrieved," or a government representative (the Attorney General or the CIPO), can apply to expunge a right, and initial grants can be opposed only under the *PBR Act* or the *Trade-marks Act*.[17] These rights of opposition are not intended as forms of social control. For example, the general public does not read the *Trade-marks Journal* (the only place pending trade-mark registrations can be found); the grounds of opposition are closely defined to exclude any matter of general public interest; and no provision exists for notifying anyone (except another registrant) possibly affected by a registration.

Meaningful public participation in the intellectual property granting process would need more than giving the public standing. Suitable grounds for opposition would need to be devised.[18] Applicants could provide an impact statement to demonstrate how the grant may affect the public. Applications could be advertised in newspapers likely to be read by potential interveners (e.g., a mark in Chinese lettering might be advertised in the Chinese language press). Applicants could carry the onus of proof that grants in their favour would, overall, benefit the public.

---

16   Westminster Institute for Ethics and Human Values & McGill Centre for Medicine, Ethics and Law, *Ethical Issues Associated with the Patenting of Higher Life Forms*, (London, Ont., 1994) at 103ff, esp. 106–7.

17   Informal "protests" can be filed in the PO and, presumably, other CIPO branches. The information may be used, but the filer is treated as an interloper: see, for example, the *Patent Rules*, 1996, s. 10.

18   Presumably more specific than making the grant "objectionable on public grounds," as is provided in some corporate names registration schemes: for example, *Business Corporation Regulations*, O. Reg. 62/90, s. 13.

Imagine how these modifications might work for trade-mark registrations. The Trade-mark Office might more quickly recognize Canada's changed demographics and stop testing the registrability of obviously foreign marks according to what the notional average bilingual Canadian might think. It might learn that there are many Japanese or Spanish speakers in Canada and that they might not all treat NISHI, KOLA LOCA, or GALANOS as meaningless arbitrary marks.[19] It might more readily decide that such marks, as well as marks in foreign characters (e.g., Chinese, Arabic, Hebrew), should be judged by the reaction of speakers of that language. The Opposition Board might also take judicial notice of the obvious — for example, that "the number of Canadians fluent in Chinese" is in fact "significant," contrary to what it has so far held.[20] It might also find that the Nisga'a people of British Columbia would have preferred to be notified of the registration of a mark like NISKA for clothing and to have been given a chance to object to it, even though their existence was said by the Board to be (then) known to "relatively few Canadians."[21]

F. FIRST NATIONS

The Nisga'a example shows how trade-mark law can affect a particular social group without its knowledge until it is too late. Sometimes this result occurs through neglect; other times the policy is quite deliberate.

Consider how copyright law affects First Nations peoples. It certainly protects the work of contemporary Aboriginal artists, writers, and their publishers and distributors, just as it does the work of their non-Aboriginal counterparts.[22] Traditional First Nations work, however, is more vulnerable. What is to stop anyone from commercializing, with or without embellishment, traditional Aboriginal stories and artwork, even when this behaviour may be deeply offensive to the group that feels these stories and their art are integral to its culture, part of the glue that binds

---

19   *Galanos v. Canada (Registrar of Trade Marks)* (1982), 69 C.P.R. (2d) 144 at 155 (Fed. T.D.); *Nishi v. Robert Morse Appliances Ltd.* (1990), 34 C.P.R. (3d) 161 at 167 (Fed. T.D.); *Krazy Glue Inc. v. Grupo Cyanomex S.A. de C.V.* (1989), 27 C.P.R. (3d) 28 (T.M. Opp. Bd.).

20   *Cheung's Bakery Products Ltd. v. Saint Anna Bakery Ltd.* (1992), 46 C.P.R. (3d) 261 at 268 (T.M. Opp. Bd.).

21   *Lortie v. Standard Knitting Ltd.* (1991), 35 C.P.R. (3d) 175 at 179 (T.M. Opp. Bd.).

22   See, for example, *Milpurrurru v. Indofurn Pty. Ltd.* (1994), 30 I.P.R. 209 (Austl. Fed. Ct.), for a sensitive attempt to reconcile copyright law with the customary law of an Australian aboriginal people.

it together? First Nations peoples have valid concerns about how their stories and their art are being taken and commercialized, sometimes by their own peoples, more often by others. Sometimes the commercialization itself may be offensive, as when the story or the piece of art is treated as sacred by the group to which it belongs; other times, the commercialization, while not in itself offensive, distorts the original story or artwork.

Copyright and moral rights pass these issues by. The objections to protection under the current law are often insuperable. The author may be unidentifiable because he or she is long since dead, or the work may have been communally made. The work may have been oral and unfixed. There may be no one who can put forward a plausible claim to be the author or the copyright owner, in the sense of having derived title from an identifiable author or authors. Any possible term of copyright may also have expired.

Protecting traditional culture in some way raises controversy because it suggests that some areas of thought and expression are off limits except to one identified group: a type of censorship that is anathema to writers and artists. First Nations peoples may respond that the act of translation itself may be a form of cultural oppression that, intentionally or unintentionally, recreates traditional stories according to the translator's perspective. The reformed stories then may be treated as the authentic expression of the group's culture, even by the group itself. Differences likes these are best settled through rules not designed in bureaucrats' offices, but coming out of discussions involving interested Aboriginal and non-Aboriginal leaders, writers, and artists.

The present situation has come about quite deliberately. The issue of bringing traditional culture ("folklore") under copyright was discussed during *Berne*'s 1967 revision process. An international consensus developed that favoured protection, and a working group was struck to look further into the matter. Immediately, the Canadian delegate was on guard, and he is recorded as saying that

> he had been unable to speak earlier on the question of folklore. His country had a very considerable body of folklore, which it had always regarded as falling within the public domain. Canada was therefore opposed to any action likely to restrict the public use of folklore material. His Delegation was extremely unwilling to enter into a discussion as to who owned or was entitled to use such material. He hoped the new Working Group would bear his remarks in mind, since the matter was of great concern to his Delegation.[23]

---

23 *Records of the Intellectual Property Conference of Stockholm (1967)*, vol. 2 (Geneva: World Intellectual Property Organization, 1971) at 877–78.

Given *Berne*'s rule of unanimity, this objection was enough for the provision on traditional culture to be watered down to an inoffensive non-binding scheme that has attracted few adherents. Needless to say, Canada is not one of them.

G. RETHINKING INTELLECTUAL PROPERTY

For the meantime, the international community has accepted the notion that intellectual property is integral to national and international economic welfare; and, at some level, the utility of intellectual property is of little doubt. Few would deny that some stimulus and protection has to be offered in some sectors to encourage production of goods that are easily appropriable, where copying avoids the producer's initial investment and deprives the producer of the opportunity of recoupment and making a fair profit. The question is what stimulus and what protection should be offered. The policy instruments for deciding these questions are readily at hand.

Whenever governments want fundamentally to review what services they provide or ought to provide, they introduce a system of zero budgeting. Under it, every department of government is allocated a budget of $0. To get more, the department has to show why it needs it and how much it really needs to achieve its goals. There is no presumption that a department has an entitlement simply because it has always had one or had one the previous year. Each project and the level of support to be devoted to it have to be justified separately. The map created by the total number of successfully justified projects is then surveyed, checked off against policy criteria, and finally adjusted for anomalies. The product is not timeless: there are periodic short-term reviews, based on the presumption of the prior budget's accuracy; there are periodic comprehensive audits to ensure that policy objectives are being achieved; and there are periodic longer-term reviews, where a return to zero budgeting and no presumptions are the order of the day.

Intellectual property seems ripe for a zero budget review, domestically and internationally. The broad questions to be asked would be:

- What activities do we as societies desire to encourage?
- What degree of stimulus needs to be offered for the activities to occur?
- Who should benefit from the stimulus? The initial producer(s)? Later distributors? In what proportions and to what degree? And who deserves to be called a "producer" in the first place: the blood donor as well as the researcher who isolates the cells and develops a cell-line from it?

Along the way, some other equally fascinating questions will no doubt need answering, for example:

- Should society simply set up a market for ideas and allow entrants in that market to sell those ideas to the highest bidder? Should it be concerned about people who do not have the resources to enter the market?
- Should society be concerned about the unequal distribution of intellectual property, nationally and internationally, in the same way it may be concerned about the unequal distribution of traditional property? Or should intellectual property laws be devised that do not entrench and enhance existing distributions of power and wealth?
- Should society be concerned that intellectual property laws may play a part in causing people to invest too much time and money in inventive and creative activity, to the detriment of more modest but as worthwhile improvements to existing technology? Or that the laws may contribute to new technology being introduced and exploited before its potential social impact can be fully and fairly assessed, because its promoters naturally want to reap the rewards of monopoly quickly? Or that intellectual property laws may need to be modified or supplemented to encourage activity in areas which society considers particularly necessary for its well-being or survival and which those laws are doing little or nothing to encourage?

In the heat of the battle between owners and users of intellectual property, such systemic questions are rarely asked. Not only should they be but attempts should also be made to answer them, so laws can be devised which have a coherent moral centre that the public can comprehend and accept.[24]

---

24 Some paragraphs of this chapter were drawn from D. Vaver, "Some Agnostic Observations on Intellectual Property" (1991) 6 I.P.J. 125; "Rejuvenating Copyright" (1996) 75 Can. Bar Rev. 69; and "Rejuvenating Copyright, Digitally" in *Symposium of Digital Technology and Copyright* (Ottawa: Department of Justice, 1995) 1.

FURTHER READINGS

ALFORD, W.P., "How Theory Does — and Does Not — Matter: American Approaches to Intellectual Property Law in East Asia" (1994) 13 U.C.L.A. Pac. Basin L.J. 8

BARLOW, J.P., "The Economy of Ideas: A Framework for Rethinking Patents and Copyright in the Digital Age (Everything You Wanted to Know About Intellectual Property Is Wrong)" (1993) 2:3 Wired 84

BOYLE, J., *Shamans, Software and Spleens: Law and the Construction of the Information Society* (Cambridge: Harvard University Press, 1996)

CONSUMER & CORPORATE AFFAIRS CANADA, *Intellectual Property: Litigation, Legislation and Education — A Study of the Canadian Intellectual Property and Litigation System* by G.F. Henderson (Ottawa: Supply & Services, 1991)

COOMBE, R.J., "Objects of Property and Subjects of Politics: Intellectual Property Laws and Democratic Dialogue" (1991) 69 Texas L.R. 1853

COOMBE, R.J., "The Properties of Culture and the Politics of Possessing Identity: Native Claims in the Cultural Appropriation Controversy" (1993) 6 Can. J. Law & Jur. 249

CORNISH, W.R., "Authors at Law" (1995) 58 Mod. L. Rev. 1

INFORMATION HIGHWAY ADVISORY COUNCIL, *Final Report of the Copyright Subcommittee: Copyright and the Information Highway* (Ottawa: The Council, 1995); council@ist.ca; debra.dgbt.doc.ca/pub/info-highway or http://debra.dgbt.doc.ca/info-highway/ih.html

INFORMATION HIGHWAY ADVISORY COUNCIL, *Final Report: Connection, Community, Content: The Challenge of the Information Highway* (Ottawa: The Council, 1995); http://info.ic.gc.ca/info-highway/ih.html

Intellectual Property Rights: The Politics of Ownership (1991) 15 Cultural Survival Q. 1

LADDIE, H., "Copyright: Over-strength, Over-regulated, Over-rated?" [1996] 5 E.I.P.R. 253

NAIR, K.R.G., & A. KUMAR, eds., *Intellectual Property Rights* (New Delhi: Allied Publishers, 1994)

PALMER, T.G., "Intellectual Property: A Non-Posnerian Law and Economics Approach" (1989) 12 Hamline L. Rev. 261 (1989)

PASK, A., "Cultural Appropriation and the Law: An Analysis of the Legal Regimes Concerning Culture" (1994) 8 I.P.J. 57

PURI, K., "Cultural Ownership and Intellectual Property Rights Post-*Mabo*: Putting Ideas into Action" (1995) 9 I.P.J. 293

U.S.A., *Report of the Working Group on Intellectual Property Rights, Intellectual Property and the National Information Infrastructure* (Washington, D.C.: Patent and Trademark Office, 1995), (Chair: U.S. Commissioner of Patents Bruce A. Lehman), iitf.doc.gov.

STANBURY, W.T., "Aspects of Public Policy regarding Crown Copyright in the Digital Age" (1996) 10 I.P.J. 131

WOODMANSEE, M., & P. JASZI, eds., *The Construction of Authorship: Textual Appropriation in Law and Literature* (Durham, N.C.: Duke University Press, 1994)

GLOSSARY

* indicates cross-reference to another entry.

Account of profits: Discretionary remedy that requires an infringer to detail the net profits made from an infringement and to pay the sum over to the claimant.

Anticipation: The converse of novelty in *patent law. An invention that has been anticipated (i.e., the same subject matter is shown to exist already at a patent application's claim date) is not new and therefore cannot be patented.

Assignment: Voluntary transfer of ownership of a right. The person transferring is the assignor, who transfers (assigns) to an assignee. Such a transfer is called "cession" in Quebec.

Berne Convention [Berne]: The *Convention on the Protection of Literary and Artistic Works* signed at Berne in 1886. The latest version is the *Paris Act* of 1971. Canada has ratified only the 1928 version, but *NAFTA and *TRIPs bind it to give a high level of *copyright protection equivalent to the 1971 *Act*. Canada will soon formally adhere to the 1971 version.

Bill C-32: The Copyright Amendment Bill of 1996, introduced into the Canadian House of Commons on 25 April 1996. The bill increases the rights of record companies and performers, gives Canadian book distributors the right to stop unauthorized imports or distribution, and provides some exemptions for libraries, archives, museums, and people with disabilities. References are to Bill C-32 as it stood at its second reading stage in June 1996. The bill was referred to a parliamentary committee to hold hearings and, at press time, was likely to be presented with a number of amendments for third reading. It is projected to be passed by 1997.

Bootleg: *See* Piracy; Theft.

Breach of confidence: The wrong of disclosing or using information confided to or improperly taken from another for a purpose not authorized by the confider. *See* Trade secret.

Canada Gazette: The periodical in which regulations and notices of the federal government are officially published.

CIPO: Canadian Intellectual Property Office, located in Hull, Quebec. The umbrella government department under which the Patent Office, Copyright Office, Trade-marks Office, and the like operate.

Claim date: Usually the date when a *patent application is filed. It can be moved back; for example, a claim in application **A** filed in Canada on 1 February 1996 can be bumped by a claim in application **B** filed as late as 31 January 1997, if **B** is based on an application filed in a *Paris Convention* or *WTO* state on 31 January 1996 (up to twelve months earlier). **B** has priority based on its earlier claim date: it will get a patent covering its claim, and **A** will not.

Clearance: *See* Licence.

Common law: Judge-made law, used here to include rules of *equity.

Consent: *See* Licence.

Copyright: The protection that literary, dramatic, musical, and artistic works receive internationally, typically for the author's life plus fifty years. In Canada, copyright includes neighbouring rights (*see Rome Convention*).

Copyright Board: A tribunal established under the *Copyright Act*, with authority mainly over rate approvals for cable retransmission, performing and broadcast rights for music, and tariff disputes between collecting societies and users. Appeals go directly to the Federal Court of Appeal.

De minimis: A shortened form of the Latin legal maxim *de minimis non curat lex*: the law does not concern itself with the trivial. For example, an act that is technically an *infringement can be called *de minimis* if it is thought to be outside the purpose of the law to catch it; the claim can then be dismissed with costs. This involves a value judgment that the complaint should either have been resolved without taking up the time of a court or is a minor irritant that, like the unintentional jostle in a crowded street, the complainant should have borne with equanimity.

Disclaimer: In *patent law, the giving up of anything beyond what the inventor truly invented.

In *trade-mark law: (1) The giving up of any unregistrable parts of a trade-mark — for example, descriptive language on a label — when seeking registration. The mark owner may, however, have common law rights in the disclaimed material, which still forms part of the mark. Disclaimers take effect on being recorded on the respective *CIPO register.

(2) A notice, such as "my business or trade-mark is not associated with firm X or mark X," that is designed to minimize confusion between two trade-names or trade-marks. A clear and prominent notice that achieves this goal may help to avoid a passing-off or trade-mark infringement action.

Employee: An individual employed under a contract of service with an employer; distinguished from a *freelancer, who is not on an employer's payroll. Employers often *prima facie* own the intellectual property rights in subject matter produced by employees on the job. This may be true even where a freelancer is working under contract (e.g., an industrial designer or ICT creator), but a specific agreement is usually required where a *patent or *copyright is involved.

EPC: Abbreviation for *European Patent Convention*, signed at Munich on 5 October 1973, governing the grant of European patents.

Equity, equitable rights: A term used here in the technical sense of rules or rights historically derived from those recognized by courts of chancery to supplement legal rules or rights — those administered by the ordinary courts of the land. For example, a writing may be required for a valid legal *assignment of *copyright; but a court of chancery accepted that an oral assignment can effectively transfer the right between the parties, although the right could disappear if the assignor resold to an innocent third party. Such an assignment is called an equitable assignment; the rights that flow from it are equitable rights. Equitable rights are not always recognized as such in Quebec, although the *Code Civil* may, through other means, redress some of the injustices equity targets.

Estoppel: A legal bar, from medieval French law, meaning "stop." For example, assignors are estopped from challenging their assignee's title, and licensees are estopped from challenging their licensor's title: the assignor or licensee sued by the assignee or licensor for infringement cannot defend by (is estopped from) showing that the right is invalid. Hence, the terms "assignor estoppel" and "licensee estoppel." Someone may be estopped without intending or knowing it. Thus, if **A** leads **B** to assume that a certain state of affairs exists, and it would be unfair to let **A** have a change of heart in the light of what has since happened, **B**'s assumption is treated as true: that is, **A** is estopped from denying its validity.

EU: Abbreviation for the European Union and the states that belong to it. The way *intellectual property laws are harmonized within the EU influences developments in other states.

Ex parte: A term literally meaning "from one side"; an application is *ex parte* when it is made to a court or a tribunal without notifying or serving anyone else with the proceedings. Because of the proceeding's one-sided nature, applicants owe the decision maker a high duty of good faith; in practice, this means they should reveal to the decision maker any objections that might result in a decision adverse to them.

Expunge: A term meaning to "strike" or "delete"; it is used in this book in relation to an entry on an intellectual property register; the same result is achieved in *patent law by a declaration "voiding" the patent. The *CIPO can expunge entries in limited specified circumstances; more usually, the Federal Court exercises this power. Expungement invalidates the right as against the world, not merely the parties to the litigation. An entry may also be amended, corrected, or rectified, a lesser remedy than expungement that changes, but does not delete, the entry.

Freelancer: An independent contractor or contracting company. An individual working as a freelancer is different from an *employee; the latter is under a contract of service with an employer.

GATT: The acronym for *General Agreement on Tariffs and Trade* of 1947, designed to eliminate discrimination in international trade relations. The latest of its periodic revisions is the 1994 *WTO Agreement.*

ICT right: Integrated Circuit Topography right, granted on registration under the federal *ICT Act* for ten years. The U.S. equivalent is a semi-conductor chip right.

Impeach: A word meaning "invalidate." In *patent law, impeachment proceedings are proceedings that seek to have a patent invalidated. Compare the term *expunge.

Industrial design: Features of shape, pattern, or ornament applied to a finished article. Mass-produced designs for most useful articles can be protected only by registration under the *Industrial Design Act*; limited protection until the fifty-first copy is made can be had under *copyright.

Infringement: Violation or breach of a statutory intellectual property right, allowing the right-holder to recover civil remedies against the infringer. Some infringements are also criminal offences — for example, certain deliberate *copyright infringements. "Substantial infringement" denotes the unauthorized taking of something less than or different from the protected subject matter — for example, using NOLEX instead of the ROLEX trade-mark, or taking a chapter from a copyright book. What takings are or are not substantial is often controversial.

Injunction: A court order requiring someone to stop doing a specified act (negative injunction) or requiring the doing of a positive act (mandatory injunction). Injunctions can be granted pre-trial (interim or interlocutory injunctions) or after a full trial (final injunction). Disobedience can result in proceedings for contempt of court, leading to a fine or even imprisonment.

Intellectual property: A term that denotes *copyrights, *patents, *trade-marks, *trade-names, *industrial designs, *PBR and *ICT rights, and sometimes rights arising from provincial law relating to, for example, *trade secrets, *misappropriation of personality, and *passing-off. Both "intellectual" and "property" may be misnomers.

Interlocutory relief: Orders granted by a court before trial. An "interlocutory injunction" is granted to preserve the claimant's rights before trial; if the claimant then loses, it may have to compensate the defendant for losses caused by the *injunction.

Intra vires: See Ultra vires.

Licence: Consent, permission, or clearance (all interchangeable terms) given by a right-holder (licensor) to someone (licensee) to do something only the licensor can legally do. The licence can be oral or written. An exclusive licence gives the licensee alone the right, to the exclusion of even the licensor (this licence usually has to be written). A sole licence is the same, except the licensor can compete with the licensee. A non-exclusive licence allows the licensor to appoint other licensees in the same area.

Limitation: Generally, a restriction placed on a right; specifically, a time-bar within which legal proceedings must be commenced, failing which a claimant can no longer sue.

Misappropriation: *See* Unfair competition.

Misappropriation of personality: The right to prevent commercial uses of one's name, voice, or image. It is roughly equivalent to the U.S. "right of publicity."

MOPOP: The PO's *Manual of Patent Office Practice:* a guide for patent applicants, outlining the rules patent examiners follow on patentability and other features of practice in handling *patent applications. The current version, effective as from 1 October 1996, is presently available only in electronic form. It may be downloaded from the CIPO website at http://info.ic.gc.ca/ic-data/marketplace/cipo/prod_ser/download/mopop/mopop-e.html. This covers applications filed since 1 October 1989.

Moral rights. Author's rights to have work properly attributed and not prejudicially modified or associated with other products; a poor, but commonly used, translation of the French *droits moraux* ("personal" or "intellectual" rights). The rights are as legally binding as any others; they have nothing to do with morals or morality.

NAFTA. *North American Free Trade Agreement* of 1992, between Canada, Mexico, and the United States. Chapter 17 obliges the parties to maintain high levels of *intellectual property protection. Canada implemented this treaty through the *North American Free Trade Agreement Implementation Act*, S.C. 1993, c. 44, mostly effective from 1 January 1994, which made substantial changes to all intellectual property legislation.

National treatment. An obligation to extend the rights a state grants its own citizens, residents, and corporations to foreign citizens, residents, and corporations without discrimination. Most international *intellectual property treaties oblige their adherents to extend national treatment to one another, but not necessarily to non-adherents. Thus, Canada as an adherent of the *Berne Convention* must extend to people from other *Berne* states exactly the same rights as it extends to Canadians. The other states do the same for Canadians.

Neighbouring rights. *See Rome Convention.*

Novelty. Inventions that are not new or novel cannot be patented: that is, if the same subject matter is shown to be publicly available anywhere in the world at the application's claim date. *See also* Anticipation.

Obviousness. A feature of an alleged invention that prevents its being patented; "invention" and "obviousness" are antitheses. Analogous requirements exist for *industrial designs and *ICTs. *See also* Originality.

Originality: Copyright's threshold requirement for protection: that a work not be copied and that it have some minimal creativity. For *industrial designs, some difference from prior designs or the adaptation of an old design to a new use is also required; for *ICTs, the topography must not be commonplace among ICT designers or manufacturers. *See also* Obviousness; Patents.

Parallel import: The importation, without the authorization of the owner of a Canadian *intellectual property right, of a product lawfully made abroad; it is sometimes called "grey marketing." It is often (controversially) barred by Canadian law, but is challenged by global technology like the Internet.

Paris Convention [Paris]: The *Paris Convention for the Protection of Industrial Property*, 1883, last revised in Stockholm (1967). It provides national treatment and foreign filing priorities for *patents, *trade-marks, and *industrial designs. Canada is a member.

Passing-off: The wrong of misrepresenting one's business, goods, or services as another's, to the latter's injury; for example, by a confusingly similar *trade-mark or *trade- name.

Patent: A term used here to denote a patent for invention, a twenty-year monopoly granted for new inventions. It is sometimes called "letters patent," from the Latin *litterae patentes* ("open letters"), meaning that the royal seal was placed at the bottom of the document, making the document a public record open for all to see. The *Patent Act* still defines "patent" as "letters patent for an invention," being one species of the genus of letters patent, which at various times covered franchises, land grants, honours, and company incorporations.

Patent Appeal Board: A tribunal of senior examiners that hears appeals from examiners' decisions in patent application proceedings and recommends what action the Commissioner of Patents should finally take. The Commissioner rarely rejects the Board's recommendation. Appeals from the Commissioner go directly to the Federal Court of Appeal.

Patentee: The owner or holder of a *patent.

PBR: Abbreviation for Plant Breeders' Right, registrable under the *PBR Act* for new varieties of stated plants and effective for eighteen years.

Permission: See Licence.

Piracy; pirated goods: Abusive terms, used by those who know no better or who have vested interests in a strong *intellectual property system, to describe the products of deliberate infringement. These terms are sometimes used more loosely to describe any acts *right-holders object to: for example, when British *copyright owners complained of U.S. "piracy" of their books in the nineteenth century, even though U.S. law permitted this activity. They are best reserved for the exploits of Captain Bluebeard, and are not otherwise used in this book.

PO: Abbreviation for the Canadian Patent Office, which examines and grants applications for *patents.

Prima facie: Literally, "at first sight." A *prima facie* position is one that prevails unless contrary evidence is presented.

Priority: (1) The right to acquire an *intellectual property right where competing applications are filed. In *trade-mark law, the earlier of the first to use or file usually has priority; in *patent law, the first to file for a claimed invention usually has priority. Both may be bumped by a later Canadian filing based on a timely foreign application with an earlier filing date.

(2) The better title to a proprietary interest when a right has been assigned or licensed more than once. So if **A** assigns the same right to **B** and then later to **C**, **C** will have priority if its title is better than **B**'s. This means that **C** owns the right and that **B** can claim against **A** only for breach of contract. Priorities for intellectual property are not standardized. Provincial law, sometimes overlaid by federal law (e.g., for *patents, *copyrights, and *PBRs), usually governs. Typically, who registers a right first, and whether **C** is a good-faith buyer without knowledge of **B**'s interest, are important factors.

Prosecution: The term sometimes used for proceedings in applications for an *intellectual property right: thus *trade-mark prosecution, *patent prosecution. It has nothing to do with criminal law.

Quia timet **relief:** Relief, typically an injunction, sought where a wrong is anticipated. *Quia timet* literally means "because he or she fears"; so a *quia timet* injunction is granted when a claimant reasonably fears it will be injured by the imminent commission of a wrong.

Registrant: The holder of a registered right; so a *trade-mark registrant is the person registered as the trade-mark's owner.

Reissue: In patent law, the procedure by which a *patent is amended. Technically, the original patent is surrendered, and a new patent is granted.

Right-holder: A term used to indicate anyone with a proprietary interest in an *intellectual property right: for example, an owner or exclusive licensee.

Rome Convention [Rome]: Rome Convention on the Protection of Performers, Producers of Phonograms and Broadcasting Organisations of 1961. It protects performers, record producers, and broadcasters through *droits voisins* ("neighbouring rights") similar to traditional *copyright. *Bill C-32, the Copyright Amendment Bill of 1996, would implement these rights in Canada. About fifty states presently adhere to this Convention, though the United States is notably absent.

Service mark: A mark used or intended to distinguish one service provider's services from another's. It is often hard to distinguish a service mark from a *trade-name.

Statute of Monopolies: The English patent law of 1624 that first curbed the Crown's power to grant monopolies at its discretion, while excepting (in s. 6) fourteen-year grants for "the sole working or making of any manner of new manufactures within this realm." This statute and the Venetian *Patent Law* of 1474 are treated as progenitors of modern patent laws. Even today, Australia's patent law, entirely revamped in 1990, continues to define invention as "any manner of new manufacture . . . within section 6 of the Statute of Monopolies"!

Sui generis: A term meaning separate, stand-alone, specialized. The *ICT* and *PBR Acts* are *sui generis* pieces of legislation since they deal separately with specialized items that may not fall easily under established protective schemes like *patents or *copyrights.

Theft: An abusive term used to describe an *intellectual property infringement or, sometimes more loosely, any act to which a *right-holder objects. An association of computer software manufacturers even calls itself the Canadian Alliance against Software Theft. But intellectual property infringement is not "theft" in Canada because, after the "taking," the right-holder is still left with the "property".[1] Still, right-holders have never let facts get in the way of a good slogan. *See also* Piracy.

TMO: Abbreviation for the Canadian Trade-marks Office, which examines and grants registrations for *trade-marks, and maintains registers of geographical indications, official marks, etc.

Trade-mark: A mark distinguishing one trader's product or service from another's. It can include *service mark. In other countries, the term is also spelled "trademark" and "trade mark."

Trade-marks Opposition Board: The tribunal that decides oppositions to trade-mark registrations. Appeals go to the Trial Division of the Federal Court.

Trade-name: The name under which a corporation, firm, or individual does business. It can qualify as a *service mark and be registrable under the *Trade-marks Act*.

---

1   *R. v. Stewart* [1988] 1 S.C.R 963.

Trade secret: Commercial information that derives its value from the fact of its not being generally known and from the protection the law erects around it, mainly through contracts and the *breach of confidence action.

TRIPs: Acronym for *Agreement on Trade-Related Aspects of Intellectual Property Rights, Including Trade in Counterfeit Goods* (Annex 1C to the *WTO Agreement* of 1994). It was probably coined by survivors of the 1960s with redirected energies. Most countries of the world (major exceptions are presently China and Taiwan) are members. Canada implemented this treaty by the *World Trade Organization Implementation Act*, S.C. 1994, c. 47, effective as from 1 January 1996.

Ultra vires: Beyond lawful authority. A statute is *ultra vires*, and therefore invalid, if Canada's *Constitution Act, 1867,* does not authorize the legislature that passed it to legislate on that matter. The opposite is *intra vires,* within lawful authority.

Unfair competition: 1. A general term describing a basket of harms — for example, *passing-off, injurious falsehood, interference with economic relations, conspiracy, *breach of confidence — that amount to torts against businesses harmed by them.

2. A synonym for "misappropriation," the wrong of unfairly taking or using business assets to the injury of their holder. It was used, for example, in the United States by Dow Jones to prevent the Chicago Board of Trade from adopting a futures trading contract based on the Dow Jones index.[2] The civil law of Quebec may recognize a similar wrong, but no Canadian common law province presently does; nor may the federal Parliament constitutionally enact it.[3]

3. An abusive, legally insignificant term an enterprise may use to describe any practice by which another manages to undersell it.

Universal Copyright Convention [UCC]: Signed in 1952 and revised in 1971, this Convention enabled the United States and other Pan-American countries that had *copyright registries and marking requirements to join with *Berne countries in an international treaty. Less demanding than *Berne*, it allowed a marking like "© David Vaver 1997" to satisfy any formalities a state required as a prerequisite of copyright. Canada adheres to the *UCC*'s 1952 version. The *UCC* is less important today because most states, including the United States, have since joined

---

2   *Board of Trade of the City of Chicago v. Dow Jones & Co.*, 456 N.E.2d 84 (Ill. S.C. 1983).

3   *Macdonald v. Vapor Canada Ltd.* (1976), [1977] 2 S.C.R. 134.

Berne, and *TRIPs* also mandates compliance with *Berne*'s higher obligations and "no-formalities" rules.

Usefulness; utility: In *patent law, the requirement that an invention must have a practical use, must relate to the "useful" (not fine or professional) arts, and do what the patent specification claims it can. In *copyright law, the design of "useful" articles receives only limited protection; further protection for their appearance may be gained by registration under the *Industrial Design Act*. *See also* Industrial design.

Waiver: The giving up of a right. It may be done expressly or may be implied from the circumstances.

WIPO: World Intellectual Property Organization. This UN agency, headquartered in Geneva, administers and holds intergovernmental conferences to revise the international *intellectual property conventions. It is a longtime promoter of the view that, without more intellectual property, the world would be a worse place (at least for some).

WTO: World Trade Organization. The *WTO Agreement* of 1994, a successor of *GATT*, contains extensive mandatory provisions on *intellectual property rights in its *TRIPs Agreement*. Breaches can lead to trade sanctions. It was implemented by Canada, effective 1 January 1996, by the *World Trade Organization Agreement Implementation Act*, S.C. 1994, c. 47.

TABLE OF CASES

INDEX

Asterisked items also appear in the Glossary

333

ABOUT THE AUTHOR

David Vaver, B.A., LL.B., J.D., is Professor of Law at Osgoode Hall Law School at York University, where he teaches intellectual property law. He taught previously at the University of British Columbia and the University of Auckland. He is the founding editor and editor in chief of the internationally respected *Intellectual Property Journal.* He also serves as an adviser to the Department of Heritage on copyright law reform, including the present Phase 2 proposals to amend the *Copyright Act.* Professor Vaver has written extensively on the law and policy of intellectual property both in Canada and internationally, and his writings are often cited by courts and legal writers.